MARTIAL POWER AND ELIZABETHAN POLITICAL CULTURE

This book studies the careers and political thinking of English martial men, left deeply frustrated as Elizabeth I's quietist foreign policy destroyed the ambitions that the wars of the mid sixteenth century had excited in them. Until the mid-1580s, unemployment, official disparagement and downward mobility became grim facts of life for many military captains. Rory Rapple examines the experiences and attitudes of this generation of officers and points to a previously overlooked literature of complaint that offered a stinging critique of the monarch and the administration of Sir William Cecil. He also argues that the captains' actions in Ireland, their treatment of its inhabitants and their conceptualisation of both relied on assumptions, attitudes and political thinking which resulted more from their frustration with the status quo in England than from any tendency to 'other' the Irish. This book will be required reading for scholars of early modern British and Irish history.

RORY RAPPLE is a visiting assistant professor at the University of Notre Dame.

CAMBRIDGE STUDIES IN EARLY MODERN
BRITISH HISTORY

Series editors

ANTHONY FLETCHER
Emeritus Professor of English Social History, University of London
JOHN MORRILL
Professor of English and Irish History, University of Cambridge,
and Fellow of Selwyn College
ETHAN SHAGAN
Associate Professor of History, University of California, Berkeley
ALEXANDRA WALSHAM
Professor of Reformation History, University of Exeter

This is a series of monographs and studies covering many aspects of the history of the British Isles between the late fifteenth century and the early eighteenth century. It includes the work of established scholars and pioneering work by a new generation of scholars. It includes both reviews and revisions of major topics and books which open up new historical terrain or which reveal startling new perspectives on familiar subjects. All the volumes set detailed research into our broader perspectives, and the books are intended for the use of students as well as of their teachers.

For a list of titles in the series, see end of book.

MARTIAL POWER AND ELIZABETHAN POLITICAL CULTURE

Military Men in England and Ireland, 1558–1594

RORY RAPPLE

CAMBRIDGE UNIVERSITY PRESS
Cambridge, New York, Melbourne, Madrid, Cape Town, Singapore, São Paulo, Delhi

Cambridge University Press
The Edinburgh Building, Cambridge CB2 8RU, UK

Published in the United States of America by Cambridge University Press, New York

www.cambridge.org
Information on this title: www.cambridge.org/9780521843539

© Rory Rapple 2009

This publication is in copyright. Subject to statutory exception
and to the provisions of relevant collective licensing agreements,
no reproduction of any part may take place without
the written permission of Cambridge University Press.

First published 2009

Printed in the United Kingdom at the University Press, Cambridge

A catalogue record for this publication is available from the British Library

Library of Congress Cataloguing in Publication data
Rapple, Rory.
Martial power and Elizabethan political culture : military men in England and Ireland, 1558–1594 / Rory Rapple.
p. cm. – (Cambridge studies in early modern British history)
Includes bibliographical references and index.
ISBN 978-0-521-84353-9 (hardback)
1. Great Britain–History, Military–1485–1603. 2. Elizabeth I, Queen of England, 1533–1603–Military leadership. 3. Great Britain–Military policy. 4. Great Britain–History–Elizabeth, 1558–1603. 5. Great Britain–Foreign relations–Ireland. 6. Ireland–Foreign relations–Ireland.
I. Title. II. Series.
DA66.R37 2009
306.2′7094209031–dc22   2008039993

ISBN 978-0-521-84353-9 hardback

Cambridge University Press has no responsibility for the persistence or accuracy of URLs for external or third-party internet websites referred to in this publication, and does not guarantee that any content on such websites is, or will remain, accurate or appropriate.

For Colm and Nuala

Contents

Acknowledgements	*page*	viii
List of abbreviations		x
Notes on the text		xii
Political map of sixteenth-century Ireland circa 1534		xiii

Introduction		1
1 Chimneys in summer		19
2 Martial men and their discontents		51
3 The limits of allegiance: English martial men, Europe and the Elizabethan regime		86
4 The captains and the Irish context		127
5 The limits of *imperium*: martial men and government		162
6 The limits of rhetoric: the captains and violence in Elizabethan Ireland to 1588		200
7 Unlimited indemnity: delegates versus viceroys		250
Conclusion		301
Bibliography		309
Index		324

Acknowledgements

Many of the debts incurred during the period spent researching this book have been to institutions. First and foremost, I must thank the Arts and Humanities Research Board and the electors of both the Robert Gardiner Memorial Scholarship in Cambridge and the Irish Government Senior Scholarship at Hertford College, Oxford for providing funding for the original Ph.D. thesis from which this work emanated. In particular, I must express my profound gratitude to the Master and Fellows of St John's College, Cambridge for electing me a 'title A' Fellow in Intellectual History in 2002. By their grace I was afforded the most splendid of berths for four years. Since leaving Cambridge I have had the good fortune to be employed first by University College Dublin (UCD) and then by the University of Notre Dame. At UCD, Michael Laffan, John McCafferty and Richard Aldous were particularly important in making things congenial, and at Notre Dame, John McGreevy, Dan Graff, Brad Gregory, Chris Fox, Jim Smyth, Breandán Ó Buachalla and Jim Turner have proved to be wonderful colleagues.

My personal acknowledgements for the most part are due to people living in two locations: Dublin and Cambridge. In Dublin I owe much to a collection of friends, most of whom I first met as an undergraduate at Trinity College Dublin; they include Ray McIlreavy, Liz McEvoy, Jim Carr, Aoibhlinn Hester, the late Patrick Cusack, Josephine McHale and Tom Flanagan. More recently, Ann Marie Long provided renewed motivation to finish this project, and much in the way of happy distraction. In St John's College, Cambridge, Sylvana Tomaselli, Peter Linehan, John Kerrigan (who has always been a great encouragement) and the wickedly funny Emily Gowers were indispensable. Throughout my time in Cambridge as a whole I relied for friendship and support on Mairi and Gerard Hurrell, Alban McCoy, Michael Ledger Lomas, Piers Baker Bates, Alderik Blom, Dougal Shaw, Joe Bord, Grant Tapsell, Marino Guida, Alison Davies and my godchild Alexandra O'Connor.

At Cambridge University Press, Michael Watson has been an exemplary editor: patient and kind.

I am fortunate that my most pressing intellectual debts are to historians, each of whom shares a common commitment to the difficult business of saying true things about the past.

In between our conversations about Brahms, Flaubert and the Great American Songbook, Ciaran Brady has proved to be an invaluable sounding board for much that is in this book. He has been the most lively and perceptive of critics.

During my year at Oxford, Roy Foster was not only a colleague with common tastes but also a great friend. Throughout the writing of the book, John Guy's encouragement has been indispensable and his advice always of great value.

When I began my Ph.D., I was under the supervision of Brendan Bradshaw. A bout of serious illness in 2000 (which he has recovered from since) meant that our formal relationship came to a halt. But in spite of this, Brendan, a great intellectual historian as well as a formidable sparring partner, proved a constant inspiration to me throughout my research and writing. I hope this book will prove just another cause for discussion in a, by now, long and rumbustious intellectual friendship.

In particular, I am blessed to have had John Morrill as my supervisor and mentor. In my experience, no one combines incisive intelligence and sheer goodness in the same way as John. I have been a constant beneficiary of both of these traits, even at times when it can neither have been convenient nor easy to assist me. I owe him heartfelt gratitude for all the encouragement, friendship and help he has given me. He cannot be praised enough.

Finally it is the greatest pleasure to thank my parents Colm and Nuala Rapple, whose patience and love surpass description. I am also grateful to them for teaching me to think, and to think again. This book is dedicated to them.

The bibliography and my footnotes show the extent of my debts to writers, scholars and archivists, living and dead. Much as I would like to blame others for the shortcomings of this book, all mistakes, inaccuracies and blemishes are my fault. I would like to thank Oxford University Press for permission to publish material from my article 'Taking up Office in Elizabethan Connacht: The Case of Sir Richard Bingham' from *English Historical Review* CXXIII, 501, April 2008, pp. 277–299.

Abbreviations

Add. MSS	Additional manuscripts (British Library)
ALC	*Annals of Loch Cé*
APC	*Acts of the Privy Council*
Archiv. Hib.	*Archivium Hibernicum*
ARÉ	*Annála Ríoghachta Éireann*
BL	British Library
Bodl.	Bodleian Library, Oxford
Cal. Bor.	*Calendar of Border Papers, 1560–94*
Cal. Car. MSS	*Calendar of Carew Manuscripts*
CPR Eliz.	*Calendar of Patent Rolls, Elizabeth I*
Correspondentie	H. Brugmans (ed.) *Correspondentie van Robert Dudley, graaf van Leycester, 1585–7.*
CPRI	*Calendar of Patent Rolls* (Ireland)
CSPD	*Calendar of State Papers: Domestic*
CSPF	*Calendar of State Papers: Foreign*
CSPI	*Calendar of State Papers: Ireland*
CSPR	*Calendar of State Papers: Rome*
CSPSc	*Calendar of State Papers: Scotland*
CSPSp	*Calendar of State Papers: Spanish*
CSPVen	*Calendar of State Papers: Venetian*
EcHR	*Economic History Review*
EHR	*English Historical Review*
Fiants	*The Irish Fiants of the Tudor Sovereigns*
HJ	*Historical Journal*
HMC	Historical Manuscripts Commission
IHS	*Irish Historical Studies*
JGAS	*Journal of the Galway Archaeological and Historical Society*
Leycester corr.	J. Bruce (ed.) *Correspondence of Robert Dudley, earl of Leycester, during his government of the Low Countries* (1844)

Abbreviations

NHI	*A New History of Ireland*
PCC	Prerogative Courts of Canterbury
P&P	*Past & Present*
SP10	Public Record Office, State papers, Domestic, Edward VI.
SP11	Public Record Office, State papers, Domestic, Philip and Mary.
SP12	Public Record Office, State papers, Domestic, Elizabeth I.
SP61	Public Record Office, State papers, Ireland, Edward VI.
SP62	Public Record Office, State papers, Ireland, Philip and Mary.
SP63	Public Record Office, State papers, Ireland, Elizabeth I.
SP Hen. VIII	*State papers of Henry VIII*

Notes on the text

All dates are Old Style, but the year is taken as beginning on 1 January rather than Lady Day. Throughout this text, spelling and punctuation have been modernised in all quotations except in the case of the titles of books.

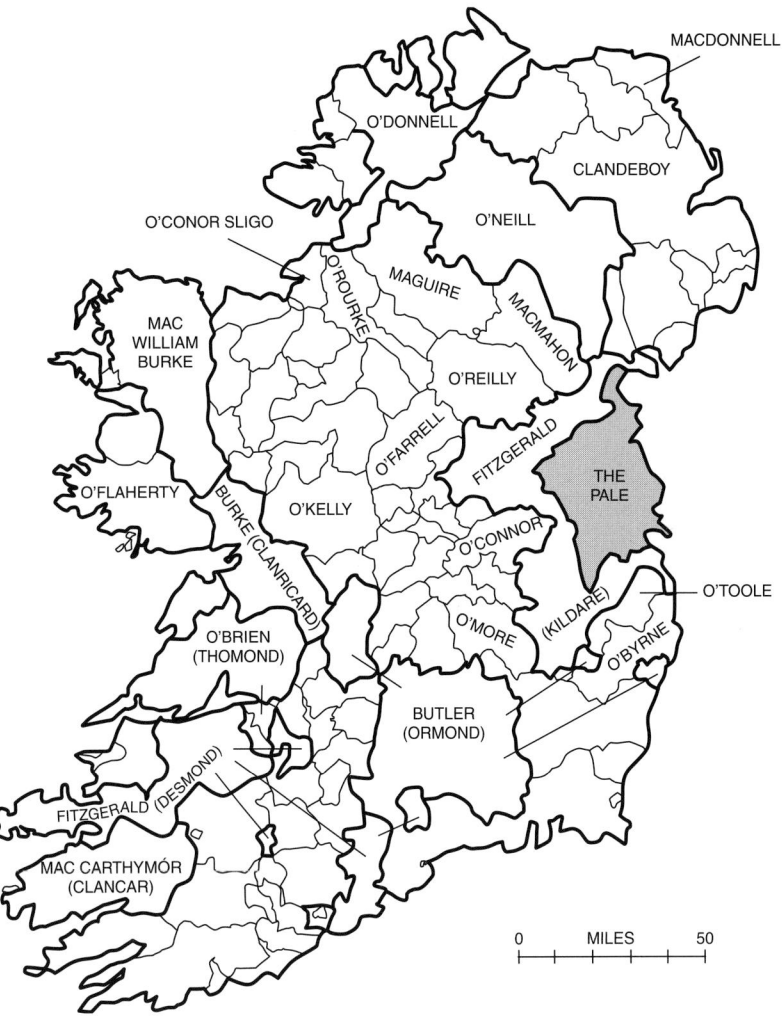

Political map of sixteenth-century Ireland, circa 1534 (after the map by Kenneth Nicholls in *A New History of Ireland Vol. III*, edited by Moody et al. (1976), pp. 2–3. By permission of Oxford University Press).

Introduction

*Yes. Why do we all, seeing of a soldier, bless him? bless
Our redcoats, our tars? Both these being, the greater part
But frail clay, nay but foul clay. Here it is: the heart,
Since, proud, it calls the calling manly, gives a guess
That, hopes that, makesbelieve, the men must be no less.*[1]

The urge to praise soldiers has proved strong in most cultures. This stems from a number of emotions commonly held: gratitude towards those who fight, kill and sometimes die for what we might identify with; sheer envy of the sudden action, the rare clarity and decisiveness of mortal combat; and, not least, the persistent belief that those who have engaged in that sudden action can attain some sort of heightened moral quality forged in them during their time in the gap of danger. Samuel Johnson famously said that 'were Socrates and Charles XII of Sweden both present in any company, and Socrates to say "Follow me, and hear a lecture on philosophy;" and Charles, laying his hand on his sword, to say, "Follow me and dethrone the Czar;" a man would be ashamed to follow Socrates.'[2] This sort of admiration has been (for a long time, anyway) particularly strong in England. The history of the engagement of Englishmen in armed conflict has been so enthusiastically followed by so many over such a long period of time that the discipline of military history – an area of study distinct from political, constitutional, intellectual or social history, yet free to borrow from them all – has long had an avid following, and England, consequently, has produced very many excellent practitioners of

---

[1] Gerald Manley Hopkins wrote '(The Soldier)' while on retreat in Clongowes Wood College, County Kildare, a Jesuit school located on the borders of the Pale, which had formerly served as a castle for the Eustace family.
[2] *Boswell's life of Johnson* (Oxford, 1934) 6 vols., Vol. III, pp. 265–6. See also Johnson's 'On the bravery of the English common soldiers' in *Samuel Johnson: the major works*, ed. D. Greene (Oxford, 1984), pp. 549–50, where he concluded that the 'courage of the English vulgar' stemmed from the fact that 'their insolence in peace is bravery in war'.

that art. This book is not a work of military history. It does, however, have fighting men at its centre.

The focus of this book is on martial officers and captains of the Elizabethan period, not primarily to sketch an episode in the broad and impressive history of English military development or to treat of the structure of 'Elizabeth's army', or even the technological accomplishment, or otherwise, of 'Elizabethan military science' (all very well done elsewhere) but rather to make a bid to redress an imbalance in the historiography of Tudor political thinking, political culture and, for want of a better term, 'mentalities'.[3] Little study has been done on Tudor martial men as individual actors in history, their assumptions, what they took for granted, even their ideas, yet, as we shall see, quite a lot has been assumed about their collective character, their passions, their opinions, the 'type' to which they conformed.[4] These assumptions invite further scrutiny.

Take, for instance, the example of the best flower of English Protestant knighthood, Philip Sidney, 'poet, soldier and statesman' who fell mortally wounded at Zutphen sconce in September 1586, hit by a musket ball in the leg.[5] Initially, his wound seemed mild, but it was deceptively so. Sidney's death was unpleasant and slow; it took three weeks for his gangrene to kill him. Subsequently, it was often held that in his person the most recognisable motifs of Elizabethan chivalry had found coherence: reformed Protestantism of a type compatible with the martial necessities

---

[3] For essential treatments on all these topics see Paul Hammer's *Elizabeth's wars* (London, 2003), C. G. Cruickshank's *Elizabeth's army* (Oxford, 1966), L. Boynton's *The Elizabethan militia* (London, 1967) and H. J. Webb's *Elizabethan military science: the books and the practice* (Madison, Wisc., 1965).

[4] In writing this sentence I have self-consciously borrowed from Peter Burke's defence of the humble and careful use of the term 'mentality': 'we need some way of speaking about human assumptions, about what people take for granted in a given place and time, as well as about the ideas which they hold consciously. If we throw out one word, we are going to have to coin another to occupy this conceptual space'. See M. L. G. Pallares-Burke *The new history: confessions and conversations* (Cambridge, 2002), pp. 154–5.

[5] Philip Sidney was described as 'poet, soldier, and statesman' in the 1885–1900 *DNB*, but has, with more sobriety, been cast as 'author and courtier' in the 2004 *DNB*. In a letter to his brother Robert Sidney, future earl of Leicester, Philip recommended two hours of practice in swordplay a day, urging him to 'play out [such] play lustilie'. Although one can assume that Philip followed this discipline to some extent, he had hardly ever drawn his sword on an enemy in battle prior to his demise at Zutphen. See J. Osborn, *Young Philip Sidney* (New Haven, Conn., 1972), pp. 81–2. On the incompatibility of artillery and honour see Ariosto's denunciation, in Book 11 of *Orlando Furioso* of 'la machina infernal', the 'scelerata e brutta invenzion' which had destroyed chivalry: 'Per te la militar gloria è distrutta/ per te il mestier de l'arme è senza onore'. See also Don Quixote's meditation on the 'vile cowardly' effect that firearms had on the 'profession of knight errantry' in Vol. I, Chapter 38 of *Don Quixote*. However Hotspur in *Henry IV*, Part 1, Act I, Scene 3, mocks those who shun the battlefield because of their fear of being killed by gunshot.

Introduction 3

of the Huguenots and Dutch rebels, an appetite for tilting, aggressive vaunting of honour and a significant literary imagination.[6] His posthumous reputation rested on a magnification of each of these qualities while his personal charm, obvious in his lifetime, died with him. During his life, Sidney had been adored by the most prominent Elizabethan statesmen. The principal secretary Sir Francis Walsingham ruined himself to honour Sidney's will and furnish him with a public funeral. Sir William Cecil once confided to the wunderkind's father that his affection for Philip was so strong that others might think it improper.[7] The shadow of Philip, the Protestant knight, loomed large over the doomed vanity and frustration of Robert Devereux, second earl of Essex; it remained to dog the steps of the young Stuart prince Henry and spurred the ambitions of Algernon Sidney.[8]

His intellectual accomplishments tended to counter the austerity of his appointed status as puritan hero. His literary merits, his best and most lively legacy, were beyond reproach. His talent and commitment as a political thinker, although somewhat forgotten with the passage of time, had impressed his contemporaries.[9] But he was not a soldier, a shortcoming he felt keenly. Despite his many accomplishments off the battlefield, it was obvious that he intensely desired to have triumphs on the field as well as off and that he regarded men of war with reverence.[10] Why else did Sidney, on seeing Sir William Pelham go into battle without leg armour (probably because he had none), in a lonely impulse of delight rip off his own greaves in emulation? This was the decision that cost him his life.[11]

---

[6] For a meditation on the significance of Philip Sidney and his literary circle to the formation of a type of Protestant knighthood see M. E. James, 'English politics and the concept of honour, 1485–1642', *Past & Present* supplement 3, (1978), pp. 68–72.

[7] Cecil to Henry Sidney, SP63/27/2, 6 January 1569: 'Your Philip is here in whom I take more comfort than I do openly utter for avoiding of wrong interpretation.'

[8] For the psychological hold that the idea of Sidney held over Essex, who was knighted at Zutphen, see P. Hammer, *The polarisation of Elizabethan politics: the political career of Robert Devereux, 2nd Earl of Essex, 1585–1597* (Cambridge, 1999), pp. 51–4. For his influence over Prince Henry, see *Culture and politics in early Stuart England*, ed. K. Sharpe and P. Lake (London, 1994). Algernon inscribed 'PHILIPPUS SIDNEY MANUS HAEC INIMICA TYRANNIS EINSE PETIT PLACIDAM CUM LIBERTATE QUIETEM' ('This hand, enemy to tyrants, by the sword seeks peace with liberty') in the signature book of the University of Copenhagen in 1659, see Jonathan Scott, '**Sidney, Algernon** (1623–1683)', *Oxford Dictionary of National Biography* (Oxford, 2004).

[9] Sidney explicitly aimed to move his concerns 'out of the limits of a man's own little world, to the government of families and maintaining of public societies'. See B. Worden's *The sound of virtue: Philip Sidney's* Arcadia *and Elizabethan politics* (New Haven, Conn., 1996), pp. 209–96, for a sustained analysis of Sidney's political thinking and opinions.

[10] In a fit of despondency in 1580 he had counselled his brother Robert, who was travelling through Europe, to seek out good wars, Worden (1996), p. 67.

[11] Crucially, neither Sidney's presence in the Netherlands nor his desire to imitate Pelham stemmed from personal success. Quite the opposite: it was only because he could not secure the circumstances of life

But what about Pelham? Can he be saved from a mere bit part in Sidney's narrative? Ironically, when he died in November 1587, it was also because of a leg wound which '[had] fallen into a dangerous case'.[12] Renowned for his martial prowess, he had served as marshal of the garrison in the Low Countries since July 1586. Previous to this, he had been lord justice of Ireland in 1579 and then lieutenant general of the ordnance in England: an apparently illustrious career. But if Philip Sidney had been frustrated at Elizabeth's disdain, his experience was nothing compared to the monarch's vindictive toying with poor William Pelham. Her treatment of the latter after his, admittedly controversial, stewardship of the Irish viceroyalty led one crown officer to reflect 'how dangerous a thing it is to disgrace an officer in so great a place'.[13] Throughout late 1585 and early 1586, she prevented him from taking office as marshal of the earl of Leicester's army in the Netherlands by refusing 'to stall his debt [or] to take as much of his land as reasonably may satisfy his debt'. Pelham was in penury. He had horrific personal debts excluding a hefty debt to Elizabeth, incurred during his service as lieutenant general of the ordnance. In a calculated bid to shame Pelham, Elizabeth had determined that she would allow him to attend on Leicester 'as a private man' but would 'charge him with no service'. Pelham offered to go to the Tower instead. This harsh treatment did not go unnoticed. William Davison later reflected on 'the hard measure [Pelham] received' and concluded that it was 'enough to break the heart of any gentleman in the world of his sort and deserving'.[14] Leicester noted that Pelham's mind 'had languished' for two to three months before his death. This depression was no doubt exacerbated by the scale of the misery that surrounded him in the Low Countries: the English troops were without hose and shoes, and the local merchants refused to have any dealings with them because the captains had taken everything upon credit and could not honour their transactions. Pelham's will, penned prior to taking up office under Leicester, shows that his personal financial arrangements were far from comfortable. Yet, despite

---

that would have best corresponded with his temperament – an aristocratic title coupled with senior government office – that he found himself in the company of hardened soldiers in the first place. See *The Prose Works of Fulke Greville*, Lord Brooke, ed. John Gouws (Oxford, 1986), pp. 76–80, 214.

[12] Leicester to Burghley, 17 November 1587, *Correspondentie*, Vol. III, p. 310.

[13] Fenton to Walsingham, 3 January 1580, SP63/71/2. Thomas Churchyard wrote of Pelham's part in the siege of Leith: 'To save the ward from harm of enemy's shot / Full many a trench, did Pelham cause be wrought' *Churchyard's chippes* (London, 1575), sig. 4 v.

[14] *Correspondence of Robert Dudley, earl of Leycester during his government of the Low Countries in the years 1585 and 1586* (ed.) J. Bruce (London, 1844), p. 45, Burghley to Leicester, 27 December 1585, Davison to Leicester, 17 February 1586, *Leycester corr.*, pp. 45, 125–6. It is Fulke Greville who tells how the desire to imitate Pelham's wonted courage led directly to his fatal injury at Zutphen.

his ruin, Pelham's military prowess and 'long experience', for what they were worth, were highly regarded.

They were not worth much. There was no public funeral for Pelham.[15] The charm and poise of Philip Sidney has counted historically (and historiographically) for more than the dogged despair of Pelham. This is understandable; whatever Pelham's talents happened to be, the writing of literary masterpieces was not one of them.[16] But even the briefest consideration of contemporary views on the treatment of Leicester's marshal shows that the subaltern role that was forced upon him and other Elizabethan martial men up to the late 1580s was a source of disquiet and no little resentment in some quarters. The status of martial officers was a source of political and social tension, and this raises questions about Elizabethan society and politics. This study aims to answer some of these questions while attempting to analyse the thinking of Elizabethan martial men who served in Ireland up to the outbreak of the Nine Years' War in 1594.[17]

Why ask these questions at all? In my case, the interest was provoked by a problem. As an undergraduate, my interest in Elizabethan Ireland gave me a list of English dramatis personae – a sizeable group of administrators, governors and soldiers between 1558 to 1603 – which I found to be of little use in trying to get a handle on the historiography of Elizabethan England. In short, figures such as Sir William Pelham, Sir Nicholas Malby and Sir Richard Bingham, all very prominent in the history of Ireland, were hardly to be found in the standard works on the politics and society of their native land. Yet, the sophistication and scope of the emerging secondary material on Tudor political culture was both encouraging and presented a challenge: to find a contextualised location for the captains in the political and intellectual spectrum of the mid-Tudor and Elizabethan

---

[15] Day, J. F. R., 'Death be very proud: Sidney, subversion, and Elizabethan heraldic funerals' in Dale Hoak (ed.) *Tudor political culture* (Cambridge, 1995), pp. 179–203.

[16] See the verse supposedly written by Pelham endorsing Sir George Peckham's plan to establish a Catholic colony in the New World (also supported by Philip Sidney) in Peckham's *A true reporte, of the late discoueries, and possession, taken in the right of the Crowne of Englande, of the new-found landes: by that valiaunt and worthye gentleman, Sir Humfrey Gilbert Knight* (1583) with the words 'To valiant minds each land is a native soil, / and virtue finds no dwelling place amiss. / Regard of honour measures not the toil, / to seek a seat wherein contentment is'.

[17] For a treatment of the nuts and bolts of impressment, payment and victualling see the relevant parts of C. G. Cruickshank's *Elizabeth's army* (Oxford, 1966), M. C. Fissel's *English warfare, 1511–1642* (London, 2001), pp. 82–105, and J. Nolan *Sir John Norris and the Elizabethan military mind* (Exeter, 1999). For a full description of the relationship between the mechanisms of the county militias and state formation over two centuries, see M. Braddick *State formation in early modern England c. 1500–1700* (Cambridge, 2000), pp. 180–232. For the pivotal nature of the mid- to late 1580s in this development, see p. 191.

world. Geoffrey Elton's posthumously published foreword to *Tudor political culture*, edited by Dale Hoak, indicated that even he, the Tudor historian most devoted to the idea that the structures of Tudor institutions and the Tudor Constitution were coterminous, was impatient with those who 'treated [the Tudor age] as essentially worked through'.[18] Elton's coda and Hoak's advocacy of work on political culture were further amplified by John Guy two years later in the introduction to a compilation of some of the most important articles on Tudor monarchy and political culture from the 1980s and 1990s, *The Tudor monarchy*.[19] Guy formulated a nine-point manifesto with a view to a 'New Tudor Political History', a call for historians to chart the constellated relationship between the different milieux in Elizabethan politics, the codes of political and social conduct, political ideas, institutional procedure, political actions and actual events.[20]

Perhaps the flagship for history written in this manner has been the work done by many of the best Tudor scholars on the shared values of the milieu known as the 'Cambridge connection' – Nicholas Bacon, Richard Sackville, William Parr, and Ambrose Cave as well as Thomas Smith and Francis Knollys – Protestants who had endured their own 'mid-Tudor crisis', having previously been forged together in opposition to Bishop Stephen Gardiner, religious conservative and chancellor of the University of Cambridge in the early 1540s.[21] This solidarity was lasting, binding not only those who went into exile, such as Knollys, but also those, such as William Cecil, who stayed and retired to the outer margins of politics. On Mary's demise, of course, they went on to institute the form of the Elizabethan church and to dominate the English polity under its new queen. This much had always been well known, but further exploration yielded particularly precious ore.

Spearheading a new approach to these familiar figures, Patrick Collinson famously argued that Cecil and his kindred spirits had been foremost in seeing England as a 'monarchical republic', and, accordingly, 'citizens were concealed within subjects' during the Elizabethan era. These 'republicans' did not constitute an anti-monarchical cabal; rather, they took the

---

[18] See the foreword to Dale Hoak ed. *Tudor political culture* (Cambridge, 1995), p. xxi. Elton conceded that 'there is a lot still to be done both by way of elaboration and by way of re-thinking'.
[19] 'The difference between politics and political culture is essentially the difference between political action and the codes of conduct, formal and informal, governing those actions', Hoak's formulation in Hoak (1995), p. 1 was endorsed by Guy in his introduction to John Guy, ed. *The Tudor Monarchy* (London, 1997).
[20] Guy (1997), p. 7.
[21] Hudson, W. S., *The Cambridge connection and the Elizabethan settlement of 1559* (Durham, NC, 1980), pp. 35–9.

Introduction 7

standards and structures of republican Rome as their model for political emulation: consciously following Cicero, they championed the virtues of the dutiful participation of citizens in the government of the realm.[22] They were also adherents of the view that the mixed constitution was the best type of government for a *res publica*, especially in one ruled by a woman.[23] Their advocacy of the mixed nature of the constitution as a radical formulation rather than as a weary truism was best instantiated by Cecil's assertion that parliament should actively address the issue of the royal succession. As principal secretary, he produced drafts for the controversial 1566 Commons' petition on the issue: parliament had a duty to counsel the queen, and the queen had a duty to listen.[24] So, far from being the taciturn bureaucrat that Conyers Read sketched in his works, he is now presented as a radical, or at least instinctive, conciliarist, an intellectually sophisticated and thoughtful man who proposed that, in the event of Elizabeth's death, the privy council should remain *in situ* as a type of council of regency endorsed by statute until such time as parliament had nominated a successor. Similarly Sir Thomas Smith, the foremost analyst of the concepts and structures of the Elizabethan polity, presented the mixed constitution as an institutionalised reality in his *De republica anglorum*, arguing, with a tone of certainty, that parliament could indeed give forms of succession to the crown, an issue that Elizabeth always maintained could and should be determined by herself alone.[25] Furthermore, the shadow of Mary Stuart in the wings and the persistent problem of

---

[22] Collinson, P., 'The monarchical republic of Queen Elizabeth I' in Guy (1997), pp. 110–35 and 'De republica anglorum': *or History with the politics put back* (Cambridge, 1990).

[23] Peltonen, M., *Classical humanism and republicanism in English political thought 1570–1640*, (Cambridge, 1995). One particularly good example of the convergence of continental classical republicanism with an English context is that of Thomas Blunderville whose translation of Furió Ceriol's treatise *A brief treatise of counselers* into English (originally printed in 1559) asserted that parliament's role paralleled that of the 'council of revenues' and council of the 'matters of law', two bridles on monarchical power prescribed by the Spanish humanist. Of course the mixed constitution was also supported by indigenous common law authorities such as Christopher St German. See 'St German's doctor and student', ed. T. Plucknett and J. Barton, *Selden society* 91 (London 1974), p. 327.

[24] Alford (1998), pp.149–50. The first draft protested that Elizabeth intended for parliament be 'deprived of at least sequestered from an ancient laudable custom always *necessarily annexed to our assembly*, and by your majesty most graciously always confirmed, that is, a sufferance and leeful liberty to treat and devise of matters honourable for your majesty and profitable for your realm' (my italics). The best work on counsel in early modern England is John Guy's 'The rhetoric of counsel in early modern England' in Hoak (1995), pp. 292–310.

[25] 'Parliament abrogateth old laws, maketh new, giveth orders for things past, and for things hereafter to be followed, changeth rights and possessions of private men, legitimateth bastards, establisheth forms of religion, altereth weights and measures, giveth forms of succession to the crown . . . etc.' in T. Smith, *De republica anglorum*, ed. M. Dewar (Cambridge, 1982), p. 78.

the succession led to the very un-English (but strangely Scottish) Bond of Association in 1584 (a 'quasi-republican statement') and the Act 'for the surety of the queen's most royal person', which, as Collinson has pointed out, implicitly located sovereignty somewhere other than in the monarch. 'Legally, sovereignty and all power to act, all offices and courts, would have lapsed with the queen to be at once transferred to her lawful successor' he reminds us, but Cecil desired that in such circumstances 'government [should] reside in a great council or grand council, acting "in the name of the imperial crown of England"'. Cecil's plans are seen as an emanation of a civic republican *geist* that gripped England, high and low, in the second half of the sixteenth century. Indeed, the emblem of the 'monarchical republic' has been the 'self-governing republic' of Swallowfield, Collinson's evocation of the town meeting in a politically anomalous part of Berkshire where the 'chief inhabitants' vowed to meet regularly, to regulate the mores of their community and to 'be esteemed to be men of discretion, good credit, honest minds, and christianlike behaviour, one towards another'. Is Swallowfield closer to Tocqueville's impeccably Protestant New England Town Hall meeting or, more traditionally, the spirit of the customs of Romney Marsh?[26]

A broadening intellectual and methodological context for the thinking of Cecil and his circle has also emerged in the works of Stephen Alford and Markku Peltonen. Alford has quarried a particularly rich seam by investigating the implications of the educational formation of Sir William Cecil, paying particular attention to how he employed the skills in rhetoric he had attained to work out his thoughts on the state of the

---

[26] Collinson (1997), pp. 125–30. Collinson does, in passing, wonder whether Burghley's plan to deploy a sovereign great council during an interregnum caused by Elizabeth's sudden death 'would have succeeded in defeating the *coup de théâtre* which brought that other Mary to the throne against all the odds, in 1553', he also drastically limits the scope of his argument with his concluding remarks. Perhaps the possibility of such a coup happening, the shape it might have taken and a plausible list of those who might have backed it, might be given more consideration. In the event of Elizabeth's death prior to 1587 might the possible survival and enthronement of Mary Stuart – bond of association and act for the surety of the queen's royal person notwithstanding – have been enough of an assertion of the primacy of dynastic succession, of sovereignty being inherent in the 'true' monarch, to prove an obvious and devastating counterblast to the acephalous republican strategies advanced on paper by Burghley? What choice would the political estate of England have made between Burghley saying 'Follow me, and institute a sovereign general council' and (say) Lord Henry Howard declaring 'Follow me and enthrone your queen'? We should not presume how Swallowfield would have reacted. Presumably Burghley's frequent memos on both Mary Stuart and his interregnal plans, indicated his fear that such a thing could happen. For more on the customs of Romney Marsh and East Greenwich as benchmarks of English legal development see L. A. Knafla 'Common Law and custom in Tudor England: or 'the best state of the commonwealth' in *Law, Literature, and the settlement of regimes* (Washington, DC, 1990), pp. 171–81.

commonwealth.²⁷ Peltonen, among other things, has looked at the phenomenon of civic republicanism in the localities. Both the methodology and results of this work on high politics and the development of republican ideas throughout the country have been exemplary, giving us not only a 'history of political thought with an historical character' but one that has an emphatically demonstrable relationship with events and people, filling out our understanding of this crucial group, their influence and what influenced them.²⁸

Yet, there are some difficulties about seeing England's constitution *solely* from the vantage point of Swallowfield, or, indeed, from the lofty official heights commanded by the 'Cambridge connection'. Donald Kelley has quite correctly reminded us that 'there is no satisfactory historical account of political theory in Tudor England' and that (echoing J. H. Baker) 'the sixteenth century continues to represent the Dark Age of English legal history and so, to a degree, of political thought'.²⁹ While not denying the possibility that the men of Swallowfield and the partisans of the 'first' *regnum Cecilianum* may have shared certain assumptions, perhaps this point can be overstretched. The Cambridge men that commanded the early Elizabethan privy council were not a representative group; on the contrary, they were a caucus of exceptionally well-educated Edwardians who had been given a second chance. They were peculiar, and, it might be extrapolated, held peculiar views. Presumably if another peculiar caucus, say, the civil lawyers that made up the society known as Doctors' Commons, had wielded the dominant influence on the privy council and thereby on the monarch, parliament and court, they might have operated according to an entirely different view of the English constitution (Sir Thomas Smith's status as a prominent civilian notwithstanding), and perhaps they would have found willing fellow travellers to acquiesce in their view: the powerful generally do.

And whatever about the view of the English constitution and polity, its boundaries, its limits and its customs which were held in Swallowfield, around the council bench or at Doctors' Commons, the view from Dublin, Carrickfergus or Iar-Chonnacht must have been different again.

---

[27] Alford, S., 'Reassessing William Cecil in the 1560s' in Guy (1997), pp. 233–52, and also *The early Elizabethan polity: William Cecil and the British succession crisis, 1558–1569* (Cambridge, 1998), pp. 14–28.
[28] The phrase 'a history of political thought with an historical character' comes from Q. Skinner, *Foundations of modern political thought*, 2 vols. (Cambridge, 1978), Vol. I, p. xi.
[29] Kelley, D. E., 'Elizabethan political thought' in *The varieties of British political thought, 1500–1800* ed. J. G. A. Pocock, (Cambridge, 1993), pp. 50, 66.

Furthermore, whatever the received opinion about the shape of the English constitution and polity accepted by the burghers of London, the gentry of Berkshire or the Protestant survivors of Mary's reign (and maybe all these views were not the same), the opinions held by English captains serving in Ireland on the matter, for a variety of political, social and cultural reasons could well have been different. In short, all Englishmen might not have (in the term usually employed when speaking of the civil law) 'received' the 'monarchical republic'. Indeed, Kelley has suggested that Elizabethan political thought was made up of 'an extraordinary confusion of tongues'. It seems correct to assert that, although events did not seem to demand articulation of difference in the sixteenth century quite as starkly as they did in the seventeenth century, there definitely were differing varieties of English political thought during the Elizabethan era.[30] While one would not want to claim too much for the scope and internal logic of the political assumptions of English captains in Elizabethan Ireland, their views and experiences in the sister kingdom certainly were the views and experiences of Englishmen and therefore add to the spectrum of what we know about thoughts thinkable by the Elizabethan English. The generational bias of this book has concentrated on those figures who dominated military service in Ireland to 1594; figures who, like Cecil and Leicester, had also survived the warp and woof of the mid-Tudor period.

Of course, the mindset of certain martial men has always sparked patriotic feeling and provoked curiosity, namely those soldiers who distinguished themselves at sea. Sir Francis Drake, Sir Walter Ralegh and, at a stretch, Sir Humphrey Gilbert have received regular historical attention and have long been deemed emblems of what the age of Gloriana was all about. The vision of England to be found in the historiography surrounding these figures differs markedly from the fundamentally dull but decent ambience suggested by the good 'citizens' of Swallowfield in conclave. Where Swallowfield suggests the measured beat of English domestic values, the pluck of Drake and Ralegh suggests the audacity and exuberance of Empire. The fêting of this pluck was hardly an innovation in 1852 when James Anthony Froude enshrined it in his essay 'England's Forgotten Worthies', one of his *Short studies on great subjects*, in which he concluded that Elizabethan mariners had been short-changed in the volumes of the Hakluyt Society, which had turned 'the Prose Epic of the modern English

---

[30] Kelley (1993), p. 47. Note also Kelley's observation, quoting Conal Condren, that much work on political thought or political thinking is done by the 'political thought community' on the thought of former 'political thought communities'.

nation' into a subject dry as dust.[31] Froude mawkishly portrayed 'Humfrey and Adrian Gilbert, with their half-brother, Walter Raleigh, [in Devonshire], when little boys [playing] at sailors ... and listening, with hearts beating, to the mariners' tales of the new earth beyond the sunset'. Here his sentimentality got in the way of accuracy – when Ralegh was born, Gilbert was at least thirteen years old – but this conceit was designed to provide a picturesque account of the origins of England's world domination.[32]

Yet, this fastidiousness had more than a merely national importance. Froude's sensibility had a pressing global significance: the stated aim of his Tudor history was 'to describe the transition from the Catholic England with which the century opened ... into an England of progressive intelligence'. He asserted that it was because of the striving of the Elizabethans, with the heroic mariners in the vanguard, that the Victorians had the privilege to 'inhale the spirit of Protestantism with [their] earliest breath of consciousness'. The apotheosis of this development had been reached in his lifetime. Britain 'has created the great American nation; she is peopling new Englands at the Antipodes; she has made her Queen Empress of India' and of course the initial tentative steps towards these achievements had been those of the forward Elizabethan mariners.[33] The reign of Elizabeth had witnessed the English nation's turning away from the regressive allure of Rome and the setting of the stage for future greatness. The seamless association of English martial or maritime men with the triumph of either 'Reason' or 'Muscular Christianity' over the superstition and effeteness of 'Romanists' (represented by the overtly sensitive John Henry Newman on one hand and grubby Irish immigrants on the other) was not merely a myth of coherence spun by Froude. Sir Henry Newbolt, in his poem 'Drake's Drum', first published in 1896, summed up the wonted mixture of patriotism, regional authenticity and Elizabethan nostalgia very well:

> Drake he's in his hammock till the great Armadas come,
> (Capten, art tha sleepin' there below?)
> Slung atween the round shot, listenin' for the drum,

---

[31] Froude, J. A., 'England's forgotten worthies' in *Short studies on great subjects* (Oxford, 1924), pp. 314–15.
[32] Froude (1924), pp. 337–8. There was a further territorial twist to his account, as Froude was ever mindful of his own regional identity as the son of a Devonshire rector. That the genesis of the British empire might have been pregnant in the lisp of an old salt in the West Country held undoubted emotional appeal.
[33] Froude, J. A., *English seamen in the sixteenth century* (London, 1907), pp. 1–4. This work was based on a series of lectures Froude delivered as Regius professor at Oxford in the Easter terms of 1893–4.

> An' dreamin' arl the time o' Plymouth Hoe.
> Call him on the deep sea, call him up the Sound
> Call him when ye sail to meet the foe;
> Where the old trade's plyin' an' the old flag flyin'
> They shall find him, ware an' wakin', as they found him long ago.[34]

The British empire at the pinnacle of its power thrived on such a stirring account of the reasons for its greatness, and the greatness of its mission. In the historiography of English martial servitors, these associations have died hard.[35]

The many popular histories of Ralegh and Drake that have been published over the decades attest to the Elizabethan era's status as a designated 'Golden Age' in England's history: the beginnings of the empire. Even W. G. Gosling's scholarly biography of Sir Humphrey Gilbert leapt from consideration of its subject to explicit reference to hopes that the imperial dominions and colonies might be constitutionally integrated into the mother polity and a 'Greater Britain' might emerge.[36] Later in the twentieth century, as a greater awareness grew of the slow and demoralising withdrawal of British sovereignty from Africa and Asia, of the waning influence of Great Britain over the globe and, for some, the ominous success of left-wing politics at home, treatments of English expansion in the high colour of its youth became an overtly reactionary way of dealing with these changes, a reaction that persisted for decades after 1952, the starting point of the second Elizabethan age.[37] Treatments of a technocratic or Marxist inflection about these Elizabethan rough diamonds were attempted by scholars such as Christopher Hill and D. B. Quinn, who showed more and more interest in topics such as Ralegh's scientific interests, his 'atheism' and his central role in the globalisation of nascent capitalism through voyages and discoveries. Although we will deal with the implications of some of these interests later, it is worth noting how this frame of reference continued to resemble Froude's, championing on one hand the anti-obscurantist and 'rational' traits of these Elizabethans

---

[34] Newbolt, Sir H., *Admirals All* (London, 1897). The poem was arranged as a popular choral piece, an English favourite, along with other verses by Newbolt, by Dublin born composer Sir Charles Villiers Stanford. For a brilliant and not wholly irreverent parody of Newbolt's verse, see Brendan Behan's 'The captains and the kings' in *The Hostage*.

[35] See N. A. M. Rodger, 'Queen Elizabeth and the myth of sea-power in English history', *Transactions of the Royal Historical Society*, sixth series, Vol. XIV, pp. 153–74.

[36] Gosling, W. G., *The life of Sir Humphrey Gilbert* (London, 1911), p. 297.

[37] David Cannadine's essay 'The haunting fear of national decline' in *In Churchill's shadow* (London, 2002), pp. 26–44, deals thematically with a strand of Conservative reaction to perceived 'decline'.

and, on the other, the heroic importance of their expansionism. In many respects their main divergence from the concerns of the Victorian pessimist rested on a distinct view about the desired terminus for England's unfolding dialectic. In this way, one man's courageous patriot could become another's heroic nascent bourgeois.[38]

Ralegh, in particular, had become *the* model of Elizabethan dash. Biographies of less well-known martial men, even those without a maritime association, as well as treatments of Elizabethan martial men as a group, contained the well-rehearsed hagiographical gestures found in treatments of Sir Walter. These biographies often featured the aggrieved tone found in Froude's 'England's Forgotten Worthies': there were obscurer figures who had played their part in the creation and maintenance of English greatness, and their contribution had been unjustly forgotten. A particular variety of treatment made these men resemble nobody so much as Evelyn Waugh's Brigadier Ritchie-Hook who 'came back from a raid across no-man's-land with the dripping head of a German sentry in either hand', a figure who encapsulated that mixture of autonomy, insubordination and violence that constitutes 'pluck': a privileged English type that biffs superstitious popery and the hopelessly backward Irish.[39] In the face of the assurance of an A. L. Rowse (or indeed a Cyril Falls) on the topic of Elizabethan policy and its execution in Ireland, it might seem obvious that to achieve a satisfying and balanced treatment of the careers, or mentality of those military officers who carried it out, one should steer an interpretation between the Scylla of portraying them as plucky buccaneers and the Charybdis of dismissing them as mere psychopaths. Nevertheless, the personalities and activities of all of the English captains in Ireland during the reign of Elizabeth I have become blended together, not only in popular accounts but also in academic histories. While one damned captain after another took turns to enforce crown rule, only a few have earned fleeting distinction, usually by virtue of some particular atrocity. The often un-self-conscious presentation of heroism and bravado in history-writing as a whole has allowed rapacity and violence to be

---

[38] See Christopher Hill, *The intellectual origins of the English revolution revisited* (Oxford, 1997).
[39] See Evelyn Waugh, *The sword of honour trilogy* (London, 1994), pp. 60–1. '[Ritchie-Hook] was the great Halberdier *enfant terrible* of the First World War; the youngest company commander in the history of the Corps; the slowest to be promoted; often wounded, often decorated, recommended for the Victoria Cross, twice court-martialled for disobedience to orders in the field, twice acquitted in recognition of the brilliant success of his independent actions . . . Wherever there was blood and gunpowder from County Cork to the Matto Grosso, there was Ritchie-Hook.'

winked at: 'he may be a murderous thug, but he is *our* murderous thug.' It must be stressed that the Irish are quite as good at employing this double standard as any other nationality, their state-builders or *banditti* attaining a glow of heroism while despatching anti-Treatyites, crown forces, informers or oppressors. This study, it should be stressed, has no agenda as part of a trite *apologia* for the actions of Elizabethan martial men in Ireland: there is no 'Gentle Black and Tan' here.[40]

Notwithstanding the jingoistic inflection of previous works, recently there has been a bid to discover more about the 'Elizabethan military world' and to present it in a satisfactory manner. Apart from Paul Hammer's essential book *Elizabeth's Wars*, which skilfully presents the story of Elizabethan martial ventures and infrastructure with exemplary clarity, examples have included John Nolan's work on Sir John Norris and Mark C. Fissel's work on early modern English warfare.[41] Nolan's biographical treatment of Norris, an honour usually bestowed on Elizabethan mariners, accurately presents the reader with the disjointed and international character of the average Elizabethan captain's life. Norris is a shrewd choice for such a study: he had been perilously close to the coalface of Elizabethan diplomacy, especially as colonel of those English troops that served in the army of the Dutch states in the late 1570s when he enjoyed a close personal association with William of Orange as well as some acquaintance with Francis, duke of Anjou. In the 1580s, he played a prominent but divisive role in the earl of Leicester's Dutch campaign, and when the invasion of England by Spanish forces was widely anticipated in 1588, he was given charge of the defence of the vulnerable southernmost counties of England. Nolan, who fulfils his remit very well, however, has a protective attitude towards his subject, lamenting his neglect by previous historians, anxious to stress that Norris 'was by no means average'.[42] Intriguingly, this tone of special pleading has become quite a common motif in recent scholarship on Elizabethan martial men. For example, many of the entries

---

[40] See the result of the Irish novelist and journalist Breandán Ó hEithir's effort to write 'a revisionist ballad' with that title in *The begrudger's guide to Irish politics* (Dublin, 1986), pp. 5–6.

[41] See Hammer (2003). Hammer's work amounts to the best work on Elizabethan martial endeavour since Cruickshank (1966) and H. A. Lloyd *The Rouen Campaign 1590–2: Politics, warfare and the early modern state* (Oxford, 1973).

[42] Nolan, J., *Sir John Norris and the Elizabethan military mind* (Exeter, 1999), p. 242. Some of these comments were anticipated in a review written by the author in *IHS*, May 2000. By far the least tendentious of biographies of Elizabethan martial men is John Wagner's *The Devon gentleman: a life of Sir Peter Carew* (Hull, 1998) which is a model of thorough and illuminating research and restrained presentation.

on captains in the *Oxford Dictionary of National Biography* are written in this register.[43]

Fissel's work, however, is particularly problematic given that it seeks to prove that 'the English approached warfare with eclecticism and adaptability' throughout the late sixteenth and early seventeenth centuries.[44] This thesis is difficult to sustain. *Pace* Fissel, it took a lot less than 'muddy strategic thinking' to 'confound the best efforts of English soldiers'. The very fabric of England's military establishment was threadbare during the Tudor era, and the crown army of the Stuarts before and after the interregnum was not a shining example of the state of the art either.[45] Comparisons with Spain or France made England's military capacity appear particularly limited. As Cruickshank has pointed out, Elizabeth's parliaments, unlike Mary's, produced no great military statute. By contrast, as early as 1439, the French Estates General had granted its crown the resources to maintain a standing army.[46] As we shall see, contemporary military commentators felt ambivalent about the benefits of being an island rather than a land-locked kingdom. On the one hand, geography granted a degree of safety, but, on the other, it seemed to encourage military complacency. Fissel somewhat breathlessly ascribes a singular heroism to the age. His qualified belief in the existence of 'national characteristics' seasons his presentation of spirited English soldiers displaying ingenuity wherever they served, whether ranging battlefields on the Continent or facing 'partially concealed Irish sharpshooters...on the terrain of Eire'. Most strikingly, he asserts that 'English warfare charts part of the story of the preservation of the reformed religion, ensuring the eventual rise of toleration. The "Christian soldiers" discussed herein helped us along the circuitous route to *Veritas, Libertas, et Religios*', a startlingly loaded statement.[47]

---

[43] A particularly good example of this tendency is to be found in D. J. B. Trim's 'Gates, Geoffrey (*fl.* 1566–1580)', *Oxford Dictionary of National Biography* (Oxford, 2004) where Gates's book *A defence of the militarie profession* is described as 'a remarkable monument to his obscure yet passionate life'.

[44] Fissel, M. C., *English warfare* (London, 2001), p. xii.

[45] For a more measured assessment see Hammer (2003), pp. 236–64; for assessments of the Stuart army, especially towards the end of the seventeenth century, see Jonathan Scott, *England's troubles: seventeenth-century English political instability in European context* (Cambridge, 2000), pp. 215–16, 466–7.

[46] Cruickshank (1966), pp. 6–7.

[47] Fissel's use of the term 'Eire' to designate the island of Ireland in the sixteenth century brings misuse of this term to a new nadir. Often used erroneously by English commentators and manufacturers to describe the twenty-six-county state known as the Republic of Ireland, the title 'Éire' was adopted by the composers of the 1937 Constitution of Ireland as the name of the state (which in their minds included the entire island and surrounding waters) in the Irish language, the

An assumption made particularly often about Elizabethan captains is that they were Protestant zealots and that their careers were lived out with the aim of advancing reformed religion abroad and strengthening it at home. David Trim, whose work on the links between English men of arms and the religious conflicts on the Continent has unearthed much that was hitherto overlooked and neglected, not only subscribes to this view but has amplified it to argue that English foreign policy during Elizabeth's 'first reign' was predominantly motivated by confessional concerns in alliance with European Calvinism.[48] While sharing Trim's frustration with the strand in Elizabethan historiography that latches on to commitment to reformed religion and interprets it as merely a promise of a future capacity for secularism, I cannot agree with his certainty about the religious zeal of many of the martial officers of the period. His ascription of firm Calvinistic commitment to certain figures such as Edward Randolph and Richard Bingham is sometimes questionable. In any case, the use of terms such as 'ardent Calvinist' is not particularly useful if these descriptions are thought to give us a total picture of the person being dealt with, his motivations and thoughts and how he adapted himself to circumstances. Commitment to Calvinism could take a multitude of forms in line with the temperament of the person who held it, running the gamut from merely a personal, but not particularly active, preference for a certain model of ecclesiology to a totalising vision of the world and the place of everything in it from kings to commoners. Particularly tenuous is the attribution of 'godliness' to the captains as a default setting; this tends to sit uncomfortably with both the distrust or disdain that Cecil and kindred spirits held for these often highly appetitive and corrupt figures and also forecloses any sustained discernment of criminality and dishonesty. The religious motivation of English soldiers, stressed in Trim's work on the service of English and Welsh mercenaries in the Low Countries and France is, as we shall see, worryingly absent from developments in Ireland where captains actually had a central role in local government and where the Elizabethan religious settlement – a Church of Ireland with merely twelve articles open to broad interpretation – could hardly be

---

first official language. The name of the state in English is the translation 'Ireland'. Since the nineteenth referendum on the Irish constitution in 1998, the terms 'Éire' and Ireland describe the twenty-six-county state in Irish and English respectively and exclusively.

[48] Trim, D., 'Fighting "Jacob's warres": the employment of English and Welsh mercenaries in the European wars of religion: France and the Netherlands 1562–1610', unpublished Ph.D. thesis (University of London, 2002), pp. 104–33; 'Seeking a protestant alliance and liberty of conscience on the Continent, 1558–85' in *Tudor England and its neighbours*, eds. Susan Doran and Glenn Richardson (London, 2005), pp. 139–77.

deemed satisfactory to convinced Calvinists.[49] So much evidence points to diversity in these matters that an open mind on the question is required.[50]

A question that will be legitimately asked is why have I opted to finish my book at the terminus of 1594, just on the eve of that climacteric known as the Nine Years' War? This decision stems from a belief, based on the documentary material, that Ireland prior to that conflict, although ragged, brutal and corrupt, was a working political society, where crown authority, although beleaguered and occasionally challenged, was never shaken to its very core as it was by the confederation of Hugh O'Neill, earl of Tyrone, and Hugh O'Donnell, lord of Tyrconnell. I believe that the experience of Englishmen as governors in Ireland, especially the experience of those generations of Englishmen who had been old enough during the mid-Tudor period to be aware of the changing political and religious environment that had surrounded them in England, is worthy of research in and of itself.[51] Furthermore the weary truism that man's experience of time, and events in time is a sequential one has led me to be wary of the temptation to deal here with the conflict that animated Elizabeth's final years, for fear that the distinct and total nature of that conflict might distort analysis of the sixty years that went before. The Nine Years' War altered the topography of Irish politics, changing Gaelic Ireland from a society the crown negotiated with from a position of relative weakness, to a broken society to be dealt with from a position of strength. The sustained and countrywide escalation of military and political tensions that the Nine Years' War brought was unprecedented in Ireland. Furthermore, the personnel that were involved in the crown administration and in the conduct of that war, had a significantly different profile overall than had been the case previously.

Maybe only Shakespeare managed to capture the diversity of types found in the English martial profession from Falstaff to Iago and from Hotspur to Othello. The garrison in Ireland threw up a similar array of

---

[49] Matthew Parker's eleven articles of 1559 for the subscription of the clergy were used as the basic doctrinal framework of the Church of Ireland until the adoption of the 105 articles of 1615. See *A brefe declaration of certein principall articles of religion set out by order and aucthoritie as well of the right honorable Sir Henry Sidney knyght* (Dublin, 1566).
[50] It should also be noted that some of the differences in interpretation between Trim and myself may stem from a difference chronologically between our studies. The centre of gravity of my research lies in the examination of an earlier generation of English martial men than the focus of his study, which runs from 1562 to 1610.
[51] In 1594 Sir William Fitzwilliam, the sixty-eight-year-old Lord Deputy of Ireland (1526–1599) handed over the sword of state to his successor Sir William Russell, who was twenty-seven years younger than him.

flawed, but recognisably human, characters. What is the best way for a historian to deal with this range of temperaments? The study of 'mental worlds', 'sets of beliefs' or 'mentalities' is looked upon with understandable suspicion by British historians, especially those involved in the history of political thought, the history of ideas and intellectual history. The prioritisation of texts (and texts that aid the study of texts) has an obvious value, but, I would argue, so has the placing of a person or a defined group (mindful of individual idiosyncrasies) at the centre of a study. The distinct and long-rehearsed place that the knight or man-at-arms held in Christendom, as well as the existence of specific officerships from general down to ensign lends a type of coherence – a coherence acknowledged at the time – to the group of men considered here. Necessarily, the subject is somewhat more chaotic, inscrutable and drab than the study of the development of an idea – say, the theory of republican liberty – over time. However, an awareness of the importance of contexts – often short-term contexts arising from basic motivations – has been particularly important in the treatment of all the materials from which this study is drawn. This is stuff about people, not movements, about attitudes, prejudices, impulses, intentions, differing temperaments and political thinking, not political thought. Patterns do certainly emerge, but to some extent the Cobbsian waiver must be appealed to: 'my main concern throughout has been to allow people to speak for themselves.'[52]

[52] Cobb, R., *Police and the people: French popular protest, 1789–1820* (Oxford, 1970), p. xix.

CHAPTER I

Chimneys in summer

> Harry Monmouth, being in his right wits and his good judgements, turned away the fat knight with the great belly-doublet; he was full of jests, and gipes and knaveries, and mocks; I have forgot his name.
> *Henry V*, Act IV, Scene 7

In 1584, Sir William Cecil, Baron Burghley, wrote his son Robert a letter containing ten common-sense precepts for ordering his life. The advice was blunt – especially where he advised his hunchbacked son not to marry a dwarf for fear he might 'beget a race of pygmies' – and betrayed much about Cecil's prejudices. 'Suffer not thy sons to pass the Alps', he intoned 'for they shall learn nothing but pride, blasphemy, and atheism'; he was also eager to add 'neither . . . shalt thou train them up to wars'. Here he was unequivocal. To train a son for war was hazardous because

> he that sets up his rest only to live by that profession can hardly be an honest man or a good Christian, for war is of itself unjust unless the good cause may make it just. Besides it is a science no longer in request than [its] use for 'soldiers in peace are like chimneys in summer.[1]

To Burghley's mind, soldiering and the life of virtue were incompatible, and martial men were quick to grow rotten once their season had elapsed. In this, he was echoing commonplaces – later in Elizabeth's reign,

---

[1] Wright, L. B., *Advice to a son: precepts of Lord Burghley, Sir Walter Raleigh, and Francis Osborne*, (Ithaca, NY, 1962), p. 11. The Erasmian tone here may also have a Machiavellian inflection. In *L'Arte della guerra*, Machiavelli had Fabrizio Colonna, the mercenary commander say of the military profession: 'It is impossible for a good man to follow this profession [i.e. soldiering] . . . Neither a republic nor a well organised kingdom have ever permitted its citizens or subjects to make it their profession . . . Pompey, Caesar and practically all those leaders after the last Carthaginian war acquired fame as brave men, not as good men', see *L'Arte della guerra* (Rome, 2001), pp. 44–5. The work was translated by Peter Whitehorne as *The Arte of Warre*, and was published in England not only in 1560, but again in 1573 and 1588. Significantly, Whitehorne claimed to have completed his translation while he was in Charles V's army in 1550, see Webb (1965) p. 13. Whitehorne also wrote *Certain ways for the orderyng of souldiers in battleray* (1560) and published *Of the generall captaine and of his office* (1563).

Shakespeare would give posterity a candid and familiar portrayal of the military servitor at his most feckless, cowardly and appetitive, on one hand levying paltry things such as Ralph Mouldy, Simon Shadow, Thomas Wart, Francis Feeble and Peter Bullcalf for military service and, on the other, bragging about martial feats never performed.[2]

But there was more substance to hostile attitudes towards martial officers, captains and lieutenants than either comedic ridicule or blind prejudice could express. There was a serious intellectual and ethical case to make against military officers, a case that not only dealt with abstractions but with plain realities. How had these men earned Cecil's opprobrium? They, themselves, affected to wonder why, complaining that their stock had unjustly fallen. In the late 1570s, Thomas Churchyard, captain and scribbler, would feel compelled to write wistfully about the reign of Henry VIII, a time when

> all chivalry was cherished, soldiers made of and manhood so much esteemed that he was thought happy and most valiant that sought credit by the exercises of arms, and discipline of war [and] he was counted nobody, that had not been known to be at some valiant enterprise [for the] advancement of his country.[3]

Why was there such a discrepancy between the treatment that the Elizabethan captains thought they deserved and the treatment they got? In the highest reaches of power England's political culture had changed, and the captains were slow to react.

Of course, if the peddlers of nostalgia were to be believed, time was when the value of martial men, as asserted through knighthood, and chivalric culture had been self-evident truths held throughout Christendom. They were largely correct. As M. E. James has demonstrated, theoretical justifications for the status of the gentleman-soldier or knight straddled two venerable and pervasive Continental traditions of thought, which together could produce many variants of mongrel offspring. As we shall see in the next chapter, traces of these traditions survived and strongly influenced the content of the captains' *apologiae* for their profession.[4] The first tradition was heavily indebted to civil and canon law. This stressed the knight's role as an agent of God's authority delegated to him by the Church or a

---

[2] Shakespeare, *2 Henry IV*, Act III, Scene 2.
[3] Churchyard (1579) sig. Ai, r. See also Sir James Croft's description of the Henry VIII 'by whose death all meanes of preferment was taken away' see R. E. Ham, 'The autobiography of Sir James Croft', *Bulletin of the Institute of Historical Research*, Vol. 50, pp. 171, 51.
[4] James, M. E., 'English politics and the concept of Honour, 1485–1642', *Past & Present Supplement 3* (1978), pp. 8–15. Russell, F. H. *The just war in the middle ages* (Cambridge, 1975), pp. 16–39.

temporal ruler, and prioritised the idea that the military profession had a specific location within a universal sacred design and posited consequently that war could be instrumental in securing justice; these ideas received their first systematic Christian treatment in the works of Augustine and Isidore of Seville.[5] Christian sacralisation of violence and recognition of the professional status of soldiers reached a state of advanced development in western Europe when Bernard of Clairvaux endorsed both crusading and the sacral knights of the Order of the Temple, a sacralisation amplified by John of Salisbury's treatment of martial men in his *Policraticus*.

In the world of jurisprudence, these spiritual and philosophical developments were complemented in the works of the Italian post-glossators of the late thirteenth and fourteenth centuries. Using scholastic dialectic and a sophisticated appreciation of the social and political context of their times, these jurists attempted to reconcile the *corpus juris civilis* with contemporary feudal, monarchical and oligarchical societal structures. Their treatment of knighthood tallied with a central motif of their project: the adoption of the maxims *rex in regno suo est imperator regni sui* (a king in his kingdom is emperor of his kingdom) and *rex qui superiorem non recognoscit* (he who recognises no superior is king/sovereign).[6] This regional distribution of God's temporal authority allowed the different monarchs of Europe to be recognised as legitimate possessors of *merum imperium*, defined by the jurist Ulpian as 'possession of the power of the sword to punish the wicked, also called *potestas*'. This provided the legal space enabling princes to impose domestic rule on their own territories and to authorise 'just war'.[7] In theory, this development in civil law, popularly assimilated in the works of Honoré Bonet (1340?–1405?) and Christine de Pisan (1364–1429), bound the sovereign and his knightly vassals closer

---

[5] See D. E. Luscombe and G. R. Evans, 'The twelfth-century renaissance', in J. H. Burns (ed.), *The Cambridge History of Medieval Political Thought* (Cambridge, 1988), pp. 396–41; p. 309.

[6] The glossators and especially the postglossators, by highlighting the pre-eminence of the king's will in creating law, instigated a crucial moment in the development of political thought, leading to the definition of ideas of the state and territorial sovereignty. See J. P. Canning's 'Introduction: politics, institutions and ideas' and 'Law, sovereignty and corporation theory' in Burns (1988), pp. 363, 365, 458.

[7] *Merum est imperium habere gladii potestam ad animadvertendum facinorosos homines, quod etiam potestas appelatur*, *Digest of Justinian*, ed. T. Mommsen and P. Kruegar, trans. A. Watson, (Pennsylvania, Pa., 1985) p. 40. I will return to the concept of *merum imperium* and its delegation in a later chapter. Russell, F. H. *The just war in the middle ages*, (Cambridge, 1975), p. 69. For reference to movement by the glossators of the twelfth century towards this accommodation in order to confine the waging of war to licit authorities, see p. 45.

together, tending to undermine the contractual nature of feudal loyalty by favouring a straightforward idea of delegation.[8]

The other traditional mode of thinking about the vocation to knighthood placed more emphasis on a communal and self-affirmative concept of the knight's place in society and the legitimacy of violence; this concept tempered, and in some respects tacitly subverted, the hierarchical nature of the formulation outlined above.[9] A key innovator within this tradition was the Majorcan mystic and logician Raymond Lull. Glorifying knighthood as an order within the tripartite division of society into clerics, knights and peasantry, Lull, in his *Libre del ordre del cavayleria* (translated by Caxton in 1484) posited that in the state of nature one 'man most loyal, most strong, and of most noble courage' out of every thousand had been given both a horse and the authority to coerce.[10] Consequently, gentility, which had always been intimately associated with knighthood, was conceived of as the perpetuation over generations of character judgements or semi-constitutional arrangements arrived at by humanity as a whole in prehistory.[11] Lull, however, conceived of the order of knighthood as spread organically by the dubbing of worthy men by attested knights, the distinctions between them being established by the struggle for pre-eminence.[12] Most of all, he emphasised a code of chivalric behaviour

---

[8] See Pisan, C. de, *The book of the fayttes of armes and of Chyvalrie*, trans. Caxton, ed. A. Byles (London, 1932), p. 10, for Chapter 3, Book 1, Here it deviseth how it is not leeful but to kings & sovereign princes to imprise was and H. Bonet, *The tree of battles*, ed. G. Coopland (Liverpool, 1949), pp. 128, Chapter 4, Book 4, 'Whether a prince other than the emperor may ordain war'. For the role of jurists, such as Raymond of Pennaforte, John of Legnano and Baldus of Ubaldo, in formulating normative late medieval thought on the just war see Keen (1965), pp. 65–6. See also Keen (1984), pp. 34–43, 111. The concept of monarchical delegation of power to knights was especially current throughout the Holy Roman Empire and Italy and corresponded well with the administrative structure of the Empire. Keen notes the existence of a twelfth century fable which claimed that Julius Caesar had instituted German knighthood.

[9] For contrasting views on the criteria for bearing arms between a stress on gentility of blood as encapsulated in *The boke of St Albans* and Nicholas Upton's (1400?–1457) emphasis on a causal relationship between virtue and nobility in his *De studio militari* see J. P. Cooper *Land, men and beliefs* (London, 1983), pp. 46–50. For the artificial nature of, and reason behind, many heraldic genealogies see M. E. Keen *Chivalry* (New Haven, Conn., 1984), p. 33, and Lawrence Stone's entertaining treatment in *The crisis of the aristocracy* (Oxford, 1965), pp. 65–128. See also James (1978), pp. 2–12.

[10] Caxton, W., *The book of the ordre of chyvalry or knyghthode*, (originally Westminster, 1484; facsimile edition, Amsterdam, 1976), sig. Avii, v. Noah's blessing on Japhet and curse on Shem, a story that carried scriptural authority, was also looked upon as the inaugural designation of the gentle and the base, see J. P. Cooper *Land men and beliefs* (London, 1983), p. 47, James (1978), p. 5. This motif is found in *The boke of St Albans* (Originally St Albans, 1486; facsimile edition, London, 1881), G. Legh, *The accedens of armory* (1568; reprinted 1576, 1591, 1597, 1612); and J. Ferne, *The blazon of gentrie* (1586).

[11] See Burke (1995), p. 9. For the resilience of a threefold division of society into knights, clerics and labourers, see Keen (1984), p. 4.

[12] Caxton (1484) sigs. Av, r.–Av, v., Cviii, v, Dii, v–Div, r. The earliest literary treatment of the practice of dubbing was the early thirteenth-century Norman romance *Ordene de chevalrie*, see

as an abstract standard by which conduct could be deemed honourable or shameful, one by which even actions of royalty could be judged. This tradition was widely disseminated in the *chansons* and romances of late-medieval chivalric literature, where the virtues of *prouesse, loyauté, largesse, courtoisie* and *franchise* were emphasised. These required a knight to be courageous in war, faithful to his word, generous to his peers and inferiors, courteous in his manner (especially with women) and frank in his bearing, shunning flattery while upholding the honour of his office. King Arthur in Thomas Malory's *Morte d'Arthur* administered an oath to his knights each Whitsunday, but the pledge was neither a test of allegiance nor a confession of monarchical supremacy but a declaration of commitment to an ethical code of practice.[13]

Following this model, the justification of knighthood did not depend on investiture by pope or prince but nourished itself on a belief in the intrinsic moral necessity of knighthood and the primeval election of knights by the peoples of the earth.[14] Furthermore, the political independence of knights was not only deemed possible but was thought to be desirable. 'So much noble is chivalry', Caxton declared, 'that every knight ought to be governor of a great country or land'.[15] In England, Magna Carta, with its stress on the baronial prerogative in relation to monarchy could be seen as a constitutional expression of this idea of *franchise*.[16] However, despite giving expression to the political and social aspirations of a feudal culture, Lull's account of the genesis of the order of chivalry, for all its individualistic swagger, based its claim to legitimacy on an idea of the 'common good' which had become a central theme of late medieval scholastic argument on politics, influencing ideas about the duties carried by political structures and institutions. In this context, the question increasingly arose as to the balance to be struck between an individual's moral worth in the eyes of God (the degree to which he could be said to be *honestum*) and his advantage to the polity (the degree to which he was *utile*).[17]

Keen (1984), pp. 7, 26. One obvious reason for the association of gentility with wealth stemmed from the fact that riches were an obvious precondition, not only for the possession of weapons and horses, but for the exercise of chivalric *largesse*.

[13] See R. W. Kaeuper, *Chivalry and violence in medieval Europe* (Oxford, 1999), p. 295.

[14] In Caxton admission to the order of chivalry, ideally takes place through the dubbing of qualified squires by knights. It is strongly hinted that the dubbing of knights by monarchs commonly leads to the assumption of knighthood by unqualified candidates. Caxton (1484), sigs. Av, v; Fii, v.

[15] James (1979), p. 5.

[16] Ullmann, W., *A history of political thought: the middle ages* (London, 1970), pp. 145–54.

[17] Of course this type of legitimating myth of origin also underwrote Justinian's civil law, where it was asserted in the *lex regia* that the emperor's authority had been granted to him by virtue of the unanimous will of the people for their own protection. See Caxton (1484), sig. Fii, v. 'To a knight

The knight was a source of true justice, the quality necessary for the maintenance of a legitimate polity. It could be argued that his role in the preservation of both national and international order, hard won from the state of nature, was a necessary precondition for the continued existence of humanity as well for the possibility of living a virtuous life.

Chivalry can best be described as a state of mind – at once a standard, a system and an aspiration. Its creative literature displayed its Dionysiac imagination, while the day-to-day 'workings' of the chivalric *geist* were often played out in the more drab surroundings of the courts of chivalry in arbitration on matters to do with the payment of ransom or the equitable distribution of spoils of war. As both Maurice Keen and Peter Coss have demonstrated, until the thirteenth century, martial prowess and a sense of chivalric vocation, above all else, were emphasised as qualifications for knighthood, but thereafter these elements increasingly came to be seen as necessary adornments to aristocratic heredity rather than the actions which conclusively proved gentility: it was often because a man came from a long line of knights that he felt the need to fight pagans in the mists of Lithuania or the overweening urge to join a crusade. Furthermore, those who accepted knighthood needed considerable financial attainments to fulfil their duties when serving their monarchs or lords; provision of a warhorse, acquisition of the skill to ride it, not to mention the weaponry and armour required. Knighthood itself had always comprehended differing social gradations within its ranks – there were dukes, earls and counts who had been dubbed – whereas divisions within the knightly class itself, between barons, bannerets and bachelors, were recognised. By the late fourteenth century, the term 'esquire', previously employed merely to describe the armed servants of a knight, was being used to designate a gentle class of landowners directly lower than knights in the social pecking order. They were entitled to hold coats of arms and to use heraldic devices on their seals; some were scions of families who were either of knightly descent or had a knight as the head of their kin; many had opted against taking up knighthood for economic reasons. In a further development, a stratification below esquires but above the yeomanry emerged, largely a class of professional administrators and wealthy freeholders who were termed 'gentlemen'. They too supplied men-at-arms and aspiring captains

---

apperteineth that he be lover of the common weal. For by the communal of the people was the chivalry founded and established.' See also G. M. Kempshall, *The common good in late medieval political thought* (Oxford, 1999), p. 347.

to armies throughout Europe out of the cohort of younger sons they produced who set their sights on such a career.[18]

While these social developments were taking place, the terms of service in warfare and the make-up of armed forces were changing radically. Edward III's armies during his wars in France increasingly relied on a system of indentures securing short-term recruitment for fixed periods rather than more immoveable feudal obligations or commissions of array. Whereas the overall command of major armies remained in the hands of militarised nobility, the maintenance of lands subdued or conquered was in the hands of professional men-at-arms from minor gentry heading smaller forces of occupation. Following the reverse of 1305 at Bannockburn, a tactical revolution took place in English warfare. There came to be less reliance on cavalry, and infantry took the primary role on the field of battle. Andrew Ayton has pointed to the apparent contradictions this posed for the aristocracy who found themselves fighting on the ground side by side with '*parvenu* men-at-arms' while archers, by contrast, were often mounted. In this logistically sensible but socially counter-intuitive environment, upward mobility within the ranks of the army from archer to captain became ever more plausible.[19] Furthermore, the legal and ritual worlds of chivalry, as well as its account of the virtues, were meant to be reverenced and respected by all men-at-arms of whatever social status. It became common to elide the distinctions between gentry and titled aristocracy on the field of battle, comprehending both groups under the common title of *miles*.[20] In time, all men who had held office commanding men would be comprehended as *milites*. While the title of knight, as Gerald Harriss has pointed out, came to be increasingly the badge of a narrow elite, the aspiration towards pre-eminence earned by the pursuit of chivalric virtues became the common inheritance of all members of the manor-holding classes who pursued a martial career.[21]

CIVIL AND CIVIC DEVELOPMENTS: THE RUBRICS OF CRITICISM

Amid the martial clamour, a more civil account of the virtues was developing in the Italian city-states, where a notion of the common good

---

[18] Coss, Peter, *The knight in medieval England 1000–1400* (Gloucester, 1993), pp. 128–34.
[19] Ayton, A., 'English armies in the fourteenth century' in *Arms, armies and fortifications in the hundred years war*, ed. Anne Curry and Michael Hughes (Woodbridge, 1999), pp. 21–38.
[20] See Keen (1984), pp. 27–8, for the shifting definition of the term.
[21] Harriss, G., *Shaping the nation: England 1360–1461* (Oxford, 2005), pp. 139–41.

dependent on political participation in the *res publica*, rather than on violent coercion, was coming to the fore. In constitutional terms, the post-glossators had not only conferred imperial authority on local monarchs but had, by extension, also made it available to the government of Italian city-states. Consequently, in those states that operated a republican constitution in the thirteenth century, such as Arezzo and Padua, and those that retained their republican status for longer, such as Florence and Venice, a discourse on the nature of legitimate citizenship flourished. As is well known, this ethos took as its talisman the corpus of Stoic writers of the Roman republic and early empire. Cicero's works in this context, especially *De officiis* (reclaimed and interpreted through the work of the great humanists Poggio Bracciolini, Pietro Bembo, Francesco Patrizi, Leonardo Bruni and Coluccio Salutati) moved the locus of virtue and honour away from ancestral lands and local jurisdiction to the centralised area of state service and high politics, be it *podestà* or court.[22] Whereas Aristotle had explicitly made riches a precondition of true nobility, Cicero had stated unequivocally that virtue was true nobility and that this virtue had to be expressed in deeds done for the commonwealth. In many respects, prowess and the arts of war were increasingly deemed less useful in facilitating secure government than *eloquentia*, a synthesis of rhetoric and philosophy expressed in *negotium* in the service of the *res publica*. *Eloquentia* was the means by which the four cardinal virtues of prudence, justice, courage and temperance were carried into a political context.

Commonwealths had to be both defended and policed, but their preservation was deemed to be dependent on the health of their constitutions. Therefore, by assuming office and serving the polity, one helped to maintain the constitution in prosperous existence. Furthermore, this shift in the definition of true nobility led to a change in opinion about the form a suitable education for aristocrats should take. The result was new enthusiasm for Quintilian's educational writings – the complete *Institutio oratoria* had been rediscovered by Bracciolini in the early fifteenth century. Their exaltation of rhetorical training provided a *cursus* that could give the learned clerk a better preparation for political life than that pursued by high-born aristocrats who had been formed through a life of hunting, tournaments and military exercises. Nobility theoretically became a property contingent on suitable training in *eloquentia* facilitating a life

---

[22] Skinner, Q., 'Political philosophy' in *The Cambridge history of renaissance philosophy*, ed. C. Schmitt, especially pp. 426–7.

of *negotium*. Stoic moral philosophy also brought a moral philosophy prioritising *decorum* in political society into increased currency. Central to this philosophy was the pursuit of a code of restraint – epitomised by the maxim *abstine et sustine* – which made explicit demands for personal pre-eminence, not to mention the culture of errantry, seem increasingly petulant, self-serving and injurious to the commonwealth.[23]

This is not to say that Italian political thought did not acknowledge the importance of military endeavour. Most of the heroes of the Roman republic had comprehended both the civil and military spheres; for instance, Plutarch stressed that the dictator Fabius Maximus when he 'came to consider the great sovereignty of [the] commonwealth did [both] use his body to all hardness' and 'gave himself much to eloquence also as a necessary instrument to persuade soldiers unto reason'.[24] *De officiis*, as well as being a statesman's primer, had been a seminal text in the formation of standard European thinking in relation to the law of war, casting war as the redress of injury and therefore a means of establishing justice.[25] Even from a purely tactical and technical perspective, the debt to Roman precedent was immense, both Sextus Julius Frontinus' and Renatus Flavius Vegetius' military treatises being a constant touchstone for martial men throughout the Middle Ages and into the sixteenth century. However, the key feature of republican discourse at this time was endorsement of the civic militia or citizens' army rather than recourse to professional soldiers. As early as the thirteenth century, Giles of Rome, in his continuation and completion of Aquinas's *De regimine principum*, had endorsed the idea of a trained militia made up of all social groups in the *res publica*, irrespective of whether they were involved in mechanical labour or not.[26] Subsequently, Italian political thinkers, from Salutati through Leonardo Bruni and Savonarola onto Guicciardini, followed Aristotle and Roman republican thought and exalted the concept of the civic militia as the *sine*

---

[23] Kraye, J., 'Moral philosophy' in *The Cambridge history of renaissance philosophy* ed. C. Schmitt (Cambridge, 1988), pp. 360–70.
[24] Plutarch, *The lives of the noble Grecians and Romanes compared* trans. T. North (London, 1579), p. 191. For the use of *eloquentia* to rouse Elizabethan soldiers (admittedly with the assistance of 'a tun of wine'), see Sir Henry Sidney's account of his exhortation to troops during the Butler rebellion of 1569, Sidney, H., *A viceroy's vindication? Sir Henry Sidney's memoir of service in Ireland, 1556–78*, ed. C. Brady (Cork, 2002) p. 68. Sallust's account of martial speeches in *Bellum Jugurthae* was also a touchstone for those who wished to integrate martial pursuits with rhetoric.
[25] Cicero, *De officiis* (Cambridge, Mass., 1997), Vol. I, pp. 13, 34–40; Vol. III, pp. 107–11.
[26] Bayley, C. C., *War and society in Renaissance Florence: the 'De militia' of Leonardo Bruni* (Toronto, 1961), pp. 181–3.

qua non of a healthy, free and secure polity.[27] Citizens, they stressed, should be prepared to fight for and defend their liberties, not least because they were deemed more effective and trustworthy in that role than hired warriors; it was recalled that Livy, employing a daring counterfactual, had asserted that even if Alexander the Great had attacked the fledgling Roman republic he would not have prevailed over its army, because 'there were many Romans equal to Alexander in glory and in the grandeur of their deeds, and yet each of them might fulfil his destiny by his life or by his death without imperiling the existence of the state.'[28]

Emphasis on republican virtue was leavened by a rising Italian patriotism, which cast foreign *condottieri* as barbarians in the tradition of Alaric the Goth, a symptomatic proof of Italy's decline from its days of martial virtue and superiority. An influential voice in this dispute was that of Petrarch, who, in his *De rebus familiaribus*, launched a tirade against mercenaries on Italian soil, branding them as a morally reprobate band capable of every wrong, who lived a slovenly life at camp in a stew of drink, whores and dice. They were cowardly, men who sated their greed and vanity in a pretence of conflict, who were incapable of any higher loyalty to country, cause or, indeed, honour but endemically broke their word and despoiled their employers.[29] It is true that the city-states of Italy had bitter experience at the hands of *condottieri*, but despite notional abhorrence for mercenaries, throughout the late fourteenth and fifteenth centuries, the skill and manpower of figures such as Sir John Hawkwood, Alberigo Barbiano, Bracchio da Montone, Musio Sforza and later Bartolomeo Colleoni proved invaluable to the republics of Florence, Padua and Venice in their struggle to defend themselves. Of course, mercenaries were also willing to uphold despotism in the form of Visconti rule in Milan, Aragonese rule in Naples, and papal control over central Italy. From a republican perspective, the most terrible abuses of power occurred when mercenaries came to exert personal lordship over a city or town as the Malatestas did in Rimini and the Baglioni in Perugia.[30] However, it was not all bad. The *condottiere* Francesco Sforza, who caused the dissolution of the short-lived Ambrosian republic, which had employed him

---

[27] Skinner, Q., *Foundations of modern political thought* (Cambridge, 1978), Vol. I, pp. 75–6, 130–1, 147. Plato had also endorsed the idea of a militia, but envisaged an order of professional soldiers formed by the republic as a permanent army. Bayley (1961), p. 179.
[28] Livy, *History of Rome* (Cambridge, Mass., 1963), Book IX, Chapters 17–18, p. 236–7; Machiavelli, *Discourses on Livy* (Oxford, 1997), Book II, Chapter 10, pp. 177–80.
[29] Bayley (1961), pp. 184–8.
[30] Mallett, M., *Mercenaries and their masters: warfare in Renaissance Italy* (London, 1974), pp. 92–3 on granting of fiefdoms to *condottieri*.

to fight the Venetians on its behalf, proved himself to a relatively benign and enlightened ruler. Whereas the Baglioni in Perugia were largely an unsympathetic group, Sforza, as duke of Milan, was a popular sagacious figure, a charismatic rejoinder to republican government.

To the north of the Alps, of course, states were, on the whole, constitutionally monarchical, yet this did not prevent the percolation of republican political philosophy along with renewed classical learning north from Italy, or the development of a counter-blast of invective against martial attitudes. Here, the application of classical humanist intellectual trends in the late fifteenth and early sixteenth centuries led to a radical scrutiny of unquestioned values of honour, military prowess and lineage in some quarters; this radical scrutiny complemented other social and economic pressures towards a reformation of manners and was more explicitly Christian in sentiment than Italian thought. In the eyes of humanists such as Erasmus of Rotterdam and Thomas More, vanity, violence and venality characterised the current dispensation, a morass from which Christendom could only extricate itself by means of education and the advancement of individuals to office solely on the basis of merit conceived of as rational virtue. Erasmus, in particular, repeatedly cast a cold eye on what he perceived as the futility and the unchristian nature of war. Augustinian just-war theory, which, following Cicero, stressed the necessity of war to redress injury, came to be unfavourably juxtaposed with Christ's injunction to turn the other cheek. Erasmus, in characteristic anti-Augustinian vein, even denied military men any indulgence as Christian professionals, maintaining instead that soldiers should be buried in unconsecrated ground.[31] He produced at least six essays explicitly condemning war; 'Querela pacis', the most renowned of these, was reprinted twenty times between 1517 and 1529. Like most Christian authorities, he stressed that peace was the precondition for prosperity, security, pleasure and the perfect worship of God, but he did not readily admit that coercive means were needed to maintain this condition. In exalting the common good and stressing the quality of *humanitas* in (generally princely) government, he also scorned the 'personal inclinations', that is the thirst for pre-eminence, that looked to honour for validation. Furthermore, Erasmian humanism's fresh emphasis on every man's resemblance with the divine, and its imperative towards its own conception of

---

[31] Erasmus, 'Querela pacis' in *Collected works of Erasmus*, ed. A. H. T. Levi, trans B. Radice, Vol. 27, pp. 289–322.

social justice, helped to undermine the age-old tripartite differentiation between knights, common labourers and clerics.[32]

While Erasmus wished to set a specific tone throughout the commonwealth by advocating a return to Christian simplicity, in northern European more pragmatic humanist sentiments came to be expressed in a way that took account of the monarchical nature of the *res publica*. Consequently, the role of *eloquentia* in the form of counsel given by individuals to princes was considered. Royal courts were never going to be particularly well disposed towards an indiscriminate reception of all elements of the Erasmian humanist project, least of all its pacifism and uncompromising insistence on merit over blood, but there was an appetite for a polished Italianate urbanity and the recasting of aristocratic demeanour and disposition through education. Baldissare Castiglione's *Il cortegiano*, written in the context of early sixteenth-century Italy, when even the most stalwart republics, apart from Venice, were being replaced by principalities, proved an opportune and readily adaptable text that applied a classical humanist ethic and aesthetic to the hoary medieval genre of courtesy books. His work was enthusiastically seized on, not least for its facility in accommodating many different intellectual strands within its scope and its stress on courtesy, which satisfied the need for a new treatment of chivalric virtues relating to courtesy in the context of the early modern court. However, it catered for other appetites also. The arbitrary nature of advancement at court stemmed from the whim and inclination of the monarch. To be attractive at court ultimately meant to be attractive to the prince, a tacit acknowledgement of the non-contractual nature of even the most casual aspects of imperial kingship.

Aristocrats, on the other hand, believed themselves to be the natural counsellors of the king, the *pares* among whom the monarch was *primus*, the living and breathing best interest of the realm. *Il cortegiano* showed itself to be readily adaptable to the aristocratic prejudices of Henrician England.[33] The most famous indigenous work mimicking the Castiglionean format was *The boke named the gouernour* (1531) by the impeccably Erasmian humanist Sir Thomas Elyot. This work marked a movement

---

[32] See B. Bradshaw, 'Transalpine humanism', in Burns and Goldie (1991), p. 126. For a different view that posits a divergence by 1533 between More and the optimism of the Erasmian programme, see A. Fox, 'Interpreting English humanism' and 'English humanism and the body politic' in A. Fox and J. Guy *Reassessing the Henrician age: humanism, politics and reform* (Oxford, 1986), pp. 19–51.

[33] Burke, P. *The fortunes of the courtier* (Cambridge, 1995), pp. 13–18, 34, 79–80. Thomas Cromwell owned a copy while he was Cardinal Wolsey's secretary and Henry Howard, subsequently earl of Northampton, also read and annotated the text.

away from the abstracted and radically communitarian model of More's commonwealth Utopia, as recounted by Hythlodaeus, towards the consideration of a 'public weale' predicated on the remoulding of the feudal nobility, by means of education, to be governors, eager to pursue virtue through office.[34] Elyot's aim was to get the de-facto Aristotelian nobility to attain true nobility the Ciceronian way – an ambitious target given the recent strife of the Wars of the Roses when England's aristocracy plunged itself into internecine bickering and self-destruction. During the late fourteenth and fifteenth century, five kings lost the throne through baronial rebellion, because of the very ethos of self-assertion that Lull and others had believed to be the linchpin of the preservation of order.[35] From the reign of Henry VII to that of Elizabeth I, 'bastard feudalism' was brought to heel through the promulgation of statutes that subjected wayward aristocrats to the rigour of the royal courts and harshly punished attempts to corrupt the legal process. The court of Star Chamber became the locus of these disputes and thereby became an emblem for the centralisation of power in London.[36] Given the fact that this court was derived from the privy council, court patronage, more and more, was perceived to be crucial in determining the success or failure of a suit. Later, Sir Thomas Smith would be remarkably frank in his treatment of the reasons why Star Chamber had been established. He argued that it had been 'marvellous necessary' in order 'to repress the insolency of the noblemen and gentlemen of the north parts of England, who being far from the king and the seat of justice made almost as it were an ordinary war among themselves and made their force their law'.[37]

It was under this new dispensation, that *The boke named the gouvernor* was composed. Elyot's intentions were less individualistic than Castiglione's had been; *sprezzatura* was licit only in so far as it advanced the 'public weale'.[38] But, at the kernel of Elyot's vision was a concern to maintain the ranking of orders: the desire to save the aristocracy by training it to be adept politically, emboldening it to seize the influence and power that

---

[34] For a treatment of Elyot's personal circumstances, his ambition and eventual frustration see A Fox's 'Sir Thomas Elyot and the humanist dilemma' in *Reassessing the Henrician Age: humanism, politics and reform 1500–1550*, eds A. Fox and John Guy (Oxford, 1986), pp. 52–73.
[35] *Cyvile and uncyvile life* (London, 1579), p. 16, v.
[36] Elton, G. R., *The Tudor constitution* (Cambridge, 1982), pp. 163–6.
[37] Smith, T., *De republica anglorum* (Cambridge, 1982), p. 127.
[38] Elyot's definition of a 'public weale' states that it is 'a body living, compact or made of sundry estates and degrees of men, which is disposed by the order of equity and governed by the rule and moderation of reason'.

was its birthright for 'where virtue joined with great possessions or dignity, hath long continued in the blood or house of a gentleman ... there nobility is most showed'.[39] Thomas Starkey in his unpublished *Dialogue between Pole and Lupset* showed a similar interest in an increased role for the aristocracy in counselling and bridling the king, proposing, through the voice of Reginald Pole, that there should be two councils of nobility to ponder the issues of the day. Crucially, Elyot, like Starkey, silently passed over the role of threatened violence in securing order. By contrast, they both stressed the 'rule and moderation of reason' as the means by which a polity should be governed.[40] Indeed, fear and pre-eminence, both of which had been central to Caxton's view of a society safeguarded by chivalry, were changed from self-affirmative, but essential, qualities to topics for ascetic contemplation.[41] Contrast Elyot's 'it is a faint praise that is gotten with fear' with Caxton's 'the knights by noblesse of courage and by force of arms maintain the order of Chivalry and have the same order to the end that they incline the small people by dread' and the difference becomes clear. Whereas in Caxton pre-eminence was pithily dealt with as a necessary phenomenon, not a topic to be agonised over ('because [of] the dread ... the common people have of the knights they labour and cultivate the earth for fear lest they should be destroyed'), by contrast, according to Elyot, pre-eminence sat the governor 'on a pillar on the top of a mountain, where all the people ... behold [him]' in both his private and public dealings.[42] In essence, law and order were being conceived of less as hard-won phenomena snatched on a day-to-day basis from chaos by ongoing aristocratic coercion than the central elements of a divinely instituted state sustained by political engagement in which physical coercion was the last resort.[43] In an Elyotan court, would there be any place for a discourse of chivalric virtues along traditional martial lines? Would everything be replaced by a mish-mash of gravity and effeteness?

---

[39] Elyot, T., *The boke named the gouvernour* (London, 1992), pp. 120–1. For a treatment of Thomas Starkey's *Dialogue of Pole and Lupset*, see T. Mayer, *Thomas Starkey and the Commonweal* (Cambridge, 1989), pp. 106–38.
[40] For a treatment of Elyot's attempts to resolve the tension between humanistic ideals and political actions, see A. Fox, 'Sir Thomas Elyot and the humanist dilemma' in Fox and Guy (Oxford, 1986), pp. 52–73.
[41] Elyot (1992), p. 113.
[42] For a treatment of the commonplace idea of a threefold division of society between knights, priests and labourers, see Keen (1984), pp. 4–6. Elyot, T. (1992), p. 113; Caxton (1484) sigs. Bii, r; Bvi, v.
[43] See Lander, *Crown and nobility 1450–1509* (London, 1976), pp. 267–300 for a treatment of the use of bonds and recognisances to bridle the nobility from the mid-fifteenth century on.

Chimneys in summer 33

Education was the key to the changing nature of political society. Elyot posited that the easiest way for members of the aristocracy and gentry to maintain influence and authority was through pursuing education with the intention of soliciting for crown office. The 1539–40 Act of Precedence seemed to bear this out. Here the old ranking of nobles by virtue of the age and description of their title was replaced by ranking according to office held on the evolving privy council – an indication not only of the degree to which royal benediction had been given to the idea of an office-holding aristocracy but also the willingness of the aristocracy to embrace this innovation as a means of retaining power.[44] An educational revolution had already begun in England prior to the writing of Elyot's *Governor*, but one that catered predominantly for minor gentry and the sons of merchants. Following the Erasmian lead, John Colet and Cardinal Wolsey had proved key figures in establishing and supporting establishments which taught a *cursus* that stressed *eloquentia* and *humanitas* through a new approach to the study of classical texts. Other establishments throughout the sixteenth century came to adopt this new educational programme, including Eton and Winchester. Whereas these institutions were devised with the minor gentry in mind, it became common for noblemen and wealthier gentlemen to employ tutors trained in the 'new learning' to instruct their children. After rudimentary training in grammar, many proceeded to Oxford or Cambridge where, from 1535, scholastic learning was discouraged in favour of a programme of logic, rhetoric, arithmetic, geometry, music and philosophy along the lines advocated by humanist German scholars of the age, notably Melanchthon.[45] Classical texts and scripture took centre stage. Significantly for English society and political culture, the men who effected and subsequently administered these changes following the break from Rome were figures such as John Cheke, Thomas Smith, Roger Ascham, Nicholas Ridley, Hugh Latimer, Walter Haddon, and William Cecil, all commoners who gained great political power and influence throughout the Edwardian period into the Elizabethan era; they were prime examples of laymen attaining virtue and preferment because of education.[46] They had attended

---

[44] Starkey, D., *The reign of Henry VIII, personalities and politics* (London, 1985), pp. 130–1.
[45] During Mary's reign, attempts were made to revive scholastic theology in English universities.
[46] Hudson, W. S., *The Cambridge connection* (Durham, 1980), pp. 26–30; for an account of the shared formation and interests of the Cambridge 'Athenians' see pp. 36–56. See S. Alford, 'Reassessing William Cecil in the 1560s' in Guy (1997), pp. 233–53. The method Cecil used to compose his many memoranda was expounded in classically inspired publications by contemporaries at Cambridge, for example, Rainolde's 'Book called the foundation of rhetoric' (1563) and Thomas Wilson's 'Art of rhetoric' (1554). Of course, Wilson was later to become joint

grammar schools and university and had consequently reaped the greatest benefits.[47]

DIFFERING VISIONS OF MILITARY CULTURE

Of course, in matters of political and social culture, it was Henry VIII who was pre-eminent in setting the tone. And Henry, anxious to be the epitome of a Renaissance prince, melded an enthusiasm for the creative possibilities that the 'new learning' brought to policy with a self-consciously revivalist passion for military prowess and chivalric values. Concerns of honour had been the overarching influence on his active pursuit of victories in Burgundy, France, Scotland and Ireland. His court was unashamedly magnificent, becoming renowned, as Churchyard wistfully recalled, for chivalric magnanimity and *largesse*. The impossibly indulgent aspect of these ambitions was best demonstrated by the scale of his efforts to impress Francis I with lavish ritual on the Field of Cloth of Gold in 1520.[48] But Henry's chivalry was of different type to that regard for pre-eminence which had animated the baronial *geist* of the fifteenth century with its internecine strife between Nevilles and Percies, Courtenays and Bonvilles.[49] In contrast to the caution and suspicion that had characterised his father's reign, Henry VIII, as is well noted, adopted a more fraternal approach to the peerage while also adopting an attitude of solicitation and patronage towards members of the gentry, not least later in his reign through the distribution of monastic lands. But the character of this relationship between the king and his gentle subjects had changed radically from the *status quo ante*. The baronial wars aside, the fifteenth century had been one of attrition for the noble families of England; a sense of horror and the waste of civil war tranquillised some of the baldly assertive culture of that era. In this context, Henry VIII was able to establish his sway over the country's aristocracy relatively easily. From early in his reign, Henry had also become increasingly preoccupied with the idea of the English

---

principal secretary himself, joining Sir Francis Walsingham, another Cambridge man, in 1577. For Cecil's relatively humble origins see Read, *Secretary Cecil* (1955), pp. 17–22. Note also the relatively humble origins of both Sir Nicholas Bacon and Sir Thomas Smith, alumni of Cambridge, privy councillors and senior officers in Elizabeth's government. For a treatment of the homogeneity of the new intake onto Elizabeth's first privy council, see Hudson (1980), pp. 18–20. The continued interest of Cecil *et al.* in the state of education becomes a constant refrain in Ascham's *Scholemaster*.

[47] Read (1955), pp. 17–22. [48] James (1978), pp. 22–32.
[49] McFarlane, K. B., 'The Wars of the Roses' in *England in the fifteenth century* (London, 1981), pp. 231–61.

monarch as a wielder of *imperium*, in line with continental civilian ideas. In 1513, he claimed temporal and spiritual sovereignty over Tournai, making reference to French legal precedent. By 1515, his caesaropapism had led him to reject the jurisdictional autonomy of ecclesiastical courts. In 1521, he asserted that he was 'of [his] absolute power . . . above the laws' in a letter to Thomas Howard, the earl of Surrey.[50] Then, in 1530, he appropriated all heraldic jurisdiction in England for the crown. This seizing of chivalric authority was in line with his eventual annexation of all sources of power in his realm. It has even been argued that Henry's legitimation of the earl marshal the duke of Norfolk's blatant breach of promises made on the king's behalf during the Pilgrimage of Grace (in Howard's words 'Whatsoever promise I shall make unto the rebels . . . I shall observe no part thereof') signalled the genesis of a new form of chivalric ethos strictly under the supreme headship of the monarch.[51] If the 'theology' of English chivalry had changed significantly, its rites and value system, in so far as they did not meddle with royal authority, appeared to remain unchanged. But at a deeper level, individual honour had become increasingly subsumed in an overarching 'state honour', a concept abstracted from, but coterminous with, the king's honour among his royal peers; in Henry's case, his status in relation to Francis I of France and Charles V of Burgundy and Spain.[52] This 'state honour', championed and enunciated in the king's foreign policy, claimed priority over every man's will and desires but acknowledged the prowess of those individuals who were foremost in its defence.[53]

Although the honour of the king and the 'public weal' coincided in scope and definition, this did not seem to profoundly affect the character or style of military service undertaken by aristocrats or 'governors'. Under Henry VIII, aristocrats restored or created by the king (for example, the second and third duke of Norfolk, the duke of Suffolk and the earl of Shrewsbury) served their king, in a manner reminiscent of the Hundred

---

[50] See Bradshaw 'The Tudor reformation and revolution in Wales and Ireland' in Bradshaw and Morrill (eds), *The British problem: 1534–1707* (London, 1996), pp. 62–3.
[51] James (1978), p. 26.
[52] See C. Cruickshank, *Henry VIII and the invasion of France* (London, 1990), pp. 159–60. For the evolution of Henry's chivalric instincts into a fully fledged doctrine of *imperium*, see T. F. Mayer 'On the road to 1534: the occupation of Tournai and Henry VIII's theory of sovereignty' in D. Hoak's *Tudor political culture*, (Cambridge, 1995). For the collapse of foreign relations into a theoretical framework based on individual relations between monarchs see D. Starkey, 'Representation through intimacy: a study in the symbolism of monarchy and Court office in early modern England' in Guy (1997), p. 56.
[53] Bradshaw and Morrill (1996), pp. 62–3.

Years' War, by defending what remained of England's territory in France or by neutralising Scotland's threat to English security. The favour to be gained by gentlemen through distinction in martial affairs was considerable and long lasting, given that financial and political preferment necessarily followed the king's approval.[54] From the earliest point in the reign, Charles Brandon (created duke of Suffolk in 1514) and Thomas Howard (created earl of Surrey in 1514, succeeding his father as duke of Norfolk in 1524) epitomised the new aristocratic chivalry, rigidly monarchical in its loyalties, careerist in its search for new achievements. Brandon had not only been a seasoned participant in domestic tournaments, he had earned his spurs at Tournai and proved remarkably successful in pursuing his king's martial aims in France in both 1523 and at the siege of Boulogne in 1544. He had also played a central role in securing the north of England during the Lincolnshire rebellion and in facing down the Scots. Howard's career covered many similar bases. He had played a major role in the victories at Flodden and Branxton Hill, served as lord lieutenant of Ireland, led forays against France in the 1520s, ravaged Scotland, declared war on France in the name of his king in 1543 and then served as lieutenant general of the army there. But this first generation, which had carved out an aristocratic niche by dint of its military prowess and service at court, was followed by a younger generation that enjoyed an even more vertiginous burst of upward mobility.

Chief among the parvenus was Edward Seymour, son of the sheriff of Wiltshire, who after a period of acquaintance and involvement with court ceremonial, proved his worth serving under Brandon in France in 1523. A knighthood, promotion to the privy council and, remarkably, an earldom followed. The 1540s brought further military endeavour when Seymour (now the earl of Hertford) intermittently served as lieutenant general in the north, devastated Scotland and captured Boulogne, holding it in the face of sustained French aggression. At the same time, John Dudley, son of the disgraced crown official Edmund Dudley, came to prominence by combining personal courage under Brandon in 1523 with a formidable reputation as a jouster. Following a period as warden of the Scottish marches, Dudley, by now Viscount Lisle, was appointed to be lord highadmiral of the royal fleet routed a French expedition which had menaced

---

[54] Keen (1984), pp. 27–8, for the shifting definition of the term. See George Whetstone's *The honorable reputation of a souldier* (London, 1585) sigs. B, r–Bii, v for a later statement (full of classical allusions) of this token disregard for social degree among soldiers. For reference to Henry VIII's policy of ennoblement see MacCaffrey 'The crown and the new aristocracy', *P&P*, 30 (1965), pp. 55–6.

Boulogne in 1544. By the late 1540s, the Howards and their clerical ally Archbishop Stephen Gardiner found themselves opposed by a group of advocates of reformed religion centred around Edward Seymour and Katherine Parr. Norfolk's son, Henry, the earl of Surrey, the epitome of aristocratic chivalry, a gallant soldier, the lieutenant general of all England's Continental possessions and an enthusiast for Henry VIII's expansionist ambitions, eventually fell foul of the king in 1546 because of his imprudent assertion of a heraldic claim to the arms of Edward the Confessor. His cataclysmic error, the assumption of an uncomfortable level of aristocratic self-sufficiency, dragged the fortunes of his house down with him and enabled the triumph of the political grouping centred around Somerset. This group had been bound together during the latter years of Henry's reign not only by its outward submission to the king's agenda but also by virtue of its commitment to the reforming aims for both church and commonwealth advocated by Thomas Cranmer and his allies, aims which would later find their champion in the boy-king Edward VI.[55]

At this point, a recalibration of perceptions of martial endeavour in influential quarters is discernible, and the influence of civic republican thinking and doctrine gained ground. Concerns for the preservation of the commonwealth or 'public weal' prompted a movement away from preoccupation with individual glory towards an evaluation of the structure of recruitment: the necessarily institutional county militia and aristocratic levies. Machiavelli, obsessed with the necessity for republics to have a native armed force, had singled out Henry VIII's 1513 expedition to France as an expression of the republican military ethos.[56] Henry's troops, according to the Florentine, had been recruited solely from his own subjects and, accordingly, had acquitted themselves admirably despite the fact that England had been peaceful for thirty years and the army 'possessed no soldiers nor any commanders and good troops who had ever served in the military'. Their success stemmed from Henry's prudence in attending to preparations for war and a 'well-organised kingdom'.[57] However, as K. B. McFarlane pointed out, the native character of Henry's troops owed more to his dependence on the retinues of his nobility than anything more rarefied, although some soldiers had been

---

[55] MacCulloch, D., *Tudor church militant* (London, 1999), pp. 40–56.
[56] For the dating of Machiavelli's *Discorsi* to the period between 1516 and 1519, see Skinner, *Foundations of modern political thought* (Cambridge, 1978), Vol. I, pp. 153–4.
[57] Machiavelli, *The discourses of Livy* (Oxford, 1997), trans. J. C. Bondanella and Peter Bondanella, Book I, Chapter 21, pp. 73–5. See P. Williams, *The Tudor regime* (Oxford, 1981), pp. 110–20.

levied at county level by crown officers.[58] From 1522, efforts were made to increase effective state intervention in the process of mustering troops and ensuring the contribution of arms and men from landowning subjects in accordance with their personal wealth. However, the old system based largely on aristocratic voluntarism remained intact. By the early 1540s, troops raised by individuals were combined into county bands, and, increasingly, crown officers acting as muster commissioners provided the nuts and bolts of the recruitment of armies for suppressing rebellion and defending the realm. Of course, the barely adequate process of centralisation in matters of military recruitment and supply had much less to do with republican discourse than the imperative for defence posed by the international repercussions of the 1534 act of supremacy, which created an unprecedentedly isolated England in a sea of anti-schismatic hostility. But this did not prevent some intellectuals seizing upon these developments in quite as precipitous a way as Machiavelli had done.

In the 1540s, it was the Protestant party at court, rather than martial gentlemen and aristocrats, who began to use civic republican thinking in writings addressing military matters. Cromwell's and then Cranmer's propagandists, former Catholic clerics such as Richard Morison and Thomas Becon, took centre stage in this matter. These men, concerned with confessional war and the influence of religion on foreign policy, stripped away virtually any connection between serving the commonwealth and individualistic glory in a series of officially ratified books. *An exhortation to styrre all Englyshe men to the defence of theyr countreye* (1539) by Morison and *A new pollicy of warre* (1542) by Becon are good examples of this new orthodoxy, works addressed to the people as a whole, not merely the gentry and aristocracy. Although *An exhortation* listed many examples of heroic self-sacrifice for the *patria* from Greek and Roman precedent, it is clear that, as far as its argument went, that the monarch was synonymous with the *patria* and its liberties. Englishmen, as Henry VIII's subjects, had a 'bounden duty' to defend their sovereign militarily to the end because of the spiritual liberty he had secured for them from papal obscurantism and the temporal victory he had won for England over papal usurpation.[59] Morison did not extoll the temporal liberties of England but emphasised the benefits of order and praised obedience as 'the knot of all common weales'. He combined his derivative republican discourse, with

[58] McFarlane, K. B., *The nobility of later medieval England*, ed. J. P. Cooper and J. Campbell (Oxford, 1973), p. 162.
[59] Morison, R., *An exhortation to styre all Englyshe men to the defence of their countreye* (1539).

an eschatological Protestantism, laden with scriptural references, which characterised the Pope as 'antichrist' and Henry VIII as the divinely appointed agent of the Pontiff's undoing. He pointed to the previous blessings God had bestowed on Henry's regime, especially the occasion in 1513 when his success at Tournai had been complemented by the devastation of Scottish forces at Flodden.[60] The debt of duty a 'citizen' might incur because of the benefits of political liberty paled into insignificance beside the obligation enjoined on English men because of the realisation of England's spiritual liberty, maintained against Romish usurpation and error. Pointing out this debt became a recurrent gesture for the post-Reformation 'commonwealth' men. Morison's jibe, echoed by Becon, that the maxim of Cardinal Pole and other adherents of Catholicism was *Roma mihi patria est* illustrated the blurred distinctions that arose between the idea of defending homeland and freedom against both temporal and spiritual tyranny. The boons to be protected had less to do with continued earthly existence or the practice of liberties than the necessity for salvation.[61]

Both Morison's and Becon's treatment of war marked a sharp break away from the idea that armed conflict was solely the speciality of soldiers qua Christian professionals. They endeavoured to motivate everyone, irrespective of social standing, to do their maximum to furnish a military force for defence or offence, and not for monetary recompense. Repudiating even Luther's neo-Augustinian view of soldiers as the sole agents competent to effect God's judgements on the battlefield, they wholeheartedly embraced the republican idea of a citizens' militia and tried to map it onto the quasi-feudal structure the state had inherited, a tendency which can be seen in Becon's enthusiasm for the gentlemen of Kent, who obediently 'laid all other business aside [and] provided the requisite amount of men [and] armed and armoured them'. Their enthusiasm was expressed through the use of a strongly Ciceronian vocabulary of duty to the *res publica;* Becon remarked that 'the studious endeavours and diligent employments of all men, tend unto this, that the commodity of the public weal and the health of the country should be sought above all things'.[62] But for all that, neither the glories nor prowess of Seymour or

---

[60] Morison (1539) sig. Civ, v.   [61] Morison (1539) sigs. D, r–Diii, v.
[62] Becon, *A new pollicy of warre* (1542), sig. Aiii, v. Note also *The ordre and duety of fyghting for our countrey* (1545) by the Irishman Edward Walshe, dedicated to Sir Anthony St Leger. While Walshe's work did not have the eschatological fervour of either Becon's or Morison's works, it contained a paean to *patria*, conceived of as territory. Citing Lucian, Walshe pointed to the natural loyalty a man must feel for the very soil of his country because of the spiritual and physical necessities it provides for him, *viz.* baptismal waters, food, and a context in which to move,

Dudley on the battlefield were subjects written up by Cranmer's ginger group. The notion of an obedient people on the march willing to defend reformed religion was more attractive and deemed more useful for the commonwealth, even if the reality was significantly different from the ideal, than any emphasis on individual prowess. And recruits were needed; for instance, during Edward VI's reign, Somerset had to employ over 7,000 mercenaries to man his newly established garrison grid in Scotland to make up the shortfall in recruitment at home.[63]

Somerset's foreign policy, effectively a war policy, was enthusiastically supported by the evangelical party at court as a means of securing the reformation in England and protecting the realm from French invasion. It was hoped that a union of the two realms of England and Scotland through the forced marriage of Edward VI to the young Mary Stuart could be secured with an economy of English force and the cooperation of Protestant allies within Scotland.[64] However, it is clear that the reform party did not prize the military profession for any inherent virtues that it might possess but only in so far as it was engaged in service of which they approved. A soldier could have use value, but this was often fleeting.

Somerset's wars were England's wars, however, and the evangelicals and the old nobility fought side by side, especially in Scotland, for example at the battle of Musselburgh (or Pinkie) on 10 September 1547, where many future Elizabethan notables served. There a closely grouped wave of Scottish pikemen – which an eye-witness later compared to an 'angry hedgehog' – punctuating its advance with yells of 'come here lounds, come here tykes, come here heretics', threatened to snuff out England's finest. William, Baron Grey de Wilton, was run through the mouth with a pike, yet survived; the Protector Somerset's horse was fatally injured; and Sir Thomas Darcy, the prominent Edwardian soldier, had his right hand crushed. A twenty-six-year-old William Cecil also found himself in the thick of it all, but he did not prove quick-witted on the field. His contemporary biographer noted that '[Cecil] was like to have been slain, but was miraculously saved by one that putting forth his arm to thrust [him] out of the level of the cannon, had his arm stricken off.' In that

---

acquire language and hear the gospel. Book 7 of Patrizi's *De institutione reipublicae* follows a similar approach.

[63] Bush, M. L., *The government policy of Protector Somerset* (London, 1975), pp. 35, 104.

[64] See Becon (1542) sig. C, v, where there is an appeal to the Scots to side with Henry VIII as their feudal overlord. In Edwardian times the proposed means of securing union between the two realms was marriage between Edward VI and Mary Stuart. Sir William Cecil inherited these 'British' concerns, see Alford (1998), pp. 59–70.

moment, it could be argued that some poor nameless soldier by sacrificing his arm had assured the Elizabethan religious settlement and the condemnation of the queen of Scots.[65]

A ZEAL FOR ORDER

Somerset's willingness to promote and defend England's church as Protestant rather than as a temporarily schismatic limb of the Catholic Church, led him, *mutatis mutandis*, to adopt the 'clerks'' programme for a thorough reformation of English society, and, of course, their alternative vision of soldiering and warfare was a part of this project.[66] Paul Slack's recent examination of the impact of 'commonwealth' thinking on England provides important insights into the laicising ethos that motivated much of the social organisation that took place throughout the sixteenth century and the continuity with which these aims were pursued under both Catholic and Protestant regimes.[67] These measures, first initiated at government level by Wolsey, were amplified in statutes devised by Cromwell and were subsequently promoted with varying degrees of eschatological fervour by later reformers from John Hales to Thomas Smith.[68] Reform was undertaken as a measure against the decay believed to have characterised late-fifteenth and early to mid-sixteenth-century society, and, although the most socially egalitarian aspects of the project fell by the wayside following Kett's Rebellion and the demise of Somerset, a zeal for order continued to grip many throughout the realm throughout the mid-Tudor period and into the reign of Elizabeth.[69] The optimistic emphasis that Erasmus and More had placed on *humanitas* was supplanted by a more pessimistic view about the potential that existed for the creation of a more 'godly' society. Despite this pessimism, it remained the divinely ordained role of government to plot a programme of improvement. Such

---

[65] Polemon, J., *All the famous battels that have been fought in our age throughout the world* (London, 1579), sig. Hhii, v–Iiiii, r. For the account of Cecil's part in the battle see Francis Peck ed. *Desiderata curiosa: or a collection of divers scarce and curious pieces*, 2 vols. (London, 1732–5), Vol. I, p. 8.

[66] See Starkey (1985), pp. 131–45 on Henry VIII's bias towards reformed religion in the latter years of his reign. Becon for instance conceived of the sacrament of the altar as the linchpin of social obligation reminding the faithful of the need for 'all to be beneficial one to another', especially the poor.

[67] See also Lucy Wooding's *Rethinking Catholicism in reformation England* (Oxford, 2000), Chapters 2–3.

[68] Statutes dealing directly with poor-law and vagrancy were enacted in 1531, 1536, 1547, 1549, 1552, 1563, 1572, 1576. See also A. L. Beier, *Masterless men* (London, 1985).

[69] Shagan, E., 'Protector Somerset and the 1549 rebellions: new sources and new perspectives' *EHR*, 114 (1999), pp. 34–63, see also his ' "Popularity" and the 1549 rebellions revisited' *EHR*, 115 (2000), pp. 121–33.

a programme, however, did not depend solely on descending power mediated through statute or patent; it began from the premise of communities policing their own morality while invoking the assistance of government in securing a full reformation.

In local communities, the pastoral and educational services previously provided by monastic establishments or chantries were replaced with institutions such as grammar schools and bridewells, financed by the laity, often organised into corporations with royal patents, using money accruing from dissolution. These cultural and social developments manifested themselves most explicitly in London but could also be detected in urban areas such as Winchester and Coventry and especially in towns in the east of the country such as Ipswich and Colchester. Protestantism and the phobia of social dissolution were pervasive influences.[70] The commonwealth, a seamless godly society that could tolerate no loose ends, was deemed to be qualitatively greater than the sum of its parts. Whereas education could train prospective office-holders to be amenable to the service of the commonwealth, the question arose as to what was to be done with those that could not be easily integrated. In 1576, the town clerk of Tewkesbury John Barston pithily testified to the homogenising tendency of urban political culture when he asserted that

Everyone should possess [not only] country love [and] care of common weal, [but also] a well disposed mind to prefer the universal of all as willingly as any private cause or singular intent . . . to join himself, by his private commodities and travails, to profit all other as well as himself.[71]

As is well known, the implications this type of thinking had for appetitive and self-assertive modes of living were considerable; both 'merry England' and the wonted fetishisation of pre-eminence were under attack.[72] A reformation of manners in line with an approach to emotions and passions informed by an ideal of Christianised stoicism was counselled, as this form of virtue taught men 'how to pacify and rule the disordered passions and perturbations of the mind and to subject the motions of

---

[70] Slack, P., *From reformation to improvement: public welfare in early modern England* (Oxford, 1999), pp. 36–7.
[71] Barston, J. *Safegarde of societie: describing the institution of lawes and policies, to preserve every felowship of peple by degrees of civil government; gathered of the moralls and policies of philosophie* (London, 1576), p. 30, v. See M. Peltonen, *Classical humanism and republicanism in English political thought 1570–1640*, (Cambridge, 1995), pp. 54–73 for a fine treatment of Barston's work.
[72] Hutton, R., *The rise and fall of merry England* (Oxford, 1994) is the standard account of the sanitisation of rural life in England in the early modern period.

[their] appetites, and unruly will, to obey reason'.[73] 'Courtly gallantness' and 'town going in good cheer' were disapproved of, as was 'outrage in apparel, huge hose, monstrous hats [and] garish colours' at court as something 'against order [and] for faction'.[74] From the 1530s, vagrancy and poor relief Acts were invoked against *fratres ambulantes inordinate* whose idleness, it was accepted, was the breeding ground for vice.[75] By the 1570s, statutes comprehended minstrels and idle retainers among the list of rogues and vagabonds to be made amenable to or excised from the commonwealth.[76] However, discomfort with the social assumptions inherent in this 'commonwealth' programme was not provoked merely by obvious outsiders: sturdy landless peasants dispossessed by enclosure, decommissioned retainers, or haughty northern nobles chary of Edwardian and Elizabethan social, religious and foreign policy. From the ranks of gentry and esquires of England, those surplus sons who followed a military career were increasingly seen as untidy elements in a pristine commonwealth. Not only were 'cheer' and 'gallantness' at stake but even the wonted stature of the gentleman soldier was under threat.

The five-year Catholic interval occasioned by Mary's reign showed signs of an attempted return to a *status quo ante*; conservative aristocrats and prelates gained confidence in the country and, as we shall see in a later chapter, the presence of Philip of Spain as the king came to provide a virile centre of patronage and power, winning the allegiance of many military captains who had previously been chary of a Habsburg influence in the English court. Dissidents fled the country, especially those who had been behind Northumberland's bid to exclude Mary from the succession; many who held fast to the reformed religion met their death as a result. Becon and Morison fled to Strasbourg; John Cheke, principal secretary and tutor to the dead king and to the heirs of Seymour and Dudley, had arrived there before them. He was later arrested in Flanders (the long arm of the Habsburgs was difficult to avoid) and sent back to England where he was forced to recant. Sir William Cecil, erstwhile principal secretary, after reading an account of Socrates' refusal to escape from prison, decided to stay in England in a type of internal exile, while Roger Ascham integrated

---

[73] Peltonen (1995), p. 63. See Ascham (1863), pp. 65–7.
[74] Ascham (1863), p. 165. See also the justice of the peace William Lambarde's frequent denunciations of alehouses as dens of iniquity in his charges to quarter sessions in the 1580s, *William Lambarde and Local Government*, ed. C. Read, (Ithaca, NY, 1962), pp. 70, 73.
[75] Slack (1999), pp. 17–19.
[76] Slack (1999), pp. 37–8. See also P. Roberts 'Elizabethan players and minstrels and the legislation of 1572 against retainers and vagabonds', in A. Fletcher and P. Roberts (eds.), *Religion, culture and society in early Modern Britain* (Cambridge, 1994), pp. 29–55.

himself fully into Mary's court, becoming the queen's personal secretary and striking up a rapport with both Stephen Gardiner and Cardinal Pole, an indication of the durability of shared assumptions among the educated.[77]

The survival of commonwealth theories about social organisation into Mary's reign is demonstrated by Humfrey Braham's *Institucion of a gentleman* (1555): a sustained mid-Tudor meditation on the ways that gentility could be achieved by dint of virtue and service to the commonwealth. Asserting that gentility as a concept was in disrepair, Braham posited the existence of three types of gentleman. The first type, the 'gentle gentle', were not only 'gentle born', but learned, 'apt in feats of arms for the defence of [their] country', and courtly in behaviour; Julius Caesar was proffered as a good example. The second type were the 'gentle ungentle', men of good lineage but corrupt manners. Last, and most startlingly, Braham presented a classification he called the 'ungentle gentle', men of poor stock and low degree, who, by virtue, wit, policy, industry, legal knowledge or valour in arms, had become 'well beloved' and 'high esteemed' and appointed to high office, thereby becoming a 'post or stay' of the commonwealth. With such a prevailing wind behind him, an 'ungentle gentle' man was bound to set up the rest of his 'poor line' on a better footing than he himself had enjoyed. Braham concluded that there were many of this sort in England and argued that it was unfair to label them 'upstarts'. Here he was referring to the judges, attorneys, administrators and estate officials that had, by virtue of their salaries and fees and 'their professional concern with land transactions', managed to attain gentry status, usually through marrying heiresses, notably widows.[78] Braham hastily added that this allowance did not mean that he denied that pretenders existed: handicraft men who were bearing coats of arms previously held by old families, men who were being referred to as esquires at each assize merely because they purchased lands by 'certain dark augmentation practices' and intruders who had flourished 'since the putting down of abbeys', a time within Braham's memory.[79]

His treatment of the martial profession and its adherents, however, contained much of the ambivalence common among mid-Tudor advocates of social reform.[80] First, Braham stated that soldiering was not an

---

[77] Ryan, L. V., *Roger Ascham* (Stanford, Calif., 1963), pp. 193–219.
[78] Harriss (2005), p. 141.
[79] Braham, H., *The institucion of a gentleman* (London, 1555) sigs. *iii, v; Dii, r; Diii, r.
[80] Braham's book was dedicated to Thomas Radcliffe, aka Lord Fitzwalter, later earl of Sussex, a Howard partisan.

inferior mode in which to serve the commonwealth, stressing the sacrifice soldiers made for their country:

A soldier with peril of his life, loss of his goods, departeth from his quiet house, his wife and dear children, going forth against his enemies to fight for the defence of his country: and coming to the wars in change of warm lodging, he taketh his rest under a cold tent (yea sometime he lieth upon the bare earth) . . . he is constrained to take evil seasoned meat, moulded bread, unwholesome drink, and sometime he hath no sustenance at all: but where he hopeth to find vitells, he findeth nothing but a spoiled country.

However Braham, obviously aware of sacrifices undertaken by soldiers, found it difficult to come to terms with their bloody work and attendant swagger. The honour of the military profession was besmirched by the widespread reputation soldiers had acquired for covetousness, corruption and faithlessness. Braham stressed their tendency to sell besieged cities under their protection to their attackers (a common republican motif). Although he argued, using examples from classical literature, that this conduct was corruption of the natural tendency of soldiers to be both liberal and faithful to their word, his true beliefs became clear when, in total contradiction to his earlier opinions – now revealed as mere tokens – he stated that 'to minister justice in a state of peace', i.e. to be a lawyer or an officer in local government, was 'an office of higher commendation' than soldiering.[81] Citing Sallust 'somewhat to depress the glory of soldiers', Braham added that ancient Rome's greatness and prosperity had not come about through war. Withering criticism followed of soldiers 'hasty to draw [their] sword' in Fleet Street, Smithfield or Charing Cross 'for every trifling cause'.[82] The same men, Braham argued, commonly undertook treacherous acts against their country in the field. All in all, his verdict was plain: the military profession was an inherently destructive influence unless confined to the minute and specific context within which it served the polity. Captains were only useful to the commonwealth on the battlefield, and the existence of the battlefield itself was lamented. It is notable that feckless 'roisters', according to Braham, commonly spoke in

---

[81] Braham (1555) sig. Fiii, r.
[82] Braham (1555) sig. Fii, r. As early as 1560, the privy council warned local authorities to move to prevent crime instigated by troops demobilised from the Scottish expedition. See I. Archer, *The pursuit of stability* (Cambridge, 1991), pp. 210–11. For examples of the discord that soldiers could cause in an urban environment see *A commentary of the services and charges of Lord Grey of Wilton by his son Arthur Lord Grey of Wilton*, ed. De Malpas Grey Egerton (London, 1847), p. xiv, and the 1890 *DNB* entry on Grey de Wilton, for reference to Arthur Grey de Wilton's confinement to the Fleet in 1574 for attempting to kill Sir John Fortescue in London.

slang from Boulogne, an indication, given English martial activities there in the 1540s, that many of the capital's louchest rascals were soldiers.[83] The truculent soldier in Charing Cross was emblematic of the common belief that professional martial men were agents of *furor*, *ira* and *impatientia* not fit for the reformed city.

If Mary's reign, with its stress on aristocracy and aristocratic values, had acted as a bridle on Edwardian enthusiasts for civic reform, the accession of Elizabeth enabled many commonwealth men who had gone to ground to return to their wonted devotion to the ideal of the ordered commonwealth. First and foremost, Sir William Cecil, whom she had long held in esteem and trust, was appointed as principal secretary and proceeded to make the office as pivotal as it had been in the days of Cromwell.[84] As Hudson has noted, the new appointees to Elizabeth's first privy council were educated Protestants of an Edwardian provenance, all of whom had a close connection to Cecil.[85] Cecil was used to acting as the convener of 'safe' Edwardian notables and assumed the leading role among them. Not only had he been indispensable to both Somerset and Northumberland, he had also hosted the first of two discussions on transubstantiation in November 1551 which John Cheke (Cecil's father-in-law), Edmund Grindal, Francis Knollys and Nicholas Throckmorton had attended; the second meeting was held by Richard Morison. Praise and flattery naturally accompanied Cecil's upward mobility. Roger Ascham, fellow alumnus of St John's College, Cambridge, described Cecil as 'the fairest spring that ever was . . . of learning', 'one of the forwardest young plants in all that worthy college of St John's', adding that 'in the temperate and quiet shade of his wisdom, next the providence of God, and goodness of one, in these our days *religio* for sincerity, *literae* for order and advancement, *Respub[licae]* for happy and quiet government, have to great rejoicing of all good men, specially reposed themselves'.[86] And, indeed, St John's in the 1530s, as well as being Cecil's haunt, was central to the formation of many of the prominent clergymen of the

---

[83] Braham (1555) sig. Biiii, v. The 'Boulogners' were deemed a particularly tough and ruthless type of soldier. William, Baron Grey de Wilton had the leading of them at the battle of Pinkie in September 1547, see J. Polemon, *All the famous battels that have been fought in our age throughout the world* (London, 1579) sigs. Hh, ii, v–Ii, iii, r.

[84] Hudson (1980), pp. 9–18 for the basis of the special relationship between Elizabeth and Cecil, notably his solidarity with her during the Thomas Seymour 'affair'.

[85] Hudson (1980), pp. 9–24; Alford, S., *The early Elizabethan polity: William Cecil and the British succession crisis, 1558–1569* (Cambridge, 1998), pp. 14–28.

[86] Ascham (1904), p. 282.

Elizabethan Church, including James Pilkington, bishop of Durham; Edwin Sandys, archbishop of York; Robert Horne, bishop of Winchester; William Bill, dean of Westminster and Andrew Perne, dean of Ely and master of Peterhouse.

Cecil continued to convene and preside. Ascham's own educational tract, *The scholemaster*, for instance, ostensibly stemmed from a discussion that took place in Cecil's chamber in 1563 while the secretary relaxed from 'weighty affairs of the realm'; the topic, the definition of successful education, was prompted by the news that harsh discipline had driven some scholars at Eton to hate learning. Ascham's familiarity with Cecil was circumscribed by a deferential attitude: 'I was the bolder to say my mind because Mr Secretary courteously provoked me thereunto: or else in such a company, and namely in his presence, my wont is to be more willing, to use mine ears, than to occupy my tongue.'[87] His *bête noire* was the Italianate Englishman, prey to perversion and papistry, rather than the captain: 'praised be God, England hath at this time, many worthy captains and good soldiers, which be indeed, so honest of behaviour, so comely of conditions, so mild of manners, as they may be examples of good order, to a good sort of others, which never came in war.'[88] Indeed, what Ascham despised was the show of braggadocio courtiers made, which led them

in greater presence, to bear a brave look: to be warlike, though [they] never looked enemy in the face in war: yet some warlike sign must be used, either a slovenly busking, or an overstaring frounced head, as though out of every hair's top, should suddenly start out a good big oath, when need requireth

as well as the culture of jostling for pre-eminence which caused them 'to face, stand foremost, shove back: and to the meaner man, or unknown in the court, to seem somewhat solemn, coy, big and dangerous of look, talk and answer'. He also saved a good deal of invective for the chivalric culture of the early Tudor period, the very dispensation for which Thomas Churchyard felt such pangs of nostalgia:

In our forefathers' time, when Papistry, as a standing pool, covered and overflowed all England, few books were read in our tongue, saving certain books of Chivalry, as they said, for pastime and pleasure, which, as some say were made in monasteries, by idle monks, or wanton canons: as one for example, Morte Arthure: the whole pleasure of which book standeth in two special points, in open man's slaughter, and bold bawdry: In which book those be counted the

---

[87] Ascham (1904), pp. 175–6.   [88] Ascham (1904), p. 207.

noblest knights, that do kill most men without any quarrel, and commit foulest adulteries by subtlest shifts: as Sir Lancelot, with the wife of King Arthur his master: Sir Tristram with the wife of King Mark his uncle: Sir Lamerock with the wife of King Lot, that was his own aunt. This is good stuff, for wise men to laugh at, or honest men to take pleasure at. Yet I know, when God's Bible was banished the court, and Morte Arthure received into the prince's chamber. What toys, the daily reading of such a book, may work in the will of a young gentleman, or a young maid, that liveth wealthily and idly, wise men can judge and honest men do pity.[89]

Despite his warm words for captains, as far as Ascham was concerned, the martial profession was respectable only as long as it was torn from its wonted hinterland of concerns to do with knighthood, prowess and pre-eminence.

In truth, jockeying for position was inseparable from the lives of many Elizabethan captains, as noted by that other Cambridge graduate, Sir Thomas Smith, in his *De republica anglorum*:

our nation being much accustomed to be either in foreign wars, in France, Scotland, or Ireland, and too much accustomed to civil wars within themselves (which is the fault that falleth ordinarily amongst bellicose nations) and, where men of war, captains and soldiers be plentiful, which when they have no external wars wherewith to occupy their busy heads and hands accustomed to fight and quarrel, must needs seek quarrel and combats amongst themselves.[90]

But the change of regime in 1558 presented military professionals with more obvious problems. Elizabeth's foreign policy typically consisted of flirtation, prevarication, caution and inconstancy. When she came to the throne, England's martial reputation was at its lowest point since the reign of Henry VI. On marrying Philip, Queen Mary had set the realm to war in the Habsburg interest against the Valois. While the English participated in the victory won at St Quentin, the subsequent loss – through sheer ineptitude – of Calais, the crown's last French possession, signalled deep humiliation.[91] Elizabeth, on her accession, inherited a battle-hardened nobility. Many of those who were peers in 1558 had once served in battle

---

[89] Ascham (1904), p. 231.
[90] Smith, T., *De republica anglorum* (1982), p. 126. See *Churchyardes Choise* (1579) sigs. Pi, r.–Pii, r, where Churchyard cites a number of cases of contention between soldiers on matters of reputation. Notably one of these spats took place between John Zouche and Edward Randolph at the siege of Leith. Zouche, after consulting with other captains in the English camp, submitted to Randolph.
[91] Davies, C., 'England and the French war, 1557–9' in *The mid-Tudor polity 1540–1560*, ed. Jennifer Loach and Robert Tittler (London, 1980), pp. 159–85.

with distinction: William Herbert, first earl of Pembroke (1506/7–1570); William, Baron Grey de Wilton (1508/9–1562); William Fitzalan, earl of Arundel (1512–1580); Edward Clinton, Baron Clinton and Saye, lord high admiral (1512–1585); Francis Russell, second earl of Bedford (1526/7–1585); and Thomas Radcliffe, third earl of Sussex and lord deputy of Ireland (1526/7–1583). Within the first four years of Elizabeth's reign, the privileged role of the nobility in martial affairs was upheld when the twenty-one-year-old Thomas Howard, duke of Norfolk, was given the office of lieutenant general of the north. But, in reality, the post was a desk job while the real military leadership was left to England's semi-disgraced *mutilado* Lord Grey de Wilton, the governor of Berwick, assisted by captains and inferior officers such as William Drury, William Pelham, Cuthbert Vaughan, Edward Randolph and John Shute.[92] The foray carried out against the French garrison lodged at Leith Castle in 1560 was profoundly embarrassing: the ladders used by the English army were too small to scale the fortifications.[93] Following the death of Mary of Guise, the stand-off was resolved diplomatically through the ingenuity of Secretary Cecil whose expertise in Scottish affairs secured a victory when martial mediocrity could not close the deal.

The crown army's next outing was even more demoralising. The attempt by English forces to relieve pressure on Huguenots led by Condé was intrinsically ideological; both William Cecil and Robert Dudley supported it, hoping to guarantee safety through force for English reformed religion from the threat of a French Catholic pincer movement. Although Elizabeth tried to ease herself into involvement in France's wars of religion in 1562, the resulting debacle at Newhaven (Le Havre) left the English army, led by Ambrose Dudley, earl of Warwick, prey to plague and mass desertions. No resuscitation of English claims in France resulted, merely surrender and retreat. It would have been much more palatable if the bungling had been cheap, but it was not. Paul Hammer has shown that Elizabeth's military expenditure from 1558 to 1563

---

[92] 'The names of such captains as best served in Scotland under Lord Grey of Wilton, both the gentlemen of the country and the old captains', June 1560. *CSPSc, 1547–63* p. 438.

[93] Churchyard gives an account of the slaughter visited on the English because of the 'lewd ladders, vile and nought' in his account of the siege of Leith in *Churchyarde's chippes* (London, 1575), p. 9 r, where he wrote 'our soldiers lack no will / To climb the walls, where they received much ill / For when they laid their ladders in the dyke / They were too short, the length of half a pike'. The same occurred at the siege of Edinburgh, as noted in a letter from Sir George Howard to Norfolk in May 1560, where there was 'no scaling ladder long enough by two yards to reach the top of the wall . . . for want of which things we have sustained a marvellous great loss', see *CSPSc, 1547–63*, p. 398.

amounted to a staggering £750,000.[94] The choice of Warwick (ennobled in December 1561) as well as the tried and tested Admiral Clinton for the Newhaven escapade did not greatly improve the martial reputation of the English aristocracy. When foreign diplomats at Whitehall speculated about the best military leaders in England, they mentioned captains such as Edward Randolph rather than any of the nobility.

Eight years later, during the northern rebellion – which, when it came to actual fighting, only generated a siege at Barnard Castle and a minor battle at Haworth – Elizabeth looked to the same aristocratic personnel to lead her forces: Sussex and Hunsdon in the north, Warwick and Clinton in the south. Throughout her reign, Elizabeth advanced certain of the existing nobility as a result of their service on the field – Thomas Radcliffe was sent back to Ireland in 1559 with the title lord lieutenant to sweeten the pill while Clinton was made earl of Lincoln in 1572 for his role as lieutenant general of the north during the rebellion – but, crucially, she consistently refrained from admitting enterprising soldiers and military leaders into the aristocracy or bestowing on them the means required to hold such a title. On the one hand, the potential for meteoric upward mobility which had formerly attached itself to a career as a martial officer had atrophied, while, on the other, the semi-martial nobility had little to look forward to except serving for a while as governor of Berwick and warden of the east marches or, at best, president of the council of the north. There would be no more Edward Seymours or John Dudleys, men who rose, by virtue of their achievements on the field and royal favour, to the helm of government; idleness and poverty seemed to be the portion allocated to martial officers during Elizabeth's first reign. The next chapter will examine the embattled social status of these figures and show how they sought to defend themselves against their critics.

---

[94] Hammer, P., *Elizabeth's wars* (London, 2003), p. 67. This sum would amount nowadays to substantially more than £100 million in expenditure.

CHAPTER 2

Martial men and their discontents

> My words are not well chosen; I care little for that. Merit shows well enough in itself. It is they who have need of art, who gloss over their shameful acts with specious words. Nor have I studied Greek letters. I did not care to know them, because they had not taught their teachers virtue. But I have learned by far the most important lesson for the good of my country – to strike down the foe, to keep watch and ward, to fear nothing save ill repute . . . to sleep on the ground, to bear privation and fatigue at the same time. It is with these lessons that I shall encourage my soldiers.
>
> Marius to an assembly of the people in Sallust's *Bellum Jugurthae*.[1]

The Christian humanist case against the 'martialist' was straightforward. There was a place for everything, even fighting, but everything had to be in its proper place; those who followed soldiering tended to bring conflict back into society with them. Simply put, Christ had told His followers to turn the other cheek. But even the import of this non-violent maxim was contentious. As far as one soldier-writer Barnaby Rich (1542–1617) was concerned, Jesus's pacifism was not unbounded; even the captains' opponents could never truly maintain that Christ meant a prince oppressed by a tyrant to meekly surrender his crown: surely Jesus – a supporter of 'civil policy' – would assert that 'he that taketh away the knowledge of feats of arms, worketh the overthrow of the commonwealth'?[2] Given the similarity of most post-Augustinian Christian thought on war, Rich's argument should have been embedded in the common mind and therefore too tedious to repeat, but in early Elizabethan England it was a common expressed belief that the honour of the martial profession was being traduced.

---

[1] Sallust, trans. J. C. Rolfe (Cambridge, Mass., 1931), p. 318. *Non sunt composita verba mea; parvi id facio, ipsa se virtus satis ostendit. Illis artificio opus est, ut turpia facta oratione tegant. Neque litteras Graecas didici; parum placebat eas discere, quippe quae ad virtutem doctoribus nihil profuerant. At ferire, praesidia agitare, nihil metuere nisi turpem famam, hiemem et aestatem iuxta pati, humi requiescere, eodum tempore inopiam et laborem tolerare. His ego praeceptis milites hortabor . . .*

[2] Rich, B., *Allarme to England* . . . (London, 1578) sig. Aiii, v.

Consequently, many of the hoary old arguments for the superior status of soldiers had to be rehearsed again.[3]

This clash of political cultures, however, cuts startlingly across the more familiar political divisions established by historians. Take, for example, the chequered career of Sir Peter Carew (1514–75), a man whose political pedigree upholding the prayer book in the West Country and whose exile during Mary's reign might have been thought to have guaranteed much shared ideological ground with Sir William Cecil. The case of Carew is worth considering in some detail as, remarkably enough, a contemporary biography of him exists written by John Hooker, alias Vowell of Exeter.[4] According to Hooker's account, Peter was a younger son of Sir William Carew, heir of the last Baron Carew, of Mohun's Ottery in Devonshire. In line with the most fashionable early Tudor aspirations Sir William had hoped to bring Peter, who was 'pert and forward', to some advancement in an Exeter grammar school, but the child's hyperactive aversion to education was so pronounced that he scaled the walls of Exeter and threatened to throw himself down in protest. Sir William punished this act of defiance by pulling his son around the town on a lead like a dog, but eventually secured a place for the delinquent in St Paul's School, Colet's model foundation.[5] Peter's 'desire for liberty', however, once more proved an obstacle to his education, and he was handed over to a family friend at the French court who assured Peter's parents that he would be raised in that glamorous environment.[6] But the French courtier quickly lost interest in Peter, 'his hot love' waxing cold as the state of Carew's clothes deteriorated. Consequently, the boy was put out of his chamber and ended up attending to his new master's mule in the stables.

Although this turn of events was a disastrous blow to Carew's prospects, Hooker informs us that 'the young boy having by these means some liberty, and [being] trained up in the company of such as he liked well ... was contented with his estate'. Fortunately Peter was rescued from the stables by a distant cousin of his father who was visiting the French court, and he was subsequently introduced into the loftier circles of the aristocracy, serving with the Marquis of Saluzzo at the battle of

---

[3] Rich (1578) sig. Bi, r.
[4] Carew has even been called an 'Evangelical adventurer', see Eamon Duffy, *The voices of Morebath: reformation and rebellion in an English village* (New Haven, Conn., 2001), p. 131.
[5] For an Elizabethan view of the importance of Colet's school, see John Stowe, *A summarie of Englyshe Chronicles* (London, 1565) sig. 172, r.
[6] See Blaise de Montluc on the *cursus honorem* for young gentlemen in France. His father, through the intercession of a friend, placed Blaise as a page in the household of Duke Antoine of Lorraine, De Montluc, B., *The commentaries of Messire Blaise de Montluc, mareschal of France* (London, 1624), p. 6.

Pavia against Emperor Charles V.[7] Following the categorical defeat of the French army, Carew deftly changed sides, 'perceiving fortune to frown on the French', and joined the retinue of Prince William of Orange. After his new master's death, he entered the English court with the commendation of Orange's wife. Henry VIII instantly took a liking to him, making him one of his 'henchmen' and later a gentleman of his privy chamber. Carew thereby became a counsellor on matters concerning the French court – an enviable job given Henry's well-attested francophilia – and one for which Carew was well qualified, given that he 'had not only the French tongue ... but was also very witty, full of life, and altogether given to all such honest exercises as do appertain to a gentleman, and especially in riding ... his behaviour tasting after the French manner'. He served the king in specific chivalric/diplomatic contexts such as bestowing the Garter on Anne de Montmorency in 1533 and then on James V of Scotland in 1535.[8] Eventually, Peter returned briefly to Mohun's Ottery to visit his father after an absence of six years. Hooker sketches the scene: Carew found his parents sitting together in their parlour and knelt silently before them proffering letters from the Princess of Orange. His parents, who believed their wild son dead, wondered 'what it should mean that a young gentleman so well apparelled, and so well accompanied [with a retinue] should thus prostrate himself before [us].' When they realised that their prodigal had returned, they received him with 'all gladness' and entertained him 'in the best manner they could': the picaresque hero triumphant.

In short, Carew's life was a horror story in light of the civic humanist and godly ethos of an Ascham, a Smith or a Cecil. Not only did the hero of the piece, a younger son, actively eschew humanist education and formation, but he prospered in their absence, giving the lie to Ascham's argument that knowledge garnered from books is better than real

---

[7] The distant cousin was Carew of Haccombe. Peter made provision that Thomas Carew of Haccombe and his legitimate male heirs would be in line to inherit his barony of Idrone in Carlow if he and five other designated Carews died without legitimate heirs male, PCC, PROB/11/58.

[8] Hooker, J. alias Vowell, 'Life of Sir Peter Carew' in, *Cal Carew MSS, 1515–1574*, (London, 1867), pp. lxvii–cxviii. For the role of monarchical representation that Henrician gentlemen of the privy chamber played in diplomatic relations, see D. Starkey, 'Representation through intimacy: a study in the symbolism of monarchy and court office in early modern England' in Guy (1997), pp. 55–6. See *L & P Hen VIII, XIV*, Vol. II, p. 202, where reference is made to the role Carew was to play as a squire at the reception of Anne of Cleves in 1540, and p. 345 for his membership of 'the spears'; *L & P Hen VIII, XVII*, p. 443 (8) for record of Carew being granted a licence to buy and export 600 unwrought cloths in June 1540. In November 1543 he was granted monastic lands in Cornwall, *L&P Hen VIII, XVIII*, Vol. I, p. 979 and lands in Devon in May 1544, *L&P Hen VIII, XIX*, Vol. I, p. 610 (44).

experience.[9] Having pursued liberty in his youth, he subsequently attained a high degree of favour at the English court on the basis of facility with French, a propensity for gossip and singing, as well as a starkly frank manner.[10] Even his submission to his parents smacked less of repentance for his previous impulsiveness than of vindication of his wilfulness, a wilfulness that enabled him to become more influential (and apparently more wealthy) than his own father. Carew ended his days in Ireland as a member of the Irish Council, as holder of the office of constable of Leighlin, and as baron of Idrone in Carlow. His earlier upward mobility had less to do with meritocracy, gravity and state service than charm, pomp and self-seeking.[11]

However, by 1571 (with a brief flurry of favour around the time of Elizabeth's accession long past), Edmund Tremayne, clerk to the privy council and former Marian dissident, could write to Burghley that Carew was to be numbered among those to be 'pitied to be seen to droop for disgrace'. The man had deserved more favour, if only because of 'the remembrance of former desserts and sufficiency to many good services which of good reason should be thought on'.[12] As a gentleman of the privy chamber, Carew had once been competent to represent the prince's body and give the prince's word, but all hope of regaining this degree of favour had faded away. John Hooker describes how Carew had given up living in London for want of encouragement and how 'her Highness seemed to conceive some unkindness against him.'[13] As we will see later,

---

[9] See *English works of Roger Ascham: Toxophilus, report of the affaires and state of Germany, and the scholemaster*, ed. W. A. Wright (Cambridge, 1904), p. 218.

[10] Contrast with Ascham's wish 'to have young men brought up in . . . some more severe discipline, than commonly they be' following the counsels of the *Cyropaedia* so that the student would remain 'under the keep . . . of some grave governor, until he was either married, or called to bear some office in the common wealth'. See Ascham (1904), pp. 200–1.

[11] Hooker does ascribe to Carew a sort of nobility commensurate with civic, or even Ciceronian duty when he relates how he preferred the service of his Prince and the doing of his duty to the 'great livelihoods' that awaited him at home following his elder brother's death. See Hooker (1867), pp. lxxxii–lxxxiii; cxiii–cxviii.

[12] Tremayne to Burghley, December 1571, SP63/37/40. Tremayne had been a servant of the earl of Devon, Edward Courtenay, was implicated in Wyatt's revolt and was imprisoned in the Tower in 1554. He remained loyal to the extreme Marian opposition on the Continent centred on Sir Francis Russell, the earl of Bedford. Carew has been served particularly well by his most recent biographer J. A. Wagner, whose *The Devon gentleman: the life of Sir Peter Carew* (Hull, 1998) has dealt astutely with Carew's changing, but surprisingly easy, relationship with the gentry of the West Country under Elizabeth and his brief success during the first few years of her reign. See especially pp. 237–76.

[13] Hooker (1867), pp. xcv–xcvi. In 1563, Carew sold his interest in his Devonshire manors to his niece's husband Thomas Southcote for £2,000. Southcote allowed Carew and his wife a life estate in the properties and undertook to observe almost all leases they made during their lifetime. See Wagner (1998), pp. 271–2.

his sins against Burghley's and even Elizabeth's sensibilities were exceptionally grave, but despite these special circumstances, his actual experience of ostracism, arising out of his indebtedness and financial instability, was not untypical.

The chivalric ethos and the Christian humanist ethos, each of which had found coherence and support in the person of Henry VIII, emperor and religious-reformer, had polarised since the reign of Mary I. The increased polarisation between these *ethoi* that marked the period from 1563 to 1584 was thought to have proved unpropitious for martial men. The foremost royal servant was no friend of the martial profession; foreign policy focused on avoiding costly engagement and failure; furthermore, Elizabeth's status as an unmarried woman, rather than an exuberant man, ruled out unseemly familiarity with soldiers. After ten years of this frosty dispensation, there was a martial backlash, not in the streets of London or Berwick but on paper, and men such as Barnaby Rich and Thomas Churchyard were at its centre.

Relative poverty and neglect ensured that many of those who later served as martial men had been marginalised educationally, excluded from the fruits of Christian humanism. Peter Carew et al. were mostly the casualties of primogeniture and liable to fall prey to the misfortunes that being a younger son presented at a time of rising inflation, growing indebtedness, burgeoning consumer culture and downward social mobility.[14] Indeed, in this context, Carew was exceptional. Apart from being fortunate that his father had been conscientious enough to give him the opportunity to receive some form of education, he had been rescued from obscurity by the favour of a hearty English monarch, an impossibility under Elizabeth. The comparative neglect that younger sons of gentry suffered, as Joan Thirsk pointed out, was eloquently expressed by Orlando's complaint in *As you like it* about his treatment at the hands of his older brother Oliver:

He keeps me rustically at home, or, to speak more properly, stays me here at home unkept... My father charg'd you in his will to give me a good education: you have train'd me like a peasant obscuring and hiding from me all gentlemanlike qualities: the spirit of my father grows strong in me, and I will no longer endure it.[15]

---

[14] See J. Thirsk 'The European debate on customs of inheritance, 1500–1700' in *The rural economy of England* (London, 1984).
[15] This, from Act I, Scene 1, is also quoted by Joan Thirsk in her article 'Younger sons in the seventeenth century' in Thirsk (1984), p. 337.

Squabbling between brothers was common. Following their father's death in 1561, Thomas Randolph, Elizabeth's ambassador in Edinburgh and his brother, the seasoned captain Edward, squared up to each other, ready to take whatever opportunity might allow. According to Thomas, 'my brother's meaning is, that either [my father] has left me nothing, or that all is too little for himself', and, while he wrote platitudes about not wanting to see his brother lose out, his concern about the adverse effect that Edward's proximity to their mother could have on his claim to the family homestead indicated otherwise.[16] Similarly, Jacques Wingfield, Ireland's master of ordnance, accounted for Lord Deputy William Fitzwilliam's attempts to oust him from office in 1573, by casting them as merely another inconvenience in a life congenitally disadvantaged: 'as a younger brother evil provided for, I be as well able to sustain [Fitzwilliam's actions against me] nevertheless before God, though the loss and hindrance, besides open discontinuance, be grievous unto me'; Wingfield had once been a lively teenager with great prospects in the entourage of Bishop Stephen Gardiner.[17]

Whereas the eldest son of a successful gentry family was likely to pursue an education at grammar school, university or the inns of court which enabled him to serve as a justice of the peace or to hold some other public office, younger siblings were frequently allowed just a small portion of land that reverted to an eldest brother at death or were left to loiter around their brother's estate in a subaltern role. For example, in 1589, Sir Thomas Fane, the formerly attainted anti-Marian, sheriff of Kent, justice of the peace and eldest son, left his own eldest son Francis all his 'manors, lands and tenements' worth £467 8s 7d per annum, while his two other sons George and Edward got a £50 annuity each. Even though Francis was but four years old, Sir Thomas was anxious that the younger sons would never challenge his eldest son's birthright. To ensure that all possible discord was suppressed, he sternly included a proviso in his will that threatened, if either son claimed a piece of Francis's inheritance, to stop his annuity: Francis, benefiting from the ingrained favouritism of the

---

[16] See Thomas Randolph's letter to Cecil, 27 October 1561, in *CSPSc, 1547–63*, pp. 567. Thomas, brought up as a 'scholar' claimed to have already bought the house where he was born 'without my father's charge'.

[17] J. Wingfield to Edmund Tremayne, 12 July 1573, SP63/41/74. See also Fitzwilliam to Burghley, 18 July 1573, Bodl. Carte MSS 56/171. For evidence that Burghley continued to hold Jacques Wingfield in disfavour, see Wingfield to Burghley, 6 May 1581 SP63/83/2, where the master of ordnance petitioned Burghley to secure his kinsman 'Anthony B. D.' the Deanery of St Patrick's Dublin, even though the lord treasurer had a while earlier ignored his petition that the said kinsman might be made a prebend of the cathedral. Wingfield was unsuccessful.

system, went on to be the first earl of Westmoreland.[18] Finally, of course, illegitimacy was also a near certain guarantee of exclusion from inheritance. Edmund's soliloquy on 'bastardy' in Act I, Scene 2 of *King Lear* provides a poignant articulation of Elizabethan resentment and rage at exclusion from riches and privilege.[19] In short, the fate of *déclassé* members of the gentry seemed to be downward mobility, public shame – perhaps even indigence – and a struggle to keep up appearances. Whereas great opportunities to make fortunes in spite of the sequence of one's birth had arisen in the heyday of the dissolution of the monasteries, under Mary and Elizabeth that sort of bonanza would not repeat itself.[20]

The anonymous work *Cyvile and uncyvile life*, published in 1579 and again in 1586, placed particular emphasis on the different treatment offered the eldest son and the younger. This dialogue between the courtier Valentine and the rustic gentleman Vincent sought to champion urban life at court as the 'order of life [that] best beseemeth a gentleman ... to make him a person fit for the public service of his prince and country'.[21] For this purpose, the verve and sophistication of Valentine was consistently pitted against the naivety and crudeness of Vincent.[22] Vincent, with 'revenues of his own' attained 'by succession', was the typical *bête noire* of the younger sons of England. His comfort, very much the ease of the dog in the manger, meant there were fewer opportunities for the advancement of worthy gentlemen who were not *rentiers*. Reluctant 'to hazard [his] children abroad' for fear of the 'licentious customs of the city', Vincent claimed that there was no dishonour in 'poor younger brethren without land (as commonly they are all)' maintaining themselves and their families 'by the plough'. He saw the utility of sending his children to the universities or inns of court, but stated that, unless 'their

---

[18] Malcolm Mercer, 'Fane, Sir Thomas (d. 1589)', *Oxford Dictionary of National Biography* (Oxford, 2004); PCC PROB/11/77.
[19] There were exceptions. Cases like that of Thomas Smith Jr, the bastard son of Sir Thomas Smith who was treated as a legitimate son up to his death in 1577 were rare.
[20] Thirsk (1984), pp. 338–9. For more about the honour attached to service in local government and how office-holding became another opportunity to assert pre-eminence, see A. Fletcher, 'Honour and officeholding in Elizabethan and Stuart England', in *Order and disorder in early modern England*, ed. A. Fletcher and J. Stevenson (Cambridge, 1985). See D. M. Palliser, *The age of Elizabeth: England under the late Tudors, 1547–1603* (London, 1992), pp. 77, 105 and H. J. Habakkuk, 'The market for monastic property, 1539–61' in *Ec HR* 2nd ser., 10:3 (1958), pp. 362–80.
[21] *Cyvile and uncyvile life* (London, 1579) sigs. Aiii, r–Aiv, r.
[22] In the dialogue, Vincent, a self-confessed 'home-bred bird ... unacquainted with disguising and superfluous ceremony', vents his suspicion of the increased adoption of the 'foreign' custom whereby gentlemen leave the country to dwell in the city rather than inhabiting 'the country, continuing there from age to age, and from ancestor to ancestor, a continual house ... nourished in justice, truth and plain dealing'. *Cyvile and uncyvile life* (1579) sig. Aiv, r.

disposition to learning' was obvious, they were pulled out 'quick'. Roger Ascham had already bemoaned this tendency, complaining that fathers rarely sent their 'hard witted' children to be schooled: 'hard-wits', he claimed, ultimately made the most successful pupils because they later turned their hands to *negotium cum labore non cum periculo* (occupations involving hard work rather than danger).[23] Vincent also looked askance at service at court, and singled out service on the battlefield for particular scorn as a calling 'rather lewd than laudable . . . [a] hazard greater than we (being born to wealth and worship) will put our babes unto'.

Yet, given a choice between eking out a dishonourable existence on a smallholding and a military career full of opportunities to travel and make money, it is easy to see how the lure of being a captain could appear attractive. Most men who served as captains in Ireland appear to have been younger sons. An, admittedly rough, survey would demonstrate that William Drury, William Pelham, Richard Bingham, John Perrot, Edward Randolph, and Peter Carew were all third sons, while Francis Cosby, Nicholas Bagenal and Humphrey Gilbert were second sons. As we shall see, rather than remain 'rustically at home', many of these officers embraced a military career in the European wars either serving their own monarch or other princes: the Habsburg-Valois wars, the Holy League's Mediterranean campaigns, the French Wars of Religion and the Dutch wars provided opportunities for employment. If imbibing classical humanist learning in the cloisters of Cambridge had worked professional alchemy for the sons of yeomen bloated by the revenues of newly acquired monastic lands, the pursuit of military service under the leadership of a monarch seemed in some ways a more gallant way of securing grace, favour and renown.

The wonted advantage of military service for *déclassé* gentry, apart from being a source of income through wages, booty and revenue illicitly siphoned off, was the opportunity it offered men to gain patronage as a reward for honourable and practical service based on prowess. The author of *Cyvile and uncyvile life* pointed to the boons of the French custom in these matters where a young gentleman might proceed from being a page at court to being a soldier in garrison before becoming an officer until finally he might be appointed the governor of a town, a colonel or a chieftain. We have already seen how this system benefited Carew. Having presented this tantalising glimpse of opportunities hitherto unimagined, and increasingly unavailable in England – the chance of one day being 'spotted' – the author asked:

[23] See Ascham (1904), pp. 190-1.

Is not this a better course for young gentlemen then tarry at home in their fathers or brothers house, and keep a sparrowhawk, or a kennel of bawling dogs, or . . . marry himself with some poor maiden and through charge of children, become a very farmer; or ploughman, which things though be honest and fit for some men, yet for a gentleman [are] utterly unmeet.[24]

In the light of perennial beliefs (discussed above) about the tripartite division of society, dropping from being a *miles* to being a hewer of wood or drawer of water was truly shameful. Churchyard, in his *Choise*, compared the relative status military men enjoyed in different parts of Europe. The French, Spaniards and Italians, he assured the reader, held soldiers and veterans in high esteem. His treatment of the English attitude to martial men, however, was necessarily disingenuous. Initially, he praised Elizabeth's munificence towards soldiers: 'Do but examine how many since her noble reign, of soldiers have had leases, gotten livings, been preferred to government, and gone from court with full hands, that began with empty purses.' This upbeat preface was followed by a condemnation of 'secret suits' coupled with an allegation that 'some by the report of their friends stole away the benefices from the fountainhead.' But he ended on an optimistic note, remarking that 'the candle is in, and not burnt so far, but may give a gracious blaze and a new light, to lighten the minds of soldiers, and such as sit in the comfortless shadow of dark despair.'[25]

The giving of leases in reversion with fines waived – in essence the gift of an income rather than capital – had replaced the grants of land in fee, common in the Henrician period, as the currency which Elizabeth used to reward subjects for their service.[26] It soon became apparent that soldiers rarely benefited from these grants. Even after the northern rebellion of 1569, gifts were scarce. For instance, Philip Strelley, Robert Gamme and the hardened veteran captain Robert Yaxley – all Berwick men – were among the very few to be rewarded; indeed, out of the list of fifty-one captains of the 'army of the north', only Yaxley received a lease.[27] The one

---

[24] *Cyvile and uncyvile life* (1579) sig. Dii, r. [25] Churchyard (1579) sig. Oi, v.
[26] See K. S. H. Wyndham's 'Crown land and royal patronage in mid-sixteenth century England', *Journal of British Studies*, 19, 2 (1980) especially pp. 28–31 and D. Thomas's 'Leases in reversion on the crown's lands, 1558–1603' in *EcHR*, 30, 1 (1977), pp. 67–72.
[27] *CPR Eliz. 1569–72*, pp. 70, 202, 265; 'The captains now serving in the army of the north', SP12/66/2i. The rapine and pillage that the army of the north inflicted in 1569 on the countryside was lucrative and notorious. See the complaint made by the earl of Sussex to Cecil, 1 January 1569, that Warwick and Clinton's army 'have, by their warrants, seized (while I lay in service at Exham) all the lands, goods, leases and cattles, that appertained to any man that was between Newcastle and Doncaster; and their marshal, master of the camp and other officers, have driven all the cattle of the country and ransomed the people in such miserable sort and made such open and common

that benefited most of all, Sir William Drury, by contrast, did quite well in this respect, although, no doubt this had something to do with his efforts on an errand close to Burghley's heart: throughout the early 1570s he played a central part as an ambassador to Scotland during that kingdom's civil wars, raising the siege of Edinburgh and bolstering the earl of Morton's regime. Consequently, in 1573, he received lands in fee in the bishopric of Durham with rents of a yearly value of £25 6s 8d as well as securing inquisitions into concealed lands in Devonshire and Buckinghamshire.[28]

The predicament of that haughty gent Sir John Perrot during the reign of Edward VI illustrates how turning towards a military career was increasingly viewed by respectable opinion as a symptom of financial desperation. According to the anonymous author of his late Elizabethan biography, Perrot (rumoured to be one of Henry VIII's bastards) had lived lavishly at court, amassing a great debt. He had run 'so far into arrearages, that he began to mortgage some of his Lands, and yet did owe some seven or eight thousand Pounds'. In a desperate bid to improve his position, Perrot stood in a part of the court frequented by Edward and loudly lamented that he had consumed 'his living, having wasted a great part of that in few years which his ancestors had gotten and enjoyed for many years'. This staged display of emotion culminated in Perrot talking to himself *magna voce* about his own fate. The options were clear: either he should 'leave the court and *follow the wars*' or hope for some grant from the king. However, as he openly exclaimed, the latter was hopeless because, even if the king was inclined to favour it, 'his governors, as the lord-protector, and the privy council, yet might gainsay it, and so he should rather run into farther arrearages, than recover his decayed fortunes.' Edward heard him and, wishing to assert his autonomy from his counsellors, licensed Perrot to seek out a concealment. The author asserted that the example

of Sir John Perrot's prodigality and recovery may serve for the young men of this age, and of time to come, to teach them (with the prodigal son spoken of in the Gospel, and with this knight, whose life is here described) to return home in time, and with the eye of consideration to look into their estates before all be spent.[29]

---

spoil, as the like, I think, was never heard of, putting no difference between the good and bad.' This amounted to a usurpation of the warrants given by Sussex to the sheriff of Northumberland and the bishopric of Durham to seize lands, goods and cattle in to the Queen, C. Sharpe *The rising in the north* (Durham, 1975), pp. 130–1.

[28] *CPR Eliz. 1572–5*, pp. 27, 37, 168–9, 224, 267.

[29] Rawlinson, R., *The history of that most eminent statesman, Sir John Perrot knight of the Bath and Lord Lieutenant of Ireland* (London, 1728), pp. 31–4. The tale concludes 'This story Sir John Perrot

The social difficulties he had encountered were more aggravated by Elizabeth's reign. In 1580, Philip Sidney famously told Edward Denny that 'the unnoble constitution of our times' kept men of action from 'fit employments'; and without employment many martial men had little opportunity to avoid chronic poverty.[30] Their indigence meant that their promises were of little value; their credit was low.[31] Burghley's withering assessment of Thomas Stukeley as a 'famous man for lewdness' shows the working out of these prejudices. Stukeley had been distrusted because he 'commonly pretend[ed] himself to be a man of value and livelihood, when in truth he never had in his own right one foot of land, but by borrowing in every place and paying nowhere'.[32] Similarly, Sir Nicholas White, master of the rolls in Ireland, had Francis Cosby, the constable of Maryborough in mind when he remarked that 'mean men advanced *by service* to great wealth serve the Queen badly.'[33]

Poverty, of course, is relative, and the networks of support open to these second and third sons afforded the resources of deeper pockets than were accessible to an agricultural labourer subsisting on 26s 8d per annum, but the opportunities to incur shame were, arguably, similarly inflated. The patterns of household expenditure, demands of service to the crown and pressures to attain a desired status within the community of gentry and better yeomanry, or (more challenging still) at a court that fetishised conspicuous wealth, expected of a man of credit, invited aspirants to fall into debt, to pursue desperate measures and hare-brained schemes to regain credit and, ultimately, led them to take financial chances and fail.[34] When Sir William Pelham, lieutenant of the ordnance and marshal of Leicester's army in the Low Countries, died in 1586, he was in debt to the crown to the tune of £8,807 14s $5\frac{1}{4}$d, despite owning manors in Lincolnshire (notably Brocklesby) and holding leases in Durham. The rents from his manors continued to service this debt after his death.

---

would sometimes recount unto his friends, acknowledging it a great blessing of God, that had given him grace in time to look into his decaying estate, and such means to recover the same by the help and bounty of so merciful and rare a young prince as this noble King Edward was, the like of whom, for learning, wit, and princely piety, hath seldom been seen in so young years.'

[30] Osborn, J. M., *Young Philip Sidney: 1572–77* (New Haven, Conn., 1972), p. 537.
[31] For a treatment of the culture of credit and its relation to ideas about reputation in early modern England, see C. Muldrew, *The economy of obligation* (London, 1998), especially pp. 148–72.
[32] 'Treatise written in defence of the Queen' a tract apparently dictated by Burghley and corrected by him in 1583, SP12/164/85.
[33] Sir Nicholas White to Burghley, 17 July 1573, SP63/41/80. Cosby was a second son from Lincolnshire, who had served in Ireland since 1548. His advance had been aided by his marriage to Lady Mary Seymour, the lord protector's daughter, a widow.
[34] Muldrew (1998), pp. 148–72.

According to his will, his son William and daughter Anne would only be allowed to receive their designated inheritance once his 'debts [were] fully satisfied and paid'.[35] Twenty years earlier, his predecessor as lieutenant, Sir Edward Randolph, following his untimely death at the fort in Derry, had left his wife Sibill merely an aggregated annuity of £55 from rents. His 100-mark annuity as lieutenant of the ordinance was discontinued. Unsurprisingly, his brother Thomas was not mentioned in the will.[36]

Creative financial fixes were the order of the day. In 1574, Sir Humphrey Gilbert, to keep his head above water, alienated fifteen manors, an advowson and church lands in Kent, only to subsequently have the recipients alienate them back to him in 1578.[37] Gilbert was renowned for living wildly beyond his means, especially when his horizons appeared to broaden in the early 1570s. He was never financially content, despite marrying a wealthy wife and holding the receivership of fines for offences to do with maintenance of armaments and horses as well as unlawful games. He tried every means of getting rich quick, from the sublime (trying to capitalise on letters patent he received in 1578 entitling him to seek out 'remote heathen and barbarous landes', which he and his heirs could 'have, hold, occupy, and enjoy forever') to the ridiculous (his cooperation with Sir William Cecil, the earl of Leicester, and Sir Thomas Smith in sponsoring William Medley's alchemical project to change iron into copper). The former led to a ruinous, but posthumously glorious, career as a transatlantic explorer, the latter led to him losing face at court among the most powerful and being mocked behind his back as a compulsive homosexual. Later, Gilbert would complain to Walsingham about his shame that 'I, a poor man, having served her the queen in wars and peace above seven and twenty year should be now subject to daily arrests, executions and outlawries; yea, and forced to gadge and sell my wife's clothes from her back, who brought me so good a living.' By the

---

[35] See Sir William Pelham's will, PCC, PROB/11/69. For details of how Pelham accumulated his property, receiving alienations from Lincolnshire, Yorkshire and Suffolk along the way, see *CPR Eliz. 1563–6*, p. 6; *CPR Eliz. 1572–5*, pp. 65, 207, 326 518; *CPR Eliz. 1575–8*, p. 356, 423, 505, 457. See Burghley to Leicester, 27 December 1585, where the lord treasurer states 'For Mr Pelham, I have dealt earnestly with her Majesty to dismiss him with her favour . . . but her Majesty refuseth either to pardon him, whereof he hath most need, or to stall his debt, which he also requireth, yea to take as much of his land as reasonably may satisfy his debt, so as he may, with the rest, live and pay his other debts' in *Leycester corr.* (1844), p. 45.
[36] Edward Randolph's will PCC, PROB/11/49. *CPR Eliz. 1563–6* pp. 188, 377.
[37] *CPR Eliz. 1572–5* p. 237, see also p. 379, and especially p. 508. *CPR Eliz. 1575–8* pp. 423, 535.

time of his death, his two transatlantic voyages and other escapades had consumed what had been a considerable estate; his widow was left petitioning for a small income from the crown.[38]

When one compares Gilbert's financial trajectory with that of a figure engaged in trade of a more conventional stamp, such as the remarkably debtless Thomas Aldersey or William Towerson, the price of maniacal social aspiration becomes clear. Aldersey, son of a Cheshire landowner and a prominent member of the Haberdashers' and Merchant Adventurers, had spent his life securing the cloth trade to Emden and thereby gained a reputation as a shrewd, pious and trustworthy figure in London's mercantile community, acting as a godly philanthropist both in London and his native county: at the end of his life, his will distributed almost £2,000 among charitable institutions and family.[39] In a similar fashion, Towerson, who had made his name trading on the Guinea coast, comfortably divided his estate equally among his ten children, leaving enough resources over to clothe over twenty of his associates, friends and family in gowns of black cloth at 15s a yard and allow for charitable works within the Skinners' Company and his parish of St Gabriel Fenchurch.[40] The lifestyle of a London merchant, or indeed a prominent lawyer such as William Bendlowes, the Catholic serjeant at law, cost less to maintain than any attempt to live at court or keep up appearances in gentle society in the country. Certainly, a younger son with an aspiring mind pursuing his ambitions around the court must have found living on an annuity or a tiny fraction of his father's rent near to impossible.[41]

The sense of social and political frustration and exclusion to be found among the military profession was given voice in a literature of complaint that emerged in the 1570s, penned by writers with soldiering experience. Barnaby Rich from Essex (his motto *malui me divitem esse quam vocari*: 'I would rather be rich than called Rich'), for instance, had served at New Haven, and accordingly in 1574 he dedicated his *Right exelent and pleasaunt dialogue betwene Mercury and an English souldier: contayning his supplication to Mars* . . . to the commander of that expedition, Ambrose

---

[38] Quinn, D. B., *The voyages and colonising enterprises of Sir Humphrey Gilbert* (London, 1939), Vol. I, pp. 20–1, 26, 102; Vol. II, p. 241.
[39] R. C. D. Baldwin, 'Aldersey, Thomas (1521/2–1598)', *Oxford Dictionary of National Biography* (Oxford, 2004).
[40] See Towerson's will in PCC PROB/11/67 and John C. Appleby, 'Towerson, William (*d.* 1584)' and J. D. Alsop, 'Towerson, Gabriel (*bap.* 1576, *d.* 1623)', *Oxford Dictionary of National Biography* (Oxford, 2004).
[41] See J. H. Baker, 'Bendlowes, William (1516–1584)', *Oxford Dictionary of National Biography* (Oxford, 2004) and his will PCC PROB/11/68.

Dudley, earl of Warwick, one 'whose valiant acts hath made him famous in his country'. The *Dialogue* stands as a statement of martial disaffection in which Rich engages directly with the civil critique of the profession rehearsed in the last chapter.

In a pose which was the rule rather than the exception for martial writers, Rich stressed his own 'ignorance in the knowledge of writing' and affected 'the base and barren style of a simple soldier ... rather than the learned lines proceeding from such as hath been trained up in schools'; here he echoed Sallust's Marius, splenetically pitting martial honesty and bluntness against the weasel words and eloquence of the senators and nobility.[42] Rich, like other martial apologists, claimed to be taking up the tone and brevity of the military dispatch – the Caesarean *veni, vidi, vici*, rather than the Ciceronian *quae vel iniusta utilior est quam iustissimum bellum cum civibus* (an unjust peace is better than a just war against one's countrymen).[43] The *Dialogue*, full of allegory and classical allusion, was based on a fanciful premise reminiscent of *Piers Plowman:* in a deep sleep, Rich (his fictional self) sees a vision of a martial parade of ghost soldiers, who appoint him to bring a message to Mars's court to tell the god of war 'how many extremities ... the unfortunate soldiers of England [had] lately fallen into'.[44] Hence, Rich is entrusted with the job of relaying the grievances of his profession to both the public and the god of war.

Rich reluctantly accepted the charge from the demoralised troops and was whisked off to Mars's castle by Mercury. While there, he beheld a sort of palatial *cinquecento* Valhalla decorated with scenes of famous battles ranging from the siege of Troy down to the surrender of Tournai and attendant English exploits around Boulogne. The castle was full of the dead who had defended their country 'to attain praise and noble fame, and not for filthy lucre's sake'. Many Englishmen were there, marked out by the standard of St George's Cross, Rich even recognised a few erstwhile comrades from Newhaven.[45] Within the walls, he saw old acquaintances Cuthbert Vaughan, Edward Randolph, Captain Cromwell and Captain

---

[42] See Marius's speech to the Assembly of the People in Sallust, p. 318.
[43] Cicero to Atticus, 25 January AD 49: *quae vel iniusta utilior est quam iustissimum bellum cum civibus*. Cicero, *Letters to Atticus* (Cambridge Mass., 1999) 4 vols., Vol. II, pp. 240–3.
[44] Rich, B., *A right exelent and pleasant dialogue, betwene Mercury and an English soldier: contayning his supplication to Mars* (London, 1574), sigs. A1r–A2v.
[45] For example, his superior officer at Newhaven Captain Sir Arthur Darcy, who was George Baron Darcy's brother and son of Thomas Baron Darcy, a knight of the garter and Henrician dissident, as well as a 'Captain Sanders', and 'young Souch'.

Audeley being led as garlanded champions in a triumph by a herald called 'Warlike Policy' – the insinuation being that they had never received that kind of treatment in England.

Learning that Mars was away at Venus's court, Rich undertook to follow him there, but before heading off he beheld a terrible vision which made him fundamentally question his martial vocation. In a hall in Mars's castle he saw an horrific vision called the 'Chariot of Deadly Debate'. On the sides of this chariot were depictions of 'sundry civil dissentions' such as the struggle between Caesar and Pompey, Condé and Guise and the Houses of Lancaster and York. The chariot, pulled by 'ill-favoured and unseemly monsters' called Malice, Strife, Contention and Discord, carried three terrifying personifications: Murder, War and Famine. The chariot-driver was called Envy. Behind this horrific vision, 'that most ugly and detestable creature Ruin' was in pursuit. 'Where before I had a kind of martial desire to serve as a soldier, as occasion did permit', Rich exclaims, 'I now protested to myself not only to leave the exercise of so vile a profession, but also to desever myself from the fellowship of any such as were followers of so filthy and hateful a service.'[46]

This distressing vision prompted a disjointed and idiosyncratic dialogue between Mercury and the disillusioned Rich (billed as the 'Soldier'). This part of *Mercury* is worth examining in some detail as it provides easy access to some topics – both abstract and circumstantial – that vexed Elizabethans when considering the spectre of war and soldiering. Neither Rich nor his interlocutor keep consistently to a pat stance; the dialogue's erratic momentum has less to do with the working-out of an argument than an obvious desire to consider a preordained list of issues one by one, irrespective of how coherently they fit together.

This *Conference* begins with the 'Soldier' (Rich) recapitulating his horror at the fruits of war and criticising princes not only for rushing into the embrace of so many vices through waging war but also for imposing oppressive taxes, subsidies and customs on their people, which provoke civil strife. Mercury, who at this stage is allotted the role of martial apologist, counters that God has always used war as a scourge on humanity, and soldiers have ever been his instruments to this end – merely a repetition of the commonplace that soldiering is just one Christian profession among others. Significantly, given William Cecil's bon mot about soldiers in peace being as useless as chimneys in summer, Rich has Mercury argue

---

[46] Rich (1574), sigs. A4, v–B2, v. Rich in his susceptibility to martial images echoes Aeneas's reaction to the frieze of the Trojan war in the Temple of Juno in Book I, ll. 454–94 of the *Aeneid*.

that to reject martial men because of the horrors of war would be like extinguishing all fire because its 'nature is to consume whatsoever it touch[s]'. Consequently, the prince who does not provide for war with 'sufficient and expert soldiers' is a monarch who, in effect, pulls down all chimneys, leaving his subjects in guaranteed distress.[47]

Rich wishes to outline the social conservatism of the garrison and its service as an epitome of all in England that is good. In response to Mercury's denunciation of abuses employed by captains in the conduct of their profession, the 'Soldier' argues that the double payment of soldiers of gentle birth, previously described as venal, serves as an incentive for more gentlemen to join up – indubitably a good thing.[48] He then outlines the paternalistic command structure of England's army, a structure that mirrors society at home in which (he claims) a gentleman captain often hails from the same shires as his soldiers – 'such as were dwellers about him, yea peradventure many of them his own tenants' – so that the proper deference of the common sort to a local gentleman – 'such a one as had government amongst them, [one who would] minister justice . . . at home in the time of peace' – would be replicated abroad. And, consequently, the reputation and honour gained by individual soldiers abroad could also be brought home and be added to or subtracted from their credit in their locality 'to the end that when the wars [are] finished it [lies] yet in the captain's possibility at their return to requite them either with good or ill according as they had deserved'. In the same way, the gentlemen captains, mindful of their reputation amongst their neighbours at home, conducted themselves with restraint while abroad.

After hearing this cosy speech, Mercury accuses the 'Soldier' of being anachronistic: nowadays, the only ones who serve in the wars are those who have to, whereas in the past gentlemen were as enthusiastic about soldiering 'as they are now studious to become Lawyers'. Ironically, it is the same economic necessity that prompts a captain to serve in the wars, that breeds corruption and the defamation of the martial profession as a whole, so that 'men . . . hate warlike service and . . . fly the conversation of such as doth profess it.'[49] And, while the 'Soldier' complains that the English are not as experienced at war as the French, Spaniards or Italians, Mercury is appalled that any gentleman could be ignorant of either the order of arms or the discipline of war: he should know about these things, if only from books and historical examples, although one experience of

---

[47] Rich (1574) sigs. Biii, v–Bvi, v. [48] Rich (1574) sig. Dii, r. [49] Rich (1574) sig. Diii, v.

the battlefield serves better than any amount of literature on the art of war.[50]

In answer, Mercury declaims a monologue peppered with classical analogies about the proper qualities and tasks appropriate to a good captain: a clement demeanour, strict drilling, a determination not to fight gratuitously but only when necessity demands, stirring oratory, policy (including the use of malicious rumours and ruses to defeat the enemy) and draconian devotion to military discipline. He supplements this with a pointed analysis of the failings of recruitment procedure in England, which places the blame on the commonwealth's office-holders rather than on the soldiers. A warrant goes from prince or council to the commissioner of the shire and then to the constable of each hundred and then to the petty constable of each parish who must provide two or three 'able and sufficient men' for the commissioner. Given the perils that soldiers face in time of war, the petty constable will generally opt for 'an idle fellow, some drunkard, or seditious quarreller, a privy picker, or such a one as hath some skill in stealing of a goose' as his nominee.[51] Once men like these are mustered and sent abroad, they lose no time in ransacking the surrounding countryside or in selling their weapons and clothes. The absurdity of such 'evil conditioned people' devoid of religion or obedience upholding their prince's quarrel is presented as striking. More care should be devoted to the selection of troops, Mercury suggests, with the chief criteria of suitability being standards of neatness and 'quickness of spirit', because pomp and show tend to intimidate enemies. For these reasons, the recruitment of labourers and peasants, who are used to regular food and are normally slow and careless in manner, should be avoided; soldiers are a caste apart from the tillers of the soil.[52]

Eventually, Mercury and the 'Soldier' arrive at Venus's court. On meeting an inmate of the court telling 'a strange and tragical story' about how the follies of love end in catastrophe, Rich reflects that love causes people 'to commit most heinous murders to imbrue their hands in the shedding of innocent blood', a dangerous passion in contrast to the *discipline* of war.[53] They then meet Mars, who receives Rich's supplication on behalf of the ghostly troops and warns that England's 'quiet state' has lulled her into negligence of 'martial men and military affairs'. Rich then inveighs against those whom he calls 'carpet-knights', men who, with

---

[50] Rich (1574) sig. Cvi, r–Di, v. [51] Rich (1574) sig. Gvi, v.
[52] Rich (1574) sigs. Gvii, r–Hi, r. [53] Rich (1574) sigs. Hii, v–Lviii, v.

a slight show of chivalry, profess the laws of Venus, poltroons who, as Mars asserts, would have no peace in which to pursue their trite end without the protection of soldiers. Venus then pledges that she will always favour soldiers in all they desire. On that erotic note, Rich informs the reader that once he received this promise, his despair was replaced with comfort, and he awoke from his slumber.[54] *Mercury*, with its barely contained nostalgia for a more militarised past and its indignation about the lack of honour bestowed on those who had already given their lives and service for the Elizabethan regime, introduces the common themes of this type of complaint literature.

Four years later, Rich, by now serving in Ireland, produced his *Allarme to England, foreshowing what perils are procured where the people live without regard of martial law*, dedicated to Sir Christopher Hatton, who was then lord chamberlain, captain of the guard and privy councillor. The complaints against exclusion and frustration remain, but the change of dedicatee is significant. Unlike Ambrose Dudley, Rich's first patron, Hatton had no military accomplishments at all. Indeed, around the time that Rich and Dudley had been serving in pestilential Le Havre, Hatton, as a handsome young member of the Inner Temple, had been successfully charming the queen at court. Following his appointment as gentleman pensioner in 1564, Hatton's upward mobility in office and swift acquisition of landed wealth and monopolies was remarkable. While this parvenu might have cut precisely the sort of feminised figure or 'carpet knight' that Rich had inveighed against at the conclusion of his *Right exelent and pleasant dialogue*, Hatton, impregnably ensconced in Elizabeth's favour, was now acting as Rich's 'master and upholder'.[55] In any case, Rich's consistent disparagement of the insincerity, ambition and unmanliness of courtiers would hardly have upset one as securely lodged as Hatton. His rise had been so vertiginous, as well as so entirely dependent on Elizabeth's favour, that unlike others he had never had to bow and scrape abjectly to grandees at court to gain preferment. Rich's polemic against courtiers became pointed in obedience to his patron's likes and dislikes: for instance, his denunciation of those at court reading Henry Cornelius Agrippa's *De vanitate scientiarum* cannot but have been the explicit mockery of a readily recognisable figure – perhaps the earl of Oxford, Edward de Vere, lately returned from the Continent, or the intellectual Lord Henry Howard,

---

[54] Rich (1574) sigs. Mii, r–Miii, v.
[55] See B. Rich, *Riche his farewell to the military profession* (London, 1581) sig. Bii, v., where Rich praises Hatton for inviting him to his palace at Holdenby.

who in 1583 published a treatise condemning occultism, neither of whom were favourably disposed towards Hatton.[56]

Hatton remains an enigmatic figure, a constant challenge to historians who attempt to find the key that unlocks Elizabethan political culture in the careers of either of the two most renowned grandees at court. He left much less paper behind him than did Cecil, and had little of the black notoriety of Leicester. He had no portentous dynastic commitments to advance, and he produced no direct heirs. He seems, in retrospect, to have been remarkably sufficient unto himself. He was also frequently a comfort to the marginal and politically desperate. For instance, in the early 1580s, he assisted, among others, the Catholic Charles Arundell (accused of involvement in the Throckmorton Plot by former co-conspirator Edward de Vere, earl of Oxford) and the widowed countess of Sussex.[57] His support for Rich and Thomas Churchyard (who dedicated *Churchyardes chips* [1575], his translations of Ovid [1578] and *generall rehearsall of warres* [1579] to Hatton) seems to demonstrate that in the 1570s Hatton's support of the captains amounted to investment in stock at its lowest value. He hoped to make a return on his 'martial' expenditure by acquiring something of the manners of the garrison without ever having been there.[58]

Rich's *Allarme* recapitulated topics introduced by his *Right exelent and pleasant dialogue:* the vindication of the martial profession relative to other callings; lamentation about the harshness of military life and the poor recompense English soldiers receive from the state; criticism of tendencies towards corruption inherent in the military machinery of the time; and ominous warnings that England will suffer grievously if she does not prepare herself better for war. Rich approached these recurring themes with some humour. He asserted that captains, rather than being

---

[56] For Hatton's rivalry with Oxford in the early 1570s, see N. Nicolas, *Memoirs of the life and times of Sir Christopher Hatton* (London, 1847), p. 18. For William Herle's speculation that Howard's book 'was conceived by some of good judgement to contain sundry heresies and spices withal of treason, though somewhat closely carried' see Herle to Burghley, 16 November 1583, BL Lansdowne 39, fol. 193r–v.

[57] See Nicolas (London, 1847) for an in-depth study of Hatton's correspondence. See especially pp. 179, 181, 216 for letters from a captive Charles Arundell indicating his gratitude to Hatton in 1581 and pp. 344–7 for grateful correspondence from Frances, countess of Sussex who had incurred the queen's disfavour.

[58] John Polemon dedicated his first compendium of *All the famous battels that have been fought in our age* to Hatton, while his second compendium contained no dedication. By contrast, Richard Robinson's *A learned and true assertion of the original, life, acts, and death of the most noble valiant and renouned Prince Arthur, King of great Brittaine* (London, 1582) was dedicated to the soldier Arthur Grey de Wilton, Henry Sidney and Thomas Smith 'the chief customer for her majesty in the port of London, & to the worshipful society of archers, in London yearly celebrating the renowned memory of the magnificent Prince Arthur'.

'bloody or cruel', made the best counsellors and prove perennially faithful: the oath 'by the faith of a soldier' had always been a watchword for fidelity, which was more than could be said for the reputation of merchants, lawyers, ministers of religion and courtiers.[59] Soldiers might spoil their enemies, but merchants rob their friends, and lawyers – commonly the sons of shoemakers, tailors, inn-keepers and farmers – 'seek by law to overthrow law', turning sons against fathers and fabricating delays in the legal process to further exploit vulnerability. In spite of all these faults, neither merchants nor lawyers had, Rich alleged, ever been subject to the type of invective that soldiers had suffered. Even the church had fallen from grace employing 'proud prelates, blind guides and lazy lubbers [so] if [even] the holy temple of God, cannot be cleansed from such Ministers of mischiefs, [Rich asserted,] they be something too nice that would have soldiers to be all saints, and much more to blame that would make them devils, because some do amiss'.[60] Finally, the foibles of court were not immune from Rich's withering gaze, especially courtiers who 'apply their pleasant wits to scoffing, quipping, . . . taunting', maintaining 'proud and haughty countenances' and playing the parasite.[61]

But for all this invective, Rich's catalogue of the discomforts of soldiering had changed little from Braham's litany of 1555. However, his own frustration at official neglect of martial men had intensified since 1574.[62] In particular, Rich pointed to the plight of those troops who had served for two or three decades without any preferment or reward, except for 'slander, misreport, false impositions, hatred and despite'.[63] This state of affairs was unfavourably compared with the indemnity from taxation and legal action that Augustus bestowed on his veterans and the privileges given to retired soldiers by Charlemagne. He testified to his shame at seeing 100 Spanish and French troops marching to war equipped more expensively than all the riches of the garrison of Berwick could have mustered, and lamented that of all the fees, pensions, stipends and many offices doled out daily in England, only an exiguous amount were awarded to 'unthrifty soldiers'.[64] Here, Rich was severely, indeed dangerously,

---

[59] Rich (1578) sig. Ciii, r.   [60] Rich (1578) sigs. Ciiii, r–Di, v.   [61] Rich (1578) sig. Hii, r.
[62] Barnaby Googe's foreword set the tone when it cites the dictum of Sir William Drury that 'the soldiers of England had always one of three ends to look for: to be slain, to beg or to be hanged'. Googe, later provost marshal of Connacht, specifically criticised those who advocated a citizen militia rather than supporting professional soldiers. Significantly, Googe singled out the late Sir Thomas More as one 'who having more skill in sealing a writ, than surveying of a camp, was not ashamed most unwisely to write . . . that the common labourer of England, taken from the plough, was he that when it came to the matter, did the deed', Rich (1578) sig. *iiii, v.
[63] Rich (1578) sig. Fi, r.   [64] Rich (1578) sig. Eiiii, v.

critical of Elizabeth and her conduct towards those who had received preferments. Those unworthy recipients used those revenues merely to build big houses, purchase livings and 'run in the Queen's debt, till they c[a]me in the thousands', secure in the knowledge that the purchase of a velvet gown or a gift of a few hundred pounds to Elizabeth's ladies-in-waiting was enough to ensure that the debt would be stalled or subsequently paid off at about £100 or £200 a year. 'This is the way to thrive, these be the fellows that do gain', Rich mewled.

Rich proposed that England's soldiers should be made to take an oath 'to defend the laws and liberties of [the] country', a device that would improve the reputation of the profession by making soldiers protect these institutions with the same zeal as men willing 'to offer [themselves] to martyrdom for the maintenance of religion'. In a pessimistic turn, he then acknowledged the difficulties of proffering an oath to the 'thieves', 'rogues' and 'vagabonds' that made up the rank and file, men who '[stood] in awe of none, neither yet are inclined to any manner of religion'.[65] Of course, for Rich, these abuses were not a sign of the turpitude of the martial profession but yet another symptom of the general neglect shown towards military affairs in England, a neglect that boded ill for the country. There were hardly any trained soldiers in England, apart from in Berwick, and there was a total lack of understanding about how vulnerable the realm was as a result. Adequate soldiers, he stressed, could not be trained up within a month.[66] The example of what had happened in the Low Countries through lack of preparedness was the bogeyman that Rich constantly dangled before his readers:

How many years continued they in peace and quietness, in drunkenness, in lechery, in riot, in excess, in gluttony, in wantonness ... they were contented to submit themselves to any manner of thraldom, and to every kind of slavery, to receive the Spaniards into their cities and towns, which were naturally seated so strong, that no foreign prince could forcibly have made entry into them ... by necessity they were enforced to go to Mars his school, and to practise the art of war, which had ever been most loathsome unto them, not without great ruin and wrack, of many noble cities and towns ....[67]

---

[65] Rich (1578) sigs. Kiii, r–Kiii, v.
[66] Rich also complained that although England could cast its own iron ordinance (a process that had consumed all the country's timber and hobbled its capacity to build ships) three times as much of this home-made ordinance was sold abroad, specifically in France and Spain, than at home. By criticising this abuse, Rich was implicitly placing blame on his former commander in arms, Ambrose Dudley, earl of Warwick, the master of ordinance, Rich (1578) sigs. Hiii, v–Hiiii, r.
[67] Rich (1578) sigs. Fiii, r–Fiii, v.

Rich's opinions were forthrightly expressed. He championed the cause of those best described as true soldiers, not unworthy political appointees, not 'carpet knights', not sighing lovers, not dull mechanics, not peasants and not criminals. In his works of the 1570s, he stressed that the martial profession correctly administered, not in its neglected form, possessed an intrinsic morality superior to others, a morality that, at its best, eschewed the delinquent and effeminate. The creeping righteousness that weighed soldiers in the balance and found them wanting was merely a sign of England's decadence: 'Peace is the nourisher of vice.'[68] Rich's moral turn led him (having run the gamut of classical analogy in his 1574 effort) to use scriptural examples of God's benediction on war and soldiering – none of which, significantly enough, refer to the didactic marginalia of the Geneva Bible. Following Augustine, he drew attention to the fact that Melchisedek gave bread and wine to Abram, the 'captain' of 318 retainers as they 'returned from the slaughter and spoil of their enemies'. He cited Moses' vendetta against the Midianites, Joshua's victory over the Amorites at Gibeon, King Jehoshaphat's blessed annihilation of the Ammonites and Moabites and God's displeasure at Saul's reluctance to do a thorough job of obliterating all the Amalekites, not to mention the examples of Gideon, David, Jephthah and Judas Macchabeus. From the New Testament, he invoked John the Baptist's advice to soldiers to be content with their wages, the faithful centurion who said to Christ *Domine, non sum dignus* and Cornelius the centurion.[69]

Rich would return to martial issues later in his writing career, when war was an immediate concern, and he still found things to complain about. He also remained loyal to Sir Christopher Hatton, and, while it is difficult to be certain about how Rich had managed to maintain the support of such an influential man, it seems that courtiers, although reluctant to exert themselves financially to support martial men, continued to be interested in the opportunity of either posing as a martial man or boosting their profile among the disaffected soldiering community of England.[70] In July 1578, the same year that Rich published his

---

[68] Rich (1578) sig. Biv, v. See also William Davison's opinion advanced in March 1578 that Elizabeth could have 'a convenient army of her own subjects, trained and experienced in the wars of this country . . . whereas they be now of all other nations the most inexpert and ignorant in that behalf', Davison to Hatton, 8 March 1578, BL Add. MSS. 15891, fol. 23. Davison was trying to convert Hatton to the support of a military expedition to the Low Countries headed by Leicester. Hatton would prove sympathetic to Leicester's 1584 expedition.
[69] Rich (1578) sigs. Ai, v–Cii, v.
[70] In the following year (1579), Rich served in Ireland and benefited from Walsingham's favour: Malby on receiving a message from Walsingham delivered by Rich in September 1579 wrote that

Allarme, Gabriel Harvey presented the earl of Oxford with an oration, which, while it praised his learning, urged him to:

throw away the insignificant pen, throw away bloodless books, and writings that serve no useful purpose; [for] now must the sword be brought into play, now is the time for thee to sharpen the spear and to handle great engines of war. On all sides men are talking of camps and of deadly weapons.

Harvey assured Oxford that he was the man to drive Don John of Austria, or 'the most powerful enemy' the Turks, from 'the gates of Britain': 'Thou art fiercely longing for the fray. I feel it. Our whole country knows it [. . .] Thine eyes flash fire, thy countenance shakes a spear; who would not swear that Achilles had come to life again?'[71] There is no evidence that the earl of Oxford, too small to be an Achilles, had any martial experience whatsoever, despite tales, most likely the fruit of his own imagination, that he had served with the duke of Alva in the Netherlands. This whiff of naughtiness, which Oxford cultivated for most of his life, appears to have arisen out of a day trip to survey the Spanish army lines in the Low Countries while on his Continental adventures.[72]

A CERTAIN DEADLY DISSENTION FALLEN BETWEEN THE SWORD AND THE PEN

It was Thomas Churchyard, soldier and hack, who proffered the most desperate diagnosis of the miserable condition in which Elizabethan soldiers found themselves; while Rich could provide wit, analysis and argument, Churchyard added to these qualities self-pity and bile. Responsible for innumerable publications from the reign of Edward VI to the very end of Elizabeth's reign, he concentrated for the most part on martial themes, a subject that frequently allowed him to tell his calamitous life story.[73] In 1579, he wrote that he made no apologies for working on his chosen subject matter, the glory of English captains: 'Before all other

---

he would 'bend [himself] in all [he] can to pleasure him or any other that shall come at any time recommended from you'. Malby to Walsingham, 10 September 1579, SP63/69/17.

[71] Harvey, Gabriel, *Gabrielis harueij gratulationum valdinensium libri quatuor ad illustrissimum augustissimámque principem, Elizabetam, Angliae, Franciae, Hiberniaeq[ue] Reginam longè serenissimam, atq[ue] optatissimam* (1578), Book IV.

[72] Ward, B. M., *The seventeenth earl of Oxford 1550–1604* (London, 1928), pp. 99–100.

[73] In 1593, Churchyard listed his compositions published and performed. They numbered almost forty. He admitted that he had also penned 'an infinite number of other songs and sonnets'. See *Churchyardes Challenge* (London, 1593) sigs. *v–**v.

things (except the honouring of Prince and public state) a true writer ought of duty to have in admiration and reverence the valiant soldiers, and men of worthy value.'[74] He conceded that 'some of the malicious sort, do marvel at my boldness herein' but countered that he thought 'the best time [he could] bestow [was] to further the fame of the honest, next to the preferment of my country's commendation.' In his *Churchyard's Choise*, otherwise known as *A generall rehearsall of warres*, he specifically set his mind, with considerable bitterness, to an attack on the 'malicious sort' by treating of 'certain deadly dissention fallen between the sword and the pen'.[75]

In a scantily veiled attack on the men who had made life in England so uncomfortable for his brothers in arms, Churchyard asserted that 'The pen is ever giving a dash against the commendation of the sword', with the result that 'the sword being disgraced, by a bald blot of a scurvy goose quill, lies in a broken rusty scabbard.' He questioned the supposedly disinterested motives of the self-appointed *noblesse de robe* and alleged that 'the scribbling pen is ever working of some subtlety more for the benefit of the writer then commonly for the profit or pleasure of the reader', a sideswipe, perhaps, at Cecil, given that Burghley, by this stage, held the two most lucrative offices in the realm (the lord treasurership and the mastership of the court of wards) and was certainly no stranger to venality. Churchyard's pejorative tone persisted as he located his ink-stained foes within an urban environment, stating that the pen is 'in chiefest pomp when it lies lurking in the town' whereas the sword 'is best ... shining in the field'. His conclusion was categorical: 'the pen and sword can never agree' and 'the advantage of them both is so much when they be kept asunder', because the sword can both disquiet the pen's ease and 'put the pen out of credit' whereas the pen can both 'persuade war and purchase peace', a resolution based on disdain. Churchyard was moving far from Caxton's earlier injunction that knights, although a distinct caste of themselves, 'ought to love the other orders', especially the clerks.[76] The generosity and mutual affection between orders to which Caxton had aspired would have been easier to envisage when the 'clerks' in question were clerics confined to cathedral chapters, parish churches, universities and monasteries. When that situation had obtained, the distinction between

---

[74] Luther 'Whether soldiers too can be saved' in *Luther's Works* ed. R. Schultz (Philadelphia, Pa., 1967) Vol. XLVI, p. 97; Churchyard, T., *Churchyard's Choise*, sig. **iii, v.
[75] Churchyard, T., *A generall rehearsall of warres* (London, 1579), sig. Miii, v.
[76] Churchyard, T., (1579), sigs. Miii, v – Ni; Caxton, (1484), sig. Biiii.

orders meant that the spiritual and secular worlds each possessed separate hierarchies and exclusive codes.[77]

Peter Carew's cousin, the notorious dissident and adventurer Thomas Stukeley, employed similar language when engaged in swaggering conversation about Cecil with other English *émigrés* at the Spanish court, according to the testimony of his manservant before the privy council in 1570. Stukeley allegedly remarked that on his return to England in glory he looked forward to troubling 'Cecil's fine head once again' and to stopping Elizabeth's 'frisking and dancing' by showing her how futile it was 'to displace a soldier, and put in one with a pen and ink-horn at his girdle'.[78] The polemicists and martial malcontents, consciously or unconsciously, desired familiar and traditional perquisites, respect for well-worn habits of thought and the unconditional favour of their prince. As already noted, Churchyard's resentment of the change of dispensation for captains was articulated through that most innocuous form of sedition: nostalgia. In seeking to affirm the captains' profession, he reappropriated the rhetoric of pre-eminence, recalling 'how soldiers were made of, and honoured in times past: and what prerogative they had above other people', how 'Princes [had] held them in admiration, and [had] given them liberties, titles and dignities far above the rest of any that lived under their laws and obedience.' However, his treatment of the concept of pre-eminence was not particularly influenced by those traditional ideas of rank-ordering that stemmed from primeval proto-constitutional arrangements. Instead, Churchyard's view hinged on the idea of a perpetual jockeying for pre-eminence in which those who displayed greater spirit won out. Even 'among children that do but play', he asserted 'there is a pre-eminence'; consequently

a [soldier] that hath coped with champions [and] buckled with conquerers ... deserveth place and pre-eminence, and is no companion for punies, nor meet to be matched with milksops, whose manhood and manners differ as far from the grave soldier, as a donkite [small hedge sparrow] in courage and condition, differs from a jerfalcon.

Churchyard also referred approvingly to the example of the treatment of soldiers in Calicut. There, martial men (he claimed) were paid a stipend

---

[77] Ockham's *Dialogus inter militem et clericum*, ed. A. Jenkins Perry (London, 1825) published by the king's printer Thomas Berthelet in 1533, not only restated the fundamental division between clerics and the military, but, using the soldier as a symbol of the secular order, asserted the primacy of the temporal sword over ecclesiastical authority.
[78] Master James Rigsby's testimony before the council, SP12/80/54ii–54iii. Simpson, R., *The School of Shakspere* (London, 1878), Vol. I, p. 75.

by the king, 'would not touch a husband man's hands, nor suffer a rustical fellow to come into their houses', and could even kill 'obstinate and proud people' who did not make way for them in the street. Here Churchyard was explicitly praising the caste system, which he claimed to have heard about from Spanish or Portuguese accounts of life in the East Indies, the central feature of which he believed involved 'mean people' giving way to soldiers and maintaining them.[79]

Although his examples were less exotic, Geoffrey Gates, in his *The defence of militaire profession* (1579), dedicated to the earl of Oxford, was Churchyard's equal when it came to vehemence.[80] Whereas Rich and Churchyard had both used the conceit of martial plain speech, the rhetoric of no-rhetoric, before launching into their defences of soldiering, Gates trumped them by claiming to be semi-literate, that is, 'an unlettered man', who had needed a notary to help him advance the martial occupation 'against all condemners of the same'.[81] Like Machiavelli, he held that a prudent state was maintained both by good laws and good arms.[82] Following the tradition of Lull, he assigned a role in society to the military profession as well, arguing that there had to be a 'profession of men whose power and prudence comprehended the maintenance and defence, not only of the seat of justice, but also of the cow and plough, of the bed and cradle, yea of the altar and of the sovereign state'.[83] Arms were first used, he stated, of necessity to 'repress the violent cruelty, and beastly disorder of men and to establish social peace and justice upon earth'.[84]

However, Gates's treatment was marked not only by traditional content but also by the ferocity with which he attacked those who detracted from the honour of a martial career. He summarised the familiar argument

---

[79] Churchyard (1579), sigs. Mii, r.–Mii, v., Pi, v.–Piii, v. See also Churchyard's *A scourge for rebels* (London, 1584), sig. Bi for further endorsement of the deferential East Indian attitude to soldiers.
[80] Gates, G., *The defence of militaire profession* (1579).
[81] Gates's bluffness was an utter affectation, but his abhorrence of the rarification of learning was constant. William Blandie in the supposed dialogue with Gates entitled *The Castle or picture of pollicy* (London, 1581) has Gates spout abstract statements like 'the mind according to the opinion of philosophy (the true and diligent searchers out of natural causes) is sorted twofoldly' and 'every man in this life (as on a Theatre or stage) plays one part of other'. Although Blandie, complaining of the disadvantage of soldiers in the world of letters, laments 'what fruit will you reap or who will the more account of us, if you and I speak or write of knowledge?' Gates responds that letters are like flowers, both 'by nature are good, yielding a sweet but yet a short scent, pleasing rather the sense of some singular persons, than profiting the soul of a commonwealth'. He concludes that their prowess as soldiers should merit them a hearing because 'simplicity is the ground and root of heavenly wisdom', sigs. Biir–Biiir.
[82] Gates (1579), p. 6. [83] Gates (1579), p. 10. [84] Gates (1579), p. 36.

of this 'vulgar multitude', who allege that soldiers go to war for spoil as well as the license it gives them to fornicate, dice and get drunk, and then they return home corrupted by these experiences so 'that they seem rather to come from Hell, . . . & therefore [are] so venomous a brood to their native country (standing in civil peace and government) that they are rather to be vomited out of the bulk of the commonwealth, then to be nourished by the same', after which the only remedy prescribable is 'to cut them off'. Gates's reply was far from innovative but was even starker than Rich's or Churchyard's: to despise the military profession would be wrong because 'military occupation doth execute the high justice of God upon earth, though all the followers of the same were most horrible and wicked (as the greater number of them [are]).'[85] All detractors, *faute de mieux*, must defer to this restatement of Augustinian functionality irrespective of the morals of soldiers. Like Rich, Gates held a grudge against 'covetous merchant[s]' and 'ambitious lawyer[s]'. Unlike the faithful soldier, these types were delicate, avaricious and wanton. Gates, after platitudinous praise for the insular state of England and its recent peaceful condition, bemoaned the military complacency that had consequently afflicted the country. Most of all, he regretted that England was not a realm on the Continent 'environed with mighty nations', because 'then would the lawyer and the merchant humble themselves to the warriors, and be glad to give honour and salary to the martialist.'[86] Furthermore, England would truly know the value of a soldier and those 'miserable drudges' who besmirched the military profession would [in a startling metaphor] 'lick the dust off the feet of [England's] men of prowess'. Gates believed that the dominant enemies of soldiering in England were rich, reserving special denunciation for those who were content to build banqueting houses and purchase large holdings rather than pay their 40s towards equipping a soldier for the wars.[87] Rich had earlier criticised the reluctance

---

[85] Gates (1579), p. 43–4. Gates was certainly a Protestant (perhaps a Lutheran). He consistently cites the example of the dukes of Saxony as exemplary warriors and places special emphasis on the defence strategies of Geneva and Strasbourg.
[86] Gates (1579), pp. 9, 18, where he states that 'England dwelling in safety and commonly in peace may seem to give the pre-eminence unto the lawyer'.
[87] This reference, although directly applicable to many nobles and gentlemen who invested in building works during Elizabeth's reign, might be directly aimed at Burghley, recently ennobled, who, as well as owning considerable lands in Lincolnshire, Northamptonshire and Hertfordshire had built two great houses, one at Stamford, the other at Theobalds. Burghley's sensitivity to jibes about his building projects was shown in a letter to William Herle on 14 August 1585, SP12/181/42: 'If my buildings mislike them, I confess my folly in the expenses, because some of my houses are to come if God so please to them that shall not have land to maintain them. I mean by my house at Theobalds which was begun by me with a mean measure'.

of the gentry to pay the money needed to provide an adequate military establishment for the kingdom:

> if they find the prince a horse to the field, they think themselves to have been at great cost, and it is done so grudgingly amongst a number of them that they cared not if he might pass musters, if he were not able to go a mile out of town ...[88]

Six years later, George Whetstone, in his *The honorable reputation of a souldier* (1585), dedicated to Sir William Russell, lieutenant general of horse in Leicester's Low Countries campaign, defended the profession as a necessity in a world where 'ambition, the imp of miscreant envy, upon desire of sovereignty, begat war'.[89] With Whetstone, however, we arrive at an intriguing contrast over and against the work of Rich and Churchyard. Whetstone was from a younger generation, and, while he treats of many of the same problems as they did, his prognosis for the profession was somewhat different. He attempted to effect a greater accommodation between the martial profession and civic republican discourse. Unsurprisingly, given the tensions already outlined, this project had to answer two questions: first, what was a soldier to do in repose, and, second, how could the excesses of martial culture – sporting individual prowess and pre-eminence – be reconciled with both a christianised stoicism and the integrative corporate ethic of the educated godly. Whetstone, conventionally enough, appealed to the Greeks and the Romans when arguing that soldiering provided a real nobility based on deeds, a form of Ciceronian virtue. This increase in worth was not abstract or notional, as he indicated by providing a list of classical soldiers of humble background who later went on to greater things.[90] Where the trademarks of chivalric *franchise* might previously have been visible, Whetstone invoked humanist meritocracy; significantly, man's thirst for pre-eminence was almost entirely subsumed by thirst for civic glory, earned by way of military service for the homeland. In Roman times, Whetstone remarked 'Sole desire of fame, & zeal to do their country service, moved many (that had no thought of the immortality of the soul) to be wilful executioners of their own lives.' He further pointed out that when Cicero was thanked by the Roman republic for undermining the Catiline conspiracy, he had received the civic crown, an award usually reserved

---

[88] Rich (1574) sig. d.
[89] Whetstone's other books, which had an exclusively civic flavour included *The rocke of regard* (1576); *A mirror of treue honour* (1585), a meditation on envy; and *The censure of a loyall subject* (1587), a treatment of traitors and rebels against the queen.
[90] Whetstone (1585) sigs. Aii, r–Bii, v.

for military heroes.[91] On the vexed question of how soldiers should occupy themselves in peacetime, Whetstone pointed to the examples of Caesar, Pyrrhus and Alexander the Great when he arrived at his conclusion: they should study. He concluded that it was a 'necessary duty' for a military man 'at leisureable times to be studious in matters of policy, and always when his hands are idle to have a working mind'. Such study was not conceived of as a mere prophylactic against insubordinate conduct in the commonwealth but was seen as a kind of training and preparedness for war. By occupying his time with suitable reading, the soldier would probably be better able to inflict harm on the enemy in time of need.[92] Education – the panacea of the civic humanists – would also prove to be the salvager of the unemployed captain. Yet, education required resources, parental care and attention and a sort of concern that English primogeniture tended to dandle predominantly upon the eldest son in each gentry family.

Here Whetstone was proffering a remedy that some martial practitioners had arrived at already, although their vision of the role of the educated martial man in the commonwealth tended to retain the characteristics of chivalric *franchise*. It was Sir Humphrey Gilbert, himself a younger son with considerable experience of military command, who proposed the most comprehensive educative remedy to the problems that faced many who had pursued a martial calling, in his plan composed in the early 1570s for an 'Academy', based in London, to be devoted to the education of the queen's wards.[93] Significantly, Gilbert, bemoaning the constant waste of 'gentle' social capital in Elizabethan England, turned his back on Oxford and Cambridge, which were gaining a reputation as a bolthole for poor scholars or sizars, seeking rather to educate a new elite in a place close to the royal court.[94] His reasons were not only

---

[91] Whetstone (1585) sigs. CI, v; Fi, v. Churchyard also treats at length of the Roman civic crown in (1579) sigs. Oii, v–O iv, v. In characteristically exclusive vein he tells the story of a man who was put to death for 'merrily' wearing a civic crown 'which was ordained for the wearing only of an honorable Soldier'.

[92] For Whetstone's treatment of the virtues see (1585) sigs. Cii, v–Eii, r; for his advocacy of learning see Eiv, v; Fi, r.

[93] BL Lansdowne MS. 98 no. 1 (henceforth Gilbert), fol. 2, r.

[94] See Oxford DNB entry on the haberdasher Thomas Aldersey for his attempts to gather sponsorship for poor scholars. Compare this activity with the elitist concerns (almost identical to Gilbert's) encapsulated in the eighth clause of a dossier of considerations delivered to the Parliament in 1559 prior to the enactment of the Statute of Artificers: 'That an ordinance be made to bind the nobility to bring up their children in learning at some university in England or beyond the sea from the age of 12 to 18 at least; and that one third of all the free scholarships at the universities be filled by the *poorer sort of gentlemen's sons*' in Power and Tawney eds. *Tudor economic documents* (London, 1935), Vol. I,

discriminatory but practical: 'The greatest number of young gentlemen within this Realm are most conversant about London where your Majesty's court hath most ordinary residence.' Gilbert committed himself to a *cursus* that shunned abstract speculation for practical application of skills. In this vein, he praised Lycurgus who 'ordained that schools should be for children, and not for philosophy' because 'such as govern common weales, ought rather to bend themselves to the practices thereof, then to be tied to the bookish circumstances of the same.' Wards, Gilbert contended, were either raised in idleness 'estranged from all serviceable virtues to their prince and country', or 'obscurely drowned in education'. Consequently, in a daring step, Gilbert not only attacked wardship but also criticised the universities, stating that the 'school learnings' followed there were unsuited to gentlemen. Gilbert's project concentrated on practice, and his sights were fixed on a higher, more applicable form of *negotium*. Although his treatment of the *trivium* concentrated on producing eloquence in the vernacular, a humanist commonplace, his approach to the study of 'civil policy' and 'martial policy' (subsets of 'moral philosophy') was more innovative. The study of civil policy involved scrutinising the structure of commonwealths past and present, comparing their revenues, legal system and political structures and assessing their advantages and disadvantages; in essence, a practical investigation of the best form of government.[95] Martial policy, similarly, examined the contending military strength, weaponry and tactical facility of European states.[96]

When Gilbert came to set out his plans for mathematical studies such as cosmography, astronomy, geometry and arithmetic, he cast the textbooks by Pliny, Strabo and Ptolemy to one side, replacing them with specifically war-related studies. For example, the geometry master would concentrate on 'Embattlings, fortifications and matters of war, with the practice of artillery' as well as the use of cannons and assembly of mines. The obvious utility of applied mathematics for war, and training for war,

---

p. 326. The drafter was piqued that 'the wanton bringing up and ignorance of the nobility forces the Prince to advance new men'. Many of the top flight of clergymen of the Church of England during the late sixteenth and early seventeenth century had been Elizabethan sizars at the University of Cambridge. Thomas Bilson, bishop of Winchester, for instance, had been supported at Oxford by a trust fund for poor scholars, see William Richardson, 'Bilson, Thomas (1546/7–1616)', *Oxford Dictionary of National Biography* (Oxford, 2004). See also R. Tuck, *Philosophy and government, 1572–1651* (Cambridge, 1993), pp. 1–4.

[95] See Skinner (1978), Vol. I, pp. 139–89, for a study of the Italian contention over the best form of government.

[96] Gilbert, fols. 2, v.–3, r.

would be extolled at length by Thomas Digges in his *Arithmeticall warlike treatise named Stratioticos* (1579, reprinted 1590) where he referred in his introduction to how he had 'spent many of [his] years in reducing the sciences mathematical from demonstrative contemplations to experimental actions for the service of my prince and country': an entirely typical commitment to soldierly *negotium*.[97] Mathematical concerns would also inform Gilbert's *cursus* in the guise of an astronomer and cosmographer who would give instruction in navigation using a model ship and also concentrate on cartography. Even the medical course, teaching 'physic' and surgery in the vernacular, was devised specifically with its military utility in mind. The products of the academy, all gentlemen of five descents, therefore, would be adept both in arms and laws.[98] His plan to devote the classes dealing with law to streamlining common law into 'maxims, as is done in the book of the civil laws entitled *de Regulis iuris*' was proffered with the explicit hope that gentlemen who attained this special training would no longer have to rely on their social inferiors in legal matters but could confidently become justices of the peace and sheriffs. Consequently, Gilbert asserted that if 'younger brothers' did not succeed after such training, they 'may eat grass'.[99] Furthermore, this training would free up places in the universities and, thus, 'better suffice to relieve poor scholars, where now the youth of nobility and gentlemen, taking up their scholarships and fellowships, do disappoint the poor of their livings and advancements'.[100] Gilbert coined a phrase to describe this broader form of *negotium*: 'Chivalric policy', the creation of a caste of all-talented governors from the previously maltreated raw material that had often spent its existence in debt or on martial pursuits.

'Chivalric policy' (to apply Gilbert's useful term) would not only predispose martial men towards action on behalf of the commonwealth but would transform the complexion of the commonwealth altogether. Gilbert attempted to epitomise the fruits of 'Chivalric policy' himself. When John Hooker wrote about Sir Humphrey Gilbert in Holinshed's

---

[97] Digges, Leonard and Thomas, *An Arithmeticall warlike treatise named Stratiotocos compendiously teaching the science of numbers as well in fractions as integers* (London, 1590) sig. Aii, r. For an excellent discussion of Digges's tract see Webb (1965), pp. 17–26.
[98] Gilbert, fol. 6, v.
[99] GIlbert, fols. 2, r.–7, v.
[100] Gilbert, fol. 6, v. For a fuller treatment of Gilbert's *Achademy*, see my M.Phil. dissertation 'The political thought of Sir Humphrey Gilbert', unpublished M. Phil. thesis (University of Cambridge, 1998), pp. 12–40.

Chronicle of Ireland, he portrayed his subject as an enlightened soldier who

> gave himself to studies pertaining to the state of government, and to navigations. He had an excellent and ready wit, and therewith a tongue at liberty to utter what he thought. Which being adorned with learning and knowledge, he both did and could notably discourse any matter in question concerning either of these, as he made good proof thereof, as well in familiar conference with the noble, wise, and learned; as also in the open assemblies of the parliaments, both in England and in Ireland.[101]

Similarly, George Gascoigne wrote of a visit he paid Gilbert in Limehouse in the winter of 1575. The author, himself '[marching] amongst the Muses for lack of exercise in martial exploits', asked Gilbert what he was doing in his 'loitering vacation' from the military life. The knight invited the poet into his study and showed him 'sundry profitable and very commendable exercises, which he had perfected painfully with his own pen.' In 1576, Gilbert himself declared that 'he is not worthy to live at all, that for fear, or danger of death shunneth his country service, and his own honour, seeing death is inevitable, and the fame of virtue immortal. Wherefore in this behalfe *mutare vel timere sperno*'.[102] Significantly, we know that Gilbert had debated on aspects of Livy's *Discorsi* with Sir Thomas Smith, Thomas Smith Jr (his son who perished in Ireland), Gabriel Harvey and Dr Walter Haddon in London in the early 1570s. The discussion had centred on whether the daring strategy of the consul Marcellus were worthier than the delaying tactics of *Cunctator* Fabius Maximus. Gilbert, recently returned from his Munster campaigns, argued for Marcellus, and Secretary Smith argued for Fabius. Gilbert yielded to Smith, but Harvey, whose marginalia note the occasion, concluded that both Marcellus and Fabius were 'worthy' and 'judicious', the former 'more powerful', the latter 'more cunning' but 'each [was] as indispensable as the other in his place. There are times when I would rather be Marcellus, times when Fabius.' The echoes of Chapter 18 of *Il principe* on the benefits of adopting the guise of the lion or the fox as circumstances demand are unmistakable and point, perhaps, to the new perspectives that an openness to 'Chivalric policy' could afford.[103]

---

[101] Quinn (1940) II, 431–434.
[102] Quinn (1940) I, pp. 131–133 and R. Hakluyt, *The principall navigations, voiages and discoveries of the English nation*, 3 vols. (London, 1600), Vol. III, p. 24.
[103] Grafton and Jardine, '*Studied for action*: how Gabriel Harvey read his Livy', *P&P*, 129 (1990).

However, Gilbert's near-Machiavellian stress on personal glory as the spur above all others towards vigorous service was recognised by some contemporaries as avowedly pagan. Thomas North, in the preface to his translation of Plutarch's *Lives*, mused that it was characteristic of the ancients, who lacked any hope of heaven, to venture all on behalf of heathen kings and glory.[104] Those who had shunned the 'new learning' of Colet and Cheke now endeavoured to embrace a regime of study tempered for action. Peter Carew, according to John Hooker, displayed a number of the qualities and skills that Gilbert had prescribed. Not only was he a man of virtue, 'prudent, wise, and circumspect, as well in civil causes as in martial affairs', but he was also adept at designing and building houses, ships and forts, as well as being a justice of the peace.[105] In *Cyvile and uncyvile life*, Vallentine, the courtier, exhorts Vincent, the rustic squire, to 'not only adventure [his] son, but [his] master, [his] heir also' pointing to the example set at sea by figures such as Columbus, Vespucci, Magellan and the Englishman Martin Frobisher.[106] Gilbert's obsession with transatlantic voyaging leading to his ineffectual annexation of Newfoundland in 1583 indicates the risks that having a 'forward mind' incurred. Humfrey Braham's assessment, thirty years earlier, that 'the merchant men of London [are well] acquainted with the infirmities of . . . gentlemen' proved to be particularly apt in this case, especially when he mused that 'when the politic devices of the merchant joineth with the simplicity of the gentleman, [they] never leaveth acquaintance nor familiarity with him unto such time as *the merchant's money hath bought the gentleman's land*' (my italics).[107] Gilbert, a younger son with sparse financial resources, was deemed by Edward Hayes, an investor in his final voyage, to be a man who was 'too prodigal of his own patrimony, and too careless of other men's expenses'.[108]

Yet, even when dressed up in commonwealth rhetoric about grand designs for upholding the *patria*, the natural self-affirmative manner of martial men, the expensive thirst for pre-eminence so hated by English advocates of civic republicanism, remained inviolate. Gabriel Harvey in marginalia to John Foord's *Synopsis politica* singled out the traitor

---

[104] Plutarch (1579), p. 2. [105] Hooker (1867), pp. cxiii–cxviii.
[106] *Cyvile and uncyvile life* (1579), p. 17, v.; See Richard Robinson's, *A golden mirrour, conteining certain pithy and figurative visions* . . . sigs. B4, r–B4, v for a further example of praise in Elizabethan times of Drake and then Frobisher (1589).
[107] Braham (1555) sig. Giv, r.
[108] Hakluyt (1600) Vol. III, p. 145. Gilbert's death before he could return from Newfoundland was something of a blessing, given that sixty-seven individuals had invested up to £3,000 in his voyage.

Thomas Stukeley as 'mightily bold, adventurous and serviceable', the possessor of a 'brave Roman nature', a 'winner of gold and wearer of gold', adept in 'all essays by sea and land'.[109] Elsewhere, he referred approvingly to Stukeley's insatiable appetite for pre-eminence, describing him as 'aspiring Stukeley, that would rather be the king of a molehill, then the second in Ireland or England.'[110] Harvey, mused in the margins of his copy of Quintilian in 1579 about 'the divine madness of great men' before referring to *huc* [*sic*] *maganimi equitis Humfredi Gilberti heroicum emblema: Quid non.*[111] The influence that Machiavelli's treatment of *virtù* in *Il principe* exerted over Harvey is undeniable, but the resilience of older ideas of chivalric *prouesse* and *franchise* loomed large also, ready always to don new clothes. In short, the godly civic republicanism espoused throughout England in both local and national government, with its abhorrence of contention for pre-eminence, left a fault-line in Elizabethan political culture which arose out of the disintegration of the Henrician legacy. Out of the wreckage and disappointment of English martial men arose a continued commitment to chivalric values: most notably an attachment to the struggle for pre-eminence.

This urge for pre-eminence was depicted to its fullest extent by Christopher Marlowe in *Tamburlaine*, composed in two parts in the years 1587 and 1588. Tamburlaine, King of Persia, epitomises the 'divine madness' about which Harvey professed such enthusiasm. Gates would have found much to admire in the career of the landlocked monarch, who ranges territory, ruining his neighbours. Gates and Churchyard, both as we have seen, fond of explicitly physical images of the superiority of soldiers over other professionals, might have regarded the Persian's habit of travelling in a chariot pulled by vanquished royal opponents with approval, as being the just reward for his devastating ambition and his martial prowess.

This tendency towards a relatively secular worldview seems to have found some sympathy among Elizabethan captains, possibly because of their wonted lack of piety, a feature which had been hardly worth noticing in a united Christendom but which was more arresting in a polarised country increasingly administered by a community committed to a renewed godliness. Gilbert's educational tract, for example, had cared little for pious pursuits. Apart from a cursory reference to the teaching of

---

[109] Harvey, G. *Marginalia*, ed. G. C. Moore Smith, (Stratford, 1913), p. 198.
[110] Harvey, G. *Works*, 3 vols. (London, 1884) Vol. II, p. 146.
[111] Harvey (1913), pp. 119–20.

Hebrew, a standard denunciation of 'papistry' and the appointment of a reader of divinity (without any description of his duties), he made hardly any reference to religious affairs. This treatment seems especially spare when compared with the religious structures that Sir Nicholas Bacon had earlier envisaged in his own plan for a house of wards. Whereas Bacon had decreed that his students would attend divine service each morning at either six or seven o'clock as well as on the Sabbath day, Gilbert provided for only two sermons at his Academy annually.[112] These sermons would not concern themselves with subject matter such as the Holy Trinity or the Body of Christ, as might be the case in colleges so nominated in either of the universities. By contrast, the Academy's sermons would treat of the founder Queen Elizabeth and would take place on the anniversary of her accession and her birthday.[113] This state of affairs, 'where both by word and example of the rulers, the ruled are taught with every change of Prince to change also the face of their faith and Religion', had been shrewdly denounced by the author of the 1572 *Treatise of treasons against Queen Elizabeth and the crown of England* as 'a Machiavellian State and Governance'. In the lifetime of Gilbert and many like him, the official religious designation of the realm – the shape of the cosmos in effect – had altered many times. Small wonder then that some looked to power, specifically monarchical power in an abstracted form, as the sole stabilising element in the universe, regarding 'true religion' as verified by royal fiat.[114]

Yet, however much they fetishised royal power, the captains' relationship with Elizabeth herself was a troubled one marked by disappointment and disillusion. The simplicity that had attended service of a king steeped in a chivalric ethos had been taken from them. There was an unavoidable tension between their desire to exert pre-eminence, to acquire the resources to secure such pre-eminence and their apparent reliance on the grace and favour of a queen surrounded by 'clerks' and aristocratic courtiers who followed the prevailing fashion. As we shall see, this tension could sometimes propel military men, especially those who had previously fought on the Continent in the service of other monarchs, along dangerous paths that jeopardised their loyalty to their prince.

[112] BL Add. Mss. 32, 379, fol. 31, r.   [113] Gilbert, fol. 6, r.
[114] *Treatise of treasons against Queen Elizabeth and the crown of England* (1572) sigs. A5–A5 v.

CHAPTER 3

The limits of allegiance: English martial men, Europe and the Elizabethan regime

> And sometimes through the greatness of their minds, [those] that gallop after glory, are carried away to seek out new kingdoms, and refuse their old habitation. A matter falling out well, worthy to be liked, but otherwise, a heavy tale to be told.
>
> *Churchyardes Choise* (1579) sig. miii.

When William Flower, Norroy king of arms, arrived incognito at the Abbey of St Remy in Rheims on 7 June 1557 carrying Mary I's declaration of war on France, he was heralding a conflict that would end with shame and defeat for England. On the same day, a proclamation displayed throughout London enjoined all Englishmen to regard 'the French King, and his vassals as public enemies ... and to harm them wherever possible'.[1] Whatever this shift in foreign policy portended for the citizens of London, it held immediate significance for Nicholas and John Malby, both of whom at that time were soldiers in Henry II's camp at Cambrai.[2] According to Thomas Churchyard (the source of the tale), the brothers had served with the French against Charles V for nine years. Despite this, the Malbys, heeding Mary's commandment, immediately defected to the imperial forces.[3] This volte-face and the cursory way in which Churchyard deals with it beg a number of questions.[4] Why did the Malbys, who worked as mercenaries for their own financial benefit, switch allegiance? Were they enticed over to the emperor's army solely by the lure of the 50 crowns a piece they received for joining up? Was their act of obedience actually motivated by simple *pietas* towards Philip and Mary and their

---

[1] *CSPSp: Philip and Mary*, pp. 293–5.
[2] Sir Nicholas Malby served as president of Connacht from 1578 to his death in 1583.
[3] Churchyard, T., *A generall rehearsall of warres wherein is five hundred severall services of land and sea*, (London, 1579), sig. Cii, v. The Malbys may have started serving Henry II after Boulogne had been handed back to the French in 1550, not in 1548 as Churchyard suggests.
[4] Churchyard, not renowned for his analytical faculty, baldly states that 'the two brothers hearing of that proclamation, took their leave of France and came to the Emperor'.

homeland, or did they fear that they might jeopardise whatever livelihood they had in England by continuing to serve with Henry II?

Most martial men, when reaching an accommodation between the demands for allegiance made by chivalry, conscience and their prince devised a personal modus vivendi. The decisions arrived at reflected the pressures of the captain's immediate situation, his past experience and his personal beliefs. The casuistry that informed these choices was informed by diverse sources: a mix and match of canon and civil law, classical humanism, reformed religion, late medieval chivalry, not to mention the officers' own economic and social conditions. But, increasingly, there was precious little official indulgence for the ambivalence caused by these conflicting influences.

Quite simply, Tudor subjects, even when abroad, were expected to stand full square behind the regime at home, in thought, word and deed. Subjects were supposed to be charged up with such loyalty that any disparagement of their monarch amounted to a personal slight. For that reason, petitions and exemplary tales which detailed demonstrations of English patriotism abroad employed the language and ritual of personal honour. Therefore, the duel, the final defence of personal honour, was understood to be the ultimate means by which an individual subject in a foreign land could show his loyalty to his prince. This point is well illustrated by a petition Sir William Fitzwilliam made to Burghley in 1572 requesting a renewed pension for Edmund Byrne, a soldier from the English Pale in Ireland. Byrne had served in Spain under Philip II's son Don Carlos before returning to Ireland with the ill-fated Derry garrison in 1566, but, according to Fitzwilliam, while in Spain he had been forced to flee the royal court in Madrid because he had slain a courtier who had uttered 'evil speeches and opprobrious language against' Queen Elizabeth. Following this, he had taken up residence at the Portuguese court where, *mirabile dictu*, he had been involved in a similar fracas with another 'slanderer of her Majesty'. Consequently, Fitzwilliam urged that Byrne deserved to be financially supported because of his demonstrably 'loyal heart'.

Byrne's was not an isolated case. A similar tale was later recounted by George Whetstone in the preface of his *The honorable reputation of a soldier* (1585) concerning an Englishman in Turin in 1580 who challenged a Spaniard to a duel on hearing him publicly brag about invading and spoiling England and ravishing the country's wives. The Spaniard initially accepted the challenge but subsequently absconded. The Englishman then learned how isolated an English patriot could be in Continental

Europe. Word about his dispute in Turin came to Rome, so when he approached the eternal city, he was detained at the gates for eight days without shelter, deprived of his letters and warrants of safe passage, threatened with hanging and then given a ticket of leave for Naples.[5] Such were the indignities that Englishmen could be forced to endure when they chose to defend the dignity of England and her crown. But this model pattern of patriotism could find itself straining to justify itself: throughout Europe Elizabeth was widely viewed as an illegitimate, lewd excommunicate.

Allegiance could also be compromised by the claims of a transnational chivalric code, a resilient sign of cultural survivalism and, increasingly, by a nascent confessionalism that demanded stark declaration of religious loyalties. Many, especially among martial men, were prey to either or both of these disruptive forces. This was particularly the case with the men-at-arms that Elizabeth inherited in 1558: men who had fought in Henry VIII's third French war, who had risked their lives at Pinkie and who had served their king and queen at St Quentin; men who had no idea that, come 1563, they would be faced with twenty-one years in which England would not embark on any major military campaigning outside the queen's patrimony.

TRADITION OR CONFUSION?

The transnational nature of chivalric culture proved to be an enduring feature in the lives of many English captains. To evaluate the health and character of the chivalric ethos during the mid-sixteenth century, it is worthwhile returning to Metz in 1557, to the point when Charles V's efforts to inflict a reverse on the Valois were frustrated. While the French forces benefited from ransoming prisoners and stealing horses, the emperor's army, outside the walls, was devastated by plague. When the siege was raised, Charles left 12,000 diseased German soldiers behind him. The duke of Guise, general of Metz, took pity on these abandoned men. He refused to put them to the sword and sent all those who survived their illness home without looking for ransom. Guise's kindness was rewarded a decade later, according to Churchyard, when some of those Germans

---

[5] Fitzwilliam to Burghley, 21 May, SP63/36/23. Fitzwilliam cites Dr Thomas Wilson as a witness of Byrne's conduct during the dispute in Portugal. Byrne drew this pension until 1601 see *Fiants*, Vol. II, 4313; Vol. III, 6503, also see G. Whetstone, *The honorable reputation of a souldier* (London, 1585) sigs. Aiii, r; Aiii, v.

who later fought in the wars of religion for the Huguenot Prince of Condé encountered the Duke in a skirmish at the battle of Dreux. They remembered the nobleman's clemency at Metz and flung their weapons aside, refusing to give him battle.[6]

Given inherited assumptions about the political prejudices of English soldiers, it seems strange that in 1579 Churchyard should write such an encomium to the virtues and gentility of the duke of Guise, the arch-Catholic ideologue; his assault on Protestants at Vassy in 1562 had been the spark that had ignited the Wars of Religion.[7] By 1579, the Elizabethan regime was attempting to consolidate some sort of alliance with France, as shown by the shadow-boxing regarding the Anjou match, but these approaches were predicated on securing toleration for Huguenots and at least tacit French support for the international Protestant cause; proposals which were anathema to the House of Guise.[8] Hostile preoccupation with the Guise faction and its agenda for both France and Europe had been a consistent feature of Elizabethan foreign policy from the start. Remarkably, Churchyard did not merely confine his provocative assessments of

---

[6] Churchyard (1579), sig. Bii, v. For the best modern account of the battle of Dreux see J. B. Wood, *The king's army* (Cambridge, 1996), pp. 184–204. Neither Michel de Castelnau's report of Guise's account of the battle at court nor the story of Dreux recounted in the duke's own memoirs refers to the episode described by Churchyard. See sig. Ki, v for another encomium of Guise. For evidence that Guise's strategy at Dreux had provoked criticism, see Montaigne's essay 'De la bataille de Dreux'.

[7] François, the duke of Guise, was one of the outstanding military men of his time. His prowess as a strategist, evident in his campaign against the Habsburgs in Lorraine in 1552, was further demonstrated when he took Guines, Calais and Thionville in 1558 following the reverse suffered by France at St Quentin. Churchyard alleged that he met him at the surrender of Guines. These victories left Henry II in a strong negotiating position for the treaty of Cateau-Cambrésis. However, despite Churchyard's treatment of him solely as a chivalric knight (J. B. Garrisson has noted his renown for 'moderating the brutality of his troops'), Guise's devotion to the Catholic cause was central to his actions. It motivated him to seek alliance with his former enemy Anne de Montmorency against Condé. Furthermore his religious zeal made him an early instigator of persecution and sectarian massacre. See J. Garrisson, *A history of sixteenth-century France, 1483–1598*, trans. R. Rex (London, 1995), pp. 164–9, 274–6, 339. The fact that Guise, unlike Montmorency, never received the Order of the Garter indicates that his religious zeal constituted some sort of impediment.

[8] The Guises, although not the richest of French aristocratic families, were certainly the most influential. They boasted a well-integrated, widespread and ideologically homogenous affinity and clientage. Elizabeth and her administration were particularly wary of their power owing to their possession of the regency of Scotland and their links with Mary Stuart, pretender to the English throne. The abortive Newhaven expedition was conceived of as an anti-Guise manoeuvre. Protestants in general feared their anti-reform zeal. Condé justified his military actions as a means of liberating Francis II and Catherine de Medici from Guise tyranny. François de Guise's assassination was the major factor that facilitated the end of the first war of religion. See MacCaffrey, 'The Newhaven expedition', *HJ*, 40, I (1997), pp. 3–6, 9–16, and Garrisson, pp. 269–78.

noted European nobility to praise for England's arch bogeymen. His treatment of the count of Horne, in a similar exemplary tale, proves equally startling. Horne, who was executed for treason by the duke of Alba's Council of Blood in 1568, became a potent symbol of the arbitrary nature of Spanish tyranny and the aristocratic Protestant martyr par excellence. At the time of his death, outrage at the English court seemed unanimous.[9] But according to Churchyard, Horne had once shot a pistol at point-blank range into the breast of a prisoner of war in his custody, the Scottish 'baron of Kyrrton'. However, Kyrrton's armour had been so sturdy that the initial blast did not kill him. Horne, despite the Scot's assurances of his own worth if ransomed, was not deterred and slew him in cold blood, an action which Churchyard (quite accurately) assures us 'was against all civil order, or law of arms'. Unsurprisingly, just as Guise was rewarded for his virtue, Horne was punished for his vice.[10] Shortly after his explicit breach of chivalric ordinances, we are told that his band was utterly devastated in an ambush by the Duke d'Aumale (Guise's brother).[11]

Churchyard's apparent ambivalence about the compatibility of his paeans to chivalry with Elizabethan foreign policy resulted from something more radical than mere personal eccentricity. Politically speaking, it is difficult to pick out a specific policy agenda in much of his work, although he enjoyed the patronage of high-ranking political figures, notably Lord Charles Howard of Effingham, Lord Hunsdon and Lord Chancellor Christopher Hatton; *Choise* was dedicated to Hatton.[12] Intriguingly, his writings resemble peace-party dramas with a war-party cast. Indeed, the writer's old-fashioned belligerence, shorn of confessional verve, may even have had some sympathetic correspondence with the

---

[9] See the report written from Guzman de Silva, England's Spanish ambassador, to Philip II on 10 July 1568. Silva relates that not only was the earl of Leicester indignant at the Count's execution, but the earl of Sussex, usually a Spanish sympathiser, was also distressed. See *CSPSp, 1568–1579*, p. 51. The French were also outraged; Montaigne in his essay 'Que l'intention juge nos actions' paid tribute to the Count Egmont for asking to be executed before Horne because Horne had handed himself over to the duke of Alba on Egmont's assurance for his safety.

[10] Churchyard had a Christian concept of Fortune's operations, 'speak not of hap, for God and good men are the distributors of desired Fortune, and the only causers of that which betideth, and must fall of necessity on some men's shoulders.' (1579) sig. Oii, v.

[11] Churchyard (1579), sig. Ciii, r.

[12] Churchyard's earliest patron was Henry Howard, earl of Surrey, and he later enjoyed the protection of Lord Hunsdon. He wrote *A scourge of rebels*, dedicated to Lord Charles Howard of Effingham, in support of the earl of Ormond in 1584. From the late 1570s on he became a client of Sir Christopher Hatton. See Henry Adnitt's 'Thomas Churchyard' in *Transactions of the Shropshire Archaeological Society*, Vol. III (1880), pp. 1–68.

attitude of certain of the Howards towards military activity on the Continent. Blair Worden has indicated that the earl of Sussex and Lord Henry Howard both advocated the Anjou match as a means of undertaking English intervention in the Netherlands along dynastic, but non-confessional, lines following the pattern of campaigning that Henry VIII had himself nostalgically pursued during his reign. Indeed, Sussex carried out a consistent correspondence with the Dutch states, and, in 1576, according to the Spanish agent Antonio de Guaras, requested leave to take an army and 'turn the Spaniards out of the States'.[13]

Be that as it may, by the time of *Churchyard's Choise*'s publication in 1579, the political landscape of Europe had changed utterly from the way things had been when most of the events described had actually occurred. The intellectual and political impact of wars of religion, especially the second Schmalkaldic war, the spasmodic disturbances in France and the Dutch revolt, had weakened royal authority throughout Europe. Not only were appeals being made to God's natural law to nullify the bonds of constitutions but monarchies (for some) came to be seen as elective, not merely in a distant and primeval sense but in an immediate and ongoing way. Consequently, it was argued by the disaffected that monarchs were answerable not alone to God but to their own people, commoners as well as inferior magistrates.[14] Elizabeth, of course, was not sheltered from these chill breezes. Her legitimacy could be questioned in many ways. After initial sluggishness, early modern Catholicism actively embraced constitutional strategies to secure political ends in keeping with God's divine will, a situation repeated in France in 1576 when the Catholic League was founded with papal benediction to ensure that a Protestant would not succeed to the French throne. Whereas Protestants generally appealed to the higher law of God when asserting the rights of true religion over and against monarchs, especially in times of persecution or in contexts where they wished to gain toleration (hoping to achieve more political and religious gains subsequently), Catholicism embraced constitutional strategies in order to obliterate Protestantism once and for all. Either way, the demands of confessionalism tended to dissolve the unitary nature of any authority in Christendom.

---

[13] Antonio de Guaras to Zayas, 30 December 1576, *CSPSp, 1568–1579*, p. 536. See also Worden (1996), pp. 105, 166.
[14] Kingdon, R. M., 'Calvinism and resistance theory, 1550–1580' and J. H. M. Salmon, 'Catholic resistance theory', in Burns and Goldie (eds), *The Cambridge history of political thought, 1450–1700* (Cambridge, 1994), pp. 193–246.

However, this shift of *Weldgeist* was not reflected in Churchyard's retrospective accounts of wars. Religious consciousness was notably absent from the scene.[15] In *Churchyard's Choise*, for instance, the European wars of the 1540s were depicted as purely dynastic affairs, with figures such as the prince of Orange and the count of Horne dutifully serving their sovereign, with the narrator apparently oblivious of the future confessional and political turmoil that awaits them. Churchyard's failure to take account of Europe's changing ideological environment was motivated by the need to satisfy antiquated urges. He was assuming an heraldic role in a vulgar fashion, seeking to record incidents of military prowess and to be the means by which England's active martial caste, the discarded scions of gentry, might attain that coveted state known as Fame.[16] On the one hand, he was attempting to capture the attention of Englishmen, informing them that the captains and military men in their midst were paragons of virtue and honour in the realm. On the other hand, he was recording the exploits of English martial men for the consideration of the 'community of honour' itself.[17]

Churchyard was not alone in his resistance to the sectarian imperative of international politics. His crude evasion of the implications of confessional trauma was mirrored in the attempts of the highest repositories of European chivalric culture, knightly orders sponsored by royalty, to prevent religion from interfering with their traditional ethos. These institutions had originally been conceived as a means to provide aristocratic solidarity behind national monarchs and their policies. For instance, Edward III had instituted the Garter to secure the support of the English

---

[15] This is not to say that Churchyard ignored religion when it played a central role in events. For example in *A lamentable and pitiful description of the wofull warres in Flanders* (London, 1578) he treats of the iconoclasm of the citizens of Antwerp and their desire for 'the liberty of the Gospel'. However, Churchyard boasts that, following the prince of Orange's orders he saved six friars and thousands of Catholic gentlemen and burgesses from the riotous mob. Churchyard's personal conformity with the Elizabethan settlement is not in doubt. See BL Lansdowne MSS, 11, no. 56 for the letter he wrote to Secretary Cecil in 1569 'discharging [his] conscience and duty to the advancement of God by informing him of Catholic activities in Bath'. Doubtlessly Churchyard was endeavouring to gain preferment.

[16] See Churchyard (1579), sig. Nii, r for his praise, and effective appropriation, of the Heraldic profession. He believed that the authority of heralds was *sui generis*. See also sig. **iv, r for his letter 'to the friendly reader' where he bemoans that 'few or none' can now 'spare any . . . spark of credit to another's praise and good report' and that 'by . . . general ambition and naughtiness of nature all good studies and noble enterprises are drowned in disdain, and little or nothing is suffered to flourish, but that which Fortune prefereth, or the fond affection of a multitude will commend.' However, in his *chippes*, he placed limits on his reportage by abstaining from mentioning soldiers 'of mean and base degree'.

[17] See Nicolas (London, 1846), pp. 172, 175, 179, 253, 304, for evidence of Churchyard's reliance on Hatton's patronage for his livelihood.

nobility for his campaigns in France. This integrative motivation continued to be central to the *raison d'être* of chivalric orders well into the sixteenth century. Soon after Philip II became sovereign of the Order of the Golden Fleece in 1555, William of Orange and the count of Horne were dubbed knights of that institution. Their induction, predictable given their local influence and military prowess, was useful for Philip, who not only wished to consolidate his hold on the Low Countries but also wanted to secure support for continued Habsburg campaigns against Henry II of France and the Pope.[18] Similarly, the bestowal and reception of chivalric honours could also be employed to signify the conclusion of international treaties or alliances. Since the late fifteenth century, the distribution of such awards to foreigners as the Order of the Golden Fleece, France's Order of St Michael and England's Order of the Garter had been a useful political tool. This was especially the case in Tudor England where diplomacy and the Order of the Garter went hand in hand. Under Mary, both Philip II of Spain and the duke of Savoy, his governor of the Low Countries, had received the Garter.[19] In Elizabeth's time, Charles IX of France was invested to mark the end of Anglo-French conflict in 1564, and later the Treaty of Blois was sealed by the Constable Francis de Montmorency's acceptance into the Order in 1572. The Emperor Maximilian and Henry III both had the honour bestowed upon them in 1567 and 1575 respectively.[20] The fact that the investiture of the latter did not occur until 1585 (when it provoked Catholic League outrage and polemic) indicates the degree to which the old chivalric dispensation was under siege from rising religious passions.

However, this fracture is hardly surprising. Thomas Churchyard may have been able to sustain (or merely affect) incomprehension of the crucial role religion played in the internecine scuffles of the late sixteenth century, European aristocrats, however, given their access to civil and military power as well as the lion's share of resources, were bound to

---

[18] Maurice, J. B., *Le blason des armoiries de tous les chevaliers de l'ordre de la Toison d'Or*, (La Haye, 1665), 249/251. See also H. Kamen, *Philip of Spain*, (New Haven, Conn., 1997), p. 41, 118. In 1567, the execution of the Counts Egmont and Horne, prompted Philip II to refrain from celebrating the feast day of the Order of the Golden Fleece in public.

[19] Unsurprisingly, Philip, an aficionado of chivalric culture, became joint patron of the order while he was Mary's consort. See W. A. Shaw, *The knights of England*, (London, 1906) vol. I, p. 25. See also R. Strong, 'Queen Elizabeth and the Order of the Garter' in *The Tudor and Stuart monarchy: pageantry, painting and iconography* (Suffolk, 1995), vol. II, pp. 57–9.

[20] Significantly, France's Order of St Michael was bestowed on both the duke of Norfolk and the earl of Leicester in Whitehall in 1566, a balanced act of diplomacy that indicates the degree to which Elizabeth's court was thought by contemporaries in Europe to be rent by faction. See Strong (1995), p. 72.

become the standard-bearers in a religious war. The political momentum of the French wars and the Dutch revolt ensured that, by the end of the period with which we are concerned, monarch-led chivalric orders became religiously biased institutions. After 1578, all foreign princes nominated as knights of the Garter (including Henry IV in 1590), were Protestants.[21] In the same year, Henry III founded the Order of the Holy Spirit which reflected the zealous ethos of resurgent Catholicism. This new order, in contravention of all traditional chivalric practice, admitted cardinals into its ranks.[22] The orders under Philip II's sovereignty – the Golden Fleece, Calatrava and Santiago – followed this confessional trend. However, the underlying conservatism of chivalric culture remained. The code of conduct remained in place. A basic reluctance to change can be discerned in the Order of the Garter's continued adherence to lavish semi-liturgical ritual, as an embellishment of a reformed church service, and the cult of sainthood, as embodied in continued devotion to St George.[23]

Churchyard's treatment was both conservative and insouciant: the tone used in his account of the exploits of John and Nicholas Malby does not alter one whit; whether describing events that occurred before or after Elizabeth's accession, the fundamental lack of regard for confessional matters remains unchanged.[24] Churchyard's work also manages to be conservative in style. His picaresque account of the Malby brothers'

---

[21] These Protestant princes were Frederick II of Denmark; John Casimir, count palatine of the Rhine; James VI of Scotland, and Frederick, duke of Würtemberg. By the time Henry IV of France was invested in 1596 and installed (by proxy) in 1600, he had converted to Catholicism. See Shaw, *The knights of England* (London, 1906), Vol. I, pp. 27–9.

[22] However, as Garrison points out, Henry III's intentions in founding the Order were aimed more at gathering a new, but loyal nobility behind his monarchy. See Garrison (1995), p. 370. See also Boulton's contention that the Order was not a chivalric body at all, *The knights of the crown* (London, 1987), p. 446.

[23] For Edward VI's unfulfilled efforts to redraft the statutes of the Order of the Garter along evangelical Christian lines (notably by eliminating reference or devotion to St George), see D. MacCulloch, *Tudor church militant* (London, 1999), pp. 30–4. Significantly, William Cecil assisted the king in his redrafting of proposed reforms to the Order. See also Strong (1995). See also Nicolas (1847), pp. 103–4, Sir Amias Paulet to Hatton, 30 December 1578, where Paulet, spinning the story somewhat, describes the celebrations at the French court surrounding the foundation of 'the new order of knighthood' and remarks that 'although this Order be especially affected by Knights of the Romish religion, yet the bishop of Rome hath not yet allowed thereof, and his ambassador hath refused to assist at the ceremonies'.

[24] Towards the end of the century, Churchyard did sometimes use explicitly anti-Catholic rhetoric in his work. A good example of this can be found in *A wished reformacion of wicked rebellion*, (London, 1598) where he declaims 'In England long here may no traytors live. / O Jesuits! Can you your selves excuse / When Jesus' name and doctrine you abuse', and he denounces 'A shameless swarm off Seminaries now / Disguised like dogs that whine before they bite.'

wanderings, punctuated by skirmishes, acts of daring and set battles, fits into chivalric literature as an account of the adventures of *chevaliers errants*, a phenomenally influential genre which later found its satirist in Cervantes. It is in his retelling of this service that Churchyard places particular emphasis on the regard in which the cream of Europe's martial aristocracy held the Malbys. Thus, he emphasised how England's military men could hold their own in an international context, but placed a special premium on documenting the praise and approbation they received from Continental Europe's 'community of honour' as a result of their prowess.

INDIVIDUALS, TRADITION AND CONFESSION

The cult of errantry, the pursuit of which led knights to travel throughout Europe serving foreign monarchs and nobles on the battlefield, had blurred the boundaries of principalities to a certain extent, allowing them to become subsumed under an assertion, by assembled knights of all cultures, of solidarity in arms. This practice facilitated admission to chivalric orders as well as opportunities for reward. It also affirmed the common legal and cultural inheritance European gentry and nobility claimed to share. Since the eleventh century, lord and vassal had met each other in a social setting which, although far from egalitarian, was laden with aristocratic indulgence and respect for military feats. The Malbys were not of noble blood, and any economic aspiration they might have had of passing themselves off as gentry had been compromised by their father's early death, leaving them wards of the king.[25] Yet, despite these handicaps, if we credit Churchyard's testimony, they were frequently to be found in the high esteem and company of Europe's leading aristocrats. For example, John Malby was brought to the attention of Henry II of France when he shot his way through an imperial troop which had cut off his route back to the garrison town of Bray sur Somme. As a result, he received an increase in pay 'for that the king would not forget such an act, nor let such service escape unrecompensed'.[26] Similarly, Nicholas, on foot of his own bravery, received embraces from the count de Montmorency and the duke of Vendôme.[27] Vendôme subsequently took Nicholas to the French

---

[25] Malby to Walsingham, 7 May, 1582, SP63/92/13. Malby, seeking evidence from a Mr Wade concerning lands concealed from him, relates that his father died when he was four years old. See also SP63/91/59 where Cecil sketches an incomplete genealogy of Malby.

[26] Churchyard (1579), sig. Bi, r; Bi, v.

[27] Anne de Montmorency subsequently led the government forces that opposed the Huguenots in both 1562 and 1567.

court and presented him to Henry II where he was 'bountifully rewarded without suing for the same (as good soldiers be in many places)'.[28] Nicholas Malby commanded considerable esteem both at home and abroad as an accomplished soldier. His military prowess, if we believe Churchyard, had brought him to assume a particularly prominent rôle in many renowned engagements: he had been the first Englishman to enter St Quentin and the last to leave Newhaven.[29] He had fought for Henry II, Charles V and Philip II, receiving plaudits and rewards from them all for his service. There was even a lasting awareness of his prowess in Gaelic Ireland: the *Annals of the Four Masters* – compiled and written in the 1630s using contemporary sources – described Malby as a *fear cróga cathbhuach*, 'a valiant and battle-triumphant man, throughout Ireland, Scotland, and France in the service of his sovereign'.[30]

According to Churchyard, after the debacle of Newhaven, the Malbys, the reader is casually informed, secured an introduction to the Spanish king, courtesy of the count of Feria – later implicated in the Ridolfi Plot.[31] Philip II then commended them to Don Garcia de Toledo, viceroy of Sicily and captain general of the campaign against the Turks. On their way to meet Don Garcia, the Malbys, according to Churchyard, were imprisoned in Sicily but were freed through the remarkable personal intercession of the Spanish king. King Philip, infuriated by the ill-treatment given the brothers, supposedly demanded that the man who arrested them should have his neck broken and be flung down a well. The brothers pressed for clemency instead.[32] The Malbys' special treatment continued: Toledo promoted them to take charge of a galley in preference to another candidate with commendation from both King Philip and Don John of Austria because 'the greatest service of Christendom, was presently to be followed, with men of most experience'.[33] After the siege of Malta in 1565, they returned to Madrid where they had a private audience with Philip II in his privy chamber, were presented with 500 ducats and 'reposed themselves a season'. Before their departure, they returned to the court where the king supposedly gave them another 500 ducats, and 'gracious speeches'. Churchyard praises Philip, stating that his

---

[28] Churchyard (1579), sig. Biv.v, Ci.
[29] Churchyard (1579) sigs. Dii, r; Diii, r. He entered St Quentin with Cuthbert Vaughan and left Newhaven with Edward Randolph.
[30] *ALC*, Vol. II, p. 459; *ARE*, Vol. V, pp. 1814–15.
[31] Parker (1998), p. 161.
[32] Churchyard (1579) sig. Diii, v.   [33] Churchyard (1579) sig. Div, v.

generosity was 'meet for such a prince, and a reward that might have pleased a right good subject', and the Malbys, we are told, 'accounted, all those soldiers happy that might serve such a king'.[34]

Of course, the proffering of *largesse* in recognition of *prouesse* was a chivalric ritual of ancient provenance, which, as well as giving recognition and respect to social inferiors, reflected glory and honour on the donor. Chivalric literature had always reserved a certain scorn for lords who did not give knights their just deserts. This common opinion is found, for example, in Rawlinson's edition of the biography of Sir John Perrot. Perrot, we are told, accompanied the marquis of Southampton to the French court when the latter was negotiating with Henry II to secure the betrothal of Henry's daughter to King Edward VI. While at court, they were taken on a hunting expedition. Here, Perrot, through the timely killing of a wild boar, saved the French king's life. Henry, seeing this, grabbed Perrot around the waist and embraced him, calling him 'Beaufoile'. Typically, Perrot believed that he was being challenged to an impromptu contest of strength and took 'the King also about the middle, [and] lifted him up somewhat high from the ground: with which [we are assured] the King was nothing displeased.' Henry II, as a token of his gratitude, offered Perrot a pension if he would enter his service, which he refused, stating (in French) that 'he was a gentleman that had means of his own ... and if he wanted aught he knew that he served a gracious and a royal Prince who would not see him want and to whom he had ... vowed his service during life.'[35] Whereas Perrot's candour and impulsiveness proved his undoing later in his career, by all accounts his approach to royalty, presented as a form of chivalric *franchise*, gained him substantial favour in his youth.[36] As we have already seen, Perrot's

---

[34] Philip also alienated courtiers through spite, neglect and tightfistedness. The count of Horne, captain of the king's bodyguard from 1549 to 1559, was especially disillusioned by his exclusion from decision-making on Dutch issues when he was in Madrid as 'superintendent of Netherlandish affairs'. Once he left the court in 1561 the king withdrew his pension of 6,000 florins per annum, see G. Parker, *The Dutch revolt* (London, 1990), p. 286, n. 28.

[35] *A history of that most eminent statesman, Sir John Perrot*, ed. R. Rawlinson, (London, 1728), pp. 29–30. See also his receipt of patronage from Edward VII, referred to in an earlier chapter. See *CSPD. Mary*, ed. Knighton, p. 48 for the grant made to Perrot of a newly acquired crown property worth £100 per annum 'in consideration of a promise made by Edward VI (as the queen is informed by divers of her councillors then her brother's)'.

[36] Richard Rawlinson tends to ascribe Perrot's downfall first to an inability 'to brook any crosses or dissemble the least injuries' (Perrot was definitely not a stoic) and second to some brand of sexual incontinence in which 'he [did] offend so far in that kind, as it drew God's displeasure towards him, which (if men may pronounce God's judgment) was the cause of his ruin'. Rawlinson, (1728), pp. 20–1.

freedom and familiarity with Edward VI had secured him wealth and a living in England, and his similarly casual and egalitarian approach to Henry II likewise gained him favour.

Such stories in this politically safe form and context were a commonplace of chivalric literature.[37] The value of devotion, or *loyauté*, to Edward VI was not besmirched by Henry II's offer of a pension to Perrot, as it afforded the English knight an opportunity to uphold his existing allegiance to his king publicly. However, it must be noted that Perrot's protestations of loyalty can hardly be deemed the unconditional submission of a subject to an imperial monarch in that they were proffered in response to Edward's concern that he would never 'want'. In a society where physical access to a king was directly indicative of influence and political clout, Henry's tolerance and understanding of Perrot's reflexive desire to exert pre-eminence over him in physical contest denotes behaviour made acceptable by common membership of the 'community of honour'.[38]

Certainly, Churchyard's treatment of the distribution of favour and *largesse* among the 'community of honour' has a discontented and subversive edge, especially when combined with his barely concealed frustration at Elizabeth's parsimony in matters of patronage. According to Churchyard, while Nicholas Malby was at the French court with the duke of Vendôme, Henry II 'bountifully rewarded' him; Malby did not have to petition for Henry's favour, it was spontaneously given to him, 'without suing for the same'. It is clear that Churchyard's reason for continually rehearsing scenes of royal and aristocratic magnanimity was to shame Elizabeth, to show that the bestowal of *largesse* to soldiers, so common abroad, differed from the normal experience of English captains at home. Malby was in receipt of grace, *largesse* and favour from royalty '*as good soldiers be in many places*' (my italics). An unfavourable comparison is being made here between Elizabeth's negligent and uncaring attitude to soldiers and the honours conventionally heaped on them by princes in western Europe. This dissatisfaction with his queen hints at more rebellious discontent when he deals with the Malbys' treatment at the hands of Philip II. Philip's impulsive generosity to these English captains as if they were 'right good subjects', the reader is assured, is 'meet for such a prince'. The conclusion reached by the Malbys (and Churchyard) was

---

[37] Keen (1984), pp. 18, 121, 207.
[38] For the implications of physical intimacy with a monarch, see Starkey, D. 'Representation and intimacy: the king's privy chamber' in *The Tudor monarchy*, ed. J. Guy (London, 1997), pp. 42–78.

that all soldiers who served 'such a king' must be accounted 'happy' – a truly dangerous observation in the context of English foreign policy. Could this have been construed as an exhortation to English soldiers to defect and serve their former king? Or even a denial that Elizabeth was the legitimate monarch?

We know that Churchyard believed that French, Spanish and Italian soldiers got a better deal than English martial men did and joined these comments with veiled criticism of Burghley and Elizabeth.[39] It is worth noting that Churchyard's frankness in his *Choise* did not escape the attention of his clerkish betters. He incurred influential displeasure and went into exile for a period at the Scottish court. While there, he was dogged by suspicions that he was an agent of Elizabeth's. He later alleged that he had suffered bad treatment from James VI's courtiers solely because of his nationality (which rings true given the rapid rise in favour of Esmé Stewart, earl of Lennox at that time), but he was also (unsurprisingly) treated coldly by Thomas Randolph, the English ambassador to Scotland. Subsequently, he returned to Berwick in 1581 under a cloud of mistrust because he had 'sworn at the council board of Scotland to be true to the [Scottish] King'. When back in England, Churchyard asserted that although he was 'sworn' at the Board 'all the lords [could] testify that [he] protested openly [he] would never be false to the queen's majesty and [his] country'. It was then suggested that he had been acting as an intelligence agent scouting out English news in Scotland for Mauvissière, the French ambassador.[40]

Yes, frustration among martial men because of a lack of royal approbation and attention was palpable throughout the first three decades of Elizabeth's reign. Once more, the case of Sir John Perrot is instructive. Later in his career, his alleged outspokenness about Elizabeth created the conditions for his self-destruction. Perrot's treason trial, as Hiram Morgan has argued, was the result of clumsy but ultimately effective manoeuvring by an unholy coalition of hostile forces. However, the aim that Burghley, Fitzwilliam and Hatton sought is less relevant than the means used to bring it to pass. Apart from the supposed existence of letters, allegedly from Perrot to both King Philip of Spain and Sir William Stanley, which provided the initial spur for his arraignment on a charge of treason, there was the testimony of Philip Williams, Perrot's former private secretary who brought a number of plausible statements

---

[39] Churchyard (1579) sig. Oi, v.   [40] Adnitt (1880), pp. 33–5.

allegedly made by Perrot into the public domain. The most notorious of these utterances ('this it is to serve a base bastard piss kitchen woman, if I had served any prince in Christendom I have not been so dealt withal') explicitly questioned Elizabeth's legitimacy and criticised her tightfistedness towards her officers compared with the more generous practice of foreign royalty. Even if these words were merely a malicious fabrication, the attitude they represented was deemed convincing enough to secure a credible indictment.[41] The threat to Elizabeth and Elizabethan loyalists was straightforward: captains and other martial officers not only felt alienated but they possessed the international contacts that could enable them to transform personal alienation into something much more dangerous.

Whatever about Churchyard's intent in 1579, Malby's involvement in the Mediterranean wars of Philip II fourteen years earlier had not been clandestine. That Malby did indeed enjoy a sojourn in Madrid can be verified by the existence of a letter he wrote to Cecil on 12 June 1565, informing the principal secretary that he was to be sent by the Spanish king to serve Don Garcia de Toledo. Furthermore, it is plausible that Malby sent other haphazard intelligence back to the English court about Spanish affairs at this time; Anglo-Spanish relations were not utterly poisoned at that point, although, as the political situation worsened, Malby and military figures like him came to be viewed and employed differently by both friends and foes of the Elizabethan regime.[42] Even as early as the 1560s, it had proved difficult for Malby to balance his reputation at home with his exploits abroad. His renown had neither ensured his financial security nor his social standing in England, and his attempts to get rich quick had merely earned him the death sentence for counterfeiting.[43] After his adventures in the Mediterranean, Malby had returned to Ireland in 1567 as sergeant major of Sir Henry Sidney's army and served with Captain Piers at Carrickfergus.[44]

Until he secured the patronage of Francis Walsingham in the 1570s, Malby's stock at court was low. Indeed, even after his elevation to the presidency of Connacht, he never commanded unanimous confidence.[45]

---

[41] Howell, *State Trials*, Vol. I, pp. 1315–27. See H. Morgan, 'The fall of Sir John Perrot' in J. Guy (ed.), *The reign of Elizabeth I: court and culture in the last decade* (Cambridge, 1995), pp. 110, 117.
[42] Malby to Cecil, 12 June 1565, *CSPD 1547–80*, p. 392.
[43] *The diary of Henry Machyn*, ed. J. Gough Nichols (London, 1848), p. 290.
[44] *Fiants*, Vol. II, 1191, 1196. Lord Justices Weston and Fitzwilliam to Elizabeth, 30 October 1567, SP63/22/16.
[45] See M. Leimon, 'Sir Francis Walsingham and the Anjou marriage plans 1574–1581', unpublished Ph.D. thesis (Cambridge University, 1989), pp. 77–105, 193–201, for treatment of Walsingham's patronage in Ireland.

Most of his early communications from Ireland with central government had been with Cecil, but Malby understood that the secretary had no real affection for him: a letter he wrote to Cecil in February 1568 from Carrickfergus tactfully accounted for the fact that he had received no answer to any of the letters he had sent the secretary by assuming that 'the same [had] not come unto your honour's hands'.[46] From the earliest days of his service, he was alienated from two of Cecil's key clients in Ireland: Sir William Fitzwilliam and Sir Nicholas White.[47] However, notwithstanding all this, Malby showed himself to be both a well-disposed and effective instrument in the earl of Essex's 'enterprise of Ulster', an initiative that looked to Cecil for support at court.[48] Malby also managed to retain his association with Leicester which had been inaugurated through his service as secretary to Ambrose Dudley, the earl of Warwick, at Newhaven, and this, no doubt, accounted for his subsequent defence of Sir Henry Sidney's record as lord deputy of Ireland and the latter's consistent praise for the quality of Malby's service.[49] The queen's disregard for Malby may well have been due to the consistent enmity that existed between Malby and her Irish favourite Thomas Butler, the earl of Ormond.[50]

It seems that the lingering suspicion that dogged Malby in the corridors of power – although in some part motivated by misgivings about his slipshod conduct in Irish politics – stemmed from distrust of his international contacts.[51] By 15 October 1571, we find Guerau de Spes, the Spanish ambassador to England, informing Philip II that he 'could easily bring Malby round to your Majesty's service if [he] had orders to do so', adding that 'there are many like him in office, very desirous of serving

---

[46] See Malby to Cecil, 12 February 1568, SP 63/23/37. However, despite this lack of favour, Malby continued to correspond with Cecil throughout his career in Ireland, for example, Malby to Burghley, 4 November 1579, SP63/70/3.
[47] For Malby's enmity with Fitzwilliam, see Sir Nicholas Bagenal to Sidney, 3 May 1568, SP 63/24/31.
[48] Essex to Burghley, 14 June 1574, SP63/46/62, for Essex's allegation that Sidney merely 'reaped ... all the fruit of [the earl of Sussex's] travail'. See also Antonio de Guaras's report, 5 December 1575, *CSPSp 1568–79*, p. 511 where de Guaras tells of the 'great enmity' caused by Leicester's affair with Essex's wife while the earl was in Ireland.
[49] For example, for Malby's defence of Sidney, Malby to Cecil, 2 June 1569, SP63/28/17; For examples of the Leicester group's solidarity with Malby, see Edward Tremayne to Burghley, 17 June 1573, SP63/41/39; Collins (1746) Vol. I, Sidney to Lord Grey de Wilton, 17 September; See also S. Adams, 'The Dudley clientele, 1553–1563' in G. W. Bernard's, *The Tudor nobility* (Manchester, 1992), p. 247.
[50] See Malby to Walsingham, SP63/82/24, 33, 44; Malby to Sidney, 11 June 1569, SP 63/29/7.
[51] See Malby to Cecil, 8 Feb, 1568, SP63/23/37 where Malby complains that he had received no communication from Cecil.

your Majesty'.[52] Perhaps Spes and Malby had met during the latter's visit to court in late March and early April of that year, when the captain had brought letters from Ireland and pressed his own suit; Malby was awaiting a grant of MacCartan's country in Ulster with a remit to plant it. It is difficult to determine his motivation for approaching the Spanish ambassador at that time.[53] His professed amenability may have been a sincere attempt to broaden his career options (crown service had not yet proved lucrative for Malby), or maybe someone, mindful of his previous service for Philip II, had sent him to the ambassador with the aim of forcing the notoriously indiscreet Spes to disclose his malicious intent towards Elizabeth. The contact may have been motivated by the fact that the privy council and Burghley in particular, were anxious at that time to discover the identities of English peers in receipt of letters from Robert Ridolfi, the main intermediary in a conspiracy between Philip II, the Pope and Mary Stuart against Elizabeth.[54] Malby may even have been but one agent in the sustained intelligence-gathering exercise that resulted in the trial and execution of the duke of Norfolk, but evidence concerning espionage, especially the activity of double agents, is, by its nature, elusive: the fog surrounding their inscrutable autonomy and their floating allegiances is difficult to penetrate. It is now commonly believed that Ridolfi himself was a double agent.[55]

However, speculation about Nicholas Malby's contacts with Philip II did not end in October 1571, the point at which they may have been most useful to the Elizabethan regime. Seven years later, in June 1578, his name emerged in a new and incriminating context when Juan de Aguirre, a member of the household of the Spanish agent Antonio de Guaras, was being interrogated in the Tower of London. William Herle, an agent of Burghley's, accused Guaras not only of favouring the 'Scottish faction' but of amassing 'intelligence with our rebels, with our papists and with our discontented sort, so as none of importance, that draw that way is unknown to him'. According to Herle, Guaras was a shrewd enemy of the Elizabethan regime:

---

[52] *CSPSp, 1568–79*, p. 346.
[53] This visit is referred to in Piers to Burghley, March 25, 1571 SP63/31/41, and Loftus to Burghley, March 25, 1571, SP63/31/42. For a reference to Malby's suit as but one among a flood that followed the first Desmond rebellion see Burghley's 1571 undated note of suits, SP63/34/45.
[54] See C. Read, *Lord Burghley and Queen Elizabeth* (London, 1965), pp. 38–43.
[55] This is the argument advanced by G. Parker in *The grand strategy of Philip II* (New Haven, Conn., 1998), pp. 160–3. MacCaffrey and Read, however suspend judgement on Ridolfi's ultimate motive. See MacCaffrey, *The shaping of the Elizabethan regime* (Princeton, NJ, 1968), pp. 415–25.

He can discern of the humours of people, as well of magistrates as inferiors. He hath searched the state of the revenues of the crown ... of the navy, of the men of service for land and sea, for home and abroad ... He hath dealt in Irish matters and been a common spy ... He hath dealt and written lazily in the d[uke] of Norfolk's cause, after his second commitment, forcing by many arguments, that it was an intolerable wrong that was offered him.[56]

The interrogators sought information on communication between specific Englishmen and Guaras. Whereas Guaras himself was examined by the privy councillors, Sir Walter Mildmay and the principal secretary Dr Thomas Wilson, Aguirre was attended to by the prison's governor and Herle. The fifth question asked of Aguirre in the interrogation related to the governor of Connacht: 'Did [you] know one Captain Malby?' the servant was asked. Aguirre replied in the affirmative, adding that Malby had approached his master, asking him to forward two Irish greyhounds to King Philip.[57] This approach to Guaras, if it ever happened, must have been made between January and May 1575 when Malby was at court as an emissary from the earl of Essex. Yet, even this notional show of obligation to a former, and perhaps current, patron is also open to ambiguity. It was also around that time that Malby first gained Walsingham's trust, a connection that would last until death.[58]

Perhaps the best way to plait the straggling threads of Aguirre's answers together is to interpret them in the light of the testimony of his master Antonio de Guaras. In this context, the tenth question put to Guaras seems revealing. Guaras noted that 'They [that is, Mildmay and Wilson] examined [him] as to who it was that was going to serve with ten thousand men, giving his son as a pledge?' and the reply he gave was: 'so far as I [recollect] it was Colonel Chester.' The answer was knowingly, and even petulantly implausible, as Thomas Wilson, referring to his recent diplomatic experience in the Low Countries, would have been aware. Not only had Edward Chester recently levied troops in England for William of Orange, he was Burghley's chief contact with the leader of the Dutch rebels. Guaras claimed to have later clarified this point in conversation: 'I told Dr Wilson apart that I wished to speak with the earl of Leicester as question number ten concerned his brother in law', that is, Sir Henry Sidney.

---

[56] Herle to Thomas Wilson, 1578, BL Cotton MSS, Vespasian CXIII fols. 301r–302v.
[57] *CSPSp, 1568–79*, p. 607.
[58] Walsingham to Malby, March 1575, SP63/49/1; Malby to Walsingham, July 1575, SP63/52/46.

Further evidence exists for the future Irish viceroy's flirtatious dealings with Philip II. In 1574, the Spanish king composed a précis of despatches from Guaras which noted that Sidney

> had asked to see Guaras and spoken in great secrecy to him [offering] a way to serve his Majesty with 6000 chosen English soldiers; and since Guaras expressed two or three times his belief as to the difficulty of doing so with the Queen's will, and even more without it, he replied . . . that as security for the fulfilment of it he pledged his only heir . . . whose name is Philip whom his majesty lifted from the font.[59]

These tendentious remarks generate more heat than light. Was Guaras, through this disclosure to Wilson, merely being mischievous? It seems certain that Sidney made an approach of this nature in 1574. However, by confiding this information four years later to Thomas Wilson, Guaras may have been trying to sow discord. Wilson, like Burghley, in 1578 supported the proposed match between Elizabeth and Duke Francis of Anjou (albeit without much enthusiasm), yet he was in a difficult situation; although he was a forward Protestant and a prolific Cambridge educated humanist, he was also a Leicester client.[60] Guaras's request that Wilson, previously instrumental in Cecil's conciliatory foreign policy towards Spain, should tell the earl of Leicester (now opposed to the Anjou match and in favour of open hostilities against Spain in the Netherlands) about Sidney's offer of military assistance to Philip II, was, perhaps, an attempt to probe the court's divisions.

Sidney's approach in 1574, in all likelihood, had probably been yet another attempt sponsored by Leicester and Walsingham to glean information about Spanish intentions for England and the Low Countries. Philip II had suffered a catalogue of setbacks that year: a naval defeat on the Scheldt, a surprisingly successful Dutch assault on the east, as well as the relief of Leiden and troop mutinies. These military reverses, when considered along with the precarious nature of Castilian finances (common knowledge at the time) made discernment of Philip's intentions extremely important to England's interests. This was even more the case given that France's new king, Henry III, seemed both hostile to England

---

[59] Worden, (1996), p. 45.
[60] Read (1965), p. 178. See S. Adams, 'The Dudley clientele and the House of Commons, 1559–1586' in *Parliamentary History*, Vol. VIII, Part 2 (1989), p. 225 for the likelihood that Leicester secured Wilson's election as an MP in the 1563 parliament; also S. Adams 'The Dudley clientele 1553–1563' in *The Tudor nobility*, ed. G. W. Bernard (Manchester, 1992), p. 245 n. 29. On Wilson's 'Cambridge connection' see S. Alford's 'Reassessing William Cecil in the 1560s', in Guy (1997), pp. 239–40.

The limits of allegiance 105

and interested in the Low Countries. The following year, 1575, Spain, through financial necessity, would enter negotiations with Orange and the States at Breda. At the same time, relations between Elizabeth and William of Orange would become strained because of Dutch detention of English ships attempting to trade with Antwerp. Orange, at that point, would also appear to be leaning towards a French alliance, a flirtation that later culminated in his marriage to Princess Charlotte de Bourbon, a match that forced Elizabeth to threaten that 'she minde[d] to bend all her forces to the assistance of the king of Spain.'[61] Ultimately, Malby's contacts with Guaras at that time can perhaps be explained with reference to his undeniably close links with Sidney and by extension Leicester and Walsingham, as well as their concern – given the state of flux in international relations – to find out as much information as possible about Spanish policy. In May 1575, these three grandees put sustained pressure on Elizabeth to appoint Malby governor of Connacht, Walsingham telling Sidney that 'if [Malby's] fortune answered to his value, I know him not in this land more fit to bear the title of president than he. If he lived in any other country than this [England], *where martial men presently bear no price*, he should not have been so long kept under foot' (my italics).[62]

Yet, if Malby's offer to send greyhounds to Philip was above board in 1574 because of England's détente with Spain (or because he was merely acting as a pawn in a game dictated by his patrons), why was William Herle concerned about it in May 1578? We know that Burghley's attitude to Malby had deteriorated once more that year, for, in July, Malby wrote to the Treasurer that he had 'sundry times written unto your L[ord] and have not had any intelligence of the delivery of my letters neither yet understood from your honour by which I might be satisfied in the same'. As a result, he sent his wife Tamsin to court as an 'assured messenger' with letters and his 'honest suits', therefore colluding in the necessary pretence that Burghley's boycott from correspondence might have been the result of the failings of previous letter-bearers.[63] The Sidney administration was provoking hostile reaction throughout the realm in its eagerness to impose a countrywide system of taxation called composition that aimed at securing extra-parliamentary funding to support a

---

[61] See Read (1965), p. 160. Elizabeth instructed Daniel Rogers to tell Orange that she would assist Philip if he proceeded with the French marriage.
[62] Collins, A., *Letters and memorials of state*, 2 vols. (London, 1746), Vol. I, p. 71.
[63] Malby to Burghley, 26 July 1578, SP63/61/41. Malby attached a petition for Roscommon and Athlone in fee farm with fifty horsemen to this letter.

permanent garrison in Ireland. Ireland's peers and their followers came under sustained attack. The earl of Clanricard had been imprisoned in Dublin on a charge of treason for failing to bring his rebellious sons John and Ulick Burke to English justice. Malby had single-mindedly reduced Clanricard's sons to obedience by means of a ruthless scorched-earth campaign. Among detractors, Sidney's policy was increasingly interpreted as a malicious strategy to undermine the earl of Ormond's influence and power in Ireland. It seems certain that Sidney's drive to extinguish the grip of the Butler affinity (of which the earl of Clanricard was a member) on Irish politics was matched by Ormond's own desire to use his weighty influence at court to blacken the names of the Lord Deputy and the prominent executors of his policy, notably Malby.[64] Burghley, motivated by an amalgamation of court politics, sensitivity to the personal bias and susceptibilities of Elizabeth and his marked caution on foreign-policy matters, may well – through Herle – have been bending his own will against Malby and Sidney, making much of initiatives which, although they looked questionable retrospectively, had made perfect sense in a previous context. Although fraternal approaches to Philip II may have been conceivable and permissible in 1574 and 1575, in 1578 Don John of Austria's presence in the Low Countries and mounting fears about his ambitions in relation to England had changed the English attitude to Spain entirely.

Malby's intrigue was far from being the only such manoeuvre carried out in diplomatic no-man's-land at the time. As Spes told Philip in late 1571, there were many hardened military men soliciting employment; those who had once posed as England's answer to *Orlando Furioso* were now opting to serve as *Orlando Curioso*. For example, throughout 1574, Richard Bingham (another future president of Connacht) tantalised the excitable ambassador with an offer to seize Rotterdam (William of Orange's base at that time) on his master's behalf.[65] Consequently, Spes informed Philip that Bingham, as well as being 'good and efficient', was a Catholic surrounded by Catholic officers, 'which inspires [my] confidence'.[66] According to the ambassador, Bingham had been in the Netherlands

---

[64] See C. Brady *The chief governors* (Cambridge, 1994), pp. 186–8. Bagwell *Ireland under the Tudors*, 3 vols. (Dublin, 1890), Vol. II, pp. 338–40. See also SP63/69/50 for the earl of Desmond's letter of 10 October 1579 to the earl of Ormond, where he alleged that Malby broke and burned the funeral monument of Ormond's mother.

[65] For Guerau de Spes's imprudent and almost insatiable addiction to conspiracies and plots, see Parker (1998), pp. 155–7.

[66] *CSPSp*, 1568–79, pp. 478, 483.

throughout the summer seeking employment from Orange (who was desperately ill at the time). However, Orange refused to recruit any Englishmen into his forces, perhaps a symptom of the Dutch leader's movement towards a French alliance.[67] Given the value that strategic control of the Netherlands was assuming for France, England and Spain, it is unlikely that Bingham's petition to Orange nor his presence in the Netherlands was conceived first and foremost as a means of advancing Philip's agenda. It seems more probable that despite a lukewarm Anglo-Spanish rapprochement, Bingham was collecting information about the intentions of both Orange and his Spanish opponents for an English patron.[68] However, after Orange's rejection, Bingham furnished Spes with 'a design about Flushing', the only deep sea port in the Netherlands – the *sine qua non* for Spanish control of the North Sea – and an 'opinion about a landing in Ireland, in which enterprise he offers to take part'.[69] We will return to the question of Bingham's allegiances and his political development later on.

Significantly, neither Malby, Bingham nor Sidney, in their attempts to tantalise Philip II, ever invoked religion as a motivation for their communication or as a cause of disaffection; the fact that Philip had been invested as king of Ireland by Pope Paul IV in 1555 however left Malby's gift-giving open to uncharitable interpretation. Likewise, the irreverent statements concerning Elizabeth attributed to Sir John Perrot (although not the forged letters which he was accused of writing to both Philip II and Sir William Stanley) pointed more to a martial, perhaps chivalric, wistfulness rather than any zeal for Counter-Reformation Catholicism.[70] This disillusion with Elizabeth stemmed more from personal irritation and ennui than any systematic doubt about her legitimacy to rule.

OLD STALWARTS?

The simple truth was that when it came to martial affairs Elizabeth was not merely outgunned and under-resourced but was (perhaps overly) careful with the resources she had. This reticence, so easily ascribable to

---

[67] During Mary's reign, Bingham served with the Malby brothers in a troop led by Thomas Stukeley, and, over a decade later, fought at the battle of Lepanto. For French approaches to Orange as early as 1583 see J. L. Motley, *The rise of the Dutch republic*, 3 vols. (London, 1896), Vol. II, pp. 434–6.
[68] Churchyard (1579) sig. Eiv, r.   [69] *CSPSp* 1568–79, p. 484.
[70] See J. Murray, 'The Tudor diocese of Dublin: episcopal government, ecclesiastical politics and the enforcement of the reformation, c. 1534–1590', unpublished Ph.D. thesis (University of Dublin, 1997), pp. 223–93, for the most recent treatment of Sidney's commitment to reformed religion.

female pusillanimousness, not only caused unease for *déclassé* swordsmen from the political periphery such as Malby but also hit the regime closer to home, at the very heart of what should have been an adamant praetorian grouping around Elizabeth's throne: those martial men who had shown their active disaffection during the reign of Queen Mary. Intimations of this had been seen in the way that, at that time, many dissidents' rehabilitation had been facilitated by the new king, Philip of Spain.

The confounding effect of Philip's leniency even penetrated the ranks of those martial dissidents based in Devon and Cornwall.[71] The ringleader of this group was undoubtably Sir Peter Carew, renowned for the violence with which he put down the Prayer Book rebellion in 1549. The savagery of his conduct against the peasantry was seen as a sign of particular commitment to reformed religion.[72] Carew initially accepted Mary's accession but was subsequently implicated in the plots that surrounded 'Wyatt's revolt' and fled England in the summer of 1554, after which he spent some time in Venice and Strasbourg, becoming the military leader of a band of English dissidents who were serving with the French. This all changed, however, when Mary was prevailed upon to grant Carew a pardon through Philip's intercession. According to the despatches of Giovanni Michiel, the Venetian ambassador at the Marian Court in 1556, Sir Peter then turned informer against his erstwhile comrades. It seems certain that he not only supplied the information that secured the execution of Henry Peckham and John Daniel, he also fingered the Dudley conspirators, John Perrot, Nicholas Arnold, John Pollard and John Chichester and – most heinously – facilitated the abduction of John Cheke, the intellectual father-figure of Marian dissent, by Habsburg agents. Carew, of course, was abducted at the same time and was subsequently held in the Tower until December 1556, which might have proved valuable cover for a man who had done the unthinkable.[73] Cheke's capture and public recantation of his evangelical views became a powerful weapon in the regime's campaign to shake the resolve of those members of the Protestant intelligentsia – Cecil and Elizabeth, in particular – still residing in England.[74]

---

[71] See C. Garrett, *The Marian exiles* (Cambridge, 1938). The West Country opposition led by Carew was made up of figures such as John Chichester, John Courtenay, Henry Killigrew, James Kirkham and the Tremaynes.
[72] Duffy, E., *The voices of Morebath: reformation and rebellion in an English village* (New Haven, Conn., 2001), pp. 131, 142, 153.
[73] Giovanni Michiel, Venetian ambassador in England, to the Doge and Senate, 12 May 1556, *CSPVen, 1555–6*, p. 447.
[74] Wagner (1998), pp. 218–26.

The question mark that hung over Carew's conduct in 1556 did not disappear. His lack of favour under Elizabeth has already been noted, but his reputation was compromised across a broad base of Elizabethan loyalists as well. In 1572, Lord Hunsdon, warden of the eastern marches, on hearing that Carew might be named warden of the Stanneries, wrote to Cecil indicating that the queen had reason to distrust the Devonman, ending 'aliquid latet quod non patet'.[75]

Broadly speaking, Philip had shown a capacity to be clement and generous which neither his wife, nor Cardinal Pole, could emulate. His indulgent attitude towards Princess Elizabeth was an example of this, plausibly self-interested, magnanimity. That Philip managed to use the Habsburg war with France to rally erstwhile opponents to his flag may say more for the sway that venerable forms of military mobilisation held over England's chivalry, irrespective of confessional or political provenance, than his own charisma, but the 1557 campaign provided an excellent opportunity for Philip to use his position to proffer sceptics an amnesty. The Dudley brothers, many of the figures previously implicated with 'Wyatt's Rebellion' and former advocates of Jane Grey's claim to the throne lost no time in seizing the opportunity of indemnifying themselves.[76] This rapprochement showed a weakness in the solidarity of those parties who had been opposed to Mary's claim and her marriage. Had the attraction of Philip's prowess as a martial leader permanently dislocated the political, religious and moral compasses of figures who later served the over-frugal Elizabeth, jeopardising their allegiance to her regime and leading them to a broader analysis of international relations than was useful to a cadre at the centre of power?

The case of Sir James Croft (who had served as lord deputy of Ireland from 1551 to 1552 and as comptroller of the household from 1570) is worth noting in this context. Elizabeth herself described him at the end of his career as a man 'more trained in martial affairs than acquainted with matters of treaties'.[77] Formerly a client of Sir John Dudley, he was sent to the Tower and found guilty of high treason because of his implication in

---

[75] *CSPF, 1572–4*, p. 56. See Wagner (1998), p. 273, for his account of Hunsdon's response.
[76] The designation of Wyatt's revolt as a religiously motivated affair was first mooted in John Proctor's *The historie of Wyatt's rebellion* (London, 1554), a work of government propaganda. Malcolm Thorp's attempts to prove the confessional basis of the rebellion in 'Religion and the Wyatt rebellion of 1554' *Church History*, Vol. XLVII, 4 (1978), pp. 363–80, tend to have the opposite effect to the one intended.
[77] BL Add MSS, 4160, fol. 85.

Wyatt's rebellion in 1554.[78] According to Heywood, Croft was suborned to implicate the princess Elizabeth in the failed coup, but on confrontation with the future queen he retracted his testimony.[79] Subsequently, he was pardoned by Mary, served at St Quentin and was appointed to serve in the north in 1557. When Elizabeth acceded to the throne, Croft was appointed governor of Berwick. However, his loyalty was queried in 1560 because of his conduct at the siege of Leith. According to the duke of Norfolk, he had constantly treated with the besieged French soldiers, encouraged dissolute behaviour among his troops and displayed wilful dereliction of duty during the assault. Cecil, who later classified Croft as one of the earl of Leicester's clients, did not rally to his defence; Norfolk's allegation was designed to expel a Dudley creature from his sphere of influence, and Croft was removed from his post.[80]

Six years later, the Spanish ambassador Guzman de Silva referred to Croft in conjunction with reports concerning the reaction at court to the death of Colonel Edward Randolph in Derry and the failure of Sidney's Ulster campaign. Silva, a man of more measured judgement than his successor Spes, told Philip II of the demoralisation of the Catholics at the death of Randolph, who was 'a faithful one', adding that 'they only had two good soldiers here who understood war, and now that Randolph is dead, the only one left is Crofts'.[81] Later, when Croft was given the post of comptroller of the household, Spes described him as a former pensioner of Philip II and a Catholic. Croft's *politique* tendencies resurfaced once more when he broke his links with Leicester in the 1570s and became a partisan of the 'peace party' with Hatton, Sussex and Burghley. In 1588, his allegiances would be questioned again because of his conduct as a member of the delegation appointed to negotiate with Philip II's

---

[78] Loades, D., *Two Tudor conspiracies* (Cambridge, 1965), pp. 19–24. Loades contends that Croft was the principal leader of 'Wyatt's' Rebellion. Croft, himself, later alleged that Sir Thomas Wyatt had proceeded '(Before God!) without my knowledge or privity' and that the rebellion was 'a mere madness' in R. E. Ham, 'The autobiography of Sir James Croft', *Bulletin of the Institute of Historical Research*, 50 (121).

[79] See 'Biographical memoir: Sir James Croft' in *The retrospective review*, 15 vols. (1827), Vol. I, p. 477.

[80] 'Biographical memoir: Sir James Croft' (1827), pp. 479–81. Croft was one of the group that Cecil in April 1566 described as Leicester's 'particular friends'.

[81] *CSPSp, 1558–68*, p. 599. See *CSPD: Mary*, pp. 46, 62, 212. Croft, when interrogated by the council of the marches following Wyatt's rebellion implicated Randolph in the affair and the latter's name appeared on lists of those 'vehemently suspected'. Randolph was pardoned in October 1554. However, in 1556, his intentions towards the Marian regime, once more came under question. In 1559 Elizabeth's privy council now steered by Cecil sent Edward Randolph to give money to the Scottish Protestants in 1559 and described him to Ralph Sadler and (perhaps with unwitting irony) to Croft as 'a gentleman of trust and knowledge', *CSPSc, 1547–63*, p. 264.

The limits of allegiance

commissioners in Flanders. On 27 April that year, he had an interview alone with the duke of Parma, a course of action he had no commission or authority to pursue. By way of a personal *apologia*, Croft – casting himself as a peacemaker – stressed that 'the necessity of time did drive [him] to the duke, when otherwise the whole treaty should have been overthrown.' He admitted that he had no warrant to do this, only 'reasonable cause' but stressed that he was 'void of all malice'. Although Walsingham had indicated in June that all had been forgiven, when Croft returned to England he was imprisoned. The immediacy of the Armada and its aftermath coupled with Leicester's death (believed by the privy council to have been procured through magic by Croft's eldest son Edward) probably eliminated whatever political will existed to punish the comptroller, who died three years later.

More suggestive is the case of Croft's brother-in-law, Colonel Edward Randolph from Kent. Curiously, Randolph, like Croft, had also been implicated in 'Wyatt's revolt' and went into exile. Subsequently he pleaded for mercy, citing fear of retribution as the reason for his flight and, like Sir Peter Carew, became a spy for the Marian government among military exiles in France.[82] He received a pardon, was granted a pension by Philip II and appears to have reconciled himself totally with the Marian regime, although suspicions about his loyalty continued to be expressed.[83] Under Elizabeth, he was granted an annuity of £40 'for his service', served as a muster-master in the county of Middlesex and was then appointed lieutenant of the ordnance, but, as early as 1560, he expressed disillusion about the new regime. Bishop de Quadra wrote to Philip in March that year detailing a conversation between Randolph and himself concerning military preparation on the border with Scotland. Randolph expressed fears about the strength of French forces in Scotland and the lack of supplies and military expertise on the English side. Quadra related that Randolph believed that 'state of things [was] doomed and, if it were not for leaving his home, he would go and serve your Majesty in Spain'. Two years later, according to the bishop, Randolph went to Cadiz 'to take

---

[82] Ambassador Wotton to Philip and Mary, *CSPF, 1553–8*, p. 113.
[83] *CSPD, 1547–80*, p. 65 for Philip's order that 200 English crowns be paid to Randolph per annum; *CSPSp 1554–58*, pp. 405, 456, for reference to the amounts owed to Randolph in 1558. David Trim has recently advanced the view that Edward Randolph was 'an ardent Calvinist', a view which I believe is difficult to sustain given the details of his Marian and Elizabethan career. See Trim's 'Fighting "Jacobs's warres": the employment of English and Welsh mercenaries in the European wars of religion: France and the Netherlands 1562–1610', unpublished Ph.D. thesis (University of London, 2002), p. 104. For the £40 annuity he received from Elizabeth see *CPR Eliz., 1558–60*, p. 27.

certain baths'. Again, his access to information and his personal dissatisfaction were stressed. Whether this opportunity to make renewed contact with Randolph was seized by the Spanish regime is impossible to gauge. However, according to Guzman de Silva in 1563, Randolph was 'so much attached to the service of [Philip II] that it [was] impossible for him to conceal it', while at court he 'came quite to high words with others of his countrymen about your Majesty' King Philip.[84] Later, Silva referred to the colonel's efforts on behalf of Spain to 'discover diligently if the Flemish rebels have any understanding here'. Randolph's good faith seems to be confirmed by the details of his conversation with Silva prior to his departure for Ulster to fight Shane O'Neill in 1566. Silva noted that he went 'very discontentedly and against his will', worried once more about lack of supplies and Elizabeth's desire 'for decisive action'.[85] Perhaps the most poignant proof of Randolph's feted military acumen was the accuracy of his prophecy of doom concerning Sidney's 1566 manoeuvres and the establishment of Derry fort, the unravelling of which was hastened by his own death there in November that year.

Both Croft and Randolph seem to have confined their relations with Spain to expressions of good will and kindly disposition. Although Croft received a pension from Philip II, it could be argued that his conciliatory tendencies towards Spain stemmed not only from affection but also prudence. Religious discomfort and regard for previous international connections resulted not in a desire to provoke quarrel but rather an effort to maintain the conditions in political culture that enabled one to hold a *politique* stance. To pick a fight with Spain was to pick a fight not with a kingdom but with an empire which, although technically in financial difficulties, still possessed resources that England could not dream of matching. To hold out the hand of friendship to Philip II could actually be construed as a pragmatic act of patriotism. All that was needed to make such a gesture was an open mind concerning the relationship between England's political interests and the cause of reformed religion internationally. However, there were military men who could not reconcile their chosen relationship with Spain with the continuance of the Elizabethan regime: men such as Thomas Stukeley and William Stanley who had already served the Spanish crown in a military capacity and, like many of their profession, felt alienated from the Elizabethan regime. However, their decision to explicitly adopt the rhetoric and cause of Counter-Reformation Catholicism marked them off from those men

[84] *CSPSp, 1558–67*, pp. 136–7, 228, 407, 540.   [85] *CSPSp, 1558–67*, p. 568.

already cited. In their cases chivalric deportment was replaced by apparent confessional fervour. More fundamentally, the chief similarity between the cases of Stukely and Stanley was that each man had had his ambitions in Ireland frustrated and each chose to read that frustration as a sign that his credit at court was irremediably low – too low for him to ever attain the goals that his talents deserved.

OPPORTUNISM AND CONFESSION

Once he absconded from Ireland in 1570, Thomas Stukeley, already notorious, took up residence as a pensioner at the Spanish court. There he made his living as an avowed opponent of Elizabeth supported by the duke of Feria, Don Antonio de Toledo and other grandees.[86] The Elizabethan regime feared his knowledge of Ireland and were concerned about his continued political connections there. Further to that, his consistent attempts to fit out a naval force, first with Spanish and subsequently with papal support, to invade the sister kingdom were a source of paranoia in Whitehall.

Despite uncertainty about his motives in this enterprise Stukeley successfully carved out a considerable career for himself as a focal point for disaffection against Elizabeth on the Continent in the 1570s. His previous experience fighting in European theatres of war was impressive but somewhat typical. He had served first under the duke of Suffolk at Boulogne in 1544, then with Henry II and subsequently with Charles V. Just as Malby had moved to Ireland under the shadow of a commuted death sentence for counterfeiting, Stukeley arrived in Ulster fleeing both a conviction from the Court of Admiralty for privateering and heavy debts to the crown following the lack of success of his state-sponsored piracy.[87] Stukeley marked himself out from other military men by his audacity and precocity in engaging with espionage and high politics and by his habit for taking immense personal risks. He first attempted to act as a double agent in an Anglo-French context when the duke of Northumberland presided over Edward VI's government; this experiment ended disastrously.[88] Disgraced on both sides of the Channel, he was sent to the

---

[86] Simpson, R., 'Biography of Sir Thomas Stucley' in *The school for Shakespere* (London, 1878), pp. 68–102.
[87] See Elizabeth to Sir Henry Sidney, March 31, 1567, in Thomas Wright (ed.) *Elizabeth and her times*, 2 vols. (London, 1838), Vol. I, p. 246.
[88] In autumn 1552, Stukeley had arrived in England bearing a letter of recommendation from Henry II of France. He then claimed to have information about the French king's plans to take Calais and invade England. The duke of Northumberland, remembering that Stukeley had been a Somerset

Tower for slandering the French king, only gaining release on the accession of Mary. This *curriculum vitae* not only exacerbated both Cecil's and Elizabeth's natural antipathy towards him but also enabled him to appear more useful to the political grandees he courted.

The seeds of Stukeley's alienation from the Elizabethan regime were sown in Ireland and were the fruit of contingency. The first breach in good relations occurred in 1563 when he embarked on a project, following Jean Ribault's example, to explore Florida for the English crown. However, this was merely a cover-up for authorised piracy against French ships off the west coast of Ireland. The extent of his commitment to settling the Americas can be measured by Elizabeth's request that he should be allowed 'bring or send in to any port [in Ireland] any manner of French ships which he shall arrest to our use'.[89] However, despite the blatant nature of Stukeley's piracy, the queen got none of the booty, much of which, it seems, was used to pay his crew, nor did she receive any recompense for the ships and ammunition she had supplied him with. Furthermore Stukeley had exceeded his remit and had harassed Dutch shipping. Political expediency prompted by détente between France and England led to him being brought to trial for his misdemeanours.[90] His standing with Elizabeth never improved, not even after his return to Ireland in 1565, when he went to serve under Sir Henry Sidney and his service was endorsed by Cecil, the earls of Leicester and Pembroke, not to mention Shane O'Neill. Stukeley had been particularly close to Shane during his visit to Whitehall in 1562, having been employed by Robert Dudley and the earl of Kildare to keep the Ulsterman entertained. Shane, on his return home, had requested Elizabeth to send Stukeley to him 'that I might use his aid and counsel against your Majesty's enemies and rebels'.[91] On his arrival in Ireland, Stukeley was employed in negotiations with O'Neill designed to elaborate on the agreement reached with him by Sir Thomas Cusack and the earl of Kildare in 1563. Shane, at that stage,

---

partisan, with the assistance of an understandably compliant Secretary Cecil, ensured that Henry II was informed of Stukeley's supposed treachery. See Simpson (1878), pp. 13–17.

[89] Haynes, S., *A collection of state papers* (London, 1740), p. 401.

[90] Stukeley was not the only convicted pirate who later found a berth in Ireland. The contrast with the case of George Thornton (a military pensioner in Ireland throughout the 1570s and 1580s) was considerable. See *CPR, Eliz. 1560–3*, p. 255 for details of how Thornton raided a French ship 'laden with linen cloths worth £4,000 belonging to merchants of Spain' at Finisterre as well as a Spanish ship off Tenerife in 1560. He received a pardon in 1562. See also *CPRI*, Vol. II, p. 116 for the increase of Thornton's pension in 1587 to 8s a day. He also received 1,500 acres in the Munster plantation 'in consideration of the great charge and trouble which [he] sustained in transporting and planting English people within that province'.

[91] Simpson (1878), p. 40.

was still so powerful that the crown could not conceive of holding Ulster, given its strategic importance, in the absence of a political settlement with him. An important part of whatever agreement might be reached was the replacement of Sir Nicholas Bagenal as marshal of Ireland on his departure from his Ulster properties at Newry, Carlingford and Greencastle. Bagenal was willing to sell his estates to Stukeley, a transaction which Sidney was happy to recommend to Cecil and Elizabeth.[92]

It was at this point that Elizabeth's disapproval of Stukeley was expressed in earnest and Cecil made the queen's feelings on the matter known. His purchase of the marshalship of the army in Ireland was unacceptable. Cecil, whose personal policy agenda prioritised the removal of Shane O'Neill, stated that 'the appointing of [Stukeley] to a place of that trust is lightly spoken of', confiding later that he sympathised with his misfortune 'for there [in Ireland] percase he might have begun to turn upward in fortune's wheel, but here [in England] I think that he shall not be able to stir the while.' Elizabeth's letter to Sidney on the matter baldly referred to the 'general discredit' Stukeley had earned, 'not only in our own realm, but also in other countries' and reminded him that he 'remaineth by bond with sureties answerable in our court of admiralty'.[93] Sidney took this refusal badly, interpreting it as a slur on his political judgement as well as an imposition on the privileges of his office. 'I know no man', he wrote, 'if the queen would have peace with O'Neill, that better could please him; nor no man, if her highness would have war, that would more annoy him.' Furthermore, he asserted his own powers, stressing that the appointment of the marshal 'was and is of the deputy's gift' and had been so even as recently as the administration of Lord Leonard Grey.[94]

In 1567, Stukeley again attempted to gain a foothold in Ireland by buying Sir Nicholas Heron's offices of constable of Leighlin Bridge and Carlow and seneschal of Wexford as well as his lands, notably the barony of Idrone. In 1568, Sir Peter Carew, himself out of favour with Elizabeth, claimed ancient rights of ownership to Idrone, recently discovered on his behalf by the Exeter lawyer John Hooker. Carew's designs on these

---

[92] See J. Hogan, 'Shane O'Neill comes to the court of Elizabeth I' in Séamus Pender (ed.), *Féilscribhinn Torna* (Cork, 1947), pp. 154–70. See also Simpson (1878), p. 40.
[93] See C. Brady, *Shane O'Neill* (Dundalk, 1996), pp. 35–47. For disapproval of Stukeley's candidacy for the marshalship of Ireland and Cecil's obstruction of attempts at a deal with Shane; see Elizabeth to Sidney, March 31, 1568, SP63/16/70, and Cecil to Sidney, March 31, 1568, SP63/16/71.
[94] See Simpson (1898), p. 49 for Sidney's assessment of Stukeley and S. Ellis, *Reform and Revival* (London, 1986), pp. 19–21, for a history of the lord deputy's rights over appointments to Irish offices.

estates tallied well with Sidney's desire to minimise military charges to the queen, as he had made known his willingness to take the expenses of the garrison at Leighlin upon himself. Consequently, Sidney cassed the band and discharged Stukeley. However, in the meantime, Cecil unsuccessfully tried to secure the transfer of Nicholas Heron's offices and possessions to his client Nicholas White, a Palesman lawyer with links to the earl of Ormond. White believed that Stukeley, Carew and Sidney had conspired to exclude him and not only continued a correspondence with Cecil that excoriated Stukeley but also moved against the prodigal locally as well. At around this time, it was reported that Stukeley, during a visit to Enniscorthy in County Wexford in early June 1568 remarked of his queen: 'I set not a fart for her nor yet for her office.' On 7 June, Thomas Masterson, constable of Ferns, a position under the nominal rule of White, charged Stukeley at the council table with conspiring with rebels to levy war against the queen's majesty and her subjects.[95] Stukeley was confined to Dublin Castle from June to October. In March 1570, he sailed from Ireland to Spain under the appearance that he was returning to England to serve against the northern earls.[96] He had had enough obstruction.

There is no reason to believe that Thomas Stukeley's foremost motivation for defecting to Spain was zeal for Catholicism. It is obvious that his opportunities for personal advancement were severely obstructed by official disapproval at the highest level and economic hardship which could not be alleviated given his dislocation from sources of patronage. In short, he was faced with a simple choice: either resign himself to ruin or seek another political context in which he might prosper. Unsurprisingly, he chose the latter. The details of Stukeley's career from here on are well known. When he first entered the Spanish court in August 1570, he received 6,000 ducats from Philip II and was attended on by a retinue and household that cost 30 ducats a day. By 1571, it was widely rumoured that Stukeley was styling himself 'duke of Ireland' and that he was attempting to put together a force that would invade Ireland on behalf of the Spaniards.[97] That year, he was dubbed a knight of the Order of

---

[95] For details of the indictment of Stukeley for provoking the Kavanaghs, see BL Lansdowne MSS, 12 fol. 9; White to Cecil, 10 June, 1569, SP63/28/24; Relation of Richard Stafford's testimony, 10 June, 1569, SP63/28/25.
[96] *CSPR, 1558–71*, p. 380.
[97] *CSPR 1558–71*, p. 381, Stukeley proposed such an invasion of Ireland to Philip II from the beginning of his sojourn in Spain.

The limits of allegiance 117

Calatrava by the Spanish king.[98] However, although all reports seem to indicate that he was given both to insulting Elizabeth and indulging in daring personal bombast during his exile in Spain, in his approaches to the Papacy he was anxious to emphasise his supposed long-standing Catholic credentials despite a wealth of evidence that tended to undermine them.[99] In a letter dated September 1570 to Castagna, the Papal Nuncio in Spain, Stukeley appealed for absolution for his life 'among the heretics ... having dealings with them in matters external, not separating [himself] from their life and society and eating meat on forbidden days'. He was very anxious to deny having sworn allegiance to Elizabeth in any other way than as 'queen and sovereign lady', stressing that although he outwardly conformed to reformed religion, he 'was ever in spirit a Catholic, and kept in [his] heart the faith and religion of the Holy Mother Church of Rome'.[100] He also claimed to have been in league with Catholics in Ireland long before he absconded to Spain and that he had contacted the king in the hope of helping him 'reclaim that kingdom to the Roman Catholic Church'.[101] He moved freely and easily in the world of English Catholic exiles on the Continent, visiting Rome, Lisbon and Brussels during the mid-1570s. He cultivated links with the papacy from as early as 1571. By 1578, he had received a number of Irish titles from Pope Gregory XIII such as 'baron of Ross and Idrone, viscount of the Morough and Kenshlagh, earl of Wexford and Catherlough, [and] marquess of Leinster' and gathered a band of soldiers under his leadership. In Whitehall, an invasion of Ireland was anticipated.[102] Walsingham, for instance, wrote to Hatton explaining official reluctance to refer to Stukeley in any 'proclamation' addressed to the nobility of Ireland in case it might be seen as 'public notification ... of any fear conceived here that so weak an instrument as Stukeley is shall be able to prevail against a prince of her majesty's power, armed with the goodwill of her subjects in that realm, as she doubted not but that she is.'[103] Subsequently, he

---

[98] *CSPR, 1558–71*, p. 381. According to the 'Narrative of Thomas Stukeley's negotiation' Philip II stated that he adopted Stukeley's son as his own and asserted 'that the world shall know how he esteems the father by the regard which he will show to the son' and then dubbed Stukeley a knight.
[99] Deposition of James Rigsby, SP12/80/154ii.
[100] Stukeley also admitted having owned monastic lands, but stressed his desire to re-establish religious houses on them. On his arrival at the Spanish court, Stukeley commenced observing fasts and going to mass. *CSPR, 1558–71* (London, 1916); Castagna to Rusticucci, 24 September 1570, p. 353 and 'Narrative of Thomas Stucley's negotiation', p. 380.
[101] *CSPR, 1558–71*, p. 381, Narrative of Thomas Stucley's negotiation, pp. 380–5.
[102] As early as 1571, papal correspondence was describing Stukeley as 'an English nobleman of the blood royal'. 'Narrative of Thomas Stucley's negotiation' *CSPR, 1558–71* (London, 1916), p. 379.
[103] Walsingham to Hatton, 3 June 1578, BL Add. MSS, 15891, fol. 35b.

perished leading these men in the service of Don Sebastian, king of Portugal, at the battle of Alcazar – far from Ireland, the kingdom he had purported to invade.

In essence, it seems that Stukeley courted Continental Catholicism for his own ends, pursuing a remarkably successful career posing as a disaffected English Catholic soldier. That he died in Morocco should not be surprising. After all, his career had been a catalogue of disparity between stated aim and subsequent action. Rather than exploring Florida, he pursued piracy. Rather than returning to England, he defected to Spain. The skill with which he promoted the enterprise against England by way of Ireland to both Gregory XIII and Philip II not only afforded him a comfortable living but also earned him the means to gain command of troops and military resources which he then employed in a freelance fashion as he wished.

The sincere affection of Sir William Stanley for the 'old religion' seems less in doubt. Stanley was the eldest son of Sir Rowland Stanley of Hooton and Storeton, Cheshire, head of the senior branch of the House of Stanley. His father, a justice of the peace and a former sheriff of Chester, had served as a military captain himself, notably at the Siege of Leith.[104] He came under suspicion of being a recusant in 1583, so William was probably raised as a Catholic. Following his schooling in the late 1560s and service in the household of his aristocratic relative Edward Stanley, third earl of Derby, Stanley pursued a military career, serving until 1570 with the duke of Alva during his coercive governorship of the Netherlands. It is impossible to know how the confessional tendencies Stanley received in his youth tallied with his actions against the reformed rebels of Flanders.[105] However, on his return to England from the Low Countries, Stanley showed himself to be first and foremost a soldier seeking employment under the crown, opting to serve as a captain in Ireland. He remained there for fifteen years, first coming to particular prominence in the 1579 campaign against the earl of Desmond. Lord Justice Sir William Pelham, who had once served with his father, dubbed Stanley a knight at Waterford that year in recognition of his service in engagements at Youghal, Monasternenagh and Adare. Subsequently, Stanley was central to the suppression of Viscount Baltinglass's rebellion

---

[104] *CSPSc 1547–63*, p. 393, where Sir Rowland Stanley is numbered as one of those picked to take part in the second assault on the castle of Leith.

[105] Wark, K. R., 'Elizabethan recusancy in Cheshire', *Chetham Society* (1971), pp. 51, 182; B. Coward, 'The Stanleys, Lords Stanley and Earls of Derby', *Chetham Society* (1983), pp. 145–6.

in Leinster in 1580. He sent Walsingham a vivid account of the rout of crown forces by the O'Byrnes in Glenmalure, and his subsequent ruthlessness against the Gaelic septs of Wicklow became renowned. His torching of Fiach MacHugh O'Byrne's house at Ballinacor and the slaughter of hundreds of Kavanaghs earned him high praise from stalwarts of Walsingham's clientele in Ireland, the vice treasurer Sir Henry Wallop, the president of Connacht Sir Nicholas Malby and the archbishop of Dublin Adam Loftus. Loftus enthused: 'of all the captains in this land I know none that either more wholly hath pursued the rebels or during these broils hath abidden greater extremities', while Wallop tried to anticipate possible objections to his advancement by remarking 'whatsoever he hath done in religion I know not, but now he maketh profession to be a Protestant and thereof giveth good outward testimonies.'[106] Stanley, aware that Walsingham had patronage in the Irish garrison under his thumb, had tried to storm his way into that golden circle and was crestfallen when his efforts brought paltry recompense: he was discharged from office without reward in September 1581. Four months later, he wrote a plaintive letter to Walsingham from his father's house in Hooton expressing disappointment about his discharge, his lack of pay and the unwillingness of his 'friends' to 'perform promises made unto [him] before [his] coming forth of Ireland'.[107]

Stanley's desire to get rich quick during this sojourn in England led him to join a syndicate run by Sir Humphrey Gilbert and Sir Thomas Gerrard that sought to exploit the anxiety of both the Elizabethan regime and its recusants by offering to carve out a settlement for them in the Americas. Martin Frobisher and Sir Richard Bingham were also to be involved, but the project lost momentum, probably because of the fundamental leniency of its approach to Catholicism, and subsequently Stanley took up an opportunity to return to Munster.[108] The earl of Ormond, the military governor of the province during the second Desmond rebellion, appointed him constable of Castlemaine and captain of the garrison at Lismore. At this stage, Stanley had sincerely desired to settle permanently in Munster. In a letter to Walsingham in March that year, he wrote of his plans to make Castlemaine 'a town of English', and he later petitioned unsuccessfully for lands adjoining the manor of

---

[106] Malby to Walsingham, 21 September 1581, SP63/85/52; Wallop to Walsingham, 22 September 1581, SP63/85/58; Loftus to Walsingham, 23 September 1581, SP63/85/59.
[107] Stanley to Walsingham, 17 January 1582, SP63/88/33.
[108] For details of Gilbert's and Peckham's plans, see Quinn (1940), Vol. I, pp. 73–5; Vol. II, pp. 257–60.

Lismore.[109] His troops played a crucial part in the mopping-up operations that brought the rebellion to a close, notably the pursuit and assassination of the earl of Desmond. In March 1584, he unsuccessfully petitioned Burghley and Walsingham for the presidency of Connacht, vacant following Sir Nicholas Malby's death. Despite the failure of this suit, he held important offices in Ireland such as the shrievalty of Cork and the reversion of a commission as master of the ordnance. He was also entrusted with politically sensitive positions such as keeper of the peace in Munster during the earl of Ormond's absence and the pro-presidency of Munster while Lord Deputy Perrot's appointee, John Norris, served in Ulster.[110]

Following the suppression of the Munster rebellion and the subsequent partition of the Desmond estates, it became obvious, for reasons both of financial prudence and political stability, that the province would have to be demilitarised. The earl of Leicester's campaign to defend the United Provinces of the Netherlands against Spain was seized upon as a convenient outlet for the redeployment of the queen's soldiers, especially those who were native Irishmen. In March 1586, Stanley, who had accompanied the earl on his initial Dutch foray the previous December, returned to Ireland to levy over 1,000 troops. Crucially, his exclusion from the lucrative Munster plantation left him little option but to continue his military career, despite his role in facilitating the preliminary survey of attainted lands. Although the placing of obstacles in the way of Stanley's career was less personally motivated than it had been in the case of Stukeley, it seemed certain that the Lancashire man had reached the highest level of advancement he could under the Elizabethan regime.[111]

When Stanley brought his band to London to be transported to the Dutch wars, he was already being referred to by some as a Catholic subversive. Gilbert Gifford, a double agent posing as a priest, told the exiled Spanish ambassador, Mendoza, that Stanley was aware of and complicit in the conspiracy associated with Antony Babington which aimed to assassinate Elizabeth and enthrone Mary Stuart with the military assistance of Spain. In mid-August, Mendoza informed Philip II that he hoped Stanley would use his regiment quartered in London to seize the queen's ships, a step that Philip himself described in his annotations to

---

[109] Stanley to Walsingham, 2 March 1583, SP63/100/1; Stanley to Burghley, 25 December 1583, SP63/106/33.
[110] *Fiants*, Vol. II, 4455, 5372. See also R. Bagwell, *Ireland under the Tudors*, 3 vols. (London, 1885–90), Vol. III, p. 135.
[111] MacCarthy-Morrogh, M., *The Munster Plantation* (Oxford, 1986), p. 192.

the memo as 'the most important thing of all'.[112] However, by the time Mendoza had written this, Stanley had already joined Leicester's forces in the Netherlands. In October 1586, Stanley's regiment – with a remarkable show of cunning – took Deventer, the third most important mercantile centre in the Netherlands, with the cooperation of a Protestant party among the magistracy. Leicester showed considerable favour for Stanley by appointing him governor of the city despite the protests of the States General. Furthermore, before his return to England in mid-November, the earl, in a public slight to his deputy Sir John Norris, granted separate commissions to Stanley and Rowland York, captain of the fort at Zutphen sconce, exempting them from obedience to anybody but Leicester.[113] In his capacity as governor of the provinces, Leicester also forbade the council of state from putting aside any of his appointees to the government of towns or forts.[114]

By December, the burghers of Deventer were complaining to the Dutch council of state about Stanley's autocratic conduct as governor. They alleged that he had violently seized the keys of the city's gates, infringed their liberties and, through his soldiers' constant menacing of the population (the council of state told Stanley that 'la rudesse des soldatz cause deffidence et dégoust des bourgeois')[115] and firm hold of all fortifications, kept the city in the grip of a reign of terror, all the time exceeding the authority of his commission which had been established 'in accordance with the laws and privileges of the Low Countries and the treaty with her majesty'.[116] It was further rumoured that Stanley's Irish troops were in league with Catholics within the walls to give the city over to the Spanish garrison at Zutphen.[117] Stanley, however, explained his conduct as the severity required to ensure his men received victuals from

---

[112] Bernardino de Mendoza to King Philip, 13 August 1586, *CSPSp 1580–1586*, pp. 603–8.
[113] Wilkes to Hatton, 24 Jan. 1587, *Correspondentie*, Vol. II, p. 65.
[114] Camden, W., *The history of the most renowned and victorious Princess Elizabeth*, ed. W. MacCaffrey, (Chicago, Ill., 1970), p. 218.
[115] Which translates as 'The roughness of the soldiers alienates and disgusts the townspeople'.
[116] Council of state to Stanley, 3 December 1586; council of state to Stanley, 8 December 1586; Wilkes to Leicester, 9 December 1586; Wilkes to Stanley, 9 December 1586, *Correspondentie*, Vol. I, pp. 290, 305, 312, 316. Wilkes admonished Stanley reminding him that 'the means of obtaining the late possession of the town grew by them that are now in office who being of the religion and well affected to his excellency's government wrought his entry into the same . . . I know His Excellency would never suffer any governor out of the cautionary towns to possess the keys of the gates of any town'.
[117] Wilkes to Stanley, 18 December, 1586, *Correspondentie*, Vol. I, p. 341. Wilkes informed Stanley of the council of Gueldres and Zutphen's allegations that 'a lieutenant of some English company at Deventer hath had access to the enemy at Zutphen and that the Irish of your regiment – being for the most part papists, as it is supposed – do enter into very straight league with the papists of

the disobedient Dutch. He also dismissed as humbug rumours that his soldiers had 'demanded a church to say mass in'.[118] Matters came to a head on 28 January 1587 when Stanley handed Deventer and the most part of his garrison over to Juan Baptista de Taxis, the Spanish governor of Zutphen.[119] On the same day, Rowland York gave the fortifications before Zutphen over to the Spaniards. These actions nullified at a stroke the gains made by Leicester's recent campaigning.[120] Overijssel and Utrecht were wide open to the Spaniards. Philip Sidney had died in vain.

The court received this news with alarm and an intense feeling of betrayal. Leicester was subject to understandable recriminations from the Dutch because he had nominated Stanley as 'a very fit man to take the charge of all the English forces' and was even deaf to their warnings about York's 'former perfidious dealings', allegedly stating that he, Leicester, 'would undertake for his fidelity as for [his] brother'.[121] Stanley's alienation, it was suggested, had not been warranted. Thomas Digges, the mathematician and Leicester client, put the betrayal down to 'ambitious grudges'.[122] However, his father Sir Rowland Stanley remarked in 1590 that his son had always thought himself an outsider, believing that Walsingham was against him and that Leicester had been displeased with him, but, far from endorsing his son's conduct, he put it down to 'brainsick rashness'.[123] Leicester, in 1587, perhaps to cover his own culpability, said that Elizabeth had been willing to entrust 'whole kingdoms' to the traitor, an indication that Stanley might at some stage have been deemed a suitable candidate to become lord deputy of Ireland. Henceforth, however, the privy council in London and the Irish council in Dublin feared that Stanley and his men, like Stukeley and his troops at an earlier time, 'over well acquainted with the service and state of [Ireland]', might return and undermine England's hold on the country on behalf of Philip II.

Deventer'. He warned him 'to have a careful eye to your Irish people that they neither deceive you or offend those that are well affected within the town'.

[118] Stanley to Wilkes, 14 December 1586, *Correspondentie*, Vol. I, p. 331.
[119] See Wilkes to Leicester, 24 January 1586, *Correspondentie*, Vol. II, pp. 60–2, for an account of Stanley's 'great joy and courtesy' at the hand-over.
[120] *Correspondentie*, Vol. II, p. 86. York's role in the whole affair was important. His apparent increasing attachment to the Catholic faith, indicates that Stanley and himself had found a shared goal in handing over Deventer and the Zutphen fortification to Taxis. Their motives may have been different, however.
[121] Wilkes to Leicester, 24 January 1587, *Correspondentie*, Vol. II, p. 63.
[122] Digges, T., *A breife and true report of the proceedings of the Earle of Leycester for the reliefe of the towne of Sluce* (London, 1590) sig. A2, v.
[123] Sir Roger Wilbraham to Burghley, 10 May 1590, SP63/152/19. Wilbraham had met Rowland Stanley 'at the seaside in Wales'.

Stanley himself stated that 'in Ireland [he would] open such a game of war as the Queen [had] never seen in her life'.[124]

Stanley, like Stukely before him, found a warm welcome among the English Catholic exiles based in Flanders, notably Cardinal William Allen. In 1587, Allen published an *apologia* for Stanley's conduct that aimed at inducing other English captains to follow his example. He shied away from using a confessionalist defence that might have stressed the redundancy of any Protestant political claims by virtue of heresy alone but instead opted to use orthodox thinking on the just war. Consequently, he argued that Stanley ceded Deventer to the Spaniards because he believed it rightfully belonged to King Philip. Stanley, in effect, had been merely doing justice by giving the Spanish king his due. Therefore, England's war in the Netherlands was, *ab initio*, unjust, and any soldier participating in it on Elizabeth's side, Allen asserted, was guaranteed that his soul was in mortal sin. The Cardinal calculated that appeals to the integrity of the one true Catholic faith against the errors of reformed religion would have less effect on soldiers than references to the traditional teachings of Christendom on licit and illicit reasons for waging war. London countered with a pamphlet that accused both Allen and Stanley of bad faith and asserted the justice of England's involvement in the conflict.[125] Rumours also abounded that the English government had already sought to eliminate Stanley by covertly poisoning him.[126] Certainly, his continued existence haunted them in much the same way as Stukely's had once done. In 1594, John Carey, chamberlain of Berwick, even reported that Stanley had turned up in Aberdeen as an ambassador with power to offer James VI 10,000 crowns a year if he would declare liberty of conscience in Scotland.[127]

But if Stanley found himself to be the bogeyman of Elizabeth's regime and feted by English Catholic exiles, he was disappointed by the lukewarm treatment he received from the Spaniards. He went to the Spanish court, hoping to receive adulation and greater military responsibilities. However, he received little favour, and, ironically, there are indications that the Spaniards held Stanley's defection to be shameful, despite the

---

[124] *Correspondentie*, Vol. II, p. 86; *CSPI, 1586–8*, pp. 250–1 266; Bagwell, (1890), Vol. III, p. 162.
[125] *A copie of a letter (written by) W. Allen concerning the yeelding of Daventrie* (Antwerp, 1587). The English rejoinder was entitled *A brief discoverie of Doctor Allen's seditious drifts* (London, 1588).
[126] See *CSPSp, 1587–1603*, pp. 239, 355, 576, 606, 626.
[127] See especially John Carey to Burghley, 10 August 1594, *Cal. Bor. 1560–94*, ed. J. Bain (Edinburgh, 1894), pp. 543–4. See also the letter of Tucher Parkins, lieutenant of Captain Clifford to Sir Henry Bagenal, 24 April 1592, SP63/164/24i for fears that a soldier in Ireland, George Cowell, was a spy reporting to both the duke of Parma and Sir William Stanley about the state of Ireland.

benefits that resulted from it. It was alleged that Stanley had been unarmed and unhorsed in Seville by Spaniards who 'reviled him for his lewd doings toward his prince'.[128] Philip II even refused to place his garrison under the direct assistance of the Spanish treasury, thereby making it difficult for Stanley to recruit more troops and pursue a successful career as a military captain. Some of the Irish soldiers who had defected with him thought better of it and received pardons from the crown in 1593 on the basis that they had been 'innocently . . . forced' into disloyalty.[129]

The remainder of Stanley's career consisted of attempts to make himself useful by proposing ways and means of invading or menacing England.[130] Following the death of Elizabeth and the accession of James I of England, the Treaty of London made all Stanley's plans for harrying England obsolete. In the aftermath of the Gunpowder Plot, he was accused by his former standard-bearer, Guy Fawkes, of continuing to harbour designs to invade England. To placate James, Stanley was arrested by the authorities in Brussels. Within a year, he was freed, exonerated from all charges and excluded from the subsequent act of attainder decreed against the conspirators. For the remainder of his life, Stanley settled into the role of governor of Malines and turned to religious matters, becoming a key figure in the foundation of the Jesuit novitiate in Liege. James Wadsworth, in his anti-Jesuit polemic *The English Spanish pilgrime*, provides a vignette of the elderly captain meditating on the repercussions of his decision to throw in his lot with Elizabeth's foes. He relates that in 1624 Stanley had to go 'cap in hand' to counsellors at the Spanish court to get a pension six years in arrears. Wadsworth further alleged that when Stanley finally got his money from the king, a Spanish Jesuit deceitfully took it from him. As a result, Stanley shunned the Society of Jesus in old age, choosing rather to enter the Carthusian community at Ostend. Quite poignantly, Stanley told Wadsworth 'that if his Majesty [James I] would grant him pardon, and leave to live the rest

---

[128] William Lyon, bishop of Cork, to Geoffrey Fenton, 17 December 1587, SP63/132/46I.
[129] *CPRI*, Vol. I, pp. 255–6. The eleven Irishmen pardoned had been given passports to return to England by Sir Francis Vere, the commander of the English troops in the Netherlands.
[130] In 1591, Stanley proposed an invasion of Alderney, and in 1597 he hoped that his regiment might be used to raid England from Dunkirk. Subsequently he attempted, with others, to secure Spanish approval for setting up an English court in exile in Flanders centred on the infanta that would champion her claims to the English throne. For English trepidation about Stanley's rumoured invasion plans see the intelligence report on Stanley, July 1589, SP12/225/51 and N. Strange's letter to Walsingham, 11 May 1590, SP12/232/17.

of his days in Lancashire with beef and bag-pudding' he would be supremely happy.[131] He died in Ghent on 3 March 1630.

Opinion about William Stanley was polarised following his surrender of Deventer to the Spanish. Again, it was unclear whether he was following the dictates of his conscience in this matter or reacting pragmatically to short-term privation. The same questions arose concerning his subsequent plots against the English crown, which could either be interpreted as expressions of pure ideology or as shrewd and cynical bids for financial and social preferment. It has been suggested that Stanley was particularly obsessed with the claim to the English throne of his relative Ferdinando Stanley, Lord Strange, later earl of Derby, grandson of Mary, the sister of Henry VIII.[132] But, as Cardinal Allen's polemic indicated, Stanley might have had strong opinions about the legitimacy of the territorial rights of princes. Certainly, during his service in Ireland, he believed that the brutal suppression of the Desmond rebellion was just retribution for those seeking to overthrow Elizabeth I, the legitimate monarch of Ireland. Despite these uncertainties, given that both his brothers were Jesuits, it is likely that Stanley did feel more comfortable, both spiritually and politically, in the confessionalist Catholic camp, although his ambitions for promotion were frustrated there quite as much as they had been in Elizabeth's service and left him permanently exiled from his homeland.[133]

In conclusion, one does not have to search far for evidence that many English military officers' loyalty to the Tudors was fragile. And, given the profusion of bewildering and ultimately inscrutable spying initiatives that involved martial men, it seems that both the Elizabethan regime and its enemies had identified the captains as a constituency of people, formerly commanders in an imperial or French interest, who could be turned. Their disaffection about their allotment of patronage, advancement and respect was well known; furthermore, their circumstances and prospects had seemed better when they had served in the service of foreign monarchs.

Notwithstanding the invocation of chivalric, *politique* or confessional justification for approaches made to foreign princes, each communication

---

[131] Wadsworth, J., *The English Spanish pilgrime* (Amsterdam, 1970), first published 1629, pp. 68–9.
[132] Adams, S., 'Stanley, York and Elizabeth's Catholics', *History Today*, July (1987), pp. 45–50. See *A golden mirrour containing pithy and figurative visions* (London, 1589) sigs. Ciii, v–C iv, v for a poem in honour of Ferdinando, Lord Strange which commended him as 'A man so fixed and firm and faith / That never yet did change'; indubitable praise of his supposed status as a stalwart of the 'old religion'.
[133] Adams (1987), pp. 45–50.

made, whether sincere or merely espionage-related, was evidence that there was a known gap between the respect and worship Elizabeth demanded of her subjects and the actual attitude of military officers towards her: religious commitment in so far as it was ever articulated, it appears, was usually alluded to so that their progress towards wealth and honour would be facilitated and not hindered. Each approach, even if made in the service of the regime, was, in many ways, as much an insult to her majesty as any of the ribald statements attributed to Perrot and Stukeley. However, during the first thirty years of Elizabeth's reign, this discontent did not seriously destabilise her government. This was due to two major factors. First, there was no proximate or plausible native male alternative to Elizabeth who could provide strong oppositional leadership for frustrated martial men: Robert Dudley, the earl of Leicester, who held influence over many military clients, was a courtier first and a leader second. His later attempts to secure royal support for an expedition to the Netherlands in the late 1570s showed that while he could attempt to move the queen to consider policies, projects or preferments that might ameliorate the lot of soldiers, by no means could he wrest such privileges, or the means of producing them, from her. Ultimately, Dudley's power was entirely reliant on Elizabeth's authority and sufferance. Second, Ireland provided an outlet for the social, political and economic dissatisfactions of captains. However, as we shall see, it was there, where they served as agents of crown government in an often hostile environment, that they found that they were dependent on their queen's authority to underwrite whatever power they could exert and whatever status they could claim. In such a situation, to undermine their monarch meant to undermine their own power.

CHAPTER 4

The captains and the Irish context

When considering English government in Ireland during the Elizabethan period, the metaphor of 'the state as a work of art' seems the least appropriate one to use. From the crown's perspective, Ireland resembled a hopelessly cluttered desk covered with remnants of pieces of work started once upon a time but subsequently abandoned, sometimes abruptly, sometimes gradually. While England had achieved a strong framework of government complete with regnal solidarity, a wealthy nobility and a confident juridical identity, Ireland seemed a place of confusion, a place where generalisations were irritatingly useless, a place where micro-diplomacy mattered more than grand design.[1]

THE FAILED CONQUEST

The English crown's constitutional claim over Ireland, based on the papal bull *Laudabiliter* of 1155, had begun in earnest from the moment Henry II of England had taken up his lordship of Ireland in 1171 coming in on the harvest of the original English *conquistadores*, Strongbow, Robert Fitz-Stephens and Hervey de Montmorency. Many of the Irish kings preferred to submit to him in the hope of outmanoeuvring the first invaders.[2] Subsequently, the English influence in the country spread far and wide,

---

[1] For the differences between the constituent polities and peoples of Britain and Ireland in the medieval period see R .R. Davies's Presidential Address on 'The Peoples of Britain and Ireland, 1100–1400' in the *Transactions of the Royal Historical Society* sixth series, 4 and 5.

[2] The usual, but avowedly partial, account of the conquest is related in Giraldus Cambrensis's *Expugnatio Hibernica* ed. A. B. Scott and F. X. Martin (Dublin, 1978). Those who submitted included the Munster princes Mac Carthaig, king of Desmond, Ua Briain, king of Thomond, Ua Mathgamna of Uí Fáelain, Mac Gilla Pátraic of Osraige; Leinster potentates such as Ua Tuathail Of Uí Muiredaig and Ua Cathasaig as well as those from Connacht and Ulster, Ua Ruairc of Bréifne and Ua Cerbaill of Airgialla. There has traditionally been some controversy about the terms under which the high king Ruaidrí Ua Conchobair submitted. F. X. Martin concluded that Ua Conchobair had merely done fealty to Henry II, rather than *foi et homage*. See *NHI* (Oxford, 1993), Vol. II, pp. 89–90.

disrupting the Irish septs, turning many of them out of their territories, engulfing them using technologically superior military might. When the country was divided up among a limited number of English families – descendants of the original conquering families as well as subsequent beneficiaries of royal favour (henceforth described as English-Irish) – much landed wealth came to be held by a few, content to feather their nests rather than invite new English colonists in. Rather than plough its Irish revenues back into the colony, the English crown often employed this wealth to harry Scotland and secure Gascony and Wales. After a century, the Irish, few of whom had any rights under English law, slowly began to reassert themselves, augmented by Scottish mercenaries, thereby unsettling the young English colony in the west and north. By the early fourteenth century, the Gaelic *revanche* was deemed so total that the Scottish king Robert Bruce and his brother Edward tried to wrest Ireland from the English crown. In 1317, certain of the Irish septs took the opportunity to appeal to the papacy to annul English sovereignty over Ireland. They argued that the terms of the papal grant had been dishonoured.[3]

Although no lasting constitutional change arose from these developments, discord, disease, dearth and dynastic fragility eviscerated the strength of the English-Irish community and placed many manorial settlements throughout the country under unbearable strain. Plague weakened the economy of the English towns of Ireland, and internecine strife among the English magnates sapped the already doubtful efficacy of crown government throughout the country. A particularly harsh blow was the death of William de Burgh, lord of Connacht and earl of Ulster, the largest single landowner in Ireland, who in 1333 was killed by his tenants, leaving no male heir – only Elizabeth his infant daughter, who was subsequently married to Lionel, duke of Clarence. The instability that resulted allowed the O'Neills and the Clandeboy O'Neills to establish themselves as resurgent powers in Ulster, counterbalancing the O'Donnells of Tír Conaill. Even Dublin, the crown's administrative hub, was menaced by the resurgent Irish septs of Leinster that bordered it to the south: the O'Byrnes, O'Tooles and the MacMurrough Kavanaghs. Throughout

---

[3] For the text of the 1317 'Remonstrance of the Irish Princes' see S. Duffy, *Robert the Bruce's Irish wars* (Stroud, 2002), pp. 179–86. As a counterweight James Lydon has also highlighted the famous statement by the court poet of the O'Maddens describing the descendants of the English colonists as 'our own foreigners' claiming that 'the old chieftains of Erin prospered under those princely English lords who were our chief rulers, and who gave up their foreignness for a pure mind, their surliness for good manners, and their stubbornness for sweet mildness, and who had given up their perverseness for hospitality'. See *NHI*, Vol. II, p. 301.

the country, Gaelic-Irish and minor English-Irish families took advantage of the opportunities open to them and forcibly took up possession of lands. In this mêlée, three English-Irish dynasties in particular came to the fore: the Butlers in the midlands, the Fitzgeralds of Desmond in southern Munster and the Fitzgeralds of Kildare, just west of Dublin; the two latter dynasties were known as the Geraldines. From the crown's point of view, the most important effect of these changes was that legal title to land in Ireland, under English law, increasingly bore no relation to actual occupancy of that land.[4]

From the crown's perspective, Ireland – a potentially very useful source of revenue – had fallen beyond its reach. This fact became particularly tantalising once Edward IV ascended the throne in 1461. By virtue of his descent from Philippa, the daughter of Lionel, duke of Clarence and Elizabeth de Burgh, Edward was the holder of the Mortimer inheritance: the earldom of Ulster, the lordship of Connacht and the lordship of Trim – territories that remained part of the crown estates after the Tudor succession.[5] Ireland, of course, could also prove a potential threat, having played a significant part in the civil disturbances of fifteenth-century England, characteristically causing dynastic instability and equally characteristically lacking due readiness to demonstrate loyalty. The punctuation that Ireland had provided to England's dynastic narrative had been significant: Henry Bolingbroke's momentous return to England in 1399 took place while Richard II was campaigning in Ireland, while in 1459 Henry VI's rival, Richard of York, the heir presumptive and lord lieutenant of Ireland, retreated to his power base in Ireland, rallying the lordship's parliament behind him in defiance of the English parliament. Despite considerable tensions in the 1460s, the mainstay of the English-Irish aristocracy, the Geraldines, especially the House of Kildare, remained Yorkist partisans even after the battle of Bosworth had brought Henry Tudor to the throne. The eighth earl of Kildare, Gerald 'Mór' Fitzgerald supported Lambert Simnel in 1487 and recovered from this faux pas only to aid Perkin Warbeck in 1491. In short, Ireland could be a fatal distraction for an English monarch, but ignoring it altogether could prove as costly; furthermore, the prospect of a resumption of control of Ireland, and the restoration of the crown estates and reignition of royal

---

[4] See W. F. T. Butler, *Gleanings from Irish History* (London, 1925) especially pp. 195–249 for his analysis of the policy of 'surrender and regrant'.
[5] See Henry VIII to Lord Deputy St Leger, 5 July 1542, *SP Hen*, Vol. II, p. 294, where he tells the viceroy that Conn Bachach O'Neill, can have any title bestowed on him *except* 'earl of Ulster'. Conn was eventually made first earl of Tyrone.

prerogatives throughout the country seemed not only to be lucrative but also potentially politically remunerative.

By the mid-fourteenth century, the English population of Ireland had long since splintered into a plurality of interests, some of which clashed with each other. In Connacht, for instance, the collateral branches of the Burkes, the MacWilliam Íochtar and MacWilliam Uachtar, along with families such as the Jenkinses and Nangles were distant from the English cultural aspirations of the Pale gentry of Meath and legal administrators of crown government. Their autonomy from crown control was signified by their adoption of many aspects of Irish cultural, legal and administrative practices. They also occasionally harboured a strong sense of alienation from the metropolis. The Fitzgeralds of Desmond, for instance, had become especially disaffected with royal government since the summary execution in 1468 of the eighth earl of Desmond, by Ireland's lord chancellor John Tiptoft. The Butlers of Ormond and the Fitzgeralds of Kildare, holders of sizeable landed wealth, remained nominally within the orbit of royal authority but fell in and out of favour with the crown throughout the late medieval period. The enmity between the Butlers and the Geraldines, which gained a particular edge in the sixteenth century, became the basis of political organisation in Ireland; both Gaelic-Irish and English-Irish notables throughout the country were usually allied to either one or other of these two magnates. The English-Irish gentry of the Pale in turn were split (very roughly) into three groups: the landowners of rich holdings in Meath and Kildare (for example Barnwell of Trimlestown and the Plunketts); the marcher lords such as the Eustaces of Baltinglass, the Daltons, and the Nugents; and the mercantile community and magistracy of Dublin and Kilkenny as well as those other pockets of English-Irish settlement around the country, in Lecale in Ulster, for instance, as well as in the royal towns such as Youghal, Galway and Limerick. What united these groups was the understanding that they were 'English', although what this meant to each of them in terms of aspirations, political practice and attitudes to the Irish is sometimes difficult to determine.[6]

By the sixteenth century, the population of wonted English-Irish areas had become increasingly heterogenous. Statutes indicate that the amount of men of Gaelic-Irish background in royal towns or the Pale who were taking up denization as English subjects was considerable, and Steven

---

[6] See V. Carey ' "Neither good English nor good Irish": bilingualism and identity formation in sixteenth century Ireland' in H. Morgan (ed.), *Political ideology in Ireland, 1541–1641* (Dublin, 1999), pp. 45–61.

Ellis has noted the frequent issuing of grants of English liberty to Irish merchants and traders.[7] Many of these – ethnically Gaelic-Irish – were almost seamlessly integrated in the economy and society of the Pale as individuals outside of the septs of Gaelic Ireland, but they were always liable to come up against disqualifying legislation in civil and ecclesiastical matters to do with holding lands or benefices. As a result they could buy a charter of 'English liberty', sales of which, no doubt, were a good source of revenue for the administration. Furthermore the eighth earl of Kildare's expansion of the Pale had established new border lands which were often populated by Gaelic-Irishmen of low status, autonomous of the septs, who may have been less particular about upholding their rights against ad-hoc exactions than the English-Irish yeoman population might have been. For those who placed such a premium on the ideal of 'English liberty', the spectacle of Gaelic-Irish settlers gladly paying protection money for Kildare's defence may have seemed like 'scabbing'.[8] By the late fourteenth century, Dublin and its hinterland relied on the might of the earls of Kildare for protection. On top of the viceregal retinue, which was his entitlement, he was assisted by the 'rising out' of the men of the Pale and the Fraternity of St George, but most controversially he installed a band of gallowglass (the martial descendants of Scottish mercenaries) and hired kern (Irish foot soldiers) in the Pale, who were to be paid by way of those notorious exactions known as coign and livery, precisely the type of arbitrary exaction that Palesmen associated with the plight of the oppressed 'gentleman' and the unfree in Gaelic society and the lot of those who laboured under the despotism of the English-Irish magnates in Connacht and Munster.[9]

---

[7] The form of a charter of denization usually ran: 'AB and all his issue (born and to be born) shall be of free estate and condition and free of all Irish servitude, shall answer and be answered in all courts of Ireland, shall use and enjoy English law in all respects in the same way in which Englishmen in the king's land of Ireland use and enjoy it, shall have power freely to acquire lands, tenement, and possessions and also goods and chattels and to dispose of them at their will and to succeed to them as the English do in the aforesaid land of the king and to accept church benefices as well in cathedrals and collegiate churches as elsewhere, their Irish condition (or any statute or ordinances) notwithstanding'. See Art Cosgrove in *NHI*, Vol. II, pp. 551–6 and S. Ellis, *Reform and revival: English government in Ireland, 1470–1534* (Woodbridge, 1986), pp. 128–30.

[8] Ellis notes that 'the fine for a charter of English liberty was commonly 6s 8d or 13s 4d at this period depending on status'. See *CPRI*, Vol. I, p. 39 for grants of English liberty to Thady Coffe of Bishopstown, Charles O'Conor of Clonnenade, Hubert MacFerrys of Glanconghour, Owen O'Morran of Mountfernan, James O'Daly, clerk, Thomas Whelan of Waterford, mariner, William O'Lawler, chaplain, Maurice Byrne of Slane, yeoman, John O'Mulryan, clerk, Abbot of Wothny, Patrick O'Connolan, husbandman, Thomas O'Rourke of Kilmake, chaplain, etc.

[9] Ellis (1986), pp. 49–66.

Within the Pale, the period of Irish history from the beginning of the sixteenth century to the accession of Elizabeth was marked by a persistent dispute over what the central organising principle of Ireland's government should be. There was a tension within the local polity between the demands of magnate rule, notably the requirement to support its retinues, and the aspiration for an independent administration, aloof of seigneurial influence, which would operate according to immaculately observed English legal norms. Some influential members of the county community of the Pale hankered after this vision. They feared that parliament, courts and English law were in mortal danger of being engulfed by the single-minded drive by the House of Kildare to maintain and expand its power. The way they expressed this fear sometimes had an ethnocentric flavour, because the form that the power of the English-Irish magnates took in Ireland was deemed to be an echo of compatible power structures and wonted practices of governance in Gaelic-Ireland: this, it was argued, was a sign of degeneracy. Less idealistically, it was apparent that whatever happened, the constitutional structures established in English-Ireland were likely to remain (in some form or other) as the organising principle of government in Ireland, but Gaelic-Ireland remained a burgeoning reversionary culture, a vigorous system, which offered sensible practices and handy solutions for those English-Irish magnates who wished both to exert and maintain their power in the country and to fix jurisdictional problems to their own advantage.

Gaelic-Ireland was not in decline: it was a vigorous and pragmatic, if structurally fragmented, political culture where, as Katharine Simms has put it, 'legitimate ownership and legitimate authority ... was not traced to a recorded contract, but was founded on physical force and to a lesser extent on immemorial tradition'.[10] Although there was commonly a strong and proud attachment to the idea of the ethnic superiority of the *Gaeil* in Gaelic-Irish culture as well as a unitary idea of Ireland as the home of the *Gaeil*, this did not galvanise any adamant Gaelic-Irish solidarity in opposition to the *Gaill* ('the foreigners', that is to say, the descendants of the medieval English colonists; post sixteenth-century

---

[10] See the conversation which allegedly took place between Sir Murrough Ne Doe O'Flaherty and his 'learned counsellor' Lynch about his right to hold certain lands. Lynch advised the chieftain that 'for form of law he must make his title', and O'Flaherty replied 'What is that? ... Why man! I got it with the sword, what title should I say else?' 'Summary of rebellion in Connacht by Captain John Merbury', 1 August 1589, SP63/146/2. For essential treatments of Gaelic-Irish culture and society see, Katharine Simms *From kings to warlords* (Woodbridge, 1987); K. W. Nicholls *Gaelic and Gaelicised Ireland in the Middle Ages* (Dublin, 2003); Marc Caball *Poets and politics: reaction and continuity in Irish poetry, 1558–1625* (Cork, 1998).

English arrivals were generally known as *Saxain*, i.e. 'Saxons'); rather, it provided a sort of rhetoric of disdain apparent in much bardic poetry and facilitated the articulation of the hope for some messianic figure who would deliver the *Gaeil* from their enemies – a motif used widely in bardic poetry and which could be easily exploited by a poet to praise the chieftain of any lineage or sept no matter how unpromising he was. The political unit known as the lineage or sept was, in theory, radically autonomous, led by a chieftain of the name, for example 'the O'Neill' or 'MacCarthy Mór'.

For all this supposed autonomy, the realities of local politics, not to mention wider factional allegiances, might mean that a poorer sept which was militarily weak would be almost totally beholden to a stronger player within the province, or even further afield (for instance, the wonted subordinate relationship of the O'Cahans to the O'Neills in Ulster). Within this political universe, there were great successes and terrible failures; some lineages fared much better than others and were much richer than others. Often this depended on the quality of the sept's landed holdings (the septs of the O'Neills of Ulster and the MacCarthys of Cork, for example, held particularly rich estates), which were, after internal consultation, distributed and redistributed among the grandees and middling sort of the lineage in proportion to genealogical, honorific and pragmatic entitlement. The most emblematic feature of the internal politics of the sept was a continuous process of enforced downward mobility. Kenneth Nicholls has described this process succinctly:

> Gaelic and gaelicised Ireland was characterised by a continuing proliferation of the ruling and other dominant lineages within a stable, or perhaps declining, population, with the result that there was a recurrent process of replacement of the constituent elements of society from the top downwards, as junior branches of the ruling lineages took the place of former chiefly houses and were in their turn supplanted by more recent offshoots, the immediate offspring and kinsmen of the ruling lords. The displaced elements, pushed down the social ladder, would in turn replace their former inferiors and eventually descend into a propertyless bottom layer of the population.[11]

The mode of succession within a lineage (a practice known as 'tanistry' to the English) relied on the designated successor to the chieftainship at any time being the next strongest figure within the pre-eminent kindred of the sept, however that individual's strength was measured, sometimes

---

[11] *NHI*, Vol. II, pp. 397–8.

according to military might and prowess, political acumen or quality of support within the clan. This avoided the power vacuums and instability caused by minorities through the law of primogeniture, although it contributed to internal instability and division as prominent figures within the sept jockeyed for position. Another aspect of Gaelic-Irish practice and process that differed from English common law norms was the use of arbitration rather than trial by jury to determine compensation for a crime. A knock-on effect of this was that in order to get someone to submit to arbitration, the party who felt wronged often had to forcibly seize some of that person's property, be it cattle, land or other goods – a form of action not tolerated at common law. The Gaelic-Irish legal system was not intrinsically ideologically opposed to English custom, but much of its procedure was plainly illegal from an English legal perspective.[12]

Of course, the extent to which a sept could hold its own against external marauders was also crucial; the O'Neills of Clandeboy, for instance, were severely weakened within Ulster once the crisis in the lordship of the isles issued in a threatening influx of MacDonnells on the Antrim coastline. The degree of autonomy that each Gaelic-Irish sept and English-Irish lordship enjoyed brought a corollary: each had to pay for its own defence, which meant that all political units in the country had to fund this military outlay from their own resources. These martial retinues were neither exiguous nor cheap, ranging from troops of 500 strong to 2,000 strong and above.[13] To support these retinues, each polity had to subject its dependants to forms of taxation, and, in turn, each needed to use military force to secure these payments: forms of tribute assessed on townlands of vassal septs, the rising out of troops, the provision of

---

[12] For more on this see Nicholls (2003) for a convincing account of Irish law's adaptability to English institutions and the versatility of the Gaelic-Irish legal profession see N. Patterson, 'Gaelic law and the Tudor conquest of Ireland: the social background of the sixteenth century recensions of the pseudo-historical prologue to the "Senchas már"' in *IHS*, 27 (107) (1991), pp. 193–215.

[13] Even when the MacWilliam Burke lordship was in crisis it was able to muster 'great troops' of up to 600 troops merely to spoil the countryside, see Edward Whyte to Sir Nicholas White, master of the rolls, 20 October 1589, SP63/147/28. See also Malby's assessment of the numbers in the retinues of the Ulster lords. 'A note of the forces waged by the lords in Ulster', 26 November 1579, SP63/70/31i, where he counted 5,800 troops not in crown service in Ulster, i.e. 'Turlough Lenough doth keep and wage in Tyrone only: 1500 footmen, 400 horsemen; Maguire by himself: 400 footmen, 60 horsemen; O'Donnell in Tyrconnell: 1500 footmen, 300 horsemen; The route, Glynns, Clandeboy and Dufferin: 1000 footmen, 200 horsemen; Maghrey, Kilwarlyn and MacCartan's country: 200 footmen, 60 horsemen; MacMahon, without Ferney and Clancarvell: 200 footmen, 100 horsemen; The baron of Dungannon, O'Hanlon, Turlough Brasselagh, Henry Og O'Neill and MacDonnell and his sept for their portion of land on their side the Blackwater: 300 footmen, 120 horsemen; The Fews: 100 footmen; 60 horsemen: Total = 4500 footmen; 1300 horsemen'.

victuals, meat, butter, oatmeal, bed and board for soldiers or the requisition of labourers.[14] These exactions were often represented as immemorial rights affixed to the office of a magnate (famously so in the cases of both the O'Neill and MacCarthy Mór) but, in spite of attempted regularisation enforcement could be patchy, dependent on military capability, internal political stability and an ability to daunt predatory neighbours who might wish to gain sway over potential new contributors to their own burgeoning military budget. English-Irish lords had long found the employment of similar exactions too alluring to pass over; the earls of Desmond, Ormond and Kildare, as well as both lineages of MacWilliam Burke, employed a slew of extortionate taxes, sometimes lumped together – once again – under the title 'coign and livery', practices abhorred by more 'reform-minded' members of the English-Irish community but embraced enthusiastically by the earls of Desmond, Ormond and Kildare.[15] Magnates sometimes vied for and clashed over the right to visit exactions on freeholders who were trying to carve out their own semi-autonomous space. The most famous example of such a conflict of interest was the case of the stand-off between the earl of Desmond and earl of Ormond caused by the former's attempts to get Sir Maurice Fitzgerald of the Decies to pay his dues; this dispute led to the pitched battle at Affane in 1565.

At the time of the defeat of the House of Kildare in 1535, a good proportion of the English-Irish gentry of the Pale felt some satisfaction at the fall of this over-mighty dynasty which, under the eighth and ninth earls, had not only monopolised the office of foremost steward of English rule in Ireland but had also subjected the surrounding area, the Pale, to extortionate exactions to support their military power. The period between 1534 and 1537 – that is, between the inception of the Kildare revolt and the execution of 'Silken' Thomas Fitzgerald and his uncles – not only marked a fundamental change in relations between Ireland and England but also led to internecine strife within the country arising from unwarranted despairs and unreasonable hopes. One of the foremost of these hopes was the Palesmen's anticipation – born out of more than a century's mental rehearsal – that a restoration of the former glories of the medieval colony

---

[14] For a compilation of these exactions as used by the earl of Clancar (MacCarthy Mór) from the crown survey of the lordship, probably taken in 1598, see Butler (1925), pp. 20–1.
[15] Ellis (1986), pp. 56–8. Coign and livery was technically illegal, but could be imposed with the consent of freeholders. For the magnates' employment of coign and livery and their attempts to abandon it see V. Carey, *Surviving the Tudors: the 'wizard' earl of Kildare and English rule in Ireland* (Dublin, 2002), pp. 67–96, 149–50 and D. Edwards *The Ormond Lordship in county Kilkenny, 1515–1642* (Dublin, 2003), pp. 175–8, 180–200.

was nigh. Members of the Pale intelligentsia (mostly lawyers) had, since the beginning of the century, produced a genre of 'reform literature' flagging up this restoration.[16]

For example, the famed 'Panderus' (the Chaucerian nom de plume of a Palesman opposed to the Kildare ascendancy) had written circa 1515, that the 'King's land' should be furnished with crossbows, horses, longbows and material for horsemen, a revitalised militia under the Pale's traditional banner of St George. This was but a portion of his strategy, a panacea entitled 'The state of Ireland and it's [sic] reformation', which had as its aim the assurance that 'all the land is conquest and subdued to the king's obeisance, to do therewith what him list, without any resistance', a remedy for the phantom pains of a down-at-heel English-Irish lordship with expansionist designs.[17] The establishment by Hugh de Lacy of a network of fortifications as far west as the Shannon in the spring of the twelfth-century conquest (the virtues of which were extolled in Giraldus Cambrensis's *Expugnatio Hibernica*) held as strong a hold on the public imagination of the English-Irish intelligentsia of Leinster as lost English sovereignty over much of northern France haunted Henry VIII.[18] During the fifteenth century, much of this area was under the indirect control of either the earls of Ormond and Kildare through factional alliances with Gaelic-Irish chieftains, but this sort of magnate control was not the type of English sovereignty that Panderus wanted. The interests of the English crown and enlightened English-Irish opinion, it was argued, were one and the same. The earl of Kildare's tyrannous exactions needed to be discontinued, exactions which not only beggared the Pale but also endangered the lord deputy's soul, and the souls of his entire Council. Panderus

---

[16] The existence of an 'Anglo-Irish reform movement' has recently been fundamentally questioned by Fiona Fitzsimons in 'Wolsey, the native affinities and the failure of reform in Henrician Ireland' in D. Edwards (ed.) *Regions and rulers in Ireland, 1100–1650* (Dublin, 2004), pp. 78–121. Fitzsimons's analysis posits that the canon of reform writings ascribed to the English-Irish reform movement were not representative of 'an Anglo-Irish reform movement, but an opportunistic attempt by the Butlers of Ormond to gain access to the king and his chief ministers'. Perhaps worthy of note here is the central role that two reformers, Sir Thomas Cusack and Patrick Finglas, played in pushing Lord Offaly, 'Silken' Thomas Fitzgerald over the edge in 1534 by delivering the summons to the Irish Council which provoked the Kildare revolt. Both Cusack and Finglas had held meetings with Thomas Cromwell a month earlier, *L&P*, Vol. VI, p. 514; Vol. VIII, p. 736. Vincent Carey has demonstrated how the Pale gentry benefited from the Kildare attainders, see Carey (2002), p. 69.

[17] 1515 was a year of widespread political opposition to the ninth earl of Kildare's appointment as lord deputy.

[18] See Giraldus Cambrensis (1978) Book II, Chapters 21–3 on Hugh de Lacy and his government over Connacht and Meath.

looked forward to the demise of those English-Irish and Gaelic-Irish magnates who had usurped 'royal' lands, holding them, as he termed it, under 'imperial jurisdiction', a neat gesture to the maxims *rex qui superiorem non recognoscit* and *rex in regno suo est imperator regni sui*. Rather than bribing them to remain tractable, Panderus suggested, their downfall should be secured by military force.[19]

Although he claimed that his plan was a 'new remedy', his insistence that one man from each parish in England and Wales should be sent to populate all Ireland east of the Bann and between Dublin and Wexford stemmed from the desire to imitate the original medieval conquest. This English militia would blaze the king's writ indelibly on all those areas of the country which had once borne its trace. Lands held by the Irishry adjoining the Pale were to be wrested back; the Kildare ascendancy over the Pale would be replaced by the jurisdiction of perpetual justices of the peace drawn from the backbone of the Pale nobility; the formerly disaffected English 'rebels' of Munster and Connacht, the MacWilliam Burkes et al., once free of their Gaelic-Irish neighbours, would resume their loyalty to their lord and king. Significantly, the implementation of the plan would be effected by a military force come from England, a troop of 500 horsemen supported by the king's charge for merely three years in order to give the initiative momentum. The supply of military material and training from England for the Palemen would supplant the voracious retinues of Kildare.

Panderus's influential and much circulated position paper centred its strategy on an appeal to the monarch over the head of the ninth earl of Kildare, offering to tie Ireland closer to the monarch. But, despite the rhetoric, the interests of the English crown and the Pale gentry and mercantile community were not one and the same, and the gap between them got larger and larger as the century passed. Furthermore, it would be wrong to assert that Panderus's jeremiad on the state of affairs in the lordship encapsulated the majority view of the English-Irish community in the Pale, or in Ireland as a whole, although two tracts, both similar in content, one by Patrick Finglas and another by William Darcy, were in circulation at the same time. It could be argued (and, indeed, cloaked rebuttals by Panderus indicate that it *was* argued) that the Kildare

---

[19] *SPHen VIII*, Vol. II, p. 9. According to Panderus, Lecale paid £40 per annum to either O'Neill or O'Neill of Clandeboy (whoever was strongest) as tribute. Meath paid O'Connor £300 per annum, Kildare paid O'Connor £20, Kilkenny and Tipperary paid O'Carroll £40.

supremacy had actually succeeded in advancing the fortunes of English-Ireland, bringing most of Gaelic-Ireland under the oblique military domination of the English-Irish. But, Panderus enquired, had Ireland been gained at the expense of the lordship's Englishness through the violation of English manners and most importantly English law?[20] Looking at it one way, English standards of administration had been adulterated by rapine and peacetime transactions with the Gaelic-Irish. However, it could not be denied that the eighth and ninth earls of Kildare had secured the southern borders of the English-Irish lordship, increased the revenues of the king's government in Ireland and proved the salvation of the English-Irish community in Ireland, leading them out of some very dark days indeed.[21]

Ultimately, the decision of Thomas Fitzgerald, Lord Offaly, son of the ninth earl of Kildare, to resort to arms to secure his dynasty's status and its hold on the viceroyalty was very badly timed; 1534, merely a year after Henry VIII's marriage to Anne Boleyn, saw the passing of the act of succession as well as both the act of supremacy and the treason act in Westminster; in short, metropolitan insecurity and paranoia were particularly high. The rebellion was crushed by the Leicestershire-born Lord Deputy Sir William Skeffington, a commoner (known as 'the Gunner') with a force of over 2,000 soldiers. The crown's military intervention in Ireland in 1534 was far from unprecedented, but, whereas the investment of men and *matériel* had never previously made much of an impact on Irish politics, Skeffington's intervention changed Ireland irrevocably. In the fourteenth and fifteenth centuries, Lionel of Clarence, Roger Mortimer, Richard II, Richard of York, the earl of Worcester, and Sir Edmund Poynings, with armies in tow, had attempted to consolidate the lordship militarily. Early in his reign, Henry VIII, following this tradition, had considered using his 'absolute power' to reform Ireland and provided a force of 500 under the leadership of Thomas Howard, earl of Surrey, lord lieutenant of Ireland, in 1520 to help effect this scheme.[22] The small gains made from this investment, despite three progresses north, west and south and the exiguous provision of local soldiery by both the Gaelic-Irish and English-Irish, showed that more subtlety was needed to crack the Irish nut. There was not even enough revenue for the crown to pay official salaries. On that occasion, Henry had been easily distracted,

---

[20] *SP Hen. VIII*, Vol. II, p. 16. [21] Ellis (1986), pp. 58–66.
[22] See D. B. Quinn's contributions to *NHI*, Vol. II, especially pp. 662–85.

and the country returned to its wonted factionalism. Surrey, resigned to reality, ultimately suggested the reappointment of the ninth earl of Kildare to the deputyship. But, fifteen years later, pragmatism and the pressures of Tudor security had demanded a different approach. Following Skeffington's intervention, the viceroyalty would stay out of Irish hands for the rest of the century. Having participated in bringing magnate power low, anti-Geraldine elements of the Pale community now placed their trust in the crown and feathered their nests, distributing the Kildare lands amongst themselves (the Irish parliament of 1536 backdated the ninth earl's attainder to 1528 in order to facilitate the maximum bonanza of land) and continuing to assume that the crown's interests and their own worked along the same lines.[23] Pro-Geraldine partisans throughout the country felt vulnerable and acted erratically towards the members of the 'king's party' and their own traditional rivals. Having arrived at as near to a tabula rasa as could be secured, the crown endeavoured to recreate Irish politics in a more biddable form, loyal to the monarch, tranquil and settled in its character.

COPPERFASTENING THE NEW DISPENSATION

In the years immediately after the Kildare rebellion, the crown used its army in Ireland to cow the country, less in pursuit of the westward expansion desired by some members of the English-Irish community but rather in the hope of forcing magnates to enter into negotiations with the regime to secure some sort of lasting modus vivendi. Lord Leonard Grey, Skeffington's successor, pursued a starkly martial mode of procedure utilising the traditional strategy of visiting hostings on enemies, by which means he secured submissions from James fitzJohn, thirteenth earl of Desmond, O'Reilly, O'Byrne, O'Connor, O'Flaherty, O'Neill, MacWilliam Uachtar (Clanricard) and MacMahon amongst others.[24] But the issue of these military excursions was stillborn. Grey's successor, Sir Anthony St Leger, no soldier but a gifted and opportunistic diplomat, used his political acumen, aided by a slush-fund of Irish monastic lands, to try and develop some of these policies further.

---

[23] Carey (2002), pp. 40–67, 219–24.
[24] See Grey to Henry VIII, 26 July 1538, *SP Hen VIII*, Vol. III, Part 3 pp. 57–63; O'More's further submission 24 August 1538, pp. 88–90; Grey and Council to Henry VIII, 8 October, pp. 99–102; 'Abridgement of the treaties between Lord Deputy Gray and the Irishry', 2 January 1540, pp. 169–73.

A good deal has been written about the policy initiative most associated with St Leger, later described as 'surrender and regrant'.[25] This pragmatic approach was central to an overall strategy to firmly anchor allegiance to the Tudors in the bedrock of Irish politics and remained procedurally key to the relations of the crown to the Gaelic-Irish to the end of Elizabeth's reign.[26] Its inauguration stemmed from the crown's desire to make the ad-hoc occupancy of land in Ireland by Gaelic-Irish septs or expansionist English-Irish lordships legitimate. In order to make Ireland comprehensible under a unitary system of English law, the crown undertook a policy of regularisation, granting title to lands to both Gaelic-Irish and English-Irish magnates – holding them by knight's service, once they had first surrendered them to the king. The constitutional keystone of this policy was the act of kingly title passed by the Irish parliament in 1541. Henry VIII, previously lord of Ireland, was transformed into king of Ireland, bestowing unto him 'another imperial crown'.[27] This innovation, motivated in part by a pressing need to supersede the previous constitutional orthodoxy – that the king of England held Ireland by virtue of a papal grant – had the effect of statutorily transforming all the Irish, whatever their designated ethnicity, into subjects of the crown: the effect was that everyone was deemed to have 'received' English law and were now free to enjoy its benefits.[28] Although the Gaelic-Irish had frequently and opportunistically acknowledged themselves to be liege subjects of the lord of Ireland in the past, notably during the expedition of Richard II, reality had dictated that they had dealt with the Dublin government most often as independent political agents.[29] The act of kingly title purported to seal the conquest of the country, not by military attrition (there were, at most, only 534 English soldiers in the country at the time) but by the power of statute; Gaelic-Irish magnates were present among the lords at the 1541 Parliament, and, implicitly, this reception of English law

---

[25] See Brady (1994), pp. 14–33, and Bradshaw (1979); Butler (1925), pp. 195–249.
[26] For example, see reference to the 1585 surrender and regrant indentures between Ewer MacRory of Kilwarlin in Ulster and the Crown, *Fiants*, Vol. II, 4649, 4650, between Cú Chonnacht Maguire and the crown, 4809, and those of O'Farrell chieftains in 1587, 5062, 5063, Hubert Burke alias Mac David of Glinsk, County Galway, 5068, and Murrough Ne Doe O'Flaherty, 5120, also in 1587, and of Conor O'Callaghan, County Cork in 1594, 5903, to name but a few.
[27] St Leger to Henry VIII, 26 June 1541, *SPHen VIII*, Vol. II, pp. 304–5.
[28] See B. Bradshaw, *The Irish constitutional revolution of the sixteenth century* (Cambridge, 1979) for an exploration of the implications of the act of kingly title. On the desire to nullify Irish regard for the papal provenance of the Irish lordship, see St Leger and Irish Council to Henry VIII, *SP Hen VIII*, Vol. III, pp. 277–8.
[29] See D. Johnston, 'Richard II and the submissions of Gaelic Ireland', *IHS*, March (1980), pp. 1–20.

heralded attempts to reform the Irish polity.[30] This new emphasis on firm acknowledgement of the jurisdiction of the king meant that henceforward, as had proved the case in England, official indulgence for feudal franchise was diminishing.[31] Surrender and regrant and, later, the composition arrangements of the 1570s became attempts to systematise the relationships between the English monarch and her Irish subjects in such a way as they became a constitutional rubric and not a political matter.

However, this was not entirely satisfactory to some English-Irish elements in the crown administration, who believed the most pressing need to be the security of the Pale and pressed for what was known as the 'reduction of Leinster', because manors bordering Gaelic and Gaelicised areas remained vulnerable to raids and depredations.[32] This demand became particularly marked in 1546 during one of Lord Deputy St Leger's increasingly frequent absences when Sir William Brabazon, operating as lord justice, devastated Laois and Offaly, expelling and dispossessing the O'Mores and O'Conors led by Giollaphadraig O'More and Rory O'Conor. This incursion was the beginning of a policy of refortifying the midlands in a bid to push the Pale westwards. Brabazon not only fortified Daingean fort (later Fort Governor in Philipstown), he established Fort Protector in Laois and even rebuilt Athlone Castle on the river Shannon. The subsequent lord deputy, Sir Edward Bellingham, and the lord lieutenant, Thomas Radcliffe, later third earl of Sussex, established a troublesome

---

[30] St Leger to Henry VIII, 26 June 1541, *SP Hen VIII*, Vol. III, pp. 304–5, St Leger informed the king that 'There was at the same consent two earls, three viscounts, sixteen barons, two archbishops, twelve bishops, Donough O'Brien and the Doctor O'Nolan and a bishop, deputies assigned by the great O'Brien to be for him in the Parliament, the great O'Reilly, with many other Irish captains and the common house, wherein are diverse knights and many gentlemen of fair possessions'. See also 'The names of the Irishemen that been cum unto the Kinges Majestie', pp. 348–50, a list that included Turlough O'Toole, Art Og O'Toole, O'Byrne, the Kavanaghs, Kedagh O'More and his brethren, MacGilpatrick, O'Carrolls, O'Conor, MacGeoghan; the earl of Desmond who answered for Viscount Barry, Lord Fitzmaurice, Lord Roche, the White Knight, the knight of the Valley, MacCarthy Reagh, MacCarthy Mór, Tibbot Burke (of the Clanwilliam Burkes of Munster), O'Callaghan, the O'Kennedys; O'Brien, Donough O'Brien, MacWilliam Burke of Clanricard, the Kellys, O'Conor Sligo; O'Donnell, Maguire, O'Reilly, all the O'Farrells, the MacMahons, Magennis, O'Hanlon. See also the 'Submission of O'Neil', pp. 421–2; and Henry VIII to St Leger and council, 9 July 1543, pp. 471–2, for a list of 'English' titles bestowed on Gaelic-Irish chieftains. For the act itself, see *Irish Statutes at Large* (1786), Vol. I, p. 176.

[31] See S. G. Ellis, *Tudor frontiers and noble power* (Oxford, 1995) for a sustained comparison between feudal lords in Ireland, the north of England and Wales.

[32] See the 1540 'Devyses of your moste humble subjectes for reformatyon of Laynster, and for contynuance of the same' an Ormondist document, which suggested the setting up of a Great Master of Leinster at Ferns Castle who would keep sessions in the province, 'would speak the English tongue, [and] would hear solemn mass for the good estate of Henry VIII, supreme head of the Church of England and Ireland', *SP Hen VIII*, Vol. III, p. 272.

and much resented plantation in Laois and Offaly. So, while Henry VIII's final French campaigns raged and William Cecil diced with death at the battle of Pinkie, opportunities were opening up for English captains in Ireland, filling a set of creatively resuscitated seneschalships, constableships and shrievalties often based in previously abandoned or decayed fortifications of the medieval colony, cheek by jowl with the Gaelic-Irish, securing a country, which, in the context of the international problems of an increasingly evangelical metropolitan government, looked ever more like a liability.

For example, in Wicklow, the three septs, the O'Byrnes, O'Tooles and the Kavanaghs, were each placed under the rule of an English captain backed by wards based in Carlow, Leighlin Bridge and Ferns, which generally numbered between ten and thirty men.[33] The seneschals were meant to take the pre-eminent position in local politics, to ensure that Irish exactions and 'jurisdictions' were stamped out, to round up felons, traitors and other malefactors, and to cross-examine them. Often they had the power to hear and determine causes.[34] They were regularly granted commissions of martial law, which were meant to be employed to excise those elements responsible for cattle raids and spoiling.[35] The range of arbitrary exactions which had been exerted by the Irish chieftains were often transferred virtually unaltered to the seneschal under the title of 'seneschal's fees'.[36]

---

[33] Smaller wards were placed in Monasterevin, Faddan, and Narrow Water Castle in Kildare.

[34] *Fiants*, Vol. II, 1415, A grant to Robert Pypho of Hollywood, County Dublin of 'the office of seneschal and chief ruler of the towns adjoining the Red mountains in the County Dublin and the cross of the same from Baile ne scorne to Imaal'. See also *Fiants*, Vol. II, 1409. For a grant of seneschalsy explicitly excluding a commission of gaol delivery see Vol. III, 5690. To see the semi-judicial procedure of seneschalsy in action see 'The deposition and confession of Donal MacVicar examined on his oath' before John Chaloner and Captain Nicholas Heron, including testimony by Lysagh MacKedagh before Heron 'whom the lord lieutenant sent and appointed to take his examination', 14 January 1561, SP63/3/2.

[35] *Fiants*, Vol. II, 2415. For examples of the institution of seneschals of Irish birth, most of them with competence to hold courts baron, see Henry Cowley, Seneschal of Carbery (1570), 1564; John Bourke, seneschal of the barony of Clare (1570), 1634; Brian MacDermott, seneschal of the barony of Moylurg (1571), 1817; Patrick Savage seneschal of the Savage lands of the Ards (1572), 2090; Conly MacGeoghegan 'chief of his name' seneschal of MacGeoghegan's country, Westmeath (1574), 2415; Richard, earl of Clanricard, seneschal of Clare in Clanricard (1574), 2501; Moyler Burke, seneschal of the barony of Kilmaine, County Mayo (1577), 2981; John MacCoghlan, seneschal of MacCoghlan's country, County Laois (1582), 4024. When trying to comprehend the role of *tánaiste* in English terms the term 'vice-seneschal' was sometimes used, see *Fiants*, Vol. III, 5098 and introduction by K. Nicholls.

[36] See *Fiants*, Vol. II, 1618 for the terms of Thomas Lestrange's 1570 seneschalsy of Dalton's country in Westmeath, where his 'fees' included a payment of 6s 8d yearly from each ploughland, which was not a freehold, with fines for non payment as well as payments from the local septs of Slíocht Mhuiris, the Daltons and the Clan Owens.

As has been well documented and noted by both Nicholas Canny and Ciaran Brady, this pattern of office-holding and garrisoning established in Leinster and in areas which had been part of the medieval colony like Carrickfergus, was extended throughout Ireland, especially under the aegis of the provincial presidencies of Connacht and Munster, which were instituted in the early 1570s with the ambit of expanding crown authority and the rule of English law throughout the country, eliminating seigneurial abuses.[37] In Connacht in the 1570s, wards were established at Roscommon, Athlone, Ballinasloe and Loughrea, while in Munster, the crown established itself militarily at Lismore, Galbally and Cork.[38] In Ulster, the private efforts of Walter Devereux, the first earl of Essex, and Thomas Smith, the bastard son of principal secretary Sir Thomas Smith, to colonise Ulster east of the river Bann between 1571 and 1575 brought some martial captains into Ireland for the first time and gave others, like Nicholas Malby, the opportunity to return to the sister kingdom.

The provincial presidencies were intended, in line with the anglicising agenda of crown policy, to facilitate the decommissioning of the panoply of the arbitrary customs and practices of Gaelic and Gaelicised Ireland. Succession by 'tanistry' was to be discontinued, to be replaced by primogeniture; the retention of large private armies was to be phased out and, of course, the crippling exactions that went with them. There also was an agenda to reform Ireland's political culture. Irish titles such as 'The O'Neill' and 'The Mac William' were to be put aside, in some cases to be replaced with English titles, in others to be merely discontinued. As far as was possible, practicable and desirable, the traditional structure of authority within a sept or English-Irish lordship would be atomised. Freeholders within the lordships would be encouraged to develop an unmediated relationship with the crown, untrammelled by debilitating obligations to a chieftain or lord of the name. All subjects of the crown in Connacht and Munster would be able to use the courts of the provincial councils, which would dispense 'impartial' justice according to English legal procedure and the common law. Rents would be paid to the crown. Lord Deputy Henry Sidney in the mid-1570s, in a bid to make the provincial administrations financially self-sufficient (as much to gain glory as to save the crown expense) attempted to institute the policy known as

---

[37] Canny, N., *The Elizabethan conquest of Ireland: a pattern established, 1565–1576* (Sussex, 1976), pp. 33–44 and C. Brady *The chief governors, the rise and fall of reform government in Tudor Ireland, 1536–88* (Cambridge, 1994), pp. 269–81. See also J. G. Crawford *Anglicizing the government of Ireland: the Irish privy council and the expansion of Tudor rule, 1556–78* (Dublin, 1993), pp. 274–80.
[38] According to the 'Book of Her Majesty's garrison' of June 1579, SP63/69/45.

'composition' in which it was envisaged that in lieu of the wonted private armies of the lordships, a crown force would be placed in each province to be supported by a land tax, the purveyance requirements being commuted to a payment in cash or kind, collected by the officers of the presidency, mostly English captains. The unhappy combination of structural circumstances that had caused so many potentates to skirt personal bankruptcy, to live under the almost unbearable pressure of catering to a multitude of constituencies – the crown, freeholders and swordsmen – were to be disposed of, left to moulder in the dustbin of history. Sir Nicholas White, Palesman and master of the rolls, who masterminded the institution of the scheme in Connacht, described the policy as 'an ingenious enigma or riddle: that all sorts were eased with their bearing, and yet her Majesty's revenue, with the livings of the lords, increased'.[39] Everybody would be a winner – everybody, of course, except the native swordsmen, whose personal experience of downward mobility, already difficult, now threatened to turn lethal. Those not selected to be part of a small seigneurial retinue – that is, the majority – faced extirpation as masterless men, as dangers to public order, unless they managed to turn to subaltern roles in farm labour, which were, of course, *infra dignitatem*.[40]

THE GARRISON AND ITS OFFICERS

The advent of the familiar cast of English captains cited so often in histories of Elizabethan Ireland was staggered over the decades. Some of the more heeled-in officers arrived in the late 1540s and early 1550s: for example, Sir Nicholas Bagenal, knight marshal, based at Newry; Thomas Masterson, constable of Ferns; Robert Harpoole, constable of Carlow; and Francis Cosby who rose from the constableship of Monasterevin in 1555 to become sheriff of Kildare and thereafter seneschal of Queen's County (Laois) and general of her majesty's kern.[41] Those who arrived in the late

---

[39] *Government of Ireland under Sir John Perrot* (London, 1626), p. 84.
[40] See Ciaran Brady (1994), pp. 136–58, 170–200, 216–44 and also Brady 'Faction and the origins of the Desmond rebellion of 1579' *IHS* 22 (1981), pp. 299–315 and Brady 'Conservatives subversives: the community of the Pale and the Dublin administration, 1556–86' in P. J. Corish (ed.) *Radicals, rebels and establishments: Historical Studies* XV (Belfast, 1985), pp. 11–32.
[41] Bagenal is first mentioned in Irish state correspondence in 1542, see St Leger to King Henry VIII SP60/10/86; Masterson, Harpoole and Malby are mentioned in the 'consignation of Leix' of 1556, SP62/1/21. Bagenal, based at Newry on the northern border of the Pale, had been knight marshal under Henry VIII at 6s 8d sterling a day with a sum of over £2 a day to pay a band of (supposedly) thirty-two horsemen 9d each. He resigned from the post under Mary for religious reasons, taking it up again in 1566, see *Fiants*, Vol. II, 809. He presided over the court martial of Ireland. In 1577 he was appointed chief commissioner of Ulster, a sort of proto-president of a crown

1550s included Henry Radcliffe, Cosby's predecessor at Maryborough.[42] Others who came to prominence in the 1560s and 1570s included Sir George Bourchier in the earldom of Desmond; Robert Pypho of Hollywood; Charles Egerton, constable of Carrickfergus from 1579; Warham St Leger in Munster and Henry Harrington, seneschal of the O'Byrnes.[43] They had all either secured a post in Ireland as viceregal clients, like Henry Radcliffe, or had secured promotion within the Irish garrison by virtue of predictable wear and tear within the establishment, like William Piers at Carrickfergus or Edward Moore at Philipstown. They generally received leases of the manors attached to the castles or forts they occupied and often received monastic lands adjacent to the fortifications; in some cases, the fortification had once served as a religious house of some kind. They also, naturally, attempted to amass a portfolio of lands within these areas and further afield when and where they could, being granted commissions of inquisition to seek out concealed monastic lands or lands formerly belonging to the attainted. This allowed them to repeat the pattern of multiple manor holding that had been a salient mark of social differentiation within the ranks of the gentry in England.[44] Like landed

---

administration in Ulster, see *Fiants*, Vol. II, 3021, 4001, From 1582 he held the impost on wines discharged at the port of Carlingford, *Fiants*, Vol. II, 4001.

[42] *Liber Munerum Publicorum Hiberniae* (1834), pp. 119, 127.

[43] All these figures are named as part of the garrison at 31 March 1586. See 'Book of the garrisons', SP63/123/21; George Harvey was in Ireland by 1566, see Harvey to King, clerk of the check, 17 January 1566, SP63/16/15 as was Warham St Leger mentioned in a memo of Cecil's SP63/14/10; Charles Egerton, an acquaintance of Lady Mary Sidney served in the first Desmond rebellion, see Sir Humphrey Gilbert's dispatch of 18 October 1569, to Cecil, SP63/29/67. Sir Henry Harrington, Sidney's nephew, came over in 1574, see Sidney to the privy council, 2 January 1575, SP63/49/2.

[44] For the commission to take inquisitions granted to many martial men such as William Drury, Edward Fitton, Nicholas Bagenal, Henry Colley, Henry Harrington, Edward Moore, Robert Harpoole, William Apsley and Anthony Colcough in 1578 see *Fiants*, Vol. II, 3490. Many lawyers in crown service also received the same commissions. On the acquisition of lands three examples will suffice, Harpoole, on top of his constableship of Carlow, which was worth £20 Irish per annum in 1574 (not to mention the 8d paid by the crown per day for each footman), received the lease of the manor, many appurtenances and lands, as well as eighty four acres of arable land in the town of Carlow at a rent of £23 3s 1d Irish. He also received a lease of the Monk's grange Kilmacgobocke in Laois and its tithes at a rent of 46s 8d Irish in 1577 (this property had previously been leased to the Eustaces of Baltinglass who had acquired it following the attainder of Sir James Fitzgerald) as well as the piecemeal but substantial acquisition of lands in the Laois plantation at a very low rent. Harpoole, in short, did quite well out of his office. Similarly Thomas Masterson, who already had a lease of the Abbey of Ferns and other properties at a rent of £12 7s 10d, received the manor of Cloghamon for £13 6s 8d per annum. Another example is Captain William Collier who began his career in Ulster in the late 1560s, received property at Sroher in County Longford, a spirituality of Cong, adding leases of monastic lands in Longford as well as, ultimately, Cong abbey in County Mayo to his estate in 1571. He also served in Kilkenny under Sir Peter Carew's command in 1569 to the chagrin of the townsmen and held commissions of martial law in the Pale in the mid-1570s, *Fiants*, Vol. II, 2532, 3164, 3294, 3786, 5895, 5896, 6793; 612, 1599, 2838; 1661,

gentlemen in England, the captains were eager to exploit the resources they hoped their Irish properties held for them. Piers's speculations in timber as well as Malby's entrepreneurial description of the potential of the land around Burrishoole, and his 1581 request for a commission for mines in Connacht and Thomond, indicate a natural desire to turn a profit out of their charges.[45]

The numbers that made up Her Majesty's garrison in Ireland were normally small. Ciaran Brady, drawing on research by Anthony Sheehan, has shown how few crown troops were actually stationed in Ireland. Whereas the establishment numbered between 2,000 and 3,000 troops during much of the 1560s, the 1570s saw numbers fall to 1,500 and below. A high point of 6,000 troops was reached during the early 1580s which was subsequently reduced to around 2,000 once more. Later, during the latter stages of the Nine Years' War, troops levels in Ireland rose to 20,000. They were distributed throughout the country and the question of how best to deploy these resources vexed many of the captains. Sir Nicholas Malby was particularly interested in these questions of man management. In October 1579, he proffered an opinion with a map on how best to keep the whole land in due obedience with only 2,000 troops. The central aim of Malby's 'plat' was the strategic placing of small wards in fortifications throughout the country: for example, in Ulster – the crucible of his plan – 800 troops would be distributed in the two forts of Coleraine and Blackwater so that within as little as eight hours, both forces could mobilise to meet each other and, if needs be, join forces with the 400 troops located in Connacht, which could also ally with the 400 serving in Munster. Of the remaining 400, half would serve in the lord deputy's retinue based in the Pale, 180 would bolster the existing wards throughout the country, and twenty would man forts along the river Bann.[46] This strategy, to which Malby made frequent reference thereafter, seemed to be part of a sustained bid to replace Bagenal as knight marshal in Ireland. Similar dissatisfaction with the leadership of the garrison in Ireland had been enunciated six years earlier when Sir John

---

1737, 1776, 2531. *CPRI*, Vol. I, p. 516; *Cal Car. MSS 1601–3*, fols. 481–2. Dunlop, 'The plantation of Leix and Offaly' *EHR* (1891), pp. 94–96, Carew to Sidney, 12 July 1569, SP63/29/10. For a treatment of multiple manor-holding as an index of differentiation between esquires, lesser knights and greater knights see Harriss (2005), p. 138.

[45] Canny, N., *Making Ireland British, 1580–1650* (Oxford, 2001), pp. 88–90. See Malby's almost lyrical account of the many qualities of Burrishoole which he wrote had 'a very plentiful iron mine and abundance of wood anyway' as well as being 'one of the best fishing places in Ireland for salmon, herring and all kind of sea fish', 8 April, SP63/72/39.

[46] Malby's opinion with a plat 26 September 1579, SP63/69/63i.

Perrot recommended the centralisation of a major force in Athlone of around 500 footsoldiers and fifty horsemen under a new knight marshal ('some lusty gent like Nicholas Poyntz').[47] Along with the allocation of resources, martial expertise, and the practical skills that went with it, was deemed specifically important in particular parts of Ireland. Many presidents of Munster had proved their mettle surveying and building fortifications, and William Drury, William Pelham and John Norris, if circumstances had been more settled, might have extensively fortified the coastal towns there.[48] But occasionally their engineering expertise was diverted to less impressive but more urgent ends: Pelham, in the spring of 1580, moved most of his army across the river Shannon using the cord of his viceregal tent as a secure line to prevent a makeshift ferry from being whipped downriver by the torrential current.[49] Some of the veterans' insights were a good deal more banal, notably Malby's request that new recruits should not be clothed in red and blue coats because 'the rebels take such heart against them, as in any fight they will avoid the old soldiers and pick out the others by their coloured coats.'[50]

Many basic aspects of the garrison's presence in Ireland – the military entrepreneurship, the corruption, the sheer incompetence and periodic misfortune – were generic to garrisons anywhere, and this typical tendency towards administrative fecklessness and opportunism was fully recognised in Whitehall, where many of the leading councillors of the queen (as we have seen) had few illusions about the martial profession. The crusading zeal of Sir Nicholas Arnold's lord justiceship in 1563, for example, was based upon an officially sponsored 'general mistrust ... of all persons that receive any pay there for the wars'. His enquiry into abuses in the payment of the Irish garrison required that 'all captains [make] ready their rolls of their bands with the distinct names and surnames of all persons as well household, servants and soldiers' and resulted – significantly – in his own downfall: a potent sign of the hold that the captains

---

[47] Perrot to Elizabeth, 13 July 1573, SP63/41/76iii.
[48] See Drury to privy council, 24 March 1578. SP63/60/25. Drury fortified Limerick castle, Cork, Kilmallock, Shannonside and Castlemaine. Pelham was particularly renowned for his skills in fortification, 'Mont Pelham' was the name of a fort erected flanking Leith during the assault of 1560, see Grey de Wilton, Scrope to the duke of Norfolk 1 May 1560, *CSPSc1547–63*, 393. For Norris's expertise see Nolan (1997), pp. 159–79.
[49] Sir Edward Fenton to Burghley, 22 April 1580, SP63/72/61. Unfortunately the rope broke before the entire force was transferred to the other side killing five or six soldiers. Captains York and Thornton transported the remainder by pinnace the next day.
[50] Malby to Walsingham, 31 August 1580, SP63/75/82.

had on crown administration in Ireland.[51] As for problems caused by incompetence, even the accidental detonation of gunpowder at Derry fort in 1566 (one of the most ignominious moment for Elizabeth's army in Ireland) was a foreseeable mishap to which military outposts full of munitions throughout Europe were particularly prone; for instance, in 1560, the castle at Leith and a good proportion of the town were consumed by a chance fire.[52] In short, it was not the military aspect of service in Ireland that set the English captains' Irish experiences apart – even the night stealths and freelance distraints of a Lysagh MacKedagh O'More, a Shane Grace or a Donal MacVicar would have been entirely familiar to any soldier who served in the north of England at Berwick or the marches facing down outlaws such as 'Black Ormston', 'John of the Side' and 'The Lord's Joke'; rather, it was the greater emphasis on the captains role as *governors* of Ireland on the crown's behalf that gave their Irish experience a peculiar complexion.[53]

Their presence in Ireland did not mean that they were entirely outside the metropolitan political loop. The captains occasionally had devoted allies in high places, who could advocate the benefits of their role in administering the sister kingdom. The devotion of sometime viceroy Sir Henry Sidney comes readily to mind. This was expressed most arrestingly in his 'Memoir of service in Ireland', where not only the captains but also certain Pale lawyers and an exhaustive roll of Gaelic-Irish and minor English-Irish lords were fulsomely praised – all artfully presented as functioning parts of a relatively stable kingdom, prepared to cover its own administrative costs, presided over by the impresario Sidney and his remarkable policy of composition. As Brady has pointed out, in Sidney's

---

[51] For Arnold's abortive record in Ireland, which merely succeeded in undermining the earl of Sussex on behalf of the earl of Leicester see Brady (1994), pp. 104–9. The quotes are from Arnold's memo of September 1563 SP63/9/12. For other examples of martial corruption see the case of treasurer at war Sir Thomas Sherley, outlined in Nolan (1997), p. 178, whose 'impenetrable book-keeping' in the 1590s hid a multitude of profiteering sins.

[52] The early seventeenth-century Catholic historian Philip O'Sullivan Beare argued that the explosion in Derry was caused by St Colmcille assuming the shape of a wolf, picking up red hot coals from a smith's forge and dropping them in the magazine; see Philip O'Sullivan Beare *Historiae Catholicae Iberniae compendium* (Lisbon, 1621), p. 84. For the fire at Leith, see duke of Norfolk to Cecil, 2 May 1560, *CSPSc, 1547–63*, p. 393.

[53] For reference to Black Ormston, etc., and their role in the spiriting away of the earls of Westmoreland and Northumberland after the northern rebellion of 1569, see Thomas Radcliffe, earl of Sussex to the Regent Murray, 21 December 1569, *CSPSc 1569–71*, p. 29; for an account of the 'secret talk' between Niall MacLysagh, Lysagh MacKedagh and Brian Fitzpatrick, baron of Upper Ossory to reconcile two warring branches of the O'Mores, see 'Confession of Donal MacVicar', 14 January 1561, SP63/3/2. The O'Mores, of course also played a central role in the spiriting of the fugitive earl of Desmond back to his lordship.

view, the captains' particular role in this commonwealth was to act as 'a set of precision tools supplementing and confirming the disaggregating negotiations [between local magnates and the crown] which constituted the central theme of his narration'.[54] Hence, William Piers (for instance) was described as 'honest, valiant and politique', Humphrey Gilbert as 'valiant and politique', William Collier as 'hardy and politique' and John Perrot as 'the most complete and best humoured man to deal with that nation that I know living'.[55] But Sidney also entered into the swaggering martial spirit of the captains, praising their prowess and, in places, their lustiness. Sidney, still smarting in 1583 about the ways in which the earl of Ormond, the Palesmen, his Irish lord chancellor and his queen had thwarted his ambitions, seemed to find some sort of solace in memories of camaraderie with the Irish garrison. Consequently, he boasted of the combination of charismatic leadership and guile that had allowed him to rouse his soldiers while campaigning in 1569:

I might see by the very countenances of as resolute men as any I had, wonderful alteration; for the private soldiers came to their officer, the officers to their captains, the captains to my counsellors and the counsellors to me, and nothing in their mouths but 'home! home! home! or else we were all undone'; so mighty were the rebels; so tickle was the English Pale; so strong was Turlough Luineach [O'Neill], and so small a company were we. I hearing of this, sent for the council and captains into my tent, and had some conference with them ... This wearisome consultation being interrupted by me, out of my pavilion I went into the market place of my camp, and with trumpet and drum sounded to the standard, the soldiers and all the rest of the camp readily came, in hope that I would forthwith have returned; I showed my resolution to the contrary, and some words I spake, and somewhat it prevailed; for they with the drinking of a tun of wine, which during the consultation was provided and laid in the market place, and after my speech ended, very diligently applied both by drawing and drinking, all my men's cowardish coldness was turned into martial-like heat, and then nothing but, – 'Upon them! upon them! Lead you and we will follow to the land's end, or die by the way; and let us go by and by' – 'Nay soft sirs' quoth I, 'it is Sunday, and it is afternoon, we will go and hear evening prayer, sup and rest, and you shall be called I warrant you, betimes in the morning, and so in the name of God we will advance forwards. That evening and all the night there was nothing but singing, casting of bullets, drying of powder, filing of pike's heads, sharpening of swords, and every man thinking himself good enough for five rebels ... .[56]

[54] Brady (2002), pp. 33–4. [55] Brady (2002), pp. 63, 73.
[56] Brady (2002), pp. 56, 67–8. A Sallustian skill as an orator was thought to be a crucial talent for military commanders at this time. The oratorical skills of Thomas Radcliffe, the earl of Sussex, while serving in the north of England were highly praised: 'At whose eloquence hearers rather stood astonished than unsatisfied in any point or parcel wherein he opened the bowels of rebellion,

Unable to implement his designs in Ireland and realise his ambitions at home, this fallen courtier, although apparently spurning the ways of Whitehall for the rough, plain-spoken and simple style of the camp was being less than honest. By his own account, even his attempts to gain some small degree of glory in arms at the margins of Elizabethan politics were the subject of disparagement. His questionable claims to have been the undoing of Shane O'Neill did not impress: 'when I came to court it was told me that it was no war that I had made, nor worthy to be called a war, for that Shane O'Neill was but a beggar, an outlaw, and one of no force; and that the Scots [who assassinated him] stumbled on him by chance'.[57] Sidney's tragedy was that he found himself adopting a manner and aesthetic that he could only endorse out of desperation. He would rather have whispered to diplomats in London than cajoled drunkards in Ireland.[58]

PATRONAGE AND RELIGION

Mitchell Leimon has shown beyond dispute that it was Sir Francis Walsingham that really dominated patronage of the Irish garrison throughout the late 1570s and 1580s, ultimately holding more sway among the captains than Sidney had ever exercised – tun of wine or no tun of wine. In Ireland, Walsingham's 'church' was broad, but his grip on his clientele was firm, and his servants were nourished by frequent letters from their patron, who, as principal secretary, was at the very heart of politics in England. Using Edward Waterhouse as his primary agent in 1575, he added Malby to his portfolio, which, by that stage, already featured Henry Davells, constable of Dungarvan, and Francis Agard, constable of Ferns, seneschal of the O'Byrnes and O'Tooles. Lord Chancellor Gerrard, Lord Justice Drury and Archbishop Loftus were subsequently co-opted, the team being augmented in 1579 by the newly appointed vice-treasurer

---

the practices of enemies, and suborning of traitors, and earnestly persuaded every honest mind, to be mindful of his Prince and country in the liberty whereof, both life and living is always to be offered.' *Churchyardes chippes* (London, 1575), sig. 38 v.

[57] Brady (2002), p. 58.
[58] Sir Henry Sidney, knighted on the same day as William Cecil, Baron Burghley, was haunted by thoughts of what his career might have been like had Edward VI not died. He had been the king's favourite, a gentleman of the bed-chamber, and chief cup-bearer. Furthermore his father had been Edward's chamberlain, his mother his governess and his aunt had been the king's dry-nurse. In 1583, Sidney remembered how he had been 'bountifully rewarded' by the boy-king who would 'always be cheerful and pleasant' with him and he wistfully recalled how 'in my absence [he] would give me such words of praise as far exceeded my desert'. All this came to an end when 'to [his] own still felt grief [and] the universal woe of England' Edward died in his arms. Brady (2002), p. 106.

Sir Henry Wallop and Lord Justice Pelham. Walsingham even reached out to the detested, but influential earl of Ormond as an attempted inoculation against political misfortune and, as Leimon has demonstrated, enjoined his clients to treat him with respect. Even Malby, whose antipathy to Ormond was of long standing, vaunted his stoical acquiescence in this difficult matter as a sacrifice offered up for Walsingham's sake.[59]

The earl of Leicester's personal role in the government of the sister kingdom, by contrast, was rather remote. Yet, his influence was palpable. Some of the captains (for example, Malby) had served under his brother Ambrose at Newhaven and had been appointed to their posts in Ireland by his brother-in-law Sir Henry Sidney; others would serve with Leicester's force in the Low Countries in 1584. The sources that remain indicate, however, that the earl preferred to confine his communication with Ireland to correspondence with viceroys, sending hectoring criticism to William Fitzwilliam or encouragement to Grey de Wilton. The influence of the earl of Sussex (lord lieutenant from 1556 to 1564), although more diffuse, remained important up until his death in 1583. After his recall, he retained martial contacts and wielded considerable influence at court on Irish affairs, especially following his elevation to the position of vice chamberlain in December 1570; in most things, especially the Anjou match, he tended to ally himself with Lord Treasurer Burghley. He was well acquainted with both William Drury, whom he knighted in 1570 (president of Munster from 1576 to 1578, then lord justice until his death in 1579) and William Pelham (lord justice from 1579 to 1580), having served with them previously in the north of England. In Irish affairs, he was also friendly with the earl of Ormond; both of them shared an ingrown antipathy to Sir Henry Sidney. His martial connections even penetrated the lowest ranks of captain in Ireland. In November 1579, Sir Henry Wallop when informing Walsingham about the drowning of Mr Lister, 'one of [Sir John] Norris's company', and eight horsemen on the causeway into Howth Head, he remarked that 'Mr Norris much lamenteth his death [and] it is said that he was towards my Lord of Sussex.'[60] Norris and Sussex seem to have had a mutual understanding. Leicester later pointed to similarities between them while voicing exasperation with Norris in 1586, by declaring that Sir John 'match[ed] the earl of Sussex, of all men that ever I hath seen' in the way he 'dissemble[s] . . . crouch[es] . . . and so cunningly carr[ies] his doings as no man living would

---

[59] Leimon (1989), pp. 77–105. [60] Wallop to Walsingham, 23 November 1579, SP63/70/19.

imagine that there were half the malice or vindictive mind that doth plainly his deeds prove to be'.[61] In short, the martial caste in Ireland was not entirely Leicester's to command. Burghley himself operated a small clientele in Ireland, and, although most officers there were correspondents of his at some time or other, he had particular intimates – Sir Edward Fitton, Sir William Fitzwilliam and Sir Nicholas White – who were prized above the others.

Both Walsingham and Leicester, of course, have become associated with a confessionally motivated strain in Elizabethan foreign policy, which strongly endorsed intervention in the Low Countries in support of the insurgents and tended to repudiate the Anjou match, fearing that in it lay the germs of the overthrow of the Elizabethan settlement and its future development into more Protestant forms. Yet this confessionalised politics, it seems, did not, to any tangible extent, percolate down to animate any *esprit de corps* among the captains of Ireland. It was only during the second viceroyalty of Sir Henry Sidney that captains became intrinsically involved in the enforcement of conformity to the religious settlement by law established in Ireland. Superficially, this appeared like a less arduous theological challenge than was the case in England; whereas the established church back home boasted its thirty-nine articles, the Church of Ireland had only twelve, based on Archbishop Matthew Parker's eleven articles of 1559, a temporary measure the prelate had devised for the subscription of the clergy until they were superseded by the articles in 1563. The twelve Irish articles, published in Dublin in 1566, were much less precise than their prolix English counterpoint. The occasionally pejorative tone of the English legislation was altogether avoided; transubstantiation was not declared 'repugnant to the plain words of Scripture', an error prey to superstition which 'overthroweth the nature of a Sacrament', nor was the use of the mass as a 'sacrifice' for the living and the dead disdained as the product of 'blasphemous fables' and 'dangerous deceits'. In true late Henrician manner, the use of the cup was affirmed, the doctrine of Purgatory was denied, as were private masses. The articles particularly asserted 'the Queen's Majesty's prerogative and superiority of government of all estates and in all causes, as well

---

[61] Leicester to Walsingham, 9 May 1586, *Leycester corr* (1844), p. 264; Leicester to Walsingham, 10 June, *Leycester corr* (1844), p. 299; the earl asked the secretary to 'break or burn' this remarkably personal letter, an indication of the degree to which the range of correspondence which remains at our disposal is an edited fraction of what was written. For a record of the earl of Sussex knighting Drury, see *Churchyardes chippes* (London, 1575) sig. 39r. For Sussex's relationship with Cecil see Worden (1996), pp. 96, 104–5.

ecclesiastical as temporal, within this Realm' and the inadmissibility of any offices or ministers 'either ecclesiastical or secular' not ordained by the 'high authorities according to the ordinances of this realm' was stressed. Yet, for all that, the language the Church of Ireland used to describe the attempted usurpation of temporal authority by the bishop of Rome was measured and more conciliarist than apocalyptic in tone and content. This was the measured language that Elizabeth liked, and Sidney hoped that the Catholic episcopacy of Ireland would like it too. His cordial negotiations in 1576 with four Catholic bishops of Ireland, recounted in his memoir, indicate his desire to establish the authority of the English monarch over the ecclesiology of the Irish church and his flexibility in virtually all else. He pointed out how the bishops 'submitted themselves unto the queen's majesty, and desired humbly that they might (by her highness) be inducted into their ecclesiastical prelacy'. According to Sidney, the discussions broke down because the bishops 'stood still upon *salvo suo ordine* etc. and I of the queen's absolute authority'.[62]

And this particular emphasis on the provenance of ecclesiastical supremacy within the Irish church rather than disagreement over doctrinal issues continued to mark religious dispute in Ireland. Even a stormy petrel and zealot like Arthur Grey de Wilton, in his correspondence with Elizabeth on Irish matters, eschewed concern for matters eschatological and stressed questions of sovereignty. This is apparent in his account of the parley that took place between himself, a Spanish captain and Alexander Bartoni, the master of the camp of papal troops at Smerwick in 1579. Grey (later a sponsor of the Lambeth articles) told Elizabeth that he subjected both men to a lecture on contemporary international relations, singling out papal usurpation of temporal authority for denunciation. He feigned surprise that subjects of 'an absolute prince' (Philip II) especially 'one that was in good league and amity with your Majesty' would maintain rebels against England's queen and he tendentiously enquired as to who had sent the soldiers to Ireland and why. The Spaniard equivocated, but Bartoni was defiant: 'they were all sent by the pope for the defence of the *Catholica fide*.' This gave Grey the opportunity to unmask himself and launch into a tirade, acknowledging that while men commanded by 'natural and absolute princes' could be embroiled in 'wrong actions' they 'should [not] be carried into unjust desperate & wicked actions by one that neither from God nor man could claim any princely power or empire, but indeed [is] a detestable shaveling

---

[62] Bray, G (ed.) *Documents of the English reformation* (Cambridge, 1994), p. 349; Brady (2002), p. 86.

the right Antichrist and general ambitious Tyrant over all right principalities and patron of the *Diabolicae fide*'.[63] When compared with the content and tone of a contemporary paper by a radicalised, but anonymous, English evangelical exhorting Ireland's government to imitate the practices of the 'godly king Jehosaphat moved by the spirit of God', Grey's invective seems remarkably moderate.[64] No English military officers expressed their views on Ireland's dilemmas in a profoundly scriptural way.

By erecting a new high commission and court of faculties in 1577, Sidney sought to secure the measurable result of outward conformity rather than the intangible fruits of internal conversion and was therefore designed to establish widespread acceptance of and acquiescence to the acts of supremacy and uniformity. Its focus was on the English-Irish community. Thus, by the end of the 1570s, it is commonly argued, the results-based approach that his high commission had taken in enforcing the acts of supremacy and uniformity, notably in the Pale, provoked indigenous rebellion, in part headed by the lord of the marches of the Pale, Viscount Baltinglass, who, in contravention of the loyalist allegiances of his forebears, formed an alliance with the O'Byrnes and O'Tooles of Wicklow and a conspiracy headed by William Nugent, also from the Pale's elite.[65] Whereas previously legislation had attempted to cajole the English-Irish gentry and aristocracy gradually into the arms of a reformed church, the new high commission asserted the privileges of the royal prerogative, and, although it increased revenue accumulated from fines, in the course of implementing this policy, the commissioners seemed to glory in publicly humiliating the scions of the best families of the Pale. An insurgency in the Pale occurred in tandem with the rebellion of the earl of Desmond, a revolt sparked by the advent of troops levied in the papal states off the coast of Kerry.

---

[63] Grey de Wilton to Elizabeth, 12 November 1580, SP63/76/29.
[64] Anonymous paper, 1579, SP63/70/82. Using the example of Jehosaphat, the author prescribed the garrisoning of cities and towns to 'prevent . . . wicked practices' and the establishment of 'Levites' and priests to instruct the natives in God's law. This policy, it was argued, would salve the sore of ignorance caused by the 'lack of [God's] sacred word' and remedy 'the lack of execution of civil laws, the handmade of Christ his gospel', leading to rebellion, insurrection, invasions, treasons, murders, spoiling, robbery, rape, whoredom, drunkenness'.
[65] Murray (1997), pp. 285–7; see also C. Brady *The chief governors* (Cambridge, 1994), pp. 204–13, C. Lennon *The lords of Dublin in the age of reformation* (Dublin, 1989), pp. 150–7, and, for a broad picture of the history of friction between the Dublin government and the Palesmen under Elizabeth, see Brady's 'Conservative subversives: the community of the Pale and the Dublin administration 1556–86', in P. J. Corish, ed., *Radicals, rebels and establishments* (Belfast, 1986), pp. 11–32.

The captains and the Irish context 155

One peculiarity of Sidney's 1577 high commission and court of faculties was that it bestowed a senior role in the enforcement of religious legislation in Ireland on a number of leading martial men. Four in particular were listed as members: Sir Nicholas Bagenal, the knight marshal; Sir Edward Fitton, the erstwhile president of Connacht; Sir Nicholas Malby, the president of Connacht; and Jacques Wingfield, the master of the ordnance. Could these men really be seen as safe pairs of hands?

Bagenal was manifestly trustworthy on matters of faith; he had an impressive pedigree of Protestant commitment. Having been appointed to his post in Ireland by Edward VI in March 1547, he lost it on Mary's accession, and the new regime held him over for a recognisance of £1,000 by an act of the privy council in 1556. His brother Ralph had been the only member of the 1554 House of Commons who had refused to receive the absolution of Cardinal Pole for England's former apostasy stating that 'He was sworn to the contrary to King Henry VIII, which was a worthy prince, [who had] laboured 25 years before he could abolish him [the pope]: and to say I will agree to it, I will not.' Nicholas later resumed the role of marshal of the army under the lord justice Nicholas Arnold, a Dudley appointee.[66] Sir Edward Fitton was an even safer pair of hands – he had previously been a commissioner to enforce the acts of supremacy and uniformity in Chester. While serving as the president of Connacht, he wrote to his patron Burghley in 1573 telling him how he spent the 'idle times' during his first winter in Ireland translating Luther's Wittenberg lecture on the book of Ecclesiastes into English.[67] Fitton charitably refrained from sending the secretary the fruits of his labours because of 'fear ... of [his] own imperfections ... and partly of Luther's errors'. Obviously, this was a continuation of a conversation begun in more comfortable surroundings which was designed to display consensus between Fitton and Burghley about the proper form that a reformed theology should take.[68] However, shared doctrinal commitments never proved to be the basis for solidarity between English administrators in Ireland. Fitzwilliam and Bagenal, for instance, were on such bad terms during the former's first lord-justiceship that Fitzwilliam took joy in publicly humiliating his knight marshal.[69] Likewise, Fitzwilliam and Fitton had a protracted falling out during the early 1570s that resulted in

---

[66] Foxe, J. *Acts and Monuments of John Foxe* ed. J. Pratt (London, 1877).
[67] Fitton to Burghley, 9 August 1573, SP63/42/2.   [68] *CPR Eliz. 1560–3*, p. 280.
[69] Bagenal to Lord Deputy Sidney, 3 May 1568, SP63/24/31.

impolitic scenes at the council board.[70] In the 1580s, when Bagenal and Fitzwilliam were finally reconciled, it was only because they were both active in the undermining of Perrot's deputyship and conspired in the process that ultimately led ultimately to his trial for treason.[71]

Two other names cited on Sidney's commission, however, pose more difficulties: those of Wingfield and Malby. Jacques Wingfield, master of ordnance in Ireland, was something of a harassed figure, as he lived for much of his career under a cloud of official suspicion. His reputation in Ireland had been destroyed by his negligent conduct while serving in the rear of the crown forces during the earl of Sussex's 1561 campaign against Shane O'Neill. When Shane almost routed the crown army, treachery was suspected: Wingfield's treachery. At the time, William Cecil warned Sussex not to 'forget . . . the notable default of Jacques Wingfield, for it remaineth here in memory and for your lack of proceeding against him, some blame is noted in you.' The allegation was never proved.[72] It is of some significance that the saviour of the day in 1561 was deemed to have been Sir William Fitzwilliam. Even Sir Henry Sidney – who cordially hated Fitzwilliam – admitted that on that occasion 'he saved the honour of our nation in this land.'[73] In the early 1570s, Dublin Castle proved to be a particularly tense place to work because of a running battle between Fitzwilliam and Wingfield over the latter's continued use of lodgings on site. In July 1573, Fitzwilliam, in a letter to Burghley, referred to Wingfield as 'Bishop Gardiner's true disciple'.[74] A more deftly poisonous remark can hardly be imagined. Of course, Gardiner had been identified with the persecution of Protestants during Mary's reign, but, more pointedly, Burghley as a young man at Cambridge had defined his own

---

[70] 'Proceedings at the council board when Sir Edward Fitton being liberated and invited to take his seat refused', 5 June 1573, SP63/41/21ii.

[71] See Fitzwilliam to Burghley, 31 July 1588, SP63/135/96 for reference to Bagenal's desire to complain about Perrot. Similarly Grey de Wilton did not stint in his disparagement of Fitzwilliam, blaming his laxness for many of the difficulties that he faced during his own viceroyalty, see Grey to Elizabeth, 26 April 1581, SP63/82/54: 'Hereunto lay for the good that pardons work that in Sir William Fitzwilliam's time there was to this now intended a grant of general pardon, and thereupon a great number were sent abroad but so much regarded as three parts of them yet lye in Kilkenny and never once asked for, as I am credibly informed to be short under your high correction pardon and protection next to the small care had of true religion and settling of God's word hath been the only destruction of this government which trial enforceth me to say that only sword will salve the sore of'.

[72] Cecil to Sussex, 18 May 1561, BL Cotton MSS Titus B. XIII, 21.

[73] Sidney to Cecil, 14 June 1566 in Collins, *Letters and memorials of state*, 2 vols. (London, 1746), Vol. I, p. 14.

[74] Fitzwilliam to Burghley, 18 July 1573, Bodl. Carte MSS 56/171.

The captains and the Irish context

political and spiritual persona in opposition to the bishop.[75] But for all that, Fitzwilliam's memory was accurate. Jacques Wingfield had been a promising member of the bishop of Winchester's household from 1527 onwards, prized for his wit and high spirits, especially during the period when the prelate served as ambassador to France in 1538.[76] Wingfield's solidarity with Gardiner was noted by John Foxe in his *Acts and Monuments*, where he gave an account of Wingfield's defence of the bishop following his notorious St Peter's day sermon in 1548 when he explicitly extolled the sacrificial nature of the mass and the substantial presence of Christ therein.[77] For these reasons alone, Wingfield seemed a strange choice to hold the line of doctrinal and jurisdictional orthodoxy in Ireland.

Much has already been said about Malby. By the late 1570s, he was unambiguously Walsingham's pet and could show an understandable desire to 'work towards' his patron by times denouncing the 'Antichrist of Rome' and referring to 'God's true religion' – words and phrases that were remarkably absent from his correspondence with anyone else.[78] In the late 1570s, Walsingham sent him to the Low Countries where he was mandated to discern what proportion of the population were Don Januists', patriots and French sympathisers.[79] This acute analytical eye, however, seemed to fail Malby when considering the political and religious complexion of his own charge, Connacht. Malby expressed surprise at the way in which religion became a politically significant factor in Irish politics when the cataclysmic implications of the second Desmond

---

[75] Hudson, W. S., *The Cambridge connection* (Durham, NC, 1980).

[76] See Germayn Gardiner to Wriothesley, 21 February 1538. *L&P Henry VIII*, Vol. XIII, Part 1, pp. 109–10 for reports of Wingfield's sharp tongue which on one hand brought French aristocrats at the court of Francis I to 'delight to talk with him' but, on the other, caused offence. Germayn Gardiner relates: 'At another time, when they were playing tennis, a Frenchman said in despite that he thought [that] all the Englishmen in England were come thither. Wingfield answered him that there were yet enough in England to beat those and all the Frenchmen in France besides. This answer was peradventure somewhat over hot, but yet such as might be borne of a young lad than such a despiteful provocation of an old knave . . . I cannot find that Wingfield has ever spoken such words except in answering merry mocks or scornful sayings.'

[77] Foxe, J. *Acts and Monuments* (1563), pp. 833–834, 852, 859. Wingfield's defence was that Gardiner's sermon, far from being inflammatory, had been received calmly, being 'quietly heard without any sign, or token of disquietness, or tumult shewed, or attempted, to this deponents knowledge: and after the sermon ended, he waited on the said bishop to his house, no word or token of displeasure of any person shewed to him, as he sayth'. For Wingfield's determination not to acquiesce in his own disgrace, see Wingfield to Burghley, 6 May 1581, SP63/83/2.

[78] See N. Canny, *Making Ireland British: 1580–1640* (Oxford, 2001), p. 93 for Malby's reference to the pope as antichrist, and see Brady (1994), p. 285 for the allegations levelled against the president on religious matters as well as 'Notes of Malby's abuses' March 1580, SP63/72/24–5.

[79] *Relations politiques des Pays-Bas et de l'Angleterre* ed. Kervyn de Lettenhove, 11 vols. (Brussels, 1882–1900), Vol. X, pp. 554–5.

rebellion for the kingdom as a whole became apparent: 'This realm since the memory of man was not so disjointed as at this day it is', he declared,

> for where ever before this time the country people devised small occasions to rebel as for private quarrelling it is now converted to a matter of religion by which it is become so general a cause throughout among them all [that] more harder it will be to quench this fire then any that ever hath been in practice before [my italics].[80]

He belatedly recognised in the unfurling of the papal banner in Ireland a new and potent force of political consolidation and solidarity which, when joined with 'the expectation of foreign forces' and the reluctance of those among the native community 'which we hold for the best' to 'do anything against the rebellious papist', had unprecedented power to subvert crown rule. But even in this climate Malby could not bring himself to anathemise all those who refused to move against the rebels, reserving for them this petition: 'I pray God amend them'.[81] Significantly, Sir William Pelham, the then lord justice, also claimed to have been surprised by the unprecedented nature of the rebellion: 'No such general [resistance] hath happened since the first conquest of this realm', he informed the privy council in November 1579, adding with quizzical alarm that 'the pretence of war is the cause of religion.'[82]

Malby was incredulous at the rapprochement the new climate of religious radicalisation had effected between the hitherto irreconcilable sons of the earl of Clanricard, Ulick and John Burke. John, in the altered climate, agreed to 'allow Ulick to be his elder and that in right', a development which the president of Connacht pointed out with some astonishment he would never have accepted 'when he professed duty to her majesty', adding that at 'that time it was as much as I could do to keep them asunder.' 'Being against her majesty', Malby conceded wearily, 'they do agree well.' Structurally, the political arrangement was arrived at by putting English law to one side and embracing the Irish custom of tanistry, with John accepting the privileges that went with the status of *tánaiste*, privileges of which the English practice of primogeniture would

---

[80] Malby to Walsingham, 31 August 1580, SP63/75/82.
[81] Malby to Walsingham, 20 July 1580, SP63/74/50.
[82] Pelham and Irish Council to privy council, 26 November 1579, *Walsingham letter book*, ed. Hogan and O'Farrell (Dublin, 1959), p. 244. Pelham listed the symptoms that epitomised the new confessional element in Irish politics: 'the weakness and evil disposition of the corporate towns, the rumours that run amongst the Irish that her Majesty will not abide the charges of a general war, the foreign aid is daily expected, how the camp of the rebels is called the camp of his holiness'.

have deprived him. But the mortar that held this arrangement together was papal rhetoric. Malby admitted to Walsingham how the Catholic Bishop of Killaloe, who had met with Sidney a few years earlier, had negotiated the Clanricard compromise. Priests in the earldom who refused to say mass were being hanged by the Burke brothers for their recalcitrance. Things looked bleak: 'your honour may see that the Pope doth all things here and [will do] all things ... if it be not provided for.'[83] Malby, believing the Gaelic-Irish to be confessionally moribund, could not quite credit that they were rallying to Fitzmaurice's and then Baltinglass's banner 'for religion sake'. He persisted in arguing that the entire dynamic of Counter-Reformation Catholic political action came from the English-Irish, telling Walsingham that *without the help of the English races the Irishry is not to be respected nor to be thought dangerous*' (my italics). He continued to believe Gaelic Ireland innocent of religious zeal and later told Walsingham that although O'Rourke now defiantly held Counter-Reformation views, he had not come by them himself: rather, he had been acquainted with them 'only by the evil persuasions of William Nugent who being with him hath established him in the Romish religion'.[84]

How had the captains managed to ignore the confessionalisation of the Gaelic-Irish? In part, it seems that they had dismissed practices such as the taking of oaths on relics and the gospels, extremely common means of cementing political compacts, as mere backward superstitions rather than indications of susceptibility to fighting for the doctrines of the faith.[85] However, some of them had also had financial motives. In 1582, a dossier of grievances compiled against Malby's administration in Connacht severely criticised his apparently uneven commitment to the Elizabethan

---

[83] Malby to Walsingham, 17 November 1580, SP63/78/41. One thing the Baltinglass rebels in 1580 stressed in order to incite general support of their cause was the unsuitability of a woman being governor of the church. For example Baltinglass's assertion to Ormond that 'He is no Christian man that . . . [can] think and believe that a woman uncapable of all holy orders should be the supreme governor of Christ's church, a thing that Christ did not grant unto his own mother'. This mode of argument, it seems had some lasting appeal as attested by Richard Bingham who during his campaign against the MacWilliam Burkes heard his opponents urge: 'What have we to do with that Caliaghe [hag], how unwise were we, being so mighty a nation, to have been so long subject unto a woman! The pope and the king of Spain shall have the rule of us, and none other'. See a discourse of the services done by Sir Richard Bingham in the County of Mayo' October 1586, SP63/126/53i.

[84] Malby to Walsingham, 31 August 1580, SP63/75/82; Malby to Walsingham, 30 June 1581, SP63/83/63. See also John Zouche to Walsingham, 26 July, SP63/20/66.

[85] See 'Confession of Donal MacVicar', 14 January 1561, SP63/3/2 for a description of a compact between two opponents within the O'More sept, Lysagh MacKedagh and Neil MacLysagh, solemnised by oaths taken on a piece of the True Cross from Holy Cross Abbey in Tipperary.

religious settlement and the way in which he used his membership of the high commission. According to his critics, whatever insurgency had rocked Connacht during the second Desmond rebellion stemmed not from religion but from discontent with Malby's 'unruly government'. 'For what need they to rebel for papistry', his chief detractor Edward Whyte asserted, 'when the president allow[s] the existence of *ten or twelve friaries stuffed full of friars* which [are] continually protected and [have] the exercise of their religion and orders without controlment' (my italics). Malby, for instance, had allegedly permitted a cleric who refused to take the oath of supremacy to hold the Abbey of Boyle in Roscommon 'by the pope's gift'. Worse still, he had 'had conference' with John Case, the papal appointee to the bishopric of Killala, allowing him scope 'to seduce the people'. Malby also surrounded himself with subordinates with disreputable backgrounds, notably Nicholas Mordaunt, a captain of footmen, who had been out in rebellion in 1569 with the earls of Northumberland and Westmoreland, gaining a reputation for himself because he had once 'thrust a bodkin through a minister's nose'.[86] Malby's insouciant reply to these allegations was startling, especially where he dealt with the allegation about friaries: he airily invoked higher authority, waxed mysterious and ultimately refused to clear himself of the charges:

I found the friars of Kilconnell and Sligo protected by the governor of the realm before I had charge of the province, who did impart the cause to me, not meet to be known to the accusant, for which cause to continue therein in that service I do renew the protection from time to time as I find them to deserve that favour, wherein also I have found great benefit to the service of her majesty . . . but for any other favour unto them as in cause of religion, I defy the pope and as many as favour him or his religion.[87]

The allegations add up to a picture of de-facto religious toleration motivated by personal ambition, greed and wilful negligence. The practice of the old religion was often tolerated, but only if a tariff was paid. When conformity was enforced, it was done unimaginatively in the search for short-term results, rather than enduring commitment. On balance, it appears that English captains in Ireland were not particularly exercised by wrangles about how reformed the Church 'by law established' was in Ireland. They did not fulminate against episcopacy, nor fret about the wearing of surplices and copes, nor insinuate that the Elizabethan articles

---

[86] Whyte to the privy council, 12 April 1582, SP63/91/24.
[87] Malby's answer to Whyte's objections, SP63/91/25.

and book of common prayer were a 'mingle mangle', nor worry that the communion service might prioritise a supposed sacrificial understanding of the Eucharist over a commemorative one. Of course, immersion in an Irish context might have distracted them from developments in England or, indeed, made it difficult to discover how England's reformation was faring. They may have believed that such matters were not really their business and may have been content to remain obedient consumers of established religion. Whatever was the case, their usual silence on religious matters in state correspondence does not indicate profound engagement with the cause of reforming religion.

But in spite of their apathy about the sincere reception of 'true religion' by the Irish, the fundamental truth, as far as the captains were concerned, was that they had the power to exercise considerable control over many aspects of their charges' lives. Whether to enforce such-and-such a law or not was their decision. They also had some control over how their own conduct, and that of others – fellow officers, native grandees and subalterns – was presented at court. If time could be found to praise allies, there were always opportunities to calumniate rivals. The political culture that resulted from the counterpoint between this regular political contact with the metropolis, the radical autonomy the captains enjoyed on the ground and the abstracted authority – crown authority – that they claimed to wield is the subject of the next two chapters.

CHAPTER 5

The limits of imperium: martial men and government

> [A]uthority was to me but a sweet poison that would in the end turn to my confusion and utter discredit, rather than to the increase of my poor reputation.
>
> Sir Humphrey Gilbert to Secretary Cecil, 18 October 1569

As is well known, Lord Treasurer Burghley spent time and effort trying to conceptualise the terms under which the Elizabethan settlement and his own political career could withstand the appalling possibility of the queen's sudden death. One problem that faced him on the occasions when he tried to square this circle was a simple constitutional one: where would sovereignty be located within the commonwealth during an interregnum? The 1585 act for the security of the queen's royal person was ambiguous about where that sovereignty might lie following the queen's assassination. Burghley envisaged that under such circumstances a great council could be created, made up of the existing privy council and recruits from the House of Lords which would hold sovereignty during the interregnum acting 'in the name of the imperial crown of England'.[1] A similar, but much more immediate, 'inter-regnal' problem had earlier vexed Sir Nicholas Malby far away from Whitehall in 1579: at the time, he was sheltering from a hail of bullets in the ruins of Askeaton Abbey in Munster. The volleys came from the castle on the other side of the river Deel, where the beleaguered earl of Desmond was lodged. Malby lacked 'imperial crown' authority to do what was necessary to bring his enemy down.

Malby could not retaliate: he had been left in the lurch because of the sudden death by flux of Sir William Drury, lord justice of Ireland. The problem was straightforward. At the onset of Drury's illness, Malby had been appointed as his lieutenant in Munster, but now that the lord justice was dead – an unanticipated set of circumstances inadequately rehearsed – he

[1] Collinson, P., 'The monarchical republic of Queen Elizabeth I' in *The Tudor Monarchy* ed. J. Guy (London, 1997), pp. 110–35.

doubted that he had the authority to proceed against the earl in the way he wished. He told Secretary Walsingham:

I thought to have proclaimed [Desmond], but, at that instant I had news that the lord justice was dead, by which I thought my authority ceased because I [am] here as his lieutenant; and so did draw the force to this place where I mind to hold them in camp until I shall hear from the lord chancellor and council how I shall further proceed.[2]

Burghley may have been uncertain about identifying a single source from which all sovereignty emanated, but Malby had no such doubts. His hesitation is telling: this caution had little to do with local pragmatism but quite a lot to do with his desire to be totally sure that when he acted he was acting as a competent minister of the crown's sovereignty in Ireland. Malby's anxieties about the provenance of his magistracy in Ireland were shared by many other English-born crown officers. Frequently, this anxiety was joined with a sense of insecurity about the future of that magistracy and political distrust of the very institution that imbued them with magisterial status in that country: the crown.[3] Carelessness in matters to do with crown authority, as Malby well knew, could result in total ruin. He had to wait for sovereignty to be transferred to a new lord justice, William Pelham, who, then and only then, could delegate.

MAGISTRACY AND PRE-EMINENCE

Care about wielding authority was heightened by the stresses and strains of holding office in Elizabethan Ireland. Of course, magistracy was not a new experience for some of the English captains serving in Ireland: Sir Peter Carew, Sir Nicholas Bagenal, Sir Edward Fitton, Sir Warham St Leger, Sir John Perrot and Edmund Eltoftes, for instance, had all served as justices of the peace in England and Wales.[4] Their approach to holding office in Ireland unsurprisingly echoed their social aspirations and self-perception as expressed in local government in England. Anthony Fletcher, in his seminal essay 'Honour, reputation and local officeholding in Elizabethan and Stuart England', has shown how officeholding in England was entwined with concerns about personal and familial honour which

---

[2] Malby to Walsingham 12 October 1579, SP63/69/52.
[3] St Leger to Henry VIII, 26 June 1541, *SPHen VIII*, Vol. II, pp. 304–5.
[4] *CPR, Eliz. 1560–3*, pp. 16, 282, 444; *CPR Eliz., 1563–6*, pp. 21, 23, 30–1. Eltoftes, who was leader of the footmen in the ward of Ballinasloe in 1582, had served on the commission for the peace in the West Riding, Yorkshire.

often issued in bids for pre-eminence over one's fellows and brutal demonstrations of precedence. It should be no surprise that the sort of seething enmities that could be generated between members of a commission of the peace in Herefordshire could also build up between the captains in Ireland, emerging in sly manoeuvres as well as obvious bids to disgrace and humiliate colleagues.[5] The appetite for petty point-scoring among the captains sometimes seemed insatiable. For instance, Sir William Fitzwilliam, during his tour of Ulster as lord justice in 1568, made an especial effort to daunt both Nicholas Malby and Nicholas Bagenal while encamped at Dunluce. Fitzwilliam summoned them both to his tent and publicly accused Malby of plotting to kill him. Malby ('amazed' according to Bagenal) asked the lord justice to repeat the allegation, and when Fitzwilliam did so, Malby, flustered, or feigning being flustered, 'answered that he refused his [own] salvation and [would] become a depraved creature if ever he thought or meant any such practice against him'. Fitzwilliam then set about humiliating Bagenal. First, he assured him that the army would lie in late the following morning. Bagenal, trusting the deputy, was happily enjoying a lazy morning, when, to his surprise, he was confronted, in his night gown, with the sight of Fitzwilliam in full martial splendour, 'booted and spurred and calling for his horse ready to depart' in the midst of a camp, all ready for the off. An apparently childish trick: Fitzwilliam was pulling rank on both Marshal Bagenal and Malby and through them, perhaps, sending a terse message to his disparagers at court, Sir Henry Sidney and the earl of Leicester.[6]

The captains' sense of honour and reputation was brittle, and Elizabeth, more than anyone, knew how to employ the humiliation of officers to devastating effect. For instance, her disapproval of Sir William Pelham was most cruelly expressed by forcing him to stay in Ireland as a retainer after he had been removed from the lord justiceship. Grey de Wilton, in a fit of compassion, observed that Pelham felt particularly sore 'that being commanded to stay here he had no other title nor place appointed unto him than [to be] a common councillor'. Grey attempted to spare his predecessor's blushes by 'giving him in sittings the highest place next to the chancellor and other Lords', but Pelham was inconsolable.[7]

---

[5] See A. Fletcher 'Honour, Reputation and local officeholding in Elizabethan and Stuart England' in *Order and disorder in early modern England* (Cambridge, 1985), pp. 92–115, see especially p. 102 for treatment of the feud between the Coningsbys and Crofts in Herefordshire.
[6] Sir Nicholas Bagenal to Sidney, 3 May 1568, SP63/24/31.
[7] Grey to Walsingham, 12 September 1580, SP63/76/28.

The limits of imperium

Incidents between minor figures affiliated to prominent individuals sometimes ramified into full-scale disruption between important crown officers leading to vendettas between their households. For example, the 'wilful murder' of Thomas Roden, the vice-treasurer Sir Edward Fitton's servant, by James Meade, Henry Harrington's servant, on Castle Street in Dublin, resulted in allegations of corruption and malice on all sides. This tortuous saga involved two coroner's inquiries and two inquiries at king's bench and resulted in Meade ultimately being granted a general pardon by Fitzwilliam. Fitton, appalled by this leniency, removed the record of pardon (the 'fiat') 'out of the office' before it could pass the great seal, ostensibly to examine it, but – once his action was discovered – he refused to return it to Lord Deputy Fitzwilliam. This resulted in a stand-off between Fitton and Fitzwilliam, which prompted the Deputy to send his treasurer to prison overnight for contempt 'against the dignity and authority of the state'. The bad feeling caused by the incident was so pronounced that Roden's vengeful father (Thomas was an only son) paced the streets of Dublin to catch the assailant, and Harrington was advised to avoid Chester, as a group of Roden's family and friends were itching for the opportunity to avenge the young man's death.[8] Despite the fact that they were both clients of Burghley, Fitzwilliam's verdict on Fitton was incontrovertible: the treasurer was so 'malicious' and 'false cowardly' that the viceroy asked that 'God [may] sooner send me into the earth or to be tied in a dungeon than to be coupled with such a venomous person.'[9] In the light of such comments, it seems unsurprising that eight years later Sir Henry Wallop would sum up the normative relationship between English captains in Ireland thus: 'Such ambition I generally find amongst our few English that inhabit here as no two of them that dwell within twenty miles can agree together. Had they nothing when they came hither they account themselves great personages here, and each to make his profit without regard of service'.[10] If disputes of this bitterness

---

[8] Fitton to Burghley, 3 June 1573, SP63/41/2; Fitton's reasons, 3 June 1573, SP63/41/2i; Fitton to Sir Thomas Smith; Fitzwilliam to Elizabeth, 12 June 1573. SP63/41/2i; Act of council, 4 June 1573, SP63/41/2ii, Fitzwilliam and Council to the privy council, 9 September 1573; Fitzwilliam to Burghley, 14 October 1573, SP63/42/51. Meade had previously assaulted Burnell, a servant of the clerk of the Irish council. Burnell was a 'great friend' of Harrington's.

[9] Fitzwilliam to Burghley, 28 June 1573, SP63/41/61. For examples of similar sentiments see Perrot's complaint about the earl of Essex and other detractors made to Sir Thomas Smith, 6 July, SP63/41/71, where he inveighed against the 'unbridled malice of the earl of Essex'. Fitton (like Fitzwilliam) was a client of Burghley's. Wallop attested to the strength of that relationship when he complained in 1583 that it was defied reason that Burghley could 'yield to grant Sir Edward Fitton's account to pass here in my time and refuse mine', Wallop to Walsingham, 17 March 1583, SP63/100/21.

[10] Wallop to Walsingham, 1 March 1581, SP63/81/2.

could be found between officeholders of English birth in Ireland, how much more likely were they to occur when English, English-Irish and Irish jostled each other for precedence and position?

This vying for pre-eminence was particularly marked between the English and the English-Irish, both of which could publicly appeal, with apparent sincerity, to their concern for the English interest in Ireland. The English-Irish of the Pale and the towns tended to point to the forms of due process and consultation current in England and placed great importance on respecting the English constitution of Ireland with its courts, customs and consultative processes. By contrast, the 'new' English servitors pointed to the real possibility that the drastically corrupt nature of the Irish polity could cause the undermining of crown sovereignty there. Necessities might arise which prescribed extra-legal or legally voluntaristic actions to deal with unexpected or dangerous events. While everyone could agree on that, the differences about when, where and how that necessity arose were paramount. The most notorious example of this confrontation was the dispute between Lord Deputy Henry Sidney and the Palesmen in 1577 over his attempt to secure the commutation of the viceregal cess (purveyance for the viceroy's army) to a fixed annual tax in the English Pale without recourse to the Irish parliament or great council, an aim that proved highly offensive to the *amour propre* of the English-Irish of the Pale. This led to intercommunal tensions which, like the dispute between Fitton and Fitzwilliam, ratcheted from being a dispute over procedure to become a battle about contempt: the Palesmen's alleged contempt for the authority of the monarch over and against Sidney's contempt for the wonted customs and constitution of Ireland.

IMPERIUM VERSUS LEX TERRAE

To Sidney's chagrin, his administrative demand, the linchpin of his bid for glory as governor, resulted in a very public debate about the provenance of his authoritarian claims. The Palesmen's protests that the deputy was acting arbitrarily without consultation were countered by the answer 'that *necessity* forced that a garrison of soldiers must be maintained for their defence, otherwise *the estate would be hazarded*' (my italics).[11] The Palesmen, eager to defend their ancient rights, feared and resented the transformation of the hitherto informal and occasional exaction of the

---

[11] 'Gerrard papers: Sir William Gerrard's notes of his report on Ireland, 1577–8', ed. C. McNeill, *Analecta Hibernica* II (1931), p. 129.

The limits of imperium 167

cess (which they had protested against under the viceroyalty of Sussex) into a perpetual *taille* without reference to the bridles that the English constitution in Ireland supposedly placed on royal power.[12] When the gentry of the Pale ignored the tax (the marcher lord and member of the Irish council, Roland Eustace, Viscount Baltinglass, notoriously declared that 'they of the country needed no garrison [and] could live to defend themselves as their fathers did') Sidney accused them of 'impugning Her Majesty's prerogative'.[13] The Pale's lawyers in retaliation cited the highest authorities of the common law 'Stanford, Brooke, Fortescue, Glanvill, Brereton and Britton', some of whom, particularly Stanford – whose widely circulated 1548 work on the supposed statute *Prerogativa regis* was published in 1567 – were recent authorities, arguing that such purveyance was not a prerogative right.[14] When they attempted to secure crown support by personally appealing to Elizabeth, they were imprisoned in the Fleet until they conceded the constitutional point. But once the 'wilful gallants' did concede, and Elizabeth felt that she had protected her prerogative, even if only in a token manner, a political compromise on the issue was hammered out that made Sidney look both power-hungry and ridiculous.[15]

This incident demonstrated that each group prioritised different aspects of the working of English law in Ireland. While both the English-Irish and the captains shared many common assumptions about the law (and indeed most of the major legal offices of the kingdom were held by English-Irish servitors until late in Elizabeth's reign) and supposedly shared the aim of extending crown jurisdiction throughout the island, ambiguities remained. These ambiguities, to a certain extent, resembled

---

[12] The terminology used here is taken from Quentin Skinner, *The foundations of modern political thought*, 2 vols. (Cambridge, 1978), Vol. II, pp. 255/260. The term *frein* was used by Claude de Seyssel to describe institutional checks he believed limited the power of the French monarch.
[13] *HMC, De l'Isle and Dudley* (London, 1934), Vol. II, p. 58. See also Viscount Roland Baltinglass, John Eustace and Robert Harpoole to the Lord Chancellor and Council, 12 August 1569, SP63/29/37, where he lists the rising out of the marches in his area as a mere twenty-eight horsemen and 100 kern.
[14] 'Book of Howth', *Cal. Car. MSS*, Vol. V, pp. 213–14. See William Staunford *An exposition of the king' prerogative collected out of the great abridgement of Justice* 'Fitzherbert' (London, 1567) and M. McGlynn *The royal prerogative and the learning of the inns of court* (Cambridge, 2003), pp. 227–34 shows that Stanford believed that the king's prerogative rights came from common law but had been confirmed by parliament in the ancient undated 'statute' *Prerogativa regis*.
[15] Brady (1994), pp. 209–44; Brady (1985), pp. 11–32. See Sidney's advice to Grey de Wilton, 17 September 1580, *A commentary of the services and charges of William Lord Grey of Wilton KG by his son Arthur* . . . ed. Sir P. de Malpas Grey Egerton (London, 1846), p. 68 where he counsels Grey 'never [to] agree without cess, for if you take money it will be made a great matter here (England) and yet not serve your turn there . . . this one particular was the thing that chiefly broke my back' and again 'compound not for any money they will offer you. I did, and, as I writ before, undid myself by the same'.

the relatively unprobed ambiguities of the unwritten constitution of England with its lack of hard and fast explanation of the provenance of royal sovereignty. The situation in Ireland was starker, however, as power, and the exercise of power in that relatively unsettled environment, took on a more unequivocal and forceful aspect. For many of the English-Irish, the constitutional integrity of the Irish lordship, its parliament and its courts of king's bench, exchequer and common pleas (supplemented in 1571 by a prerogative court, the court of castle chamber) was key and retained a beleaguered majesty: English law in Ireland, of course, was almost as old as the English presence in Ireland and had always been deemed emblematic of English superiority. By contrast, the captains' legal experience in Ireland was disconcerting, their actions less part of an organic progression than an arbitrary intervention: in short, their role in the unfolding of crown government and English law across the country seemed more like a rough graft than an inevitable emanation. Ireland was not Romney Marsh.[16] The procedures and commissions used – oyer and terminer, gaol delivery, martial law – were familiar to them, but their application to the reality of Irish politics and political structures on the ground brought new challenges. Great emphasis was implicitly put on the seneschals' and presidents' qualities of discernment and discretion. Despite the precise nature of the commissions to hear and determine causes, informal licence was explicitly given at times, in the words of one description, to 'govern all the shires and other parts . . . by order of her laws and otherwise by their discretions as causes in equity and conscience should move them whereas the rules of the laws should be too strait and hard.' Therefore, the venerability of legal procedure was in counterpoint with the wisdom of a commissioned delegate of the crown, usually a captain, and his decision to punish or pardon.[17] This discretion, it did not have to be stated, was to be in line with the tenets of universal reason: the natural law by which even monarchs and popes were bound.[18]

---

[16] Knafla, L. A., 'Common law and custom in Tudor England: or "the best state of the commonwealth" in *Law, Literature, and the settlement of regimes* (Washington, DC, 1990), pp. 171–81.

[17] This definition of the powers of the members of the provincial presidential council of Connacht in 1572 was written down as a preface to an analysis of earl of Clanricard's charges against President Fitton, see Bodl. Carte MSS 57/616, also quoted in Crawford (1993), p. 317. See also Harrington's instructions of 1578 in HMC *De L'isle and Dudley MSS*, Vol. II, p. 82.

[18] For a treatment of the application of natural law by magistrates 'because it is not necessary always to consult with the written law in all judgements' see Geoffrey Fenton's *A forme of Christian pollicie* (London, 1574), p. 78, a translation of Jean Talpin's *La police chréstienne* (Paris, 1572). No resonance with Talpin's highly biblical conception of magistracy can be found in the correspondence of the constables, seneschals and presidents.

The captains believed that they were governors, reformers of a corrupt commonwealth instantiating the external force for reform and equity needed to incline the inhabitants of Munster, Ulster and Connacht to live in a society ordered towards the common good of all, a society where there would be 'embracing of justice and English civil order and conversation' where poor petitioners could sue against the powerful (that is the local magnates) and receive common justice.[19] On the one hand, the captains were like localised lords chancellor in that they acted as the conscience of the monarch, but, on the other, they were the shock troops sent in to initiate the procedures through which the standing down of the seigneurial armies and the shiring of the counties with the establishment of local government along English lines (replete with sheriffs and the paraphernalia of common legal practice) would be secured. The main obstacles to reform were the native magnates and their power, those figures who had corrupted Ireland by a constant seeking after their own gain through menaces. In an easily understood borrowing from vocabularies common to scholastic political thought, civic republican discourse, scriptural study and monarchomach theories, the lords of Ireland were designated as 'tyrants' who ruled through fear. The influence of the native lords had perverted the natural instincts of the freeholders, violated their liberties and kept the country teeming with churls without any prospect of manumission. The rude health of serfdom as a social category in Ireland offended the sensibilities of the English, who viewed such oppression – a very visible feature of Irish society – with a mixture of indignation, insecurity and contempt. It stood, quite simply, as an indictment of the Irish polity. This provoked apparently incompatible responses among English officers: on the one hand, an impulse arose to bring the lords so low that they were forced to free their serfs, but, on the other hand, remarkably little concern was evinced about the killing of serfs if, say, a scorched-earth policy were enacted.[20] Fitzwilliam's pithy analysis ran like this:

---

[19] Malby's instructions 1578, BL Add MSS 4786 fol. 1r.
[20] See Sir William Gerrard's 'Notes of his report on Ireland' ed. C. McNeill, in *Analecta Hibernica 2* (1931), pp. 93–291, for the former lord chancellor's enunciation of English concern about the state of the Irish commons who 'live in such thraldom, misery, and poverty as they do and of long time have' and contrast this with Gilbert's pragmatic belief in the necessity during a scorched earth campaign of liquidating the rural labouring class 'so that the killing of them by the sword [would be] the way to kill the men of war by famine' in Churchyard (1579) sig. Qiii, v. See also D. MacCulloch 'Bondsmen in Tudor England' in Cross, Loades and Scarisbrick (eds.), *Law and government under the Tudors: essays presented to Sir Geoffrey Elton on his retirement* (Cambridge, 1988), pp. 91–110.

The great ones have heretofore in the Irishry borne all the sway (their wills standing for law and reason) which they see, by law and justice manifested to the meaner, will in time be abated. This makes them all, tooth and nail what semblance soever they bear . . . to spurn, kick and practise against it, whereunto they are the rather emboldened for that they assure themselves that (without a greater charge than I see her Majesty disposed to) the authority of the laws will not be maintained against their violence.[21]

The presidents and seneschals, in contrast to the native lords, were to rule by means of the law, or legally delegated powers upheld by the rightful authority of the monarch of Ireland. That they sometimes performed distraint of goods in lieu of the payment of rents to the queen, that they billeted their troops on the population as necessity demanded and performed acts of devastating violence was all true, but the captains' conceit was based on a simple, but inviolable difference between themselves and the local magnates: their authority came explicitly from the crown.

THE FRUITS OF GOOD GOVERNMENT

As early as 1567, the Lord Justice Robert Weston felt that he could point out the early fruits and high promise of government by the captains in Leinster and east Ulster. He praised many of the captains elevated to the position of seneschal – men such as Agard, Colley and Cosby as well as Piers, Malby and Bagenal – and stressed the vigorous health of the body politic in the areas they governed. Where the captains held sway, coign and livery had been all but abolished, the booking of men as avowed followers by Irish lords proceeded at a brisk pace, hand in hand with the discreet use of martial law to deal with the remaining chaff. Above all, there was a burgeoning acceptance of common-law jurisdiction, and Irish society was, allegedly, enjoying its benefits. Quarter sessions were 'growing on into an ordinary in those remote shires', banishing 'all the vagabonds' as well as encouraging 'the husbandmen and true labourers'. Consequently, an increase in tillage, the invaluable sign of successful English government, had occurred, which meant 'plenty and cheap of corn and other victual to be sold' to the great convenience of the 'poor true labourers'.[22] Weston, a man with no military qualifications, counselled the consolidation of Sidney's gains in Ulster by means of severe action. 'The sword hath brought them in and the sword (in my opinion) must keep them in

---

[21] Fitzwilliam to Burghley, 25 September 1572, SP63/37/60.
[22] Fitzwilliam and Weston to Elizabeth, 30 October 1567, SP63/22/16.

and not depart', he argued. But severity had to be complemented by 'merciful justice, which once tasted, will then through love, (as I think) work in them more true and faithful obedience, than the fear of the battle sword, hath, or can do'.[23]

Elizabeth's personal attitude to the indigenous elite and its authority, following the spirit of 'surrender and regrant', was much more tractable and probably more pragmatic.[24] Time and time again it had been demonstrated that standing inflexibly on the technical privileges of crown office in defiance of Ireland's peerage resulted in rebellion, costly repression and burgeoning unrest and bitterness. Sidney's repeated exercise of his viceregal franchise in carrying out common-law sessions in the patrimony and liberties of the earl of Ormond during 1567 and 1568 had been presented as key provocation for the Butler revolt of the following year. Malby's ultimatum to the earl of Desmond forced him into rebellion in 1579.[25] Earlier, Sidney, avid for success, had tried to learn from the mistakes of his first deputyship and his composition scheme of the mid-1570s with its explicit accommodation for the lords appeared to be the acme of deference to the seigneurial interest in Irish politics. But ultimately the garrison shared Sidney's impatience and frustration with the indigenous peerage, their ambitions, and the way they defied the captains' authority; this anger was often expressed against the unimpeachable earl of Ormond, 'Black Tom' Butler, an established favourite of Elizabeth's.[26]

Indeed, despite the collegiate philosophy that theoretically underwrote the presidential councils – local magnates and bishops were designated members alongside the crown's martial and legal servitors – the establishment of judicial sessions in both Connacht and Munster in the late 1560s and early 1570s was achieved by crown officers in the maw of opposition from local elites.[27] Both Fitton and Ralph Rokeby, chief justice of Connacht, shortly after sending their upbeat reports to Cecil in January 1570 about the presidency's alleged successes in the province securing 'process obeyed, justice received, very good appearance in sundry sessions and all revenue shewed', had a startlingly different tale to tell.

---

[23] Weston to Elizabeth, 9 October 1567, SP63/22/7. Weston's distinction here between the 'sword' and the 'battle sword', a subset of the powers of the 'sword' is telling.
[24] See the account of the perfectly orthodox ceremony by which Donough MacCarthy was created earl of Clancar in 1565 in BL Egerton MSS 2642, fol. 8.
[25] Edwards, D., 'The Butler revolt', *Irish Historical Studies*, 38 (1993), pp. 243–5.
[26] Edwards, D., *The Ormond lordship in County Kilkenny* (Dublin, 2003), p. 99.
[27] In Munster, for instance, apart from legal and secretarial assistance the council was made up of the earls of Clancar, Thomond, Desmond and Ormond as well as the archbishop of Cashel and bishops of Cork, Waterford and Limerick.

Not only had the chieftain Brian O'Rourke refused to come before president Fitton when summoned but also Conor O'Brien, the earl of Thomond, had proved positively hostile to the presence of the president and officers of the presidency within his territories. When Fitton attempted to hold sessions in Thomond, he found himself opposed by 300 of the earl's own retinue. Fitton had a mere following of fifty-two men, some of whom were killed in the subsequent confrontation. Fitton alluded to the contrast between his successes from Michaelmas to Christmas and this disaster. 'All fell upside down', he exclaimed, 'no reverence shewed, no process obeyed, no justice received.' He placed great emphasis on the personal slights he had suffered, slights directed through him at crown jurisdiction. Not only had he been 'abused' but also his 'officers and soldiers (being messengers from us) [had been] taken prisoner'. The bad example set in Thomond had 'provoked ... all the rest of the light heads in Connacht ... as no corner is free from open sedition'.[28] In short, the office of president had been inaugurated without much indigenous enthusiasm and with merely grudging consent, yet this, as far as the president and his staff, both civil and military, were concerned, could not detract from the royal provenance of Fitton's authority. The native political estate's chariness about accepting the concept of a provincial presidency worth the name was underscored by the obstruction Sidney encountered trying to get Irish council endorsement for Fitton to cess the country in the same manner as could a viceroy. Fitton, already surrounded by opposition on the ground in Connacht, thus had to endure the refusal of the council – the very body one might have expected to have succoured him in his distress – to cede him this licence; they stated for good measure 'that they had one queen, and her majesty had but one deputy, and should have the prerogative, and none other'.[29] In short, political failure secured by Irish obstruction tended to undermine the authoritarian pretensions of crown officers. Royal authority was theoretically theirs, but it had to be carved out on the ground with vigour.

The presidential councils in Munster and Connacht continued in tremulous existence. The crown's stop-start commitment to the scheme during its first decade never encouraged confidence among the captains.[30] Occasionally it seemed that the initiative would be discontinued. As a

---

[28] Fitton to Cecil, 15 April 1570, SP63/30/43.
[29] Sidney to Cecil, 17 October 1569, Collins (1746), Vol. I, p. 42.
[30] The actual title of provincial president lapsed in Munster between September 1573 and June 1576 and in Connacht between September 1575 and May 1579, although Nicholas Malby served in Connacht as chief commissioner from July 1576 before being given the presidential title in 1579.

result, dispatches from those captains and their allies involved in the establishment and administration of the presidential councils tended to be fulsome in their endorsement of the institution and the policies it enacted. For instance, Sir Peter Carew, writing to his kinsman Edmund Tremayne in February 1574, was high in his praise for Perrot's presidential government, stating that the province was 'in better cast than it had been in long time before by the means of ministering the sword and justice'.[31] A good proportion of Perrot's own letters from Munster was given over to the enumeration of executions carried out under his rule as he mopped up the aftermath of the first Desmond rebellion; the headcount had allegedly reached 800 by the spring of 1572. In what would become a common motif of correspondence with Whitehall, Perrot's pride in his achievements in government was articulated by contrasting them with what he saw as the more disturbed state of the rest of the country. His gains had not been easily won. Like Fitton, Perrot had faced opposition from both local and metropolitan sources in maintaining his government. He wrote to Fitzwilliam in May 1571 outlining how he had found it necessary to endure stonethrowing, to threaten his starving soldiers with execution and even to grant a personal loan to the inhabitants of Kilmallock so that disaster could be averted.[32] A year later, he wrote to Fitzwilliam again desperately trying to stave off mooted plans to disestablish the presidency. He protested that although the 'presidents of Wales and the north did not achieve perfection in seven years', he was expected to proffer the queen like results in a fraction of the time.[33] He stressed, in defence of both the presidency and his own record as president, that the Dublin government had previously had little control of the province and that power which it had enjoyed had been 'kept by letters which were seldom obeyed and the sending of commissioners on riding journeys who made orders which were not executed'. He contrasted this degree of misrule with the results that his government had already produced. He had overseen the execution of 180 rebels and had received pledges from most of the lords and freeholders of Munster. The effects of good government were already discernible: gallowglass were eager to turn to tillage, the people, 'lords and followers' were beginning to observe the law – for instance, in November 1573, Cornell O'Driscoll and Owen MacArt had recourse to the arbitration of the president and council over the

---

[31] Carew to Tremayne, 6 February 1574, SP63/45/51.
[32] Perrot to Fitzwilliam, 14 May 1571, SP63/32/41ii.
[33] Here Perrot was unconsciously echoing the sentiments expressed by Sidney to Cecil, 17 April 1566, Collins, Vol. I, p. 10, about the councils: 'I wot not what it should be looked for in Munster which was never had in Wales, nor the North of England'.

proctorship of Ross Cathedral (handed down by Perrot, Nicholas White, the second justice of Munster and the bishop of Cork).[34] Most importantly for Elizabeth, Perrot forecast an inevitable increase in crown revenues through the collection of rents and fines. But the only way of consolidating these results was by means of the presidency 'ready with her majesty's sword of justice'.

Perrot's belief in the necessity for the presidency went hand in hand with his disparagement of the native lords. Indeed, it would become clear, after the return of the earl of Desmond, that a bitter struggle over authority was raging between the English-Irish peerage and the presidency; one could only gain strength at the other's expense. He alleged that many rebels who *had* been willing to submit to the crown, once they heard of the earl's potential release, 'excused themselves', admitting that they were afraid of Desmond's inevitable anger at their submission to crown authority.[35] Perrot even claimed that he had only accepted James Fitzmaurice Fitzgerald's submission because he believed it necessary to secure his surrender before the earl of Desmond returned to Munster. The truth was that crown authority in Munster would be totally undermined if James Fitzmaurice Fitzgerald remained aloof from the provincial president's presence only to submit to his wonted overlord, the earl of Desmond.[36] At this time, Perrot was particularly wary that Whitehall, content to allow the earl to come into his own, might suddenly discontinue the president's office, and he was startled by Desmond's boasts that the presidential experiment would be finally wound up by Michaelmas 1573. It is indicative of the presidents' paranoia that it was thought likely that the earl of Desmond might be better informed about the state of crown policy in Ireland than its foremost officers.[37]

Despite these reverses, Perrot's paeans to the wonders of the law remained consistent. In summer 1573, he wrote from Cork boasting about the success of the sessions he was holding there 'at the which', he stated, 'great appearance hath been from all part of my rule.' He claimed to have executed approximately sixty people for offences ranging from treason to felony as well as enforced rules for the anglicisation of dress and manners. Again, the benefits were tangible. No 'two picking thieves' could be found in Munster; highway robbery was a thing of the past; 'perfect

---

[34] MacCormack, A., *The earldom of Desmond 1463–1583: the decline and crisis of a feudal lordship* (Dublin, 2005), p. 138, *Fiants*, Vol. II, 2382.
[35] Perrot to the privy council, 9 April 1573, SP63/40/6.
[36] Perrot to Burghley, 30 April 1573, SP63/40/19.
[37] Perrot to Burghley, 21 May 1573, SP63/40/50.

obedience and thorough quiet' were the order of the day; and the concomitant monetary gains were substantial. Crucially, the local elite had allegedly accepted their duty to provide 'the cess of beeves, horsemen and carriage'. Perrot had high hopes for revenue from pardons, revived rents and customs, the first fruits and twentieth parts, as well as hitherto unsurveyed abbey lands and escheated properties. Ireland could be won 'with less difficulty than slothful minds would make it'.[38] In July, when he entreated Elizabeth to maintain the presidency, he couched his argument as an appeal for the queen to treat those who had 'the liberties of *ius regale* . . . in some reasonable sort'. The bad tendencies associated with seigneurial government were withering away:

The plough (in this province) doth through your Majesty's goodness now laugh the unbridled kern and rogue to scorn. The poor do pray for your highness and the rest such as be able for the war (being as I take it, eight or nine thousand) do now honour you only and are sworn to your Majesty. Their hands begin to wax as hard with labour as their feet were before in running to mischief.[39]

Within three years, he claimed, the presidency in Munster would be financially self-sufficient.

Perrot's successor emulated his enthusiasm for the establishment of justice. William Drury, a noted soldier who had served as deputy governor of Berwick and had famously harried Mary Stuart's partisans in Scotland in the early 1570s, proved even more ebullient than Perrot during his presidency of Munster from 1576 to 1578, attempting to levy the cess as a preliminary stage in securing the implementation of Sidney's composition initiative. Under Drury's aegis, Owen MacCarthy Reagh, Lord Barry, Cormac MacTeig MacCarthy of Muskerry, MacDonough MacCarthy of Duhallow and the earl of Clancar all cooperated in Sidney's scheme.[40] As had been the case with Perrot, Drury, in his correspondence with Walsingham and the privy council, prioritised the benefits of judicial sessions held in Tralee and Cork. Whereas the 'common people' were most 'ready to embrace justice', the local magnates, he said, 'do impatiently bear and hardly digest the English government no further then force and heavy hand construeth'. For example, he was particularly pleased with the

---

[38] Perrot to Burghley, 18 June 1573, SP63/41/43; Perrot to Burghley, 2 July 1573, SP63/41/68; Perrot to Thomas Smith, 6 July 1573, SP63/42/71.
[39] Perrot to Elizabeth, 13 July 1573, SP63/71/76ii.
[40] See MacCormack (2005), pp. 139–44. MacCormack has pointed out how the revived presidential council under Drury – unlike the previous dispensation under Perrot – incorporated the earl of Desmond, yet, strangely excluded Clancar and Thomond.

success of the sessions he held on the border of the earldom of Ormond and the earl's liberty of Tipperary. Even though he had little legal training, he 'dealt in matters of justice betwixt the gentlemen of those borders' after which they all 'departed well satisfied for and in their private actions'. Drury's correspondence, like Perrot's, was full of vignettes of administrative achievement, governmental success and local enthusiasm. For instance, while he was administering law, Sir William O'Carroll brought in a pledge for good behaviour 'to the great admiration of the common people thereabout who never saw, as they alleged, so much committance of justice in that place, nor, ever had so long space of quietness among them'. Much hinged on the degree to which the lower orders of the population believed that the highest power effectively resided in the royal magistrate rather than the local magnates. In any case, the impartial justice given them by the crown, it was contended, truly liberated them from the self-interested designs of the local lords. Drury acknowledged as much when he stated that 'this manner of dealing and executing of justice, [is] grievous to some whose former lives depended chiefly upon extortion.' He anticipated further resistance to 'the countenance of justice' from the lords who might 'move trouble of intent to drive things into their wonted course of rule over the common sort'.[41] But he claimed to lead by example in Munster by taking a more confrontational approach to local government. 'The nobility and gentry', he told Walsingham, '[do] nothing more ... than to maintain their idle persons and thieves ... which wicked kind I have indifferently weeded out since my coming to the number of four score put to execution.'

Drury's defiance of the claims of sept honour and loyalty was ritually displayed when a captain of the 'MacSweeneys', a gallowglass, after being convicted at assizes in Cork was led to his place of execution with the banner of his clan carried before him. The flag was subsequently sent to Walsingham as a trophy.[42] He boasted how he had 'caused all the nobles, gentlemen and others in this province to book their men and to stand answerable for them'. He also ensured that the sheriff of each county and the provost marshal had a copy of this book. 'The marshal rides from place to place' he wrote ominously, 'and is not idle'. He hoped to establish an English-born sheriff in Limerick.[43] Drury defended the

---

[41] Drury to the privy council, 24 March 1578, SP63/60/25.
[42] Drury to Walsingham, 24 November 1576, SP63/56/51. Drury claimed to have had forty-two 'malefactors' hanged at these assizes.
[43] Drury to Walsingham, 24 November 1576, SP63/56/51.

severity of his administration by stressing his integrity in spite of local attempts to corrupt him. He 'could have had large sums to have consented to ... pardoning', he stated, 'if he would have regarded more his own commodity than the profit of the commonwealth.'[44] Most importantly, he emphasised the royal provenance of his judicial powers, refusing praise for 'the worthiness of [his] service' seeking rather to ascribe it

as of right I ought unto the virtue of justice placed and maintained by her majesty among her subjects, which shall and doth win her eternal fame, and great good unto the common wealth, whereby her majesty is made known in places in this province where before her officer was not seen.[45]

It seemed that Ireland was becoming the kingdom it was officially meant to be.

Malby, as governor of a newly shired Connacht, employed similar rhetoric.[46] In his case, his chronic opposition to the passively uncooperative earl of Clanricard and his insurgent scions gave the putative struggle between her majesty's justice and local privilege a sharp edge. This was never more obvious than when Malby presided over sessions in Galway at which William Burke, another of Clanricard's sons, and Turlough O'Brien, the earl of Thomond's brother, were tried and executed. Burke, already under protection, had allegedly 'spoiled and robbed her majesty's good subjects'. He was arrested in Galway and nine men of his retinue of twelve horsemen were instantly despatched by martial law. The account Malby sent to Walsingham is businesslike:

I took the justice with me and repaired thither to examine the cause and there holding sessions did put [Burke] to his trial, who being indicted for his former treasons did confess the same upon which he received sentence of death for treason and so the twenty seventh day of May was executed.

Turlough O'Brien suffered the same fate. Malby, like Drury, asserted his probity. Despite O'Brien's status as 'a very ill liver and a mischievous person ... a thousand pound was offered unto [him] for his life'. Malby claimed to have turned down the bribe, not merely because of a desire to be incorruptible but because there was 'no hope of [O'Brien's] amendment'.[47] He further noted that many in Connacht during the

---

[44] Drury to Walsingham, 24 August 1578, SP63/61/58; Drury to the privy council, 24 March 1578, SP63/60/25.
[45] Drury to the privy council, 24 March 1578, SP63/60/25.
[46] See Malby's Instructions 1578, BL Add MSS 4786, fols. 3–7.
[47] Malby to Walsingham, 30 June 1581, SP63/83/63.

rebellion of the *mac an iarlas* in 1576 were terrified to do their duty to the the crown for fear of what might happen to them when the earl of Clanricard returned.[48] The benefits of loyalty to the crown were not evident to those who feared the backlash of their wonted masters, their heavy-handed retainers and allies. Having faced down a drastic situation in Connacht between 1576 and 1577, Malby bragged about the initial passivity of Connacht during the early part of the second Desmond rebellion in 1579, which seemed especially notable given that he was absent from the scene: 'the settled and continuing government there duly executed is the very foundation and pillar of upholding obedience to the prince'.[49] Just before his death, he still wrote of the compelling properties of government by due process, stating how the queen's subjects having experienced justice were 'now the most inclined to seek for it of any Irishmen in this land, as some of her majesty's council here who have been with me at sundry sessions will and can well testify'. The hoary old motifs were rehearsed again: the lords were quiet; the poor ploughed without fear; former malefactors under stay of execution were placid; and, crucially, the 'poor man' was not afraid 'to complain against his lord'.[50]

The captains' reception of well-worn Aristotelian motifs about good government was typical: moral virtue was acquired through habituation, and the means of instilling habituation was law. Any other state of affairs bred unhappiness. Sir Henry Sidney wrote in 1575 about how the Irish grandees of Munster were 'ashamed of their wilful misery' and how the province's 'ancient English inhabitants' whose ancestors had produced writings and built 'monuments' were now 'all in *misery*, either banished from their own, or oppressed upon their own' (my italics).[51] Despite this conservatism, we know that English captains were not entirely naive of speculations about the best form of commonwealths and the role of magistracy in reforming flawed polities. A discerning eye for the health or corruption of states had featured as a central aspect of Sir Humphrey

---

[48] Malby to Elizabeth, 20 September 1576, SP63/56/34.
[49] Malby to Walsingham, 10 September 1579, SP63/69/17. See also the reference to the garrison in Connacht circa the first of June 1579, numbering 136 paid troops, which was 'wholly to be paid and borne of the revenues of that province' in 'The book [wherein] is contained the numbers of her Majesty's garrison in pay, SP63/69/45.
[50] Malby to the privy council, 24 March 1583, SP63/100/44.
[51] Sidney to the privy council, 27 February 1575, Collins (1746), p. 91. In 1584 Perrot is reported to have referred to the sister kingdom as 'miserable Ireland'. See Rawlinson, R., *History of that most eminent statesman Sir John Perrot* (London, 1728), p. 134. See the treatment of Aristotelian moral philosophy as received in the sixteenth century in J. Kraye, 'Moral philosophy' in *The Cambridge history of Renaissance philosophy* (Cambridge, 1988), pp. 330-9.

Gilbert's recommended academy for Elizabeth's wards with classes on civil policy consisting of a close examination of the structure of monarchies, commonwealths and principalities past, present and future with reference to each state's revenues and system of justice. Gilbert had also audaciously outlined the application of the same method 'as near as conveniently may be ... to the present estate and government of this realm', that is England – the sort of anatomy of English government that Thomas Smith had produced in *De republica anglorum*. In the same spirit, Philip Sidney recommended certain books to Edward Denny before he went to 'bend [him]self to soldiery' in Ireland. The titles, presumably chosen to enhance and inform Denny's experience of Irish service, included Aristotle's *Ethics*, 'Tully's offices', Herodotus, Thucydides, Xenophon, Diodorus Siculus, Quintus Curtius, Polybius, Livy, Dionysius, Sallust, Caesar, Dion and Tacitus as well as more modish works such as Languet in French and Machiavelli in Italian. Anyone au fait with Machiavelli's *Discorsi* might have found the lesson proffered in Book I, Chapter 7, namely that 'a corrupt people which becomes free can remain so only with the greatest difficulty', apt for a country and a people corrupted at every hand's turn by local tyrants. Significantly, Machiavelli's remedy in such a case was the enaction of laws by a man 'with enormous power' who could ensure that those laws are observed in such a way 'that the material becomes good'.[52] The captains, in their conceit, whether they followed venerable Aristotelian motifs or modish Machiavellian ones could easily muster the conceptual wherewithal to believe that they instantiated the external force needed to direct the Irish towards their social end and to ensure that the society that resulted from such engineering would produce the common good of its members.[53] And yet, whatever certainty there was about the mission of the seneschals and presidents in Ireland, the provenance of their authority, especially that of the provincial presidents, was not without its political and constitutional ambiguities.

THE REALITY OF '*PRECARIUM IMPERIUM*'

In December 1573, Edward Waterhouse, only recently recruited as the first earl of Essex's personal secretary, sent former lord deputy Sir Henry

---

[52] Machiavelli, N., *Discourses on Livy*, eds. J. C. Bondanella and P. Bondanella (Oxford, 1997), p. 67. Osborn (1972), p. 538.
[53] See Thomas Aquinas *Summa Theologicae prima secundae* q 91, a. 1–2, and *De regimine principum*, chapters 1, 14.

Sidney a note telling him about Irish matters at court.[54] According to Waterhouse, in the aftermath of Sir William Fitzwilliam's lacklustre performance and, given the difficulties the earl of Essex was facing in his 'enterprise of Ulster', inaugurated three months earlier, Elizabeth and the privy council were seeking an overhaul of government in the sister kingdom and were having a no-holds-barred examination of the options open to Elizabeth.

Three plans, in particular, were being considered. The first was explicitly military. Waterhouse remarked that the appointment of 'a lieutenant, or a general, over the armies' was suggested, one to 'be sent with such authority, as the earl of Pembroke had in Picardy, in Queen Mary's days'. Once the military governor 'had appeased all stirs', he would be replaced by a civil governor. Another plan, Waterhouse related, entailed the exaltation of the presidents of Munster, Ulster and Connacht 'under particular regimen *distinct* from the controlment of the deputy'. This autonomy, it was hoped, would lead to 'a certain virtuous envy in these *monarchs*' (my italics) who would, by competing for Elizabeth's favour, employ all their energies to establish better government in Ireland. The social pressures and appetites that made Fitzwilliam slight Bagenal and Malby vie with Drury in Thomond would be turned to good use: the urge for pre-eminence made policy. Lastly, there was an alternative proposal that was thought 'more perilous'. It recommended that 'the sword [should be] put into the hands of the Irish lords . . . as the earls of Ormond and Kildare' with the deputy merely managing 'causes of Justice and law'. This idea – effectively a return to the ideal of 'aristocratic home rule' – was thought to be a very plausible prospect, not only by the Irish but also by the crown's servitors themselves.[55] Indeed, governors and captains often desperately asserted that it was the de-facto pattern of crown government in Ireland.

Five months before Waterhouse wrote his paper, John Perrot, president of Munster, had written to principal secretary Thomas Smith complaining about jurisdictional tension arising between himself and the earl of Ormond, his 'former friend'. Whatever personal affinity had existed between them in Edwardian times was now threatened by the commonplace discovery that the office made the man. Perrot was wounded

---

[54] See Waterhouse's pitch for a royal salary to be paid for serving Essex in Ulster, SP63/41/66. Brady (2002) p. 100.
[55] Waterhouse to Sidney, 17 December 1573, A. Collins, *Letters and memorials of state*, 2 vols. (London, 1746), Vol. I, p. 62. The plan for a shock military governor was in some ways attempted during the second Desmond Revolt with the appointment of Lord Deputy Grey de Wilton in 1580.

The limits of imperium

and dismayed at the high-handed attitude the earl had taken towards his attempts to exercise crown rule in the liberty of Tipperary. He was indignant about the principle of the matter, despite the fact that Lord Treasurer Burghley had enjoined Perrot to be more politic in this affair. Ormond's officers had alleged that the lord president had done 'sundry things ... prejudicial unto [the earl's] liberties', but Perrot protested that 'it were within this province [of Munster], and I had good authority so to do', adding that he was 'warranted to call for [the sheriff of Tipperary] or any other officer within any part of this province' by virtue of the tenth and eleventh articles of his instructions 'and other commissions granted by the state here'. He stated that his only concern was the preservation of the integrity of crown government in Munster, not 'private gain' and stressed, for good measure, that his actions could not be perceived as self-interested as he 'neither had patrimony in Ireland nor will have any'.[56] Perrot had a pejorative term for crown government characterised by careful deference to seigneurial interests in Ireland: he called it *precarii imperii*. He obviously assumed that Thomas Smith, a leading civilian, agreed that the informality of such a careless political and constitutional policy had already done 'hurt' in Ireland and that its further pursuit would only produce greater harm. Consequently, he asked that 'the governor might be *so abled* as he should not be driven to use it' (my italics). In short, Perrot, like Fitton, wanted increased powers, in spite of what he saw as the crown's policy of appeasing corrupt Irish lords. Seven days later, in the same vein, he exhorted Elizabeth to take the 'sword' wholly into her hands in Ireland.[57] Perrot's reference to the 'sword' – although sometimes used to signify martial law – was in this context an explicit reference to the legist Ulpian's definition of *merum imperium* cited in the Digest: to hold *merum imperium* was to possess 'the power of the sword to punish the wicked, also called *potestas*', that is the power to coerce.[58]

---

[56] Perrot to Burghley, 12 April 1573, SP63/42/11. Perrot added that he 'would God there were no liberties in Ireland so as [Ormond] and other owners thereof were otherwise recompensed in lieu of the same' and refers to his 'former friendship' with the earl. Perrot later imprisoned the sheriff of Tipperary, see Perrot to Burghley, 11 May 1573, SP63/40/35. See also the instructions 'for the establishing of a council in Munster' in Collins (1746), Vol. I, pp. 48–59, which indicate that the earl of Ormond was allowed 'the regalities, knights fees, and other liberties' in the County of Tipperary, with the exceptions of four pleas: burning, ravishing, treasure found, and a customary exaction to the crown' but under something of a caution from the president.

[57] Perrot to Elizabeth, 13 July 1573, SP63/41/76II.

[58] Waterhouse to Sidney, 17 December 1573, Collins, Vol. I, p. 62. Here the use of the emblem of the sword refers to *merum imperium* as referred to in the Digest: *Merum est imperium habere gladii potestam ad animadvertendum facinorosos homines, quod etiam potestas appelatur*, *Digest of Justinian*, ed. T. Mommsen, P. Kruegar, trans. A. Watson, (Pennsylvania, Pa., 1985), p. 40.

In Ireland, the image had further resonance as the sword of state held by the viceroy was the chief symbol of royal power in Ireland; appointees to the viceroyalty did not accede to the viceregal office until they received the sword of state. Waterhouse would later inform Sidney that many believed that the 'sword' had been alienated to the Irish overmuch.

Perrot's use of Latin or civil-law terminology, however, was not a rarefied pretension on his part. *Precarium imperium* had become a common phrase. Connacht's Lord President Edward Fitton, finding his authority frustrated in the recalcitrant earldom of Thomond, declared to Burghley in February 1570 that

> we have but Imperium precarium [and thus] we are favoured to suffer every man to do what he list, disobey process, break orders, commit forces make unlawful assemblies and we, driven to speak fair, which our lack of power must needs be supplied otherwise we shall be but like Aesop's block which Jupiter threw down among the frogs instead of a king.[59]

Fitton's successor Nicholas Malby used the term when telling Walsingham of his achievements in garrisoning Connacht and cowing Ulick Burke. The province he declared was 'wholly at her majesty's devotion', a state of affairs which had been 'wrought only with extreme travail and not by *precarii imperium* which I never saw do any good in Ireland'.[60] Even when Perrot became lord deputy in 1582, after Grey de Wilton's tour of duty, he maintained that 'the state, as it is, may well be called *precarii imperium*', a condition that 'was neither godly nor honorable'.[61]

Precarium imperium was mongrelised terminology for an apparently hypocritical policy. Although referring to informal bridles placed on the royal prerogatives, it did not refer to the benign checks on royal power envisaged by Fortescue's *dominium politicum et regale*; rather, it mixed languages peculiar to distinct areas of civil law in a provocative manner. *Precarium* appeared in the Digest as the description of anything granted or lent upon request at the will of the grantor, and *imperium*, as explained earlier, was the central concept of Roman law, the power that underpinned every maxim and piece of legislation.[62] The meaning of this coinage,

---

[59] Fitton to Sidney, 22 February 1570, SP63/30/15.
[60] Malby to Walsingham, 30 June 1581, SP63/83/63.
[61] In contrast Burghley, with his constant eye for economy, tended to counsel indulgence of the native magnates, both English-Irish and Gaelic-Irish. See his 1574 memorandum on the government of Ireland, SP63/44/65.
[62] See Digest 43, 26, 1 for this definition of *precarium*: *Precarium est, quod precibus petenti utendum conceditur tam diu, quamdiu is qui concessit patitur: quod genus liberalitatis ex jure gentium descendit, et distat a conatione eo, quod qui donat sic dat, ne recipiat: qui precario concedit sic dat, quasi tunc recepturus, cum sibi libuerit precarium solvere.*

a hybrid of private law and public authority, seemed perverse, and this was how it was meant to appear. *Precarium imperium* referred to the way the captains felt about the status of crown sovereignty in Ireland, a status that resulted directly from crown policy there. What they were asserting by using the term was that *imperium* in reality, if not in constitutional fact, appeared to be the possession of the native Irish lords, who resided de facto in their own 'imperial jurisdiction[s]' lending authority to rule the country to their queen and her delegates on sufferance. In short, Ireland's 'imperial crown' operated in Ireland in such a timid way that an observer might think that the generic *lex regia* of Roman law, the conferral of all the people's command and power to the prince, had been merely conditional rather than perpetual.[63] In this way, as far as the captains were concerned, Ireland seemed to be in a state of *lèse-majesté*. Jealous of the regal nature of their appointments, they wished to secure total submission to crown authority and the elimination of any hint of baronial supremacy.

These frustrations were of long standing. Early in Elizabeth's reign, the earl of Sussex had indicated his anxiety to protect the privileges of the crown, and, by extension, those of its officers, from Irish encroachment. He told the new queen that he had governed through the use of both the civil law and martial law 'by keeping the obedient people in fear of the laws and the disobedient in fear of the sword' and then boasted that under his viceroyalty 'many rights and prerogatives belonging to the crown (and by them [the Irish] usurped) [had] been resumed'. Significantly, he indicated that he had the 'better brought [this] to pass for that [he] had force sufficient to do this with'.[64] To the frustration of successive seneschals, constables and presidents, the queen seemed resolutely unconcerned about the degree to which her power and authority had been alienated in Ireland. She certainly did not seem anxious to provide the sort of augmentation of the garrison that had enabled Sussex to defend the monarch's poise there, as the many unsuccessful calls for augmentation of the garrison in Ireland would indicate. Lord President Drury in 1576, using particularly daring language, wrote to Walsingham that he hoped Elizabeth would 'not let slip that princely prerogative whereof they [the Irish peerage] woulde [dis]robe her, that themselves might the more largely empose coign and livery and many other Irish exactions'.[65] But the

---

[63] The designation of the Irish lordships as 'imperial jurisdictions' comes from Panderus' 'State of Ireland and it's [sic] reformation' in *SP Hen VIII*, Vol. II, Part 3, pp. 1–3.
[64] Sussex's notes for Elizabeth I, February 1559, SP63/1/13.
[65] Drury to Walsingham, 24 November 1576, SP63/56/51.

only weapon the captains could use to counter the slights they suffered because of *precarium imperium* and their queen's toleration of it, was the exercise of the *imperium* they believed they had, often in an ever more extreme manner.

Imperium, as wielded by English military men in Ireland, found governmental expression in two ways. The first, martial law, was either granted on a short-term commission or as an intrinsic discretionary aspect of the exercise of an office. Within the purview of a provincial presidency, it was, unless necessity dictated otherwise, usually meant to be used with the agreement of at least one other member of the presidential council, but an amenable figure who was not a native magnate was generally easy to find. 'The sword' in this context could be conceived of as a crucial element of any successful attempt to reform a polity. Second, many captains, specifically provincial presidents, wielded *imperium* by virtue of their judicial role. The queen's law in Ireland was often meted out at sessions by military men, of uneven training in the law, assisted by a justice and legal clerks. On occasion, as was the case for Nicholas Malby from 1576 to 1578 and Humphrey Gilbert in 1569 and 1570, when the title of president was not assumed, the more Caesarean title of colonel or military governor was employed, but this martial designation did not exclude the use of the president's wonted judicial powers and procedures.[66] The titles of provincial president and governor were hallowed ones burnished by remembrance of how the Roman senate had sent out consuls, dictators and other military officers with almost unfettered authority to rule over errant possessions. The example outlined in that most basic of Latin texts, Caesar's Gallic Wars, replete with tyrannical Gaulish or Gothic kings defined either as 'friends of the Roman people' or barbarians, had echoes in the variegated and semi-autonomous political landscape of Elizabethan Ireland.[67] Of course, the actual title of provincial president, *praeses provinciae*, was enshrined in the *Institutes* of Justinian.[68] Barnaby Googe's famous remark, made while convalescing in 1583, that Malby's 'common

---

[66] Gilbert's appointment as colonel of the forces in Munster followed Henry Sidney's unsuccessful attempts to have Warham St Leger appointed provincial president. St Leger's proposed promotion was blocked by the earl of Ormond who alleged that Warham's father, Lord Deputy Antony St Leger, had murdered his father. Malby's unpopularity with Elizabeth, the earl of Ormond and Baron Burghley has already been referred to.
[67] Brady has brought attention to the Caesarean style of Sir Henry Sidney's 1583, *Memoir of service* in Brady (2002) pp. 9–10.
[68] See Title VIII in the *Institutes*.

dalliance' with the potentates of Connacht and 'over mighty monarchs of Ulster' was *'veni, vidi, vici'* was not a careless one.[69]

The attempts of the captains to maximise their ministration of the *imperium* may well have been a self-serving manoeuvre, but, notwithstanding this, their belief that they could exercise such power had a corollary in their frequent attempts to skip the niceties of due process in their private causes. This audacity was expressed most strongly when they sought the judgement of crown authority through equitable jurisdictions rather than common law. For instance, Jacques Wingfield in 1561 obstructed all attempts by Robert Nangle, the chancellor of St Patrick's Cathedral in Dublin to get courts of common pleas, queen's bench and exchequer to hear and determine a suit between them over the parsonage of Finglas despite the fact that the queen's attorney, the chief justice and the chief baron upheld Nangle's claim, by 'claim[ing] the privilege of trial by martial law . . . as one of the army in Ireland'.[70] Another example of special pleading was Sir Peter Carew's legal bid to 'recover' the farm of Maston in Meath from Sir Christopher Cheevers, a pillar of the Pale gentry. Carew's claim to the property, discovered by his agent John Hooker alias Vowell of Exeter, was so plainly arbitrary and insulting to the county communities of the Pale that Carew protested that 'he could not have his just trial at the common law', because no jury could be empanelled in Ireland that would find in his favour, and therefore he asked that the lord deputy and council should adjudicate. Cheevers declared that the matter, being a land dispute, was outside the jurisdiction of the deputy and council, while the common-law courts were still in term, and the chief justices of Ireland (both English-Irish) Sir Robert Dillon and Sir James Plunkett tended to agree with him. But in reply, William Peryam, Carew's lawyer, stated that Elizabeth 'by her prerogative, might and did use to call before her all matters whatsoever depending on any court', and her viceroy could do the same.[71] What resulted amounted to a low-level constitutional crisis.

---

[69] Googe to Cecil, 11 March, 1583, SP63/100/14. Significantly Googe also referred to the fact that Malby could not cow the earl of Ormond: 'if my lord of Ormond beats earnestly the bushes of Munster it is not unlike but our berries will be more pested with vermin than they have ever been before'.

[70] *CPR Eliz. 1560–3*, p. 113. The dispute was over the parsonage of Finglas. 'The matter was submitted to master Gerrard, the Queen's attorney, when he was in Ireland, and he and the said chief justice and chief baron gave their opinions in favour of [Nangle]; but he cannot recover the premises by means of the common law, because Wingfield as a councillor in Ireland is too powerful, and is also liable to be called away on military service, and also because Wingfield, as one of the army in Ireland, claims the privilege of trial by martial law.'

[71] Hooker (1867), pp. 99–101. A particularly good account of this event can be found in Wagner (1998), pp. 296–302.

In Carew's case, the Dublin inns and the chief justices bowed to pressure and determined that the lord deputy and council had the competence to adjudicate on the matter. In the tribunal that ensued, the 'ancient' documents that upheld the controversial claim trumped Cheevers' occupancy and the opinion of his neighbours. Cheevers, touchingly, persevered in asserting the council's incompetence to consider the question citing Chapters 11 and 29 of Magna Carta, which declared that common pleas did not follow the king's court and that no freeman could be disseised of his freehold or liberties but by lawful judgement of his peers. As a result, he was blasted for persisting in an assault on her majesty's prerogative.[72] When Carew's claim prevailed, he allowed Cheevers to remain on the land because, in Hooker's words, he made 'more account of the conquest, and that he had made him to confess before the lord deputy and council and the chiefest of the realm then present that he had no title to the land, than he did for the value of the land': an apparently trite return – merely the demonstration of pre-eminence – for so much anxiety caused.[73] Directly afterwards, Carew pursued his claim for the lands of the Kavanaghs at Idrone. The three principal members of the sept appeared before the lord deputy and attempted to uphold their freehold of the land using the same arguments that Cheevers had used, but to no avail; even their descendancy from Diarmait 'na nGall' MacMurchada, the king of Leinster who had first invited the English to Ireland, did not wash. In short, Carew effectively asserted his pre-eminence not only over Cheevers but also over English-Irish custom and usage in general. This was a denial of the admissibility of an Irish *lex terrae*, or, at least, its admissibility in cases where the interest of an English crown officer was in question. It was thus implicitly asserted that the stuff of the country and its courts was so partial and corrupt that an Englishman could not receive justice there except by equity. And yet, paradoxically, the very idea of an impartial common law and common justice was the ideal that the seneschals and presidents had pledged to establish throughout the country.[74]

---

[72] Cheevers also pointed to 28 Edw 3 cap. 3 'That no man, of what estate or condition that he be shall be put out of land or tenement . . . without being brought in answer by due process of Law' and 42 Edw 3 cap. 3 'That no man be put to answer without presentment before Justices or matter of record, or by due process and writ original according to the Law of the Land, and if anything from henceforth be done to the contrary, it shall be void in the Law, and holden for error'. See Richard Cox's *Hibernia anglicana* (London, 1689), Vol. I, p. 328, and *Statutes at Large* (London, 1706).
[73] Hooker (1867), pp. 99–101.
[74] John Hooker's account of his own intervention in the Irish parliament of 1569 indicates the level of contempt that could be expressed by Englishmen for the substance of the Irish polity. Hooker, Peter Carew's secretary and a close friend of Humphrey Gilbert, by his own account, was attacked

Waterhouse's sketch of a proposed plan to give each of the presidents a distinct 'regimen ... from the controlment of the Deputy' alludes to the question as to what degree the presidents' and seneschals' power depended on the extent of the lord deputy's authority.[75] Within the kingdom of Ireland up until the cess controversy of 1577, there was an apparent lack of consensus on this matter. Philip Sidney remarked in his *Discourse on Irish affairs* how the Palesmen had only latterly conceded the point 'that such things granted to the queen, fall now to be the deputy's'.[76] Certain of the Irish learned to hold Henry Sidney's attitude to his office in particular suspicion. It was alleged by his Ormondist detractors that he was using the royal *imperium* in a factional interest for the earl of Leicester. He himself recalled in 1583 how, fourteen years earlier, Sir Edmund Butler had warned his followers that 'the earl of Leicester ... should marry the queen and be king of England, and that [Sidney] should be king of Ireland.' The lord deputy, it was claimed, would 'hold Ireland (as might appear) by bearing the ragged staff'.[77] Divisions at court percolated easily into the factional politics of Ireland. When Conor O'Brien, the earl of Thomond, was standing aloof from President Edward Fitton in Thomond, he allegedly announced his defiance by declaring openly at supper 'that he would do nothing with the lord deputy nor lord president but as the duke of Norfolk would say'.[78] And Elizabeth, aware of such polarities and fearing their implications, was wary of Sidney's ambitions and sometimes openly sought to curb them. For example, when she expressed disapproval of Philip Sidney's diplomatic and strategic match with Mary, daughter of William of Orange in 1577, she stated that she would not assist in 'the withdrawing [of] the

---

by two English-Irish lawyers Edmund Butler of Callan, attorney for the liberties of Tipperary, and John Bathe of Drumcondra, as well as Sir Christopher Barnwell, MP for County Dublin for 'naughtily compar[ing] Philip and the Queen [i.e. Mary I] unto Pharaoh'. Their rage was no doubt enhanced by the Speaker James Stanyhurst's injunction against anybody who attempted to leave the house during Hooker's speech, an oration allegedly peppered with references to the Irish members as 'kerns'. Hooker's irreverence stemmed from the perception that Ireland was a flawed commonwealth *tout court* and a concomitant superiority he felt as one English officer amongst others, all agents of reform. See V. Treadwell, 'The Irish parliament of 1569–71', *Proceedings of the Royal Irish Academy* 65, sect. C (1976), pp. 69–70 and John Hooker's Memorandum Book, Cambridge University Library MS Mm. 1.32.

[75] Waterhouse to Sidney, 17 December 1573, Collins, A., *Letters and memorials of state*, 2 vols. (London, 1746), Vol. I, p. 62.
[76] Sidney, P., *Miscellaneous prose of Sir Philip Sidney*, ed. K. Duncan-Jones and J. Van Dorsten (Oxford, 1973), p. 11.
[77] Brady (2002) p. 66.   [78] Fitton to Sidney, 22 February 1570, SP63/30/15.

subject from the sovereign' in the Netherlands, arguing that 'we could not like that any foreign prince should enter into *any such secret combination with our president of Wales or deputy of Ireland or any governor under us*' (my italics).[79] The castigation of the ambitions of both Sidneys was pointed. Much as it was deemed necessary to defend her prerogative against the legal pretensions of the Palesmen, Elizabeth suspected that Sidney's zeal for her *imperium* in Ireland was fundamentally partial in its ambitions. Caesarean ambition, it appears, was never far from Henry Sidney's mind. The bridge at Athlone, which he had erected following his 1568 progress through Connacht, was not only adorned with a bust of Elizabeth but also sported two effigies of the viceroy complete with a biblical exhortation to be obedient to the demands, financial and otherwise, of the English crown's spiritual and temporal prerogatives: 'Give to Caesar that w[hich] / Is Caesar's, and to God / That which is God's.'[80] Such conceit was endemic at Penshurst, as can be deduced from Philip Sidney's practice on his 1577 embassy to Germany of adorning each residence he stayed at with a tablet announcing that he was son of the *pro-rex* of Ireland, a description of his father's office that implied substitution rather than delegation.[81]

That delegated *imperium* was central to the understanding the captains had of their own status and authority is clear, but what was the nature of the delegation which they believed took place? In such matters, everything hinged on the proposed definition of *imperium*. The political vocabulary of imperial monarchy had already proved particularly useful in an English context following Henry VIII's break with Rome, allowing the increased use not only of the anti-papal, anti-hierocratic political thinking of figures, such as Marsilius of Padua, but of civilian idiom and vocabulary, allowing him to assert that all authority, spiritual and temporal, within his realms resided ultimately in the English imperial crown.[82] Of course, there had been no formal reception of civil law in England but in matters of the *arcana imperii*, the mysteries that dealt with the king's right, the vocabulary used was often Roman in character and meaning

---

[79] Worden (1996), p. 44.
[80] Loeber, R., *The Geography and practice of English colonisation in Ireland from 1534 to 1609* (Athlone, 1991), p. 34.
[81] Worden (1996), pp. 43–7.
[82] The language of imperial monarchy was frequently employed in the composition of statutes. For example see *The statutes at large passed in the parliaments held in Ireland . . .* 13 vols. (Dublin, 1786), Vol. I, pp. 176–7, 302–3.

and could be maximal in intent.[83] As early as 1515, Henry was declaring that 'kings of England in times past have never had any superior but God alone'; by 1521, Henry stated that that '[we] of our absolute power be above the laws', and, although he relied on parliament to institute the act of supremacy (1534), he never believed that this implied any constitutional restraint on his sovereignty.[84] All exercise of *imperium* hitherto alienated from the will of the English crown was to be re-annexed: in 1536 Henry formally resumed 'certain liberties and franchises heretofore taken from the crown', declaring by statute that

no person ... shall have any power or authority to make any justices of eyre, justices of assize, justices of peace, justices of gaol delivery, but all such officers and ministers [as] shall be made by letters patents under the king's great seal in the name and authority of the king's highness.[85]

The annexation of 'supreme' authority over the Church in England had a lasting effect on views of the scope of the monarchical power of the Tudors issuing ultimately in the judgement by the common law judges on Cawdry's Case in 1591 which declared that far from being a 'mixed polity', 'by the ancient laws of this realm this kingdom of England is an absolute empire and monarchy'.[86] In this context, it is important to realise that the designation of the English monarch as an emperor was not a mere embellishment of royal titles extant. It signified the acceptance of a whole political discourse that could advance constitutional propositions which differed markedly from common-law and classical republican assumptions about limited monarchy. But what did such claims mean in the context of Irish governance? To answer this question, it may be useful to consider briefly some developments in Continental thought concerning the delegation of *imperium*.

---

[83] See T. F. Mayer 'On the road to 1534: the occupation of Tournai and Henry VIII's theory of sovereignty' and Dale Hoak 'The iconography of the crown imperial' in Hoak ed. (1995) 11–30, 54–103 and John Guy 'Tudor monarchy and its critiques' in Guy (1997) pp. 78–109.

[84] For the debate between Thomas Cartwright, a Presbyterian, and John Whitgift, later archbishop of Canterbury and the verdict of the common law judges in Cawdry's Case (1591), see J. Guy, 'Tudor monarchy and its critiques' in Guy (1997), pp. 99–101. For Henry VIII's statement see the same article pp. 83–4. See also J. Morrill 'The origins of the British problem' in B. Bradshaw and J. Morrill (eds.) *The British problem c. 1534–1707: state formation in the Atlantic archipelago* (London, 1996), p. 63.

[85] See 27 H8, cap. 25 in *The whole volume of statutes at large* ... (London, 1587), pp. 720–3 and also Chapter 5 of W. Lambarde, *Eirenarcha or the office of the justice of the peace* ... (London, 1582), pp. 26–32, entitled 'by whose authority and by what means, justices of the peace be appointed: and of what sort they be'.

[86] Guy (1997), pp. 101–3.

QUESTIONS OF DELEGATION

One of the abiding disputes of civil law was a debate on whether the *merum imperium* belonged solely to the monarch who delegated it to his or her magistrates who thereafter merely exercised it, or whether the magistrates of themselves had a measure of *imperium*. This notorious conundrum, a cause of disagreement between the jurists Azo and Lothair, had been revived and revised in the sixteenth century. The trend for centuries had been to state that Azo, who argued that magistrates held proprietorial rights over some *merum imperium* themselves, had been legally correct. This changed markedly when the renowned civilian and humanist Andreas Alciatus (1492–1550), an anti-Bartolist professor of law at Bourges, declared that *imperium* was, indeed, vested solely in the monarch.[87] Such a conclusion accounted for the arbitrary and high-handed treatment that the *parlement* of Paris and the French estates general suffered at the hands of Francis I. This assessment was given further weight by the legal works of Jean Ferrault and Charles Dumoulin and many others whose absolutist view of monarchy almost totally supplanted the 'mixed polity' tradition best represented by Claude de Seyssels.[88] The extent to which 'absolute' power could be delegated in any state was a topic of dispute. Alciatus believed on one hand that only the exercise of *merum imperium* could be delegated to a magistrate, but held, on the other hand, that any magistrate equal in rank to a *praeses provinciae* ought to be granted the administration of the *merum imperium*. The central difference between *exercitatio* and *administratio* was expressed through the extent of an officer's powers to delegate. Crudely put, one who was merely an executor of the *imperium* could not re-delegate his powers, while a minister of the *imperium* could.[89]

In Ireland, provincial presidents had the power to make provincial appointments, a useful means of establishing crown rule throughout the land. For example, in 1583 Sir Nicholas Malby delegated the establishment of justice in Thomond to the young earl.[90] A similar assumption of

---

[87] See M. P. Gilmore, *Argument from Roman Law in political thought, 1200–1600* (Cambridge, Mass., 1941), pp. 48–57. For the context in which Alciatus made his contribution see P. Stein, *Roman Law in European History* (Cambridge, 1999), pp. 77–80.
[88] Skinner, Q., *Foundations of modern political thought*, 2 vols. (Cambridge, 1978), Vol. II, pp. 254–67.
[89] Gilmore (1941), pp. 49–57.
[90] Malby to Leicester, 6 July 1583, SP63/103/41. Thompson, G., *Lords lieutenant in the sixteenth century* (London, 1923), pp. 60–7. From the beginning of Elizabeth's reign many lords lieutenant in England – trusted members of the privy council given extraordinary authority over a county at the queen's pleasure – had clauses of deputation inserted in their commissions. Normally, but not uniformly, the lord lieutenant was responsible for the choice of his deputy.

delegation in the Clanricard lordship occurred in 1577 after John Burke, one of the *mac an iarlas* (the contemporary moniker for the sons of the earl of Clanricard) claimed that he had rights over 'half of those castles [that Malby had] committed to [his brother] Ulick's custody'. Ulick, in turn, refused to acknowledge his brother's complaint, telling John that the castles were 'not his [own] but the queen's, and . . . he [that is, Ulick] hath but the *use* of them during pleasure' (my italics). The appetite for power and pre-eminence may have led figures to act as if the president had the power to delegate his powers entirely. In 1577, Edward Whyte, clerk of the earl of Clanricard, wrote to Nicholas Malby, then governor of Connacht, warning him that during his absence at court in England, Robert Dillon, constable of Loughrea, 'when he is in the tavern . . . will say he hath more authority from your worship than Ulick [Burke] and taketh upon him as vice-president in your absence.'[91] Although Malby's appropriation of the power of delegation may have stemmed from notions about the powers of appointment that a colonel in the field might enjoy, more plausibly, this sense of empowerment came from the fact that the viceroy of Ireland was, in truth, a *pro-rex*, an actual incarnation in Ireland of the fount of sovereignty, not a delegate. This understanding had powerful knock-on effects for officers appointed by him.

As things stood, the limitations placed on the authority of the Irish viceroys by their commissions determined that appointment to certain offices within the kingdom were reserved to the queen herself; furthermore, there were procedural limits in the viceroy's relationship with the Irish council, but otherwise, as Sir John Perrot himself attested:

his patent was as all other deputies, not with limitation of years, or time of government but during pleasure, containing power to make war and peace, to levy arms and forces for that purpose, to punish and pardon offenders, to confer all offices and collate all spiritual promotions and dignities (a few of them excepted) concluded with the greatest latitude of authority which can be given a subject, which is to do all things in cases of justice and government, as the prince might do being present.[92]

J. G. Crawford has acknowledged that there was some disagreement as to whether the authority of the Irish council subsisted in the lord deputy or was solely held in a collegiate manner. Certainly, when Sir William

---

[91] Whyte to Malby, undated, 1577, SP63/59/70.
[92] *The government of Ireland under Sir John Perrot* (London, 1626), p. 5.

Fitzwilliam moved to Maryborough in 1573, he brought two civil officials with him but left the council in Dublin apparently powerless to legislate in his absence; by contrast, seven years later, in 1580, Lord Justice Pelham determined that decisions made by the council remaining in Dublin during his absence in Munster were to be deemed 'as available, perfect and permanent as if all we the body of the whole council were or had been altogether present'.[93] But, as Perrot expounded, it appears to have been the orthodoxy that the viceroy's powers were of the same magnitude as the monarch's, and therefore the deputy delegated the administration of *merum imperium* to Ireland's provincial presidents and other officers. On the other hand, it seemed evident as the century wore on (especially during Perrot's term of office, marred, as we shall see, by a fierce rift with his president of Connacht) that Waterhouse's 1573 suggestion that the governors of the provinces might become as 'monarchs' was no flight of fancy.[94] Given the increasing divergence between each of the provinces of Ireland in the 1580s it seemed plausible that the authority of presidents could be expanded so that their relationship with the monarch would be of the same character as that between the viceroy and Elizabeth: direct and unmediated.

There were, however, metropolitan voices abroad that dissented from the legal voluntarism and opportunism characteristic of the English constables', seneschals' and presidents' approach to Irish government and which looked to due process for amendment of Ireland's woes. Loudest of these was the voice of Sir William Gerrard, Sir Henry Sidney's lord chancellor. Although Gerrard defended Sidney's right as viceroy to exact cess and its commutation without consent from a 'grand council', he did so by virtue of legal precedents from the reign of Henry III to the deputyship of Edward Bellingham, not by virtue of the viceregal office per se. However, notwithstanding this, Gerrard counselled a political climbdown on Sidney's part, alluding to his vain-glory in carrying out his policy. Following Sidney's recall, Gerrard, warming to his new role as protector of Irishmen's English liberties against the conceit of Englishmen, campaigned vigorously for judicial, legal and civil reform in Ireland in a way designed to respect indigenous constitutional structures. But his programme for reform, paring down an expansive view of *imperium* was cut short by the rebellions of the late 1570s and early 1580s and,

---

[93] Crawford, J. G., *Anglicizing the government of Ireland* (Dublin, 1993), pp. 59–60.
[94] Waterhouse to Sidney, 17 December 1573, A. Collins, *Letters and memorials of state*, 2 vols. (London, 1746), Vol. I, p. 62.

ultimately, by his death in 1581. Later, Sidney could write scornfully of Gerrard and his faith in the applicability of constitutional bridles in Ireland, unsympathetically contrasting his cunning with the martial virtue of Lord Justice Sir William Drury:

> It irked me not a little to see the ambitious and disdainful dealing of the chancellor, who glorying of the great credit that he had won of her majesty (which indeed was more than his worth) that he would not let to say, but not in my hearing, that he had brought over such warrant for himself and restraint for me, as I could do nothing without him; he still hastening me away, gloriously braving behind my back that if I were gone, and the new justice ruling by his direction, Ireland should be governed with a white rod. But the noble knight and warrior Sir William Drury, not many months after my departure found that he had need to rule with white rods as long as spears and morris-pikes and swords whited as white as blood would whiten them; in which service he died.[95]

MAXIMISING *IMPERIUM* IN PRINCIPLE

It was some years after the ruination of Sidney's best-laid plans that Grey de Wilton, ready for war, arrived at Dublin on 12 August 1580 and demanded the sword of state. The disgraced Lord Justice Sir William Pelham, in Munster at the time, insisted on personally surrendering the sword but did not hurry back to the capital directly, choosing rather to loiter in the west for almost a month, as if to savour his last weeks of wielding *merum imperium*. Quite simply, Gerrard's vision of Ireland, ruled with a civil politician's white rod, was much less compelling for men like Pelham and his subordinates than the savour of coercive power and authority that Ireland's sword of state and the delegation of its *imperium* offered. In October 1569, Humphrey Gilbert, serving as colonel in Munster entrusted with the 'whole government in [his] hands of all that province', spoke eloquently of the vertiginous effect that *imperium* could have on those who wielded it. He wrote to Cecil asking to be revoked stating that 'authority was to [him] but a sweet poison that [he knew] would in the end turn to [his] confusion and utter discredit, rather than to the increase of [his] poor reputation'.[96]

---

[95] Brady (2002) p. 102. Gerrard's boast had some constitutional grounding, however. See J. G. Crawford *Anglicizing the government of Ireland* (Dublin, 1993), p. 60 for evidence that the lord deputy and the lord chancellor were usually present at meetings of the council. If neither of them could attend, no meeting of the council was possible. For an account of the whole cess controversy of Sidney's second viceroyalty see C. Brady, 'Conservative subversives: the community of the Pale and the Dublin administration 1556–86' in P. J. Corish (ed.), *Radicals, rebels and establishments* (Belfast, 1986).
[96] Gilbert to Cecil, 18 October 1569 SP63/29/67.

And indeed, Gilbert, in attesting to his fetishisation of authority, was baring his soul. During his term as colonel in Munster in 1569, eager to devastate the crown's enemies, he had flagrantly infringed the liberties of the chartered cities and towns of the earldom of Desmond, which provoked outrage among the citizens of Kilmallock, Kinsale, Cork and Limerick. He had also added insult to injury by dismissing their protests, telling them that he cared 'little for their charges of trespassing or their bills of complaint'. More significantly, he chose to justify his actions theoretically by 'answering them that the prince had a regular and absolute power, and that which might not be done by one *I* would do it by the other in cases of necessity' (my italics).[97] In saying this, he was claiming not only the competence to wield special powers when necessity demanded but also the authority to discern when a specific situation qualified as a case of necessity.[98] This could easily be dismissed as mere braggadocio in the field, a pose calculated to daunt opponents, except for the fact that less than two years later, on 14 April 1571, Gilbert further elaborated his views on the constitutional scope of the *imperium* in the House of Commons – the same *imperium* that had given him the power that he had wielded in Munster.[99] It seems that the voluntaristic understanding of *imperium* that the captains held while in Ireland, although seldom articulated in such a highly conceptualised way, could have ramifications for the understanding of regal authority at the very heart of England's constitution.

Gilbert attacked Robert Bell, MP for King's Lynn, for remarks he had made about the difficulties the queen's officers might face collecting the

---

[97] See Captain John Ward's letter to Cecil, 18 October 1569, SP63/29/68 where he states that Gilbert was in 'great doubt of the fidelity of the townsmen' and so ordered Ward and his men – again 'upon pain of death' to man all the gates and posterns of Kilmallock. For evidence that Lord Justice Drury had similar problems with the corporate towns see Drury to Burghley, 11 February 1579, SP63/65/37.

[98] *CPRI*, Vol. I, p. 537. Significantly Gilbert sought for additional 'allowances' to be added to his commission, such as the right to grant safe-conducts to strangers, which Sidney, jealous of his own authority, withheld stating that it was 'such an absolute royalty as is proper to be only in the hands of the Governor'.

[99] Gilbert's articulation of the state of play in the field, although highly conceptualised, was orthodox enough. It is worth noting that in *De republica anglorum* Smith when treating of the dual quality, regular and absolute, of the royal prerogative, treated martial law as an occasion when the absolute prerogative came into play. In this context, he argued, the monarch's word was law; he could put to death or maim anyone without recourse to due process. Like Gilbert, Smith also employed the language of necessity to describe cases in which martial law could be invoked, 'where the time nor place do suffer the tarriance of pleading and process, be it never so short, and the important necessity requireth speedy execution'. Smith, T., *De republica anglorum*, ed. M. Dewar (Cambridge, 1982), pp. 85–8.

The limits of imperium

subsidy latterly voted by parliament. According to Bell, the queen's subjects in England already felt sufficiently 'robbed' by men holding royal licences of purveyance and 'promoters' who used close readings of penal laws and statutes to catch unsuspecting subjects in breach of the law.[100] Gilbert accused Bell not only of 'vain derogation of the prerogatives imperial' but also of marking himself out as 'an open enemy' – a dangerous allegation given that the 1571 parliament was convening under the shadow of Pius V's excommunication of Elizabeth. The journal-keeper reported that Gilbert continued, warming to his subject:

for what difference is it to say the queen is not to use the privilege of the crown, and to say she is not queen, since they are so linked together that the one without the other possible may not be. We are (said he) to give to a common constable the right and regard of his office, which if we shall deny her, what is it else than to make her worse than the very meanest? And albeit experience hath proved such and so great clemency in her majesty as might make us perhaps to forget ourselves, yet it is not to sport or venture much with princes; yea, let be that our meanings be good and right honest . . . *if we should in any sort meddle with these matters, her majesty might look to her own power and thereby finding her validity to suppress the strength of the challenged liberty, and to challenge and to use the same her own power any way, and to do as did Lewis of France who delivered the crown there out of wardship (as he termed it), which the said French king did upon the like occasion.* He also said other kings had absolute power as Denmark and Portugal, where, as the crown became more free, so are all the subjects thereby rather made slaves [my italics].

Gilbert's speech 'was many ways disliked'; six days later, Peter Wentworth denounced him for his 'disposition to flatter and fawn on the prince' and called him a 'chameleon' able to 'change himself to all fashions saving to honesty'. He was thrice denied an opportunity to reply by the house. His attack on Bell was particularly resented because afterwards Bell 'was sent for [by the privy council] and so hardly dealt with that he came into the House with such an amazed countenance that it daunted all'.[101]

But, whatever about the irascibility of Gilbert's speech, the constitutional assertions he made about the implications of undermining the queen's authority, even when wielded by a 'common constable', deserve serious scrutiny. First and foremost, Gilbert was not improvising these opinions. The rather high-handed nature of his statement stems largely

---

[100] *TRP*, Vol. II, p. 288. See also G. R. Elton 'Informing for profit: a sidelight on Tudor Methods of Law-enforcement', *Cambridge Historical Journal*, 11 (1953–5), pp. 149–67.
[101] Hartley, T. E., *Proceedings in the parliaments of Elizabeth I, Vol. I, 1558–81* (Leicester, 1981), pp. 224–5, 436.

from the nature of the real debate in which he was trying to engage and the interlocutor at whom he was aiming. That interlocutor was not Robert Bell, it was, in fact, the principal secretary Sir Thomas Smith. In essence, Gilbert was showcasing the disagreements between Smith's view of the fundamental nature of the English constitution and his own.

Although Smith's tract *De republica anglorum* was not published until 1583, it had been written while he was ambassador to France between 1562 and 1565. The contrast between English and French conditions had been very much on the author's mind. His central assertion of the superiority of England's constitution was obviously made with an eye to Fortescue's precedent. Famously, Smith had asserted in Book II that the differentiation between England and France pivoted on the fact that the

> most high and absolute power of the realm of England is in the Parliament ... That which is done by this consent is called firm, stable and sanctum and is taken for law ... For every Englishman is intended to be there present, either in person or by procuration and attorneys ... from the Prince ... to the lowest person of England.

Smith numbered the establishment of forms of religion and forms of succession to the crown among the tasks that 'the Parliament' was competent to undertake.

Gilbert, in April 1571, was attacking Smith's large claims, but obliquely rather than head on, choosing to take issue with some of the propositions he had made in Book I on the 'definition of a king and a tyrant' and the nature of 'the absolute king'. Here Smith had asserted that the Holy Roman Emperors held absolute power by a deceitful provenance, which he chose to call 'tyrannical power', and that some authorities had also claimed that the kings of France ruled absolutely, because 'they make and abrogate ... laws and edicts, lay on tributes and impositions of their own will ... without the consent of the people ... the whole body and the three estates of the commonwealth.' Most significantly, he then added that those authorities

> blame Lewes the XI for bringing the administration royal of France, from the lawful and regulate reign to this absolute and tyrannical power and government. *He himself was wont to glory and say, he had brought the Crown of France hors de page, as one would say, out of Wardship* [my italics].[102]

The echoes between Gilbert's speech and Smith's text are unmistakable, but the degree of disagreement between them is profound. Each was

---

[102] Smith (1982), pp. 53–5, 78–9.

The limits of imperium

making a contradictory claim about the actual truths that lay behind the superficial constitutional forms of the English commonwealth. While Smith alleged that the mixed form of the English constitution tallied with an actual split in sovereignty, Gilbert, in effect, was asserting that the monarch held total and undivided sovereignty – *imperium* – and, just as Henry VIII, by virtue of his claim to imperial kingship, had declared ecclesiastical jurisdiction in England to be trespassing upon his authority, Elizabeth could in a moment suppress parliament for good, thereby reclaiming the full measure of what had always been her proper sovereignty. The fact that both Gilbert and Smith gestured to the example of Louis XI of France was telling. Both were addressing points which had been raised by Louis's critical biographer Commines, most notably where he had dealt with the enhanced powers of monarchs in Chapter 18 of Book V of his *Memoirs*. There, Commines had placed particular emphasis on the powers that the French monarch had gained by virtue of his large standing army: justice and, most importantly, taxation, he argued, had become more arbitrary, resulting in a plummeting standard of living for all three estates: clergy were molested; nobility were mulcted without consent; and commoners were brutalised by soldiers' whims. Significantly, he had suggested that it would be best for the country to pay the army a fixed stipend directly every two months than be subject to such arbitrary, if royally sanctioned, proceedings.[103]

Gilbert's gloss on Commines's condemnations was remarkable: he accepted the more expansive view of royal power to be a universal fact – there was no mixed constitution in England – but he also ignored criticism of the attendant excesses, a blind spot that had implications on both sides of the English Channel. Commines was very much on people's minds at this time. In 1572 the Huguenot lawyer Innocent Gentillet, in the aftermath of the massacre of St Bartholomew's Day, himself meditated on the implications Commines's treatment of royal authority had for the relationship between ordinary and absolute prerogatives in his *Discours sur les moyens de bien gouverner et maintainer en bonne paix un Royaume ou autre Principauté Contre Nicolas Machiavel*, a work later published in 1576. Gentillet came to acknowledge that all sovereignty resided in the king and that, theoretically, the sovereign could override the 'ordinary right' by virtue of his royal power, but he counselled that the *lex digna*, that 'express law' enacted by Emperor Theodosius, should be followed. That law stated (according to Gentillet's 1602 English translator):

[103] Commines, P. de, *Memoirs* ed. A. R. Scobie (London, 1855), Vol. I, pp. 378–84.

It is the majesty of him that governeth, to confess himself to be bound under laws, so much doth our authority depend upon law. And assuredly, it is a far greater thing than the empire itself, to submit his empire and power unto laws. And that which we will not to be lawful unto us, we show it unto others by the oracle of this our present edict.[104]

In that same year, Bodin, in his *Six livres de la république*, holding to the ideas that the king's authority was imperial (by virtue of the fact that it recognised no earthly authority greater than itself) and asserting that sovereignty was indivisible, would reiterate this point, using the example of Theodosius to state that a king's acquisition of the consent of the estates was 'not a matter of necessity but of expediency'. '[T]he sovereign majesty and absolute power had the right to impose laws generally on all subjects regardless of their consent', but political pragmatism dictated that it was not expedient for a monarch to 'levy taxes at will on his people or seize the goods of another arbitrarily'. Significantly, Bodin chose to cite Commines in his defence on this point.[105] In this context, it is remarkable that five years before Bodin and Gentillet published their works, Gilbert, in his intervention in parliament, was suggesting that Elizabeth's tolerance of her parliament's business, an ongoing demonstration of discretionary restraint emanating from her absolute power, could not be taken for granted, because it was merely a sensible concession, not some indelible right. In short, Elizabeth could shut parliament down for good.[106] It seems characteristic of Gilbert to place so little value on the monarch's expedient self-restraint, to spy the canker of *precarium imperium* in even a pragmatically self-imposed bridle.[107]

---

[104] See Innocent Gentillet, *A discourse on the means of well governing and maintaining in good peace, a kingdom, or other principality* (London, 1602), sigs, Di, r–Dii, r. See also Francis Oakley, 'Jacobean political theology: the absolute and ordinary powers of the King' in *Journal of the History of Ideas*, 29, 3 (1968) pp. 323–46.

[105] Oakley (1968), pp. 323–46. Bodin, J. *Six books of the commonwealth*, ed. and trans. M. J. Tooley (Blackwell, Oxford, 1955), pp. 32–3.

[106] Fifty-five years later when Dudley Carleton MP for Hastings, in almost exactly the same manner, warned the Commons that Charles I might seek 'new counsels' if it encroached on his prerogatives, he also proffered the examples of defunct assemblies in Europe as a warning. That confrontation, of course, ended in the Forced Loan, which although extremely controversial (as billeting of soldiers in Ireland was in Elizabethan times), was successful in its aim of raising the value of over four parliamentary subsidies. Charles I, of course, proved to be an inept and unpopular king, so one wonders what a more charismatic and shrewd English king might have established in terms of widely accepted extra-parliamentary funding.

[107] Of course, Gilbert was not the only critic that seemed to threaten the Commons's notions of its own importance. Later in the 1570s Arthur Hall notoriously questioned the antiquity of the House's authority stating that perusal of past legislation dissuaded 'the antiquity of our third voices ... and also will show a light of the admitting of the third person in this trinity'. See

The limits of imperium

This exchange between Gilbert and Smith, like their more famous discussions on Livy, which also touched on matters to do with expediency, should not just be seen as a megaphonic debate within the Elizabethan political thought community. Gilbert was articulating what he thought were truths about crown sovereignty, truths that tallied with his experience of wielding *imperium* and seeing it wielded. The way that English institutions in Ireland, parliament, courts and chartered towns, were treated by the crown's delegates seemed to underline these facts about crown authority.

The embracing of an expansive vision of crown sovereignty had serious implications for the character of Irish government, especially given the views that crown officers there held about the provenance of their own authority. Poignantly, Gentillet, as France descended into sectarian horror in 1572, appealed to officers to observe the voluntary constraints on *imperium* dictated by the *lex digna* against the example of 'many magistrate lawyers of our time, [who] not only excuse, but also cause to be executed unnatural murders and massacres against all law divine and human'; however, in matters of coercion, many crown officers in Ireland, as we shall see, sought to exploit every benefit that they believed wielding an all-competent *imperium* offered them.[108]

A. Hall, *A letter sent by F.A. touching the proceedings in a private quarrel and unkindness* . . . (London, 1579?) sig. D iv, r, and G. R. Elton, 'Arthur Hall, Lord Burghley and the antiquity of Parliament' in *Studies in Tudor and Stuart politics and government* (Cambridge, 1983), Vol. III, pp. 254–74.
[108] Gentillet (1602) sig. Di, r.

CHAPTER 6

The limits of rhetoric: the captains and violence in Elizabethan Ireland to 1588

The notoriety of Colonel Humphrey Gilbert's 1569 campaign in Munster is beyond dispute.[1] The stark image of rebels forced to submit to Gilbert by shuffling on their knees through an avenue marked by the decapitated heads of their loved ones (as described by Thomas Churchyard in his *general rehearsal of warres*) will never lose its power to shock. But even Churchyard, writing ten years after the event, seems to have realised that Gilbert's flamboyant conduct begged some questions, hence the quickness with which he offered a list of explanations and justifications for his subject's behaviour. First, he turned the charge of cruelty back against the Irish, stating that Gilbert 'did but then begin that order with them, which they had in effect ever tofore used toward the English'.[2] Next, he vindicated the Colonel's approach by pointing to its positive results: the widespread fear that these actions engendered ensured that more forts were surrendered to him in one day 'than by strong hand would have been won in a

---

[1] The details of Gilbert's campaign have been well catalogued by Irish historians. The most recent presentation of his campaign as emblematic of Elizabethan rule in Ireland can be read in J. F. Lydon's *The making of Ireland: from ancient times to the present* (London, 1998), p. 150; see also N. Canny, *The Elizabethan conquest of Ireland: a pattern established, 1565–76* (Hassocks, 1976), p. 122; T. Bartlett, *"The Academy of Warre": military affairs in Ireland, 1600–1800*, O'Donnell Lecture (2002), p. 24. For near contemporary views of his conduct, see Lord President John Perrot to Lord Justice Fitzwilliam, SP63/34/4i, where Perrot unfavourably compares Gilbert's campaign with his own. At the height of his campaign Gilbert had around 100 horsemen under his command. At Killmallock a chartered town in the very midst of the earldom of Desmond he was besieged by combined forces of James Fitzmaurice Fitzgerald and the earl of clancare which numbered up to 1,500 footmen and sixty horsemen. He then rode out of the town to get reinforcements from Cork. After this bold manoeuvre he had both Captains John Ward and Shute's forces with him, which would have made up 100 gallowglass (Irish mercenaries originally of Scottish origin) and around forty more horsemen. It is probable that a large fraction of his horsemen were of Irish birth. When his band first arrived in Ireland in January 1568 it had sixty-eight ill-furnished members. By August a full complement of one hundred had been attained. These may have come from England or been recruited in Ireland along the way.

[2] See below for how the earl of Essex used this motif to justify his slaying of Sir Brian MacPhelim O'Neill while the latter was under protection.

year'. Gilbert's most outrageous actions – the grisly *carneval* of the decapitations, for instance – were motivated, we are told, '*ad terrorem*, the dead feeling nothing the more pains thereby: and yet did it bring great terror to the people when they saw the heads of their dead fathers, brothers, children, kinsfolk and friends, lie on the ground before their faces'.[3] Horrible, certainly, but was it typical or not? In what ways were the English martial men who governed Elizabethan Ireland violent? How can we know?

This chapter is given over to scrutinising what the captains themselves wrote about their use of violence in Ireland up to 1584 – the final suppression of the second Desmond rebellion – and investigating their stated values and scruples about the subject. Priority is given here to the contexts in which the statements were made because, unsurprisingly, these contexts often suggest different meanings and intentions than a bald acontextual quotation might suggest. The wonted use of state correspondence and especially calendars of state papers (indifferently indexed) to answer well-rehearsed questions about anthropological attitudes and confessionalisation has meant that a more nuanced, micro-contextual, approach to data found in state papers has been neglected.[4] In short, in pursuit of these overly abstracted questions of anthropological and religious prejudice, some scholars have, unsurprisingly, found the dualistic attitudes that they were looking for. This has tended to obscure the fact that Elizabethan Ireland was, in many respects, a political society and that violence as employed by both the Irish (Gaelic-Irish, English-Irish and Palesman) and the English was very often a component of attempts, albeit brutal attempts, to gain local advantage in the working out of a political process.

---

[3] See Captain John Ward to Cecil, 10 October 1569, SP63/29/68 where Ward enumerates at least twenty-two castles won by Gilbert.

[4] Because the aim of this chapter is specifically to determine the attitudes of Elizabethan martial men to their violent actions in Ireland I have given relatively little treatment of Gaelic-Irish sources – for this period largely annals and poetry. Carey suggests that professional Irish historians' reluctance to trust 'folklore' as a source has led to the downplaying of 'the more traumatic aspects of popular memory', yet he himself points out many of the limitations that folkloric testimony lends itself to – inflationary claims, inaccuracy, not least its capacity to borrow from other sources without acknowledgement, see Carey (1999), pp. 324–7. Carey's use of folklore, it must be stressed is methodologically faultless, yet the skein of problems that arise from oral testimony and the context of its transmission is daunting. A particularly interesting and relevant example of the dangers can be seen from the citation of the 'folk-song' 'Follow me up to Carlow' by Patrick Joseph McCall (1861–1919), which contains the lyrics 'From Tassagart to Clonmore / Flows a stream of Saxon gore' – as a 'traditional' source about the battle of Glenmalure. See for example the statement that 'folk memories of Saxon gore flowing from Tasagart to Clonmore are exaggerated' in Richard Brooks' *Cassell's battlefields of Britain and Ireland* (London, 2005), p. 332. For an exemplary treatment of Gaelic-Irish source material of this period see Caball (1998).

English captains throughout Ireland interpreted their patents of office and commissions of martial law in the most personally beneficial and inflationary way and, always mindful of their status as crown officers, sought personal and local pre-eminence. The Irish, similarly, took the utmost advantage of the opportunities that the procedures of English law and the wonted diplomatic lulls in conflict afforded. Ultimately, friction resulted less from the 'othering' of the Irish or their exclusion from the process of government than the determination through negotiation and attrition of what were the terms under which Irish potentates might cooperate with the crown on the one hand and come to an accommodation with the captains on the other. Furthermore, any assumption that English captains and Irish subjects were naturally opposed to each other, as we shall see, is not helpful: there were many occasions when Ireland's Herods and Pilates became firm friends.

Before proceeding further, it is necessary to address a philosophical point: to deal adequately with issues that involve other people's pain, especially dead people's pain in a historical context, is an impossible task. These subjects can be approached with a lot of emotional significance and empathetic gesture. A thirst for justice can manifest itself in a desire 'to speak the truth to power', even though the power being addressed has been wielded in the distant past.[5] Despite this urge, grief and pain, two of the most personal and complex aspects of human existence, are phenomena that cannot be quantified or systematised intelligently, and, in the absence of verifiable accounts by those individuals who endured or succumbed to them, elude attempts to accurately represent them. To filter the suffering out of Irish history might result in distortion, but to inject suffering back into the narrative as a compensatory strategy for victims' silence leads to similar if not greater distortion.[6] Both of these approaches make individual cases of killing, maiming or atrocity vulnerable to stratification in accordance with present-day understanding of categories such as race, political loyalty, religious creed or social status.[7]

---

[5] Said, E., *Representations of the intellectual* (London, 1994), pp. 63–76.
[6] There is an obvious allusion here to Brendan Bradshaw's phrase 'filtering out the trauma' used in seminal article 'Nationalism and historical scholarship in modern Ireland', *Irish Historical Studies*, 26 (1988–9), pp. 329–51. For a treatment of the epistemological perils of writing Irish history see Ciaran Brady's *Constructive and instrumental*: the dilemma of Ireland's first *New Historians*' in C. Brady (ed.) *Interpreting Irish history: the debate on historical revisionism* (Dublin, 1994), pp. 3–31.
[7] For a surprising echo of this view see the statement of apology made by the Provisional IRA on the thirtieth anniversary of the 'Bloody Friday' atrocity: 'The future will not be . . . achieved by creating a hierarchy of victims in which some are deemed more or less worthy than others'. In this vein, although certainly not causally related, by far the most moving achievement endorsing the

Consequently, an 'exchange value' of lives can emerge, where the worth of one life relative to another is dependent on prejudicial calculations in accordance to our doctrines and the ends towards which they are oriented, be they historical inevitability, profit or justice. Each individual's sufferings are, by definition, personal, non-transferable and, consequently, not open to comparison with any accuracy, although such comparison often has stirring rhetorical effect. In truth, histories that absolve or condemn cannot in any sense serve as reparation for a lack of human compassion on the part of an individual at a crucial moment. The silence the dead leave behind them is unnerving. We must accept that whatever attempts are made to fill this void will be inadequate. Our voices will never be their voices. Their anonymity and silence cannot be compensated for by ventriloquising.

THE UTILITY OF VIOLENCE

Just how useful was violence to the ends of crown policy in Ireland? Elizabeth had basic priorities when it came to her Irish kingdom: the smaller island, above all, had to be secure against invasion by other European powers that might use it as a foothold to menace England; furthermore, government in Ireland should cost the least amount of money possible.[8] Viceregal policies and programmes of government, in their variety and uniformity, were formulated with these aims in mind. For instance, whereas Sir William Fitzwilliam's government tended to save money by being moribund and quietist, Sir Henry Sidney's in the 1570s aimed to ensure that the kingdom would become a going concern and provide an ongoing revenue to the treasury through attempting to implement his grand taxation policy, composition, throughout Ireland. However, it is important to note that neither the mandarins at Whitehall

---

common humanity (irrespective of difference) of victims has been *Lost lives*, eds. D. McKitterick, Seamus Kelters, Brian Feeney and Chris Thornton (Edinburgh, 1999) a thorough detailed index of all the victims of the Northern Irish 'Troubles' to the end of July 1999, written with passion, but without any particular agenda of condemnation.

[8] Elizabeth's parsimony was so renowned that English captains occasionally held that the Gaelic-Irish committed outrages and pursued their own interests violently because of their assumption that the crown's tightfistedness meant that no serious action would be taken against them. See Drury to Walsingham, 11 February 1579, SP63/65/38, where an overstretched Drury remarks that 'the governor to spare her Majesty's charges was forced to lay [the expense] upon the subject toward the maintaining of those great companies which were waged to follow the O'Mores and the O'Connors in their rebellion: *whereunto I suppose they would never now lastly have entered, had they not hoped that the limitation of the governor would have tied them rather to have yielded to any their unreasonable request than make war with them for fear of charges*' (my italics).

nor the queen had a particular emotional attachment to any specific Irish policy, they just knew what difficulties they wanted to avoid in Ireland. In short, the aims of keeping the sister kingdom from becoming a strategic bolthole for a foreign power, maintaining quiet possession and promoting financial self-sufficiency were paramount. With such concerns foremost in the minds of the London government, it seems obvious that large-scale political destabilisation in Ireland was the least welcome state of affairs.[9] To attempt a total resolution of the problems of Ireland by force would cost too much, and the disaffection caused by the consequent suppression of unrest or the provocation of local elites might make Ireland even more likely to be alluring prey for England's enemies.

This metropolitan indifference had the most profound influence on crown government and its officers in Ireland, consistently – as we shall see – proving to be both a source of licence and frustration and indubitably affecting not only the use of violence in Irish affairs but also the justifications proffered for its employment. This indifference did not amount to automatic indemnity for crown officers, especially not when bad reports reached Whitehall or supposedly avoidable crises imperilled the stability of the realm. Diametric opposition between the monarch's limited objectives and the conduct of her martial officers in Ireland could and did occur.

Perhaps the most obvious example of such a clash (already rehearsed) happened late in 1579 as Munster was engulfed by the initial stages of the second Desmond rebellion when Sir Nicholas Malby, president of Connacht, and Sir William Pelham were subjected to royal disapproval for their treatment of the earl of Desmond. Malby, ebullient after a victory over rebels at Monasternenagh in September, was deemed to have hounded the earl into an untenable position, and Pelham, unforgivably, proclaimed him a traitor – as we have seen, Elizabeth took a dim view of Pelham ever after.[10] As a result, Desmond, who had been steadily reconciling himself with crown government and, perhaps even at that late stage, attempting to remain aloof from his defiant brother Sir John, was forced into rebellion.[11] This mess, it could be argued, effectively turned

---

[9] See BL Add. Ms. 37, 536, fol. 1 for Elizabeth's opinion that her officers in Ireland should not 'proceed to that severity of punishing [rebels] . . . as might deservedly be inflicted upon them'.

[10] In Malby to Walsingham, 12 October 1579, SP63/69/52, Malby claimed to Walsingham that he had 'most manifest proof' that the earl reinforced the rebels with '600 choice gallowglasses'.

[11] Desmond, just prior to throwing in his lot with the rebels, sketched a rather grim picture of the pressure he was under from his defiant kinsmen; he said he feared that his wife and son would be killed by them. See the earl of Desmond to a member of crown government, 10 October 1579, SP63/69/51.

what might have remained as low-level unrest into chronic, and expensive, military crisis and confessional war.[12]

Significantly, whatever indulgence these captains might have normally received in Whitehall at that time was nullified by the fruits of a crisis at court: their greatest ally Walsingham had been excluded from the royal presence in November as a result of his opposition to the Anjou match. Their patronage network was decapitated; Walsingham told Waterhouse that 'by reason of my absence from the court I cannot so well resolve you touching Irish causes.'[13] Elizabeth's disapproval of her officers' actions in Munster had a bad effect on officer morale in Ireland. Edward Fenton complained to the secretary about Elizabeth's 'displeasure' towards Lord Justice Pelham whose 'care and travail' was solely to serve his queen, 'neither yet to live or breathe without her gracious countenance and favour', reflecting 'how dangerous a thing it is to disgrace an officer in so great a place.'[14] Later, Sir Henry Wallop, vice treasurer, would ask Walsingham: 'Who is it that hereafter will so willingly adventure themselves in the like action having for reward but hard opinion and displeasure?'[15] Captains in Ireland had long known that Elizabeth's views on severity in crown government, although changeable, were generally pacific. The barque of crown government in Ireland was supposed to sail on as even a keel as possible.

For all that Elizabeth had been known to endorse violent actions perpetuated in her name, notably following the northern rebellion of 1569. Although estimates of the precise numbers of those put to the sword after the revolt of the earls of Westmoreland and Northumberland vary, what is certain is that decisive and unrelenting pressure towards severity came from the monarch herself.[16] For instance, she sent irate messages to the earl of Sussex while in his northern command, ordering the seizure of rebel lands and goods (some of which, no doubt to Sussex's chagrin, later ended up in the hands of Ambrose Dudley, earl of Warwick) and carped

---

[12] Brady, C., 'Faction and the origins of the Desmond rebellion of 1579', *Irish Historical Studies* 22 (1981), pp. 299–312. See SP63/69/51 for Desmond's statement of his innocence of treachery, his service against the Queen's enemies and his molestation by Malby. See SP63/69/52i–ix for Malby's correspondence with Desmond in late September/early October 1579 demanding the earl's presence and Desmond's reluctance to comply.
[13] See Walsingham's letters to Malby and Waterhouse, SP63/70/7 and 10: 6 and 8 November 1579 where he admits his impotence while absent from court. See Leimon (1989), pp. 194–6.
[14] Fenton to Walsingham, 3 January 1580, SP63/71/2.
[15] Wallop to Walsingham 6 March 1583, SP63/100/5.
[16] McCall, H. B., 'The rising in the north: a new light upon one aspect of it', in *The Yorkshire Archaeological Journal*, Vol. xviii (Leeds, 1905), pp. 74–87.

that she was 'a stranger to her own cause'.[17] On the matter of severity, she was prescriptive, telling Sussex in January 1569 that she found it 'strange' that he intended to return to York before the job was 'thoroughly executed' to her satisfaction, later adding that she was displeased that she had heard of no execution of the 'meaner sort' by martial law 'as was appointed', adding that 'if the same be not already done, you are to proceed thereunto, for the terror of others with expedition and to certify us of your doing of the same.'[18] H. B. McCall has indicated that Sussex, mindful of his monarch's intentions, 'allowed himself to speak of executions ordered as though they had actually taken place'. Sir George Bowes in 1573 concluded that approximately 700 were executed, most of whom perished as a result of his infamous circuit of January 1569; however, it seems certain that he put to death fewer people than were appointed to be executed.[19] Whether this shortfall in numbers stemmed more from appreciation of Sheriff Sir Thomas Gargrave's opinion that unless leniency were shown the country would become bare of inhabitants, or Bowes's foreboding that the 'executions [would] be very long in doing' and his certainty that the queen would 'find cause for offence with her charge continued so long for that purpose' is impossible to gauge.[20] Camden attested to Elizabeth's capacity for bloody-mindedness on matters of smaller scale when writing about the occasion in 1573 when she called for martial law to be used against a fanatical religious 'innovator' called Peter Burchet who had stabbed Sir John Hawkins believing him to be the queen's favourite Sir Christopher Hatton. Elizabeth, to her disappointment, was informed that that particular course of action was reserved for use 'in camps' and 'in turbulent times', and, otherwise, the correct mode of procedure was 'by form of judiciary process'.[21] Three

---

[17] For a discussion of the constraints of Sussex's power and patronage, especially after the northern rebellion, see Susan Doran, 'The political career of Thomas Radcliffe, 3rd Earl of Sussex, 1526?–1583', unpublished Ph.D. thesis (University of London, 1975), pp. 384–5.

[18] Sharp, C., *The rising in the North, the 1569 rebellion* (Durham, 1975), p. 167. Elizabeth to Sussex, 11 January 1570, in *CSPD, Add 1566–1572*, p. 188. Elizabeth desired particular thoroughness, telling Sussex, 'We understand that some in those parts have remained at home or shown great slackness in our service, having brethren and children with the rebels; have an earnest regard to such and spare no offenders in that case but let them come to trial and receive due punishment. See also J. G. Bellamy, *The Tudor law of treason* (London, 1979), pp. 231–5 for a treatment of martial law in England.

[19] For Bowes's modus operandi and his reliance on the cooperation of the communities through which he went on his circuit, see Sharp (1975), pp. 143–4, 154–5, 175. Bowes told Gargrave that he felt in as much personal danger on his circuit as he had ever done during the 'first rebellion'.

[20] Sharp (1975), pp. 153, 173 and McCall (1905), p. 87.

[21] Bellamy (1979), pp. 231–5. For the story about Burchet see the entry for 1573 in W. Camden, *Annales rerum gestarum Angliae et Hiberniae regnante Elizabetha* (1615 and 1625) at http://www.uci.edu/~papyri/camden.

years later, Arthur Hall, sometime MP for Grantham, noted Elizabeth's views on the rigour of the law as expressed to Melchisidech Malory who was appealing against the pardoning of one of Hall's servants who had attacked him. Apparently, she replied that the accused 'should have justice, [but, she reassured Malory] *she never was hasty in pardoning*, neither need he fear the same' (my italics).[22] Certainly, the queen believed that there was a time to kill.

The initial manoeuvres against Desmond – the actions that propelled Malby and Pelham into disfavour – had the queen's name, in one respect, written all over them, but, ironically, did not win her approval. The ultimatum Malby had presented to the beleaguered earl was a stark one: either Desmond submitted to him – Malby – thus demonstrating his allegiance to the crown, or he did not, in which case he was deemed to have displayed unequivocal opposition.[23] Malby, as we have seen, believed his ultimatum carried royal authority because he was acting as lieutenant to Lord Justice Drury. This posed difficulties for Desmond. These were caused, first and foremost, by the abstraction of crown authority and its delegation to Malby and, second, by his own understandable inability to cope with the fact that what was being called for amounted to personal submission to the same Malby, a man who undoubtedly hated him. In short, this was the problem of Sir Nicholas Malby's two bodies. According to Sir Nicholas, he only got word of Drury's death after he and the earl had dropped diplomacy and started firing on each other.[24] It was Desmond's understandable reluctance, following rough treatment at the hands of Malby, to submit to the new lord justice, Pelham, that led to him finally being proclaimed a traitor.

Once Pelham proclaimed Desmond a traitor, the earl, apparently having nothing to lose, defaced the queen's arms in Youghal courthouse: the gesture was unequivocal because the earl needed to demonstrate a new and irreversible commitment to the rebels; the question of disloyalty had by that point become so explicit as could hardly be ignored.[25] The stern

---

[22] Hall, A., *A letter sent by F. A. touching the proceedings in a private quarrel and unkindness* (London, 1576) sig. Di, r.
[23] Malby to Desmond, 4 October 1579, SP63/69/52vi. For the context in which the last exchanges of correspondence took place see Malby to Walsingham, 12 October 1579, SP63/69/52.
[24] Malby to Walsingham, 12 October 1579, SP63/69/52.
[25] *The Walsingham letter book or Register of Ireland 1578*, ed. J. Hogan and N. McNeill O'Farrell (Dublin, 1959), p. 257. Sir N. Walsh to Walsingham, 19 December 1579. Walsh depicts the earl stating that 'his [own] arms should hang there and not those . . . because they yielded him a chief rent, they should not acknowledge any prince but him'. The story was corroborated by witnesses examined before Ormond and Walsh in December 1579.

and unyielding constitutional test which Desmond had been forced to address had looked for explicit protestation of loyalty, when complicit silence and patience would have been cheaper and easier. But, as we have seen, Malby, like most captains who acted as crown officers, was extremely possessive of the aura and trappings of delegated crown authority. This identification with the honour and authority of their monarch was not merely abstract but was often expressed in a personal (and, of course, frequently self-interested) way. One needs only to look at some of Malby's messages to Desmond written in October 1579 to realise this: 'I stand so assured of God's promises as all the rebels in Ireland can *never* have the upper hand of her Majesty's forces be they never so many against never so few, which doth give *me* that heart as no rebel, I thank God, can daunt *me* be they never so many' (my italics).[26]

THE DIGNITY OF THE STATE AND ITS DEFENDERS

This type of 'state honour', or as contemporaries called it 'the dignity of the state' was a very flexible concept that could be employed by crown officers to render politically distasteful actions licit and to label politically viable initiatives illicit.[27] For instance, at the broadest level, maintaining crown possession of Ireland was not solely a matter of political necessity from the point of view of security but also a matter of honour. For a monarch to alienate or lose any patrimony during his or her reign was the greatest shame imaginable, one that would be remembered for centuries.[28] The implications of losing control of Ireland were fully understood. For example, Sir Henry Sidney warned Cecil in 1566 that if Elizabeth did not move against Shane O'Neill she would lose the kingdom as her sister lost Calais; the same analogy was made by Fitzwilliam in 1572, and Pelham in 1579 told Walsingham that 'unless there be speedy redress had, Her Majesty may say she *had* a country' (my italics).[29] This approach,

---

[26] Malby to Desmond, 4 October 1579, SP63/69/52vi.
[27] The term 'dignity of the state' was used by Lord Deputy Grey de Wilton in his letter to the privy council, 12 August 1581, SP63/85/13.
[28] Skinner, Q., *The foundations of modern political thought*, 2 vols. (Cambridge, 1978), Vol. II, p. 260 for Claude de Seyssel's statement of a fundamental law bridling the French monarch that 'the domain and royal patrimony may not be alienated without absolute necessity'. This was a constitutional statement of beliefs about a king's relationship with his territorial kingdom and God.
[29] Sidney to Cecil, 9 June 1566, SP63/18/9; Fitzwilliam to Burghley, 15 April 1572, SP63/36/4. Where the lord deputy warns 'If Spain possess Ireland with 6, 000 soldiers I fear England may look after it as Calais and that once gone two parts of that which now does make the queen mistress of the narrow seas is taken from her'; Pelham to Walsingham, 6 September 1579, SP63/69/9.

although probably instinctive in Pelham's case, was in line with well-established modes of argument. For instance, the Pseudo-Ciceronian textbook in rhetorical instruction *Ad herennium*, a basic textbook in the sixteenth century, placed political deliberation into two classifications: that demanded by security and that demanded by honour. The tenuousness of the crown's hold over Ireland ensured that the compelling nature of both types of political action justified and supported each other.[30] Hence, much of the exculpatory rhetoric employed in Ireland at this time generally invoked royal or state honour coupled with security.

Such arguments, for instance, could be used by a servant of the crown in many different contexts to justify actions or to protest against government inaction. In January 1568, Sir William Fitzwilliam, writing to Burghley, stressed the unpalatable necessity of observing a truce with the Scots in Ulster. This was necessary because it 'were not fit' to do otherwise as 'breaking the same it would give occasion that commissioners hereafter shall hardly again be trusted in Ireland.' Government actions should command trust.[31] Similarly, when the earl of Ormond resisted Pelham's plans to divide up his troops in November 1579 by arguing that if he did such a thing 'then [I] shall not be able to do the service as I would both for her highness's honour and the credit reposed in me', he was employing the same type of argument.[32] Likewise, three years later, an overstretched Lord Deputy Grey de Wilton registered his unhappiness with the conciliatory policy Elizabeth wanted him to pursue with Turlough Luineach O'Neill by arguing resignedly that 'a war ... might have brought forth both an honourable and a perpetual assurance against the north'.[33] So, the language of state honour was one that was frequently used in putting a case to superior officers or even a monarch in order to protest for or against a policy or action. Furthermore, thinking on state honour was primarily informed by supposed monarchical concerns – a particular zeal for the monarch's interest and reputation – but the manner in which this was expressed could comprehend, mimic or overlap with the tone and content of an assertion of personal honour. As stressed before, casual (and often self-interested) elision from concerns for

---

[30] Baldwin, G., 'The self and the state, 1580–1651', unpublished Ph.D. thesis (Cambridge University, 1998), pp. 51–4.
[31] Fitzwilliam to Cecil, 22 January, SP63/23/15. Fitzwilliam would return to the theme of the importance of preserving trust in Irish politics in his criticisms of the presidency of Sir Richard Bingham.
[32] Ormond to Burghley, 7 November 1579, SP63/70/8.
[33] Grey de Wilton to the privy council, 12 August 1581, SP63/85/13.

Elizabeth's honour to matters of personal honour was far from uncommon among delegates of crown authority in Ireland. Vanity had a serious role to play in this.

As noted in a previous chapter, the language of crown authority in Ireland, although discernible during earlier periods in Irish history, had been renovated and extended in the sixteenth century when the act of kingly title of 1541 transformed Henry VIII from lord of Ireland into king of Ireland. At the local level, throughout Ireland, the military captains were the delegates of the power of the crown: they were the men responsible for the execution of crown policy and the brokerage that went with it; they instituted composition arrangements, held sessions throughout the country, and executed martial law; and, consequently, their treatment of all Elizabeth's Irish subjects was meant to be impartial. All were theoretically to be judged on their individual merits and their loyalty, or, at least, the official record should not register any deviation from that standard. Even in the highly tense environment of east Ulster in the early 1570s, the earl of Essex (as a prelude to a more severe course) made sure that the privy council was informed that his 'first action' had been 'nothing but leniency, plainness and an equal case of both nations'.[34] In all cases, descending power gave regal value and status not only to English military office-holders in Ireland but also to their discretion.

Sir Humphrey Gilbert's conduct in 1569, for example, flamboyant though it was, as we have seen, was strictly located in such a regalian context. The colonel's actions were ostensibly motivated by a particular reverence for his monarch, in his own case highly conceptualised, and a zeal that that reverence should be emulated. Churchyard informs us that Gilbert held the 'prince's mercy' to be so sacred that it should not be lightly given out to suspected rebels. During his colonelship, in 1569, Gilbert's patent stated that he could execute anyone save 'lords and captains of countries'. It is important to remember that the bestowal of such destructive powers was coupled with the potential to refrain from using them. Gilbert's capacity to 'annoy . . . any malefactor by fire or sword, or any other kind of death' was explicitly granted 'at his discretion' balanced by licence 'to treat or parley with any traitor, rebel or outlaw, when and, as often as to him shall seem good for the service of her Majesty'.[35] So, in effect, Gilbert's commission offered the ability to be as severe or as clement as he thought fit, the criterion by which this decision was to be made being his own discretion informed by concern for the better service of his queen.

[34] Essex to the privy council, 29 September 1573, SP63/42/32.   [35] *CPRI*, Vol. I, pp. 535–7.

Churchyard's account of the manner in which Gilbert availed of these powers is best supplemented by the colonel's own letter of 6 December from Limerick city to Lord Deputy Sidney. Crucially, it was written three days after the personal submission of the earl of Clancar and Mac Donnchadh, recounted in *Churchyard's Choise*. Gilbert stressed that he had forced the rebel leaders to acknowledge their treasons, beg for mercy on their knees and promise to give up their male heirs as hostages. He defended himself by admitting that he had little practical 'experience in politic government'. Here Gilbert's use of his discretion informed the tenor of his service. Although the terms of his commission allowed it, Gilbert refused to treat or parley with any of his opponents. He adamantly refused to recognise the rebels through direct or indirect contact or to give anyone protection unless they first submitted to him, swore an oath to the queen and entered into pledges of good behaviour on the basis of land or hostages. Following this code, he had refused to parley with James Fitzmaurice Fitzgerald, despite rebel efforts to secure some type of negotiated settlement. Moreover, he prided himself on his unyielding approach which enabled him, the younger son of a Devonshire gentleman, to ignore the earl of Clancar's presence in Limerick prior to his submission. He reasoned that he 'would not have them to think that the queen's majesty had more need of their service, than they had of her majesty's mercy'.[36] A similarly inflexible approach characterised his behaviour in the field. If a fort refused to yield itself to him immediately, he boasted that he would besiege it 'how many men's lives soever it cost', refusing to accept any of his opponent's subsequent efforts to surrender. Consequently, the engagement would culminate with Gilbert's men storming the fortress, 'putting man, woman and child of them to the sword'.[37]

Gilbert's defence of royal authority and the *arcana imperii* in Ireland, discussed in the last chapter, as well as his annexation of the regular and absolute prerogatives and the power to discern between them, of course, amounted to an irrefutable defence of himself and his actions. Gilbert's self-conscious appropriation of this plenipotentiary status, although distinct in the bookish form and overtly intellectual wording he adopted,

---

[36] Gilbert to Sidney, 13 November and 1 December 1569, SP63/29/82; Gilbert to Sidney, 6 December 1569, SP63/29/83.
[37] See Captain John Ward to Cecil, 18 October 1569 SP63/29/68, where he describes the siege of the castle of Garrystown, where Gilbert ordered him 'upon pain of death to put them all to the sword'. Gilbert praised Captain Shute's conduct because he was the first to enter the castle and kill the first man, Gilbert to Cecil, 18 October 1569, SP63/29/67.

was, de facto, not all that rare.[38] The captains' government of Ireland – in its enshrinement of the royal prerogative as something more than the sum of its feudal parts – was full of arbitrary action, but this was because so much of it was based on arbitrary principle.

SIGNS OF 'LÈSE-MAJESTÉ'

Concepts of abstracted monarchical power and state honour found particularly easy correspondence with the legal rituals and expectations that defined martial practice. An examination of siege warfare is particularly important to any examination of violence in Tudor Ireland. Until the Nine Years' War with its set pieces at the Yellow Ford and Kinsale, pitched battles between crown forces and Irish armies were rare – Monasternenagh was exceptional. Indeed, the native elite usually resorted to the field only when settling hostilities among themselves. The battle of Affane in 1565 between the earls of Desmond and Ormond, for example, controversially sported all the trappings of feudal war, including the unfurling of banners. In the same year, Shane O'Neill claimed that he was serving his queen when he took to the field against the Scots at Glenshesk with devastating results.[39] But when confronted with belligerent government forces, the Irish tended to avoid giving battle. For example, when Nicholas Malby, recently appointed president of Connacht, pursued John and Ulick Burke, the infamous sons of the earl of Clanricard (called the *mac an iarlas*) in 1577 with a band of kern, he marched 'hard by the mountains' hoping that they would fight him but ended up complaining that 'the cowards would not show themselves'.[40] Similarly, Sir John Perrot found during his tenure as president of Munster in the early 1570s that James Fitzmaurice Fitzgerald would only fight him for 'light skirmishes, and that upon great advantage'.[41] This Irish policy of prudence had some notable successes, not least the morale-deflating reverse Shane O'Neill inflicted on the viceregal army in 1561 by ambushing their rearguard and the humiliating overthrow of Grey de Wilton's forces at Glenmalure in 1580.[42]

---

[38] Ciaran Brady has identified Gilbert's inflexible association of supplying crown forces with victuals with loyalty to the monarch as one of the main influences in the formulation of Sidney's composition project. See Brady (1994), p. 139.
[39] Brady, C., *Shane O'Neill* (Dundalk, 1996), pp. 56–7.
[40] Malby to Walsingham, 17 March 1577, SP63/57/40.   [41] Rawlinson (1728), p. 58.
[42] Brady (1996), see also Sir William Stanley's account of the battle of Glenmalure, 31 August 1580, SP63/75/83.

However, by contrast, the prevailing nature of armed conflict in Ireland between crown representatives and the Irish was dictated by the omnipresence of the tower house. From the early fourteenth century to the sixteenth century, the most favoured and cost-effective method of fortification chosen by Irish magnates and chieftains was the erection of simple fortified structures, usually of stone but occasionally constructed out of wooden beams and sods.[43] These buildings afforded defence of life, livestock and valuables while an enemy force occupied the surrounding territory. They could form a network of resistance to counter the attempts of the crown, from the reign of Edward VI onwards, to control the country using a grid of garrisons. A commonplace of early modern government stated that a recalcitrant people could only be kept in check by a policy of systematised fortification. The Protector Somerset had endeavoured to do this in Scotland, and Philip Sidney, Fulke Greville and Hugh Languet accused the Spaniards of employing this policy to tyrannise the Dutch. However, fortifications, as Machiavelli had pointed out, had a double-edged quality lending their strategic advantage to whoever held them, be they rebel, loyal subject or occupying power.[44] Hence President Sir John Perrot's annoyance that just four years after the 1569 crisis in Munster the earl of Desmond's officers were placing wards in the territory's castles once again, castles that belonged to the queen as a result of acts of attainder.[45] Irish magnates were careful on this question as well. Turlough Luineach O'Neill razed his own castle at Strabane and Con O'Donnell's at Lifford to the ground in 1581, destroying them in the light of rumours that the crown was to send a battery into Lough Swilly to

---

[43] The Irish used the word *caisleán* to designate a fortification of any sort. See Sir Thomas Wroth's comment to Leicester in 1564 about Shane O'Neill's fortifications erected in O'Donnell's lordship. He refers to O'Neill building 'two castles, as O'Donnell calleth them, of earth'. Wrothe to Dudley, 23 July 1564, SP63/11/35.

[44] See Worden (1996), pp. 249–50. See also Machiavelli's *Discorsi*, Book II, Chapter 24 for a discussion on the utility of fortresses in keeping a conquered people in place. He concluded that they were a liability.

[45] When told to hand over fortifications to Captain Bourchier the earl's ward refused 'until they [might] hear their master's pleasure'. Perrot also protested at the earl's officers' lack of concern to replenish the earl's lands with tenants. He accused the earl, in captivity at the time in Dublin, not only of being content to 'let his own land lie waste but also to enter upon the queen's right', Perrot to Fitzwilliam, 18 July 1573, SP63/41/92i, also Fitzwilliam to Burghley, 13 October 1573, SP63/42/49. For evidence that the fort was handed over to Bourchier see Nicholas Walsh to Fitzwilliam, 24 November 1573, SP63/43/6iii. See also the seizure by partisans of the MacWilliam Burke's of the castle of Ballyloughmask from Gerald Comerford, the attorney of Connacht in October 1589. They claimed to be holding it for the newly invested MacWilliam Burke, the Blind Abbot, asserting that it was his by right, Edward Whyte to Sir Nicholas White, master of the Rolls, 20 October 1589, SP63/147/28.

persecute him. Later, Sir Richard Bingham razed castles in Connacht because 'they were not fit to be kept by the English, and very dangerous to be in the possession of the Irish'.[46]

Castles were important as a simple quantifiable currency of martial advantage in Ireland. Sir William Fitzwilliam, writing to Burghley in November 1572 about President Fitton's campaign against the lower Burkes in Connacht, marked its success in terms of the number of castles seized and noted that 'one only of those castles was kept in defence'. This fortification was taken, and 'the ward ... were all slain which execution made all the rest of the wards to fly and leave their castles open.' Subsequently, Fitton entered MacDermott's country where they took 'in one day three of his strongest holds manned for defence'. Fitzwilliam claimed that eighty of the defenders were slain and 'diverse drowned in the moat'.[47] In 1577, Malby wrote of a castle that had been taken from a 'good subject' by rebels. Within two days, Malby boasted '[we] did win it by sapping it so as the rebels finding the castle ready to fall did rather choose to put their lives into my hands then to fall with the castle and so came down.'[48] However, the winning of castles necessitated dealing with their defeated ward in an appropriate manner. In the latter case, the defenders' amenability did them no favours as they were 'put to the *misericordia* of the soldiers who had lost their lieutenant there' who opted in a fit of vengeance to kill all twenty-two of them. Similarly, three years later, President Malby wrote casually of his conduct in taking the castle of Donamona from Shane MacHubert, counsellor to Risteard an Iarainn of the Mac William Burkes, where he 'put the ward both women and children to the sword whereupon all the other castles in the enemies' country were given up without any resistance'.[49] Likewise, when President Richard Bingham described his foray against the MacWilliam Burkes and the Scots in 1586, he paid special attention to the disloyal sentiments of those who held castles against him. When he allegedly called on the holders of

---

[46] 'A discourse of the services done by Sir Richard Bingham in the county of Mayo' October 1586, SP63/126/53i and Grey de Wilton to the privy council, 12 August 1581, SP63/85/13. For the proliferation of tower houses in both Gaelic-Irish and English-Irish lordships, see R. Loeber, 'An architectural history of Gaelic castles and settlements, 1370–1600' in Duffy, D. Edwards and E. Fitzpatrick (eds.) *Gaelic Ireland* (Dublin, 2001), pp. 271–314. See also R. Loeber, *The geography and practice of English colonisation in Ireland from 1534 to 1609* (Athlone, 1991), pp. 19–20, 23–4. In Elizabethan England, by contrast, castles and fortifications were not regarded as threats and were usually neglected, occasionally they were thought of as relics of old decency, see H. M. Colvin, 'Castles and government in Tudor England', *EHR*, 327, pp. 224–34.
[47] Fitzwilliam to Burghley, 25 November 1572, SP63/34/29.
[48] Malby to Walsingham, 17 March 1577, SP63/57/40.
[49] 'Discourse of Malby's service', 8 April 1590, SP63/72/39.

O'Kelly's castle 'to remember the obedience which they owed unto her majesty, and to yield themselves unto her highness's mercy and carry themselves within the course of dutiful subjection assuring themselves they should find that favour in all things, which others her Majesty's subjects did', they explained their defiance, not in terms of any disrespect for Elizabeth but rather because they dared not 'trust her majesty's officers, alleging many frivolous and impertinent causes moving them to stand upon their guard'.[50] This was the very type of distrust for commissioned officers which Sir William Fitzwilliam, during both his first and second viceroyalties, claimed he wanted to avoid.

As far as the captains were concerned, to doubt the honour of one of Elizabeth's officers, or to defy him in any way, was to doubt the monarch's honour itself and to defy the crown. In any case, the laws of siege warfare were well rehearsed internationally. Montaigne, for instance, dedicated two pieces in his first book of essays to the etiquette and harsh realities of the early modern siege, the first tellingly called 'The hour of parleying is dangerous' and the second entitled 'One is punished for stubbornly defending a fort without good reason'.[51] In an Irish context, sieges had an enhanced political and constitutional significance. To hold a castle against the forces of the Dublin government was an act of *lèse-majesté* against Elizabeth in her capacity as sovereign of Ireland. The same was demonstrably true, of course, in England. For example, the quixotic Thomas Stafford who seized Scarborough Castle with a small force on 25 April 1557 in defiance of Mary I and the proposed Spanish match had been tried, condemned and executed for treason and was subsequently attainted.[52] To be responsible for such a slur against the queen's majesty, be one Irish or English, was to forfeit one's life. Consequently, once a tower-house was held against crown forces, the lives of the defenders were entirely at the discretion of the besieging captain. Furthermore, if a castle was taken by assault, a third of all goods and chattels remaining, under martial law, belonged to the attacking soldiers. Native resistance and self-defence therefore became excuses for devastating reprisals because they signified rebellion. Fitzwilliam, Malby and Essex presented violent actions

---

[50] 'A discourse of the services done by Sir Richard Bingham in the county of Mayo' October 1586, SP63/126/53i.
[51] Montaigne, Michel de, *The complete essays* (London, 1991), pp. 25, 73.
[52] The case of Stafford is referred to *en passant* by the fictional but emblematic English common lawyer Anglonomophylax in the civilian William Fulbecke's *The parallele or conference of the civil law, the canon law and the common law of this realm of England* (London, 1601), p. 87 in the section on 'Treason and rebellion'.

by crown forces in this context and thereby justified those actions by that context. Fitton's killings, Fitzwilliam claimed, were carried out on those that had the temerity to hold out against him. The eighty defenders done away with in MacDermott's country were by definition rebels against the queen and had forfeited their lives. Yet, the use of such unyielding analysis and action was discretionary and not mandatory. Lord Deputy John Perrot, for example, received the defenders of Dunluce Castle into his mercy following the commencement of the siege 'because he would save the charges of repairing again that piece, which otherwise he must have beaten down: and for that he would not spend the provision [and] weaken the forces.'[53]

Significantly, the protocol of siege warfare, with its implicit royal benediction, was used to explain away the otherwise controversial conduct of renowned 'massacres' such as the assault by Sir John Norris and Francis Drake on Rathlin Island executed 'on the sudden' under secret command from the earl of Essex. Essex's account of the assault, which he had not witnessed, in a letter to Elizabeth, stresses the aspects of the attack that corresponded with the formalities of siege warfare. According to the earl, when the troops landed, 'they found they were discovered by the island men which had put themselves in readiness with all their sort to make resistance.' The English captains charged the defenders 'so hotly as they drove them to retire with speed chasing them to a castle'. A siege commenced. Within three days, the walls of the castle were breached, and the occupants of the castle called for a 'parley'. Norris 'wisely considering the danger that might light upon his company and willing to avoid the killing of the soldiers which in such cases doth often happen although he saw the place likely enough to be taken with some loss of men' accepted the parley. The Scots made 'large requests' for their goods and persons to be allowed to return to Scotland. Norris refused these and was only willing to guarantee the lives of the constable, his wife and child, whatever goods were found in the castle were 'to be at Captain Morgan's disposition' and 'the lives of all the rest within to stand upon the courtesy of the soldiers'. The constable of the Scots handed his company over to the soldiers who 'being moved and much stirred with the loss of their fellows which were slain' killed them all. Crucially, they refrained from killing Alexander Óg MacAlaister Harry, a hostage Sorley Boy MacDonnell had taken from a recalcitrant client, thereby honouring promises previously made by their enemy. Essex, probably because of the precarious nature of

[53] Rawlinson (London, 1728), pp. 158–61.

royal approbation for his enterprise of Ulster, was given to emphasising his captains' and soldiers' zeal for Elizabeth: 'They think themselves happy', he stated, 'when they may have any occasion offered them that is to be your highness's acceptable service.'[54] It was necessary to couch this action on Rathlin as a siege because Sorley Boy and 'others of the Scotch Irish race' had been granted denization in April 1573. Up to that point, the Scots in Antrim and Down, despite their flirtations with the administration, had been deemed to be invaders and squatters.[55]

THE ANTICIPATION OF CLEMENCY

Another thing that profoundly affected the pattern of both low and high intensity conflict in Ireland was the expectation – shared by both the English and the Irish – that pardons would be liberally used in official procedure and that protections and safe-conducts would be employed during respites in fighting. These methods to defuse and limit violence relying (as they did) on consensus were commonly employed in Ireland. The sheer frequency with which pardons were issued can be seen by looking at *The Irish fiants of the Tudor sovereigns*. Of course, not all pardons were issued as indemnities against punishment for violent crimes, but the theory of justice that underwrote them followed the same norms as it did in England, and that theory was well understood in Ireland. For example, one scion of the MacWilliam Burkes in 1586, as he went to the gallows, allegedly displayed his outrage at President Sir Richard Bingham's violation of form by yelling, 'I have heard that scholars and such men as could read ought to have the benefit of their clergy.'[56] Hostilities, as pointed out above, were rarely instigated to secure devastating victory but as a type of negotiation to determine how favourable an accommodation might be arrived at with central government after an armed demonstration. In such a context, one of the sweetest fruits of victory was the opportunity it afforded the victor to define the conflict

---

[54] Essex to Elizabeth, 31 July 1575, SP63/52/77.
[55] See *CPRI*, Vol. I, p. 553 for the patent of denization. Sorley Boy swore an oath 'as the denizen strangers do in the chancery of England'. He claimed during a conference with Thomas Smith Jr held in May 1573 that he held his lands in Scotland in the right of Lord Misset, an Englishman, whose descendants had married into the MacDonnells, 'The colloquy of Thomas Smith, colonel of the Ards and Sorley Boy', SP63/40/77.
[56] For more on benefit of clergy in an Henrician English context, see K. J. Kesselring, *Mercy and authority in the Tudor state* (Cambridge, 2003), pp. 46–8, 62–3. The Burkes' book of complaints, 20 November 1589, SP63/148/15; Book of matters presented by juries versus Bingham, 24 November 1589, SP63/148/20.

that went before.[57] An officially ratified settlement would have to be arrived at.[58]

This mechanism of pardons and protections therefore constituted the shared plateau from which allegations by officers and Irish subjects about trustworthiness, violation of solemn undertakings and cruelty could be levelled against each other. Malby's correspondence about his vigorous campaigning in Connacht in 1576 is illuminating on the question of the limits of trust between subjects and crown officers, the violation of expectations about that trust and how these issues were practically resolved. Writing to Walsingham in March 1577, he outlined his attempts over the previous year to bring his struggles with the sons of the earl of Clanricard, John and Ulick Burke, to a satisfactory end, using and then discarding these methods of resolving conflict. Typically, he began by indicating his awareness of 'her majesty's disposition to bring this people to obedience by fair dealings and courteous usage', which he claimed to have embarked upon 'albeit he had some experience of their faithless former doings'. He arrived at a truce with them 'upon conditions tending to the dignity of her majesty and the honour and credit of my lord deputy'. Both sides met – eight to eight – and the *mac an iarlas* asked for a month's truce under protection, which Malby granted, petitioning for the viceroy's favour towards them. Towards the end of the month, Lord Deputy Sidney replied negatively to the petition, thereby withholding any further extension of the earl's sons' protections beyond the time already granted. He insisted that they should 'simply submit themselves unto him and stand to his courtesy'; if they thought him 'too severe a judge', they should go to Westminster and submit to Elizabeth themselves. Malby met with them 'at a place appointed, six to six' and told them the bad news. They asked for eight days to 'consider of it with their friends', a period that they also used to take in their harvest.

Two days before the agreed time was to elapse ('when I least looked for it', Malby claimed), John Burke entered 'sundry villages' at ten o'clock at night killing sixteen or seventeen horsemen, ten or twelve of 'her Majesty's kern' and taking a captain of horse, his lieutenant and 'a young gentleman that served in that company' prisoner. This was a breach of faith, an 'unlooked for outrage'. Malby moved fast to rescue the soldiers with ten shot and thirty horsemen, 'which I had made up and gathered of my

---

[57] Malby to Walsingham, 17 March 1577, SP63/57/40.
[58] See K. J. Kesselring's brief, but perceptive treatment of the use of pardons in Tudor Ireland (2003), pp. 192–9, and Kenneth Nicholls's introduction to the 1994 re-issue of *Fiants*, Vol. I, pp. v–xi.

friends'. On receiving further reinforcements from the lord deputy, he related,

> finding that good and courteous dealing with them had like to have cut my throat I thought good then to take another course and so with a determination to consume them with fire and sword, not sparing neither old nor young I entered their mountains which was their chiefest strength and greatest hope.

Malby's retaliation over the 'Christmas holidays' of 1576 was to be calculated usuriously. He devastated the territories of both John and Ulick Burke, 'sparing none that came in my way which cruelty did so amaze their followers as they could not tell where to bestow themselves'. But Malby intimated to Walsingham that his actions were for political effect. John Burke, seeing the president 'so bent to revenge', pleaded with him to stop his rampage, promising to make amends for his action 'if he could not prove he did commit it in time of war': significantly, John continued to stand on the assertion that he had acted in time of war rather than during a truce and persisted in arguing this point for quite a while until he was forced to concede. Through offering protections piecemeal to the gentlemen of Clanricard and thereby eventually achieving Ulick Burke's submission, Malby managed to isolate John. He told Walsingham that the defecting gentlemen had been informed 'that it [had lain] in them if they had any mind of loyalty unto her majesty to suppress the rebels', adding 'but I saw no willingness in them and therefore her majesty having appointed me to see her people brought to obedience by fair means, if it might be, *had given me authority to use force where good dealing could not take place*' (my italics). On the other hand, Malby extolled his own harshness: 'Your honour may see how in twenty-one days journey used with cruelty, the strong rebellion and private enemies were brought under foot.' The severity would not work without the leniency, the leniency would not work without the severity. The severity, in this case, according to Malby, was motivated and justified by a breach of etiquette towards both Malby, the man and, in his person, the crown.[59]

FRATERNISATION AND ETHNICITY

However, the Irish were not thought to be necessarily untrustworthy, and, indeed in many respects, the intimacy of Irish politics at both the

---

[59] Malby to Walsingham, 17 March 1577, SP63/57/40. Malby had changed his attitude to John Burke by 1580, see Malby to Walsingham, 4 November 1579, SP63/70/2.

local and national level made systematic ethnic discrimination unworkable. Vincent Carey has himself acknowledged the central role that Owen MacHugh O'Dempsey, a prominent colonist in the Laois plantation, played in the massacre of Mullaghmast; being 'pro-government' does not mean that he was less 'Gaelic-Irish'.[60] For centuries, Irish kern and gallowglass had been a central part of the military retinues of English-Irish magnates and the crown government.[61] The complexities and elisions obvious in sixteenth-century military life in Ireland are hinted at in the English-Irish rebel Edmund Butler's remarks to the earl of Ormond (at the time outraged and determined to demonstrate his loyalty in spite of Edmund's insurrection) in August 1569 about a costly engagement between his troop of gallowglass and that recent arrival in Leinster Sir Peter Carew. Sir Edmund related that thirty gallowglass and two of their captains had been killed in the skirmish but asserted that 'those [who] were slain [had done] the queen in all her wars better service under your leading than ever Peter did.' Intriguingly, when Sir Edmund went on to loudly declaim his loyalty to his queen, he asserted that in order to clear his name he had sent out a challenge for trial by combat between five of his own kinsmen and five named opponents: Sir Peter Carew, Sir Barnaby Fitzpatrick, Sir William O'Carroll, Francis Cosby and Sir Humphrey Gilbert – all of whom, he alleged, had 'persuaded my lord deputy thus to deal with me, and upon their ale benches betraitor me at their pleasure'. Disavowing his status as a proclaimed rebel, he insisted that all he wanted to do was to wage private war against his enemies on a private matter.[62] It may have been paranoia that made Sir Edmund describe these three Englishmen (two of whom have been portrayed as near-genocidal by

---

[60] Carey (1999), p. 319. Owen MacHugh O'Dempsey managed to pass on his estates in Ballybritish to his successor Sir Terence O'Dempsey. Other Gaelic-Irish figures with estates in Laois included Charles MacTurlough with 998 acres at 'Tenekill', Hugh MacCullogh with 332 acres at 'Acregar', Ferganym O'Kelly with 120 acres at Corbally. This arrangement did not always last. Grants to Kedough Mac Piers O'More, Frayne O'Kelly and Murtough O'More were forfeited in 1601. Lord Deputy Fitzwilliam described O'Dempsey as 'a dutiful Irish subject' in his 'Device for recovering the Queen's County from the O'Mores' SP63/30/38.

[61] For instance Sir Edward Fitton in August 1573 noted how Lord Deputy Fitzwilliam after the death of Robert Colley at Philipstown was pursuing O'Conor confederates of Rory Óg O'More accompanied by most of the garrison, as well as '500 or 600 of this country's birth'. This inclusion of troops, no matter how ragged, of Irish birth differentiates the make up of forces loyal to the metropolis in Tudor Ireland from the profile of the forces of the commonwealth and protectorate in Ireland less than a century later, which by contrast were homogenously English. This radically differentiates the character of conflict in Ireland in the sixteenth century from conflict in Ireland during the war of the three kingdoms.

[62] Sir Edmund Butler to Ormond, 24 August, SP63/29/47i.

historians) and two Gaelic-Irishmen as drinking companions, but maybe he was referring to a culture of real conviviality across ethnic divisions between partisans of the Sidney regime. Certainly, Sir Henry Sidney's 1583 'Memoir' underlined the former viceroy's stated fondness for both Gaelic-Irish figures amenable to the crown and English captains whom he had met during his terms of office.[63]

Whatever about the loyalties of magnates and chieftains, many disaffected or *déclassé* individuals of Gaelic-Irish stock worked particularly closely with English captains in a military or administrative capacity. The captains not only found it suited their own ends to exploit indigenous political or social conflict, they often found themselves enmeshed in it themselves because of marriage or political alliance. Such Gaelic-Irish *fidèles* were valued lieutenants; perhaps this was because of their relative lack of concern about overstepping the boundaries of English law and their wonted rapacity. In certain areas, the captains and Irish strongmen seemed to have everything stitched up, much to the chagrin of those landed gentlemen and householders who were forced to submit to their exactions. For instance, Robert Harpoole, the constable of Carlow from 1567 to 1594, had as his trusted bailiff his brother-in-law, a shady and threatening man called Owen Dowlagh O'Byrne, described by contemporaries as a 'common extortioner'.[64] Harpoole also had in his employ Donal Mac Gerald Mac Shane Óg of Mothill, whose troop of 100 kern frequently joined forces with Art Duff, captain of Henry Davells's kern, to distrain goods and impose exactions based on the 'pleasure' of Harpoole's sub-sheriff, a certain William Beg.[65] Between them all, they

---

[63] See Brady (2002), pp. 14–16. Sir Barnaby Fitzpatrick, baron of Upper Ossory, and Sir William O'Carroll, son of the baron of Ely both bordered on Ormond territories and were wonted opponents of the earl of Ormond.

[64] Owen Dowlagh, brother of Gráinne, Robert Harpoole's wife was probably a member of the Kiltimon branch of the O'Byrne sept, see Kenneth Nicholls' genealogy of the O'Byrnes in 'Feagh McHugh O'Byrne: the Wicklow Firebrand' ed. Conor O'Brien, *Journal of the Rathdrum Historical Society* (1998), Vol. I, pp. 278–80. See also the 1574 'Survey of Ireland' in *Cal Car MSS 1601–3*, 446–54, which remarks that 'Harkepoole [is] matched with a Coltyneon . . . (alias Byrnes) a maintainer of rebels'.

[65] See 'The book against Robert Harpoole', 21 August 1571, SP63/33/108. Harpoole's son William took over as constable of Carlow in 1594, see *Liber Munerum Publicorum Hiberniae* (1834), p. 118. For further reference to the 100 kern and fifty boys serving under both Harpoole and Davells see Fitzwilliam to Davells and Harpoole, 24 September 1573, SP63/42/25, where he outlines the degree of cess they can levy on Ormond's lands in Forth O'Nolan, which amounted – after royal exemptions – to a levy on a third of his lands. Harpoole on this occasion may have been using the commission of martial law issued to both himself and Henry Davells on 29 March 1570, *Fiants* II, 1505. It was renewed in 1571 (1829), 1572 (2117) and 1576 (2775).

kept Carlow's hinterland including areas in the earl of Ormond's estates under Harpoole's thumb while remunerating themselves handsomely.[66] For example, Harpoole was believed to be sponsoring and providing safe haven for Donal O'Meagher and the Keatings, who widely spoiled kine and swine, even from the sheriff of Carlow, not to mention John Rowe and members of the Eustace family. When the situation in Carlow got too hot, O'Meagher, being attached to the crown forces, probably with Harpoole's connivance, transferred his billet to Carrickfergus. Ormond partisans such as Sir Nicholas White and others alleged that this sort of intimacy entirely compromised the captains' service to the crown: in 1573, White alleged that Francis Cosby was a 'winker or maintainer of every rebellion' who should be called 'to a severe account' for the loss of Laois and criticised him as well as Captain Edward Moore (deemed 'a great favourer of the O'Mores and O'Conors') for 'their commerce with the Irishry'.[67]

The relationship between English captains and the Gaelic-Irish could even be sentimentalised. For example, Churchyard tells the story of a kern in the crown forces, who, having attempted to assassinate Malby during his time in Ulster, took advantage of a proclamation of safe conduct to submit before the captain. Malby's 'heart stirred' at this display of courage, 'courtesy and truth' when the kern explained that he had submitted because he 'heard that the captain never brake his word [and therefore he had] ventured to try his fidelity, not caring for [his] own life'. According to the tale, Malby retained this kern within his household from then on

---

[66] Sir Nicholas Malby also used Irishmen, even kern, as bailiffs in his administration of Connacht in the late 1570s and early 1580s. Part of the beauty of using kern was that Malby was able to distance himself from allegations that he encouraged excessive extortion by blaming the unruliness and natural exuberance of the natives in his administration. See the fifth point in 'The answer of Sir Nicholas Malby to Edward White's objections' April, 1582, SP63/91/25: 'There was no barony exempted from the sheriff's jurisdiction, but where the sheriffs did place strange kern, which they call the sheriff's kernty, to be their bailiffs in the sundry baronies within their bailiwick, which bailiffs being commonly kern of no honest behaviour, but such as exact and spoil the people without any conscience, the chief gentlemen and the rest made petition unto me that I would ease them from those wicked officers and that the head or chief of the barony might by appointed to be the bailiff or officer to the sheriff promising to be a diligent to obey the sheriff, as any other should be, whereupon I have granted to diverse their said request with this clause in their warrants "That they shall answer the sheriff at all times and in all things as his officers, that he shall require them to do for the service of her majesty and that if they shall fail in so doing then the sheriff shall appoint the same bailiffs that before he did"'.

[67] For the case of Donal O'Meagher, see the accusations made against him by John Rowe before the Irish council and his answers in Bodl. Carte MSS, 56/532, 56/536. See also White to Burghley, 17 June 1573, SP63/41/80. For Fitzwilliam's attempt to explain his continuing favour for Cosby the man 'chargeable with the cause of the disorder in that country of the O'Mores, Fitzwilliam to Burghley, Sussex and Leicester, 15 April 1574, SP63/45/72.

to the chagrin of other military captains. Similarly, according to Churchyard, a Gaelic-Irish chieftain 'Brian Ballowe' (probably Brian Ballagh) submitted to Malby, despite pressure from his people who 'took hold of his mantle to stay him'. Brian declared 'I will go keep my promise, for I hope Captain Malby will not see me suffer death, which keeps my word: The only credit of a man's life.'[68] And indeed, for all his severity and adamantine rhetoric, Malby had little time for discourses that stressed ethnological and anthropological distinctions between the Irish and English. For instance, in 1577 he stressed how dutiful the Irish could be as soldiers, even those who 'at the first taking of his charge were either open rebels or doubted subjects', stating that they were now 'very willing to spend their lives for the service of her majesty'. He further argued that such a trusting attitude towards the Irish was useful and necessary '[for he] who will not hazard some times in these services or that standeth doubtful of every thing shall prevail little in this land.'[69] The next year, he declared that he had 'seen by experience that the assured subject of England do some time fall from their duties much more [than is] to be looked for at this people's hand'. He hoped that 'time and good usage' would bring the Irish to 'more conformity than hitherto they have lived'.[70]

He was not the only one, even Sir Henry Harrington, seneschal of the O'Byrnes, who had previously been kidnapped and mutilated by Rory O'More during disturbances in the Irish midlands in 1577, found that he could intercede for the dead rebel's erstwhile comrade Fiach MacHugh O'Byrne six years later, stating that 'there is no time I send for him but he will come without protection'. This openness roused the scorn of Sir Henry Wallop, vice-treasurer of Ireland from 1579 to 1599. He dismissed Harrington as in 'many ways a good natural gentleman but over credulous to Irish promises, which hath cost him dear'.[71] Harrington, it was

---

[68] Churchyard[1579] sigs. Eiii, v–Eiv. But contrast Malby's alleged confidence with Barnaby Googe's remark to Burghley on his fears about leading a troop of kern. These 'people of the country' not only were 'more naturally given to spoil and extortion than the Englishman is'. They served for food alone rather than pay, a source of discomfort for Googe who felt as a result that he had little control over their 'evil demeanour' and was 'always in danger to have [his] throat cut amongst them'. Googe to Burghley, 11 March 1583, SP63/100/14. See also Wallop's stark statement about the massive influx of Irishmen into the crown forces in Munster in 1581, which had been decimated by illness. He hoped that the practice would be given over 'for . . . those we train become our dangerousest enemies', Wallop to Burghley, 13 May 1581, SP63/83/12.
[69] Malby to Walsingham, 10 November 1577, SP63/59/43.
[70] Malby to Walsingham, 12 April 1578, SP63/60/37.
[71] The most notorious example of Irish faithlessness was the killing of Captain Henry Davells, constable of Dungarvan, in his bed-chamber by the English-Irish grandee Sir John Fitzgerald, the earl of Desmond's brother. Bernardino de Mendoza wrote to Philip II from London in August

alleged, had hopes that he might be 'well thought of' in England 'for travailing in any peace, be it never so dishonorable'.[72] And Grey de Wilton was similarly withering about the young Captain William Piers's noted rapport with Turlough Luineach O'Neill and doubted that the captain had 'any credit at all with Turlough (but in the way of good fellowship which lasteth no longer than that humour continueth)'.[73] It seems that young Piers, in his frank dealings with Gaelic Ireland, was merely following in his father's footsteps: in 1573 the first earl of Essex had imprisoned old Captain Piers, constable of Carrickfergus, because of his continuing contacts with Sir Brian MacPhelim O'Neill. But Grey disparaged 'what[ever] golden mountains' young Piers promised as mere 'patched stuff that cannot long hold' – although Grey was not immune from criticism himself. Wallop, disgusted by the administration's major concessions to Turlough Luineach O'Neill – a necessity in 1581 while Munster was still in crisis – accused him of a tendency to 'patch up things' before his hasty revocation.[74]

THE QUEEN, PARDONS AND HER IRISH SUBJECTS

Of course, this capacity to trust the Irish and court their friendship, taken in tandem with the queen's refusal to be overly fastidious about matters to do with her honour, majesty and prerogative in Ireland, were deemed by some to be the gravest threats to state honour and government in the sister kingdom. Some, indeed, lamented that Elizabeth remained over-anxious

---

1579 about the stir this action caused at court. Because Davells was 'very popular with the Irish' and, indeed, had been 'the principal means of saving [Sir John's] life' the conclusions drawn from the murder were that a general rising was imminent. Sir John, who indeed had been on very cordial terms with Davells, allegedly answered the captain's pleadings for mercy saying that 'it was enough . . . that he was an Englishman', see Bernardino de Mendoza to King Philip, 15 August 1579, *CSPSp, 1568–1579*, p. 685. For Sir John's despair as a result of abandonment by the Crown he had served well and his alienation from the pardoned earl of Desmond see Brady (1981), pp. 308–10.

[72] Harrington to Burghley, 14 November 1583, SP63/105/65; Wallop to Walsingham, 28 August 1581, SP63/85/27. For details of Harrington's capture by O'More see Churchyard (1579), sig. Rii, r. See also Sidney to the privy council, SP63/59/57, 26 November 1577. As late as 1588, Harrington was used along with Sir Thomas Lestrange the pro-president of Connacht to proffer a vicegeral safe-conduct to the increasingly defiant Brian O'Rourke of Breifne, see 'Articles of treason and disloyalties committed by Fergus O'Farrell', 24 October 1589, SP63/147/37. See also the recommendation of Captain William Collier that many members of the O'Molloy sept should be pardoned, 18 September 1578, and an array of O'Dempseys, O'Kellys, MacDonoghs and others, 23 August 1582, *Fiants*, Vol. II, 3508, 3962; see also a pardon of some MacMurroughs, O'Kellys and O'Bolgers at the petition of Thomas Masterson, *Fiants*, Vol. II, 3901.

[73] Grey de Wilton to the privy council, 12 August 1581, SP63/85/13.

[74] Grey de Wilton to the privy council, 12 August 1581, SP63/85/13; Wallop to Walsingham, 28 August 1581, SP63/85/27.

to make political life easy for her prominent Irish subjects and denounced the tendency of some of her officers to capitalise on the loopholes occasioned by their sovereign's alleged anxiety. These conciliatory tendencies came at the cost of her honour and authority and, by extension, the honour and authority of all crown officers in Ireland. They warned that familiarity and casualness in government would breed contempt, and a reputation for leniency, it was often whispered, signified spinelessness or corruption. For instance, in the early 1570s, Edward Waterhouse, then the earl of Essex's secretary, alleged that the sometime rebel Hugh MacShane O'Byrne had prayed openly that Lord Deputy Fitzwilliam (hated by Essex) 'might long continue in the office as the best friend that ever he had of a deputy, because there never came to Ireland so good a lord for men of his occupation, for every man might do what they list and have their pardons whensoever they would ask it'.[75] 'This was the varlet's speech', Waterhouse wrote, 'since if there be once an opinion conceived that men shall neither be prosecuted nor punished, it makes the ill disposed bold to attempt all the wickedness that they think themselves able to perform.' Waterhouse's proposed antidote to this regime of licence was stern military government, 'whensoever any alterations shall happen let all offices be given to soldiers of experience and to none other' presumably it was anticipated that these 'soldiers of experience' would come from Essex's ever more fragile 'Enterprise of Ulster'.[76]

Similarly, Robert Dudley, the earl of Leicester, wrote Fitzwilliam a hectoring and tendentious letter in December 1572 stating that to his

> own judgement ... those governors who sought to keep those unconstant and rebellious nations most under and in fear, had them at most commandment and greatest obedience ... [as distinct from those who] gave them most the bridle by courteous and gentle manner ... by feeding them with too oft pardons upon their famed and subtle submissions.

He added disingenuously, 'I do verily think yourself [are] of the same mind and I am deceived if I had not always found you so in your discourse of that country.'[77] Leicester's pointed reference to Fitzwilliam's

---

[75] However, Fitzwilliam's leniency to O'Byrne had been anticipated by the earl of Sussex in December 1563 when Hugh MacShane O'Byrne and a medley of followers from among the O'Nolans, O'Byrnes and O'Naughton were pardoned for 'the capture and detention of George Harvey (constable of Maryborough) and Henry Davells (constable of Dungarvan).' Davells and Harvey were, no doubt, central to securing the pardons. *Fiants*, Vol. II, 579.
[76] The outrages committed by the earl of Essex during his 'enterprise of Ulster' occurred during Fitzwilliam's viceroyalty. The accusations of lenience can be seen in Waterhouse to Walsingham, 14 June 1574, SP63/46/64.
[77] Leicester to Fitzwilliam, 5 December 1572, Bodl. Carte MSS 56/39 fol. 103r.

wonted rhetoric rather than his actions shows that he knew well how large the divergence could be between accounts of government in Ireland and what actually happened there. It seems that Fitzwilliam's severe tone (as he put it three months earlier, '[until] the sword have thoroughly and universally tamed (and not meekened) [the Irish] in vain is law brought among them') had not convinced Leicester of his *bona fides*.[78] In short, it was well known that appeals for indiscriminate severity were often either merely a justification for a vendetta against a particular individual or a flimsy cloak obscuring the pursuit of a policy of scandalous lenience towards some other Irish potentate. The irate tone usually lasted as long as suited the writer, a fact underlined in the case of the ill-fated earl of Desmond who noted, while bitching to the earl of Essex in April 1574 about his treatment at the hands of Fitzwilliam that '[s]uch extremities might be with better consultation ministered or served out to such as be both traitors and rebels more near home, whose honours are daily fed with pardons and protections, sooner than justice executed to punish their desert, to the undoing of the Pale, and the great danger of the whole estate', alleging further that the viceroy was acting like 'the careless physician who seeks with great diligence to cure his patient of a morphew, being in danger of death, with an inward impostume'. In 1583, Desmond would, of course, end up impaled on his own scalpel.[79]

In his desire to demonstrate beyond doubt the faithlessness and contempt of the Irish for Elizabeth's authority, Wallop, in August 1581, sent Walsingham a list of examples of broken faith and irreverence for the crown. Deviations from proper devotion to crown authority, he believed, had become distressingly common. The starkness of procedure that Wallop desired was consistently being undermined by negotiations undertaken between the crown and erstwhile rebels in order to secure a speedy peace. He acknowledged Elizabeth's complicity in this flexible policy when he conceded that 'the avoiding of charge is the chief cause that moveth her Majesty'. The queen's stinginess played into rebel hands as all advantages won by crown forces were, he contended, subsequently squandered. The notorious rebel Fiach MacHugh O'Byrne, it was pointed out, had refused to submit abjectly to Grey de Wilton, to accept terms put to him by Henry Harrington or even to put in the pledges that crown authorities

---

[78] Fitzwilliam to Burghley, 25 September 1572, SP63/37/60.
[79] Desmond to Essex, 4 April 1574, SP63/45/55. Desmond's denunciation of Fitzwilliam may have been a pre-meditated bid to secure support from those elements at court who were seeking to bring Fitzwilliam down.

demanded of him, because he claimed to fear for his life. Theoretically, of course, O'Byrne's life was less his own possession than that of his queen, but this amounted to a piety mocked by political realities. One of the pledges Grey had demanded was that O'Byrne should bring in the rebel Hugh Duff MacDonnell. O'Byrne claimed that this was beyond his power: a lie, according to Wallop, who reckoned that such a handover could easily be carried out. Wallop drew a moral from all this: even when the Irish entered into pledges, they did not feel bound in any way by them. For example, the treasonous activities of the earls of Desmond and Clancar had not been curtailed by the fact that they had ceded their respective heirs to the crown as pledges; Phelim O'Toole, in a demonstration of particular insubordination, had entered into rebellion the very day after he had handed his brother over as a pledge for good behaviour.

Even more scandalously, the Irish were ungracious when the crown offered them pardons, often refusing to take them in person being willing only to accept them 'by way of attorney', an audacity which Wallop stated 'hath seldom been seen between so mighty a prince and so disloyal a subject'. Crucially, and no doubt much to the vice-treasurer's chagrin, a precedent had been set for such virtual submissions by President Malby in Connacht in his dealings with the *mac an iarlas*. Wallop announced that he had brought these grievances to the council table but had been voted down. In a fit of despondency, Wallop believed that two options lay open to crown policy in Ireland: either 'her majesty were better to give them over to their own government and let them one cut another's throat' or she should 'daunt these people ... by the edge of the sword and ... plant better in their places'. Anything was better than 'this style to conserve treason to no purpose seeing no action is followed to the end'. Although Wallop's subsequent rant in favour of wide-scale plantation seems prophetic (he himself mentally rehearsed and played an active role in the facilitation of the Munster plantation), it is clear that this was more of an expression of frustration than a considered policy proposal: he deemed this course of action much less likely to happen than a return to indigenous rule, and he anticipated that *precarium imperium*, which had long compromised the honour of the crown, would continue to be followed.[80] In 1581, Wallop felt increasingly marginalised within the crown administration.

[80] Wallop to Walsingham, 28 August 1581, SP63/85/27. Some of the English-Irish of the Pale were also critical of the conciliatory policy that followed the upheavals of the early 1580s. A petition written in March 1582 complained about 'the often protecting of the Irishry to save further charges

By contrast, Malby came to embrace his queen's conciliatory preferences. His pragmatism and his desire to nest down in Connacht ensured a change of heart. In December 1581, Malby cited Elizabeth's 'pleasure . . . that all parts [should] be brought to pacification by the best means' as the justification for his appeal that both Ulick and John Burke, formerly his deadly enemies, should be granted the queen's 'gracious pardon under the broad seal of England'.[81] By September 1582, he wrote to Walsingham telling of both Ulick's (now the earl of Clanricard) and John's 'determination to establish all their country people and followers in assured obedience to her Majesty'. Malby was annoyed that Wallop, who was acting lord justice, was trying to obstruct the conciliatory policy that would allow them to take advantage of a general proclamation of pardon by Elizabeth. The Burke brothers wished to have their pardons 'gratis', whereas Wallop insisted that they should pay the requisite fine. Malby, disingenuously, expressed his admiration for Wallop's probity but warned that this 'difficulty [would] establish a stubbornness in the rude people to hold on their evil dispositions which [would] be more chargeable to her majesty then the fines can be any way available to her highness' adding that the treasurer was 'of nature and condition somewhat sore.' The iron had to be hit while it was still hot, so he asked that the privy council, and especially Walsingham, Wallop's patron as well as his own, might put pressure on the vice-treasurer to submit to *realpolitik*, 'considering her Majesty's course of pacification'. But he wanted this done in a private manner that would not endanger the lord justice's credit. Malby, who at this stage in his career felt ill used and unappreciated, but did not wish to add to his store of enemies, requested Walsingham to keep the complaint to himself and commit his letter 'to the fire'. Malby could be more 'regal' than his queen when he so desired, but when personal circumstances dictated that a flexible approach towards Irish subjects might be advantageous, he could advocate it no matter how politically awkward it appeared.[82]

---

after many offences committed on the Pale'. See 'A remembrance for Ireland', 31 March 1582, SP63/90/69.
[81] Malby to the privy council, December 1581, SP63/87/74.
[82] Malby to Walsingham, 14 September 1582, SP63/95/44. It is worth noting, however, that in June 1581, Malby had told Walsingham how appalled he was by Elizabeth's general pardons. 'I have the pledges of all the principal men of Connacht saving from O'Rourke which with very force I have won from them, and not by entreaty and do find it the only means to govern this people', adding, 'I have this day seen the proclamations for pardoning offenders which shall accept of her Majesty's gracious offer. I doubt much they will rather procure a greater charge than any way to work means

Of course, the usual dispute between the captains and the Irish – whether Gaelic-Irish or English-Irish – centred around each group's attempts to use the system of pardons and protections to gain advantage over the other. In July 1573, Sir Edward Fitton, first president of Connacht, after securing an initial 'show of submission' by which the Irish made themselves 'free from all peril', noted that he believed that they felt themselves 'bound no longer to obedience than themselves list'. He remarked resignedly that the normal acceptance of this state of affairs occluded crown officers' sense of right and wrong, but, with typical resignation, he concluded that 'this kind of quiet is no new thing to be holden for politic in Ireland.'[83] Malby paid particular attention to Irish opportunism, observing in April 1578 that the 'Irishman's policy' was to seek advantage by 'winning ... time' because 'time won in this country ... is half a conquest.'[84] In short, the Irish were thought to merely use the opportunity afforded by pardons and protections to temporise, to watch and wait for crown policy to self-destruct and ultimately to collect and augment their own position, rather than using it – as theoretically envisaged – to prepare for and canvass widely within their sept or affinity in favour of abject submission to crown officers. As Irish subjects sought to eke the utmost advantage out of elements of crown procedure, crown officers consistently tried to interpret the terms of their commissions as broadly as possible and to seek similar advantage.

DESPERATION, POLITICAL VACUUMS AND MASSACRE

The case of the first earl of Essex's conduct during the 'enterprise of Ulster' is a good example of this. By November 1573, four months after his arrival in Antrim and Down to institute the 'enterprise of Ulster', Essex had given notice to Elizabeth that he was discarding his initial 'mildness' towards the native inhabitants, a kindness that 'might have allured and thoroughly won any nation well affected to your obedience'. In what, by now, will seem a familiar rhetorical trope, Essex, outraged, informed the queen that her beneficence had been repudiated by the people. And, indeed, Sir Brian Mac Phelim, after supplying cattle to Essex – a significant act of good will orchestrated by Captain Piers of

---

of pacification'. Malby to Walsingham, 30 June 1581, SP63/83/63. Malby preferred to employ pardons and protections according to his own will and discrimination.
[83] Fitton to Burghley, 6 July 1573, SP63/41/70.
[84] Malby to Walsingham, 12 April 1578, SP63/60/37.

Carrickfergus – decided to seek his advantage in opposition to the earl. On the night of Saturday, 17 October, in the darkness, next to woods, an inaugural skirmish between Essex and Sir Brian, typical of the type preferred by the Gaelic-Irish, ensued: the earl's first real experience of Irish warfare. Sir Brian's default had run counter to all of Captain Piers's assurances. Piers blamed his servants for the mess, while they in turn blamed him. Subsequently, Essex imprisoned the captain, accused him of causing £20,000 in crown expenditure and delated him to Burghley. After his plans had been thus upset, Essex told his queen that he had decided that

> since this people have refused your mercy, and taken upon them wilful war and rebellion, I trust to be the instrument, under you, to punish their breach of faith, and to compel the most obstinate of them to confess your greatness and your sovereignty here.

The consistently unnerving thing for Essex, however, was his sneaking belief that the Irish were more patient, better informed and more accurate at analysing the situation in Ulster than he. He was irritated that they knew that his first batch of hired soldiers, 'pressed by persuasion' not commission, were dissatisfied with pay and conditions and wanted to leave as soon as possible. Worse still, he told Elizabeth, the native population was 'fully persuaded that this war is altogether mine, alleging that if it were yours it should be executed by the lord deputy, being your chief general here'. Consequently, they were 'confederated in arms', waiting for Essex to run out of money and give up.[85] On the same day, he wrote to Burghley that the Irish themselves believed 'that the queen is indifferent whether this country be theirs or ours, that she esteems not the planting of Englishmen, so long as she might have obedience and rent'. But, worst of all, the Irish – it was rumoured – found him slight and ridiculous: 'I have good proof', he told Burghley 'that (Sir Brian) could be contented to hear me ill spoken of openly in his chamber by his own servant, and he to show countenance as though he took pleasure in his man's words.'[86] In short, the captain general of the 'enterprise of Ulster', away from court, isolated from the Dublin government and unable to

---

[85] Essex to Elizabeth, 2 November 1573, SP63/42/64. On Piers's imprisonment see Essex to Burghley, 9 December 1573, SP63/43/10, and Piers to Burghley, 26 January 1574, SP63/44/17, where Piers states 'Having spent my time long in the queen's service with many cold journeys upon her enemies in this country and elsewhere I did not think being old and grey headed to have this reward for my good will', he claimed to have lost all his worldly goods in a shipwreck off Dublin.
[86] Essex to Burghley, 2 November 1573, SP63/42/68.

trust many around him, but commissioned to hold extraordinary powers, was in a position where action in accordance with paranoia was a constant temptation.

Essex, beleaguered, was remarkably inconsistent in the ways he sought to advance his cause. What Elizabeth believed his strategy to be – first, the securing of an alliance with Turlough Luineach O'Neill and Brian MacPhelim to expel the Scots, and second, the consensual bringing of Clandeboy to obedience followed by the planting of adventurers – did not tally with the earl's actions on the ground nor the ideas he advanced. For instance, in November 1573, Essex suggested that Sorley Boy Mac-Donnell might be granted land in the Glynnes by the queen and then used against the Irish 'who wilfully have refused the grace and mercy of her majesty, broken their fidelity, and vowed confederacy in rebellion'. He recommended that Sorley be made a denizen and assigned 'service in lieu of rent, as captain of her majesty's kern, which he 'being a mercenary man and a soldier, will easily consent to' – the diametric opposite of his initial strategy.[87]

There were notable, but normal, limits to Essex's scope for action. For instance, his commission of martial law did not permit him to condemn any freeholder of England to death, unless found guilty by twelve freeholders born in England, nor to condemn any freeholder of Ireland unless found guilty – significantly – by twelve freeholders of either English or Irish birth, nor, finally, any 'mere Irishman' or 'Scottish Irishman' or 'mere Scot or man born elsewhere unless he be found guilty by twelve persons born in one of the said realms or [he] *be taken in the act*' (my italics).[88]

Maybe Essex relied on this final clause to justify the act for which his 'enterprise' is now best remembered: the ambushing of Sir Brian Mac-Phelim O'Neill, a figure one would have thought would have been counted an 'Irish freeman' rather than 'mere Irish' in November 1574. The earl of Essex justified this coup by alleging that Sir Brian had invited him to dinner at his castle in Belfast in order to kill him. Of course, in order to have been caught *in the act* of perpetrating such a crime, all Sir Brian had to do was welcome the earl to his country and then to his table. Indeed, Essex's account of the scene in a letter to Fitzwilliam was ludicrously tendentious: Sir Brian and some of his kinsmen 'after their dissembling manner' welcomed Essex to his territory – his wife even came to

---

[87] Elizabeth to Essex, 30 March 1574, SP63/45/42; Burghley, Sussex and Leicester to Essex, 30 March 1574, SP63/45/43. Essex's instructions to Waterhouse, 2 November 1573, SP63/42/66.
[88] *CPR Eliz, 1572–3*, 506, dated 24 July 1573.

greet the earl ('the more to blind me', Essex alleged) – then, later in the evening, 'sundry persons of credit' informed him of 'Brian's intended treachery'. Having received the 'advice and consents of all the captains in the camp' – an important fact as we shall see – he had Sir Brian arrested. According to Essex, Brian's kinsmen who were lodged in the town then offered 'resistance', and 125 of them were killed.[89]

Soon thereafter, Essex published an exculpatory proclamation justifying his conduct, specifically countering charges that Sir Brian had been under protection at the time of his arrest.[90] First, he dismissed this as the opinion of 'sundry evil men who have no disposition to allow for good anything that is well done', and, second, he launched a rhetorical offensive to retrospectively besmirch O'Neill's character, providing a list of his past breaches of trust in dealing with crown officers. He referred to Brian's previous 'shameful murdering of her majesty's subjects in a time of peace' after invitations to 'eat and make merry with him', an offence made worse by subsequent depredations carried out on the bodies of his victims: 'his cruelty showed in mangling their dead bodies as cutting of their privy members and setting up of their heads with the same in their mouths.' What makes the recitation of this list bewildering is that Essex admitted that Sir Brian had been pardoned of all these offences against hospitality. He brushed the charges aside (albeit after numbering them in pornographic detail) to stress his own proper attitude to the mechanism of protections and pardons and acknowledged that these acts could not excuse any punitive measures whatsoever.

The actual justification Essex seized on for O'Neill's execution rested on supposition and rumour about the chieftain's intentions and state of mind following the pardon. The earl alleged that Sir Brian had intended – with the collusion of the Scots – to cut the throats of English soldiers in his territory but had deferred this 'horrible treason' because there was no 'man of great account among the English' and was content to wait 'until he might get a more chosen company to perform it upon'. He had also allegedly invited Nicholas Malby to dine with him in Belfast, an invitation Malby had decided not to take up having been informed that O'Neill intended to kill him.[91] In May 1573, when canvassing royal

---

[89] Essex to Fitzwilliam, 14 November 1574, SP63/48/52iii.
[90] See Bagwell (1860), Vol. II, p. 288–9 for a frank assessment of Essex's ethics in relation to the killing of Sir Brian MacPhelim.
[91] See Essex to Fitzwilliam, 14 November 1574, SP63/48/52 iii; Memorandum entitled 'The manifest actions committed by Brian MacPhelim', SP63/48/52iv; Advertisements given against Brian MacPhelim SP63/48/52v; and Proclamation by Walter Devereux, earl of Essex, SP63/48/57i.

support for the 'enterprise', Essex had asked Elizabeth for 'authority, with the assent of any such twelve Englishmen as he shall publish by proclamation to be his assistants in counsel, to make laws and ordinances for the good government of the said country, and also to repeal the same 'in which case he only to have a double voice and not otherwise'.[92] Was his reference to canvassing his captains before killing Sir Brian's kinsmen a gesture to this procedural fig leaf? In any case, Essex wrung every bit of licence possible from his patents and commissions.

The areas where tit-for-tat violence between the captains and the Irish became most endemic were those places where crown officers, following the old expansionist fantasies of the Palesmen, had entirely undermined the normal political framework: Laois/Offaly, for instance, and the earldom of Ulster. In the case of Laois/Offaly, where there had been a power vacuum since the expulsion and imprisonment of Brian O'Conor and Giollaphadraig O'More in the late 1540s, attempts over the next three decades to maintain the plantation against the expropriated foe (known as the 'naturals') left a festering wound in the midlands which at its worst could infect a hinterland that spanned from Wicklow to Tipperary.[93] The plantation established in 1556 and bolstered in the early years of Elizabeth's reign, created a bolthole of weak crown government that had to be defended for reasons of honour, but which was universally acknowledged to have been a ludicrous idea, especially as it was an area of consistent unrest during the 1570s. The impatience of many elements of crown government in Ireland with colonising projects must be stressed. For instance, Lord Deputy Fitzwilliam's exasperation with the Chattertons' clumsy and indiscreet attempts to take O'Hanlon's country in Armagh 'as if [they] had been taking of a farm in Meath' led him to complain that 'there is no need for firebrands kindled in England to be thrown into Ireland', adding for good measure that such plans caused too much instability in Gaelic Ireland when military resources were scarce, for 'to have rumours spread [of colonisation] and beef salted to mad men ... and to have no men come to tame mad men with, I must think to be some practice to disturb quiet government'.[94] Later, Lord Deputy

---

[92] 'The offer of Walter, earl of Essex', *Cal Carew MSS 1515–74*, 439–440. See Sidney to Burghley, May 1573, SP63/40/60, for Henry Sidney's objection: 'I like not that any subject of his own choice should be able to make laws and less like that with consent of another twelve he might revoke the same'.

[93] See the first point of Sidney's 'Articles', 20 May 1565, SP63/13/46.

[94] Fitzwilliam to Burghley, 26 October 1572, SP63/38/24. See Sidney's subsequent exasperation with the waste of lives and resources over sustaining the Chattertons' claim, Sidney to the Privy Council, 14 November 1575, SP63/56/47. For the terms of the grant to Thomas Chatterton of

Sidney (also expressing abhorrence of the number of lives and the amount of resources that had been wasted in sustaining the Chattertons' claim) repined at the drain that the Laois/Offaly plantation had been to the crown's revenues: 'two hundred men at the least in the prince's pay lie there to defend [the plantation]', he explained, adding that 'the revenue of both the countries countervail not the twentieth part of the charge.' Sidney wearily noted that there was a moral to this story: 'this may be an example how the like hereafter is attempted considering the charge is so great and the honour and profit is small to win lands from the Irishry so dearly.' Of course, for Sidney, part of the joy of condemning the plantation may have stemmed from the fact that his rival the earl of Sussex had initiated it.[95] Seven years later, Edward Whyte, the disaffected secretary of the council of Connacht, would attempt to darken official attitudes towards Nicholas Malby's attempts to organise his estate at Roscommon Castle by claiming that he 'taketh any lands near Roscommon for his own without order or justice whereby he driveth the inhabitants adjoining in jealousy to be supplanted, where in Leix and Offaly may be an example for breeding her majesty's charge'.[96]

CUPIDITY AND VIOLENCE

It would be naive to think that the captains, so many of them second or third sons or fugitives from England, did not see in their service in Ireland an opportunity to gain landed wealth, even to acquire a sizeable estate, thereby transcending the limitations that social customs placed on their prospects in England. In both the Laois/Offaly plantation and the enterprise of Ulster, the role of English captains and soldiers was prioritised, and it was envisaged that soldiers would administer and maintain

---

O'Hanlon's country, 'Gallyglas country' and the Fews, dated 10 June 1573, see *CPR Eliz., 1572–5*, p. 48. For the commission granted to Bagenal and others in March 1571 to survey O'Hanlon's country see *Fiants*, Vol. II, 1736. See also Fitton's pessimism about the prospects for Essex's 'enterprise' which, from the very start, he thought unlikely to prosper, Fitton to Sir Thomas Smith, 19 July 1573, SP63/41/60. For a more optimistic view of the possible benefits of colonies in Ireland see Sir Thomas Smith to Fitzwilliam, 8 November 1572, SP63/38/30. See Fitzwilliam and the council's regrets about Smith Junior's arrival and anxieties about Essex's advent: 'the like bruits of Mr Smith's coming over last summer bred trouble not yet appeased. What this may do – the great difference of the person, credit, calling and ability considered – is to be thought of. If there is any such matter in determination, we wish the action should not be long behind the bruit', Fitzwilliam and council to Elizabeth, 12 June 1573, SP63/41/21. See also H. Morgan 'The colonial venture of Sir Thomas Smith in Ulster, 1571–75', *HJ*, xxviii (1985), p. 261–78.
[95] Sidney to the Privy Council, 15 December 1575, SP63/54/17.
[96] Whyte to the Privy Council, 12 April 1582, SP63/91/24.

these colonies; their potential usefulness in defending demarcated areas against attack was obvious. For instance, in the case of Laois/Offaly, the constables of Philipstown and Maryborough, Henry Colley and Francis Cosby, had each been granted profound control over the lives of the colonists, receiving a plough-day's labour for each plough owned by a tenant as their due. Each also had power to determine, with the consent of a majority of the free tenants, the number of Gaelic-Irish in the colony, both those under arms and those unarmed, and to enforce the ruling that no one married any Irish 'not amenable to the laws of the kingdom'.[97] But for all this, the captains' cupidity for land led them to lobby for the securing of offices, constableships or seneschalships that brought with them particular castles or fortifications that belonged to the crown. The use of violence, in and of itself, to secure lands was ineffective.

The question obviously arises as to whether the captains opted to harass magnates with the aim of forcing them into rebellion, thereby ensuring that they would be liable, if defeated, to lose their lands by act of attainder. To pursue such a strategy, the captains would have had to have been sustained by the hope that they would become recipients of sizeable tracts of land as a reward for bringing a traitor low.[98] The precedents for such a plan, however, were not promising. After the northern rebellion of 1569, the crown distributed the lands of the earls of Northumberland and Westmoreland in a way that was most useful to its own interest, bestowing them on prominent partisans of the regime, favourites of the queen, or local figures who had sided with the crown, not, as we have seen, on the captains of the 'army of the north'. In Ireland, Warham St Leger's sophisticated plans for the establishment of a plantation on the lands of the earl of Clancar, O'Sullivan, O'Driscoll and MacDonough, advanced in early 1569, were definitively short-circuited when those grandees were pardoned in 1571.[99] But, despite these unpromising

---

[97] *Fiants*, Vol. I, Eliz., 474.
[98] Ironically, given his later criticisms of Malby's manner of organising his lands around Roscommon Castle, Edward Whyte wrote to Malby in 1577 speculating about the opportunities for a possible attainder arising from the conflict between Ulick Burke and MacNamara: 'the taking of this prey containeth a great mystery and is like to yield such fruit to the advancement of her Majesty's service as no man without the secret providence of God could devise', Whyte to Malby, 1577, SP63/59/70.
[99] St Leger consolidated his hold on Kerrycurrihy as an undertaker in the Munster Plantation, see the proceedings of the undertakers of Munster, 29 October 1589, SP63/147/51i. Initially, Warham St Leger and Richard Greville having leased lands from the earl of Desmond in 1568 or early 1569, intended to establish a very minor colony between Cork and Kinsale, this was quickly inflated to a plan to plant all of Gaelic Munster which was ultimately rejected by the privy council. St Leger never managed to overcome severe indebtedness despite his attempts to appear useful to the

precedents, the opportunities to secure attainders in Ireland may occasionally have seemed widespread: the title that septs and even English-Irish lords had to their lands, officially ratified little more than two or three decades previously, were constantly imperilled by political infighting and succession disputes, not to mention the inadequacy and thinness of the legal infrastructure of the country. But, as already noted, the very distance of Ireland from the metropolis, while allowing the captains free rein to extort and seize, actually tended to undermine their capacity to provoke massive unrest in order to gain wealth officially. Elizabeth's anxiety about her capacity to hold Ireland, her desire to avoid expense as well as her abhorrence for the opening up of a political vacuum meant that serious unrest was tremendously unwelcome.[100] The captains' vaulting ambition also met with disapproval because of other destabilising tendencies it posed to social standards in general. One of Elizabeth's main 'dislikes' in late 1579 was the increased amount of knighting in the field which was taking place in Munster – one of those who was a beneficiary of this assertion of martial *esprit de corps* was William Stanley. However, Walsingham informed Edward Waterhouse in November that it would be difficult to express 'how offensively the making of knights is taken', adding that it was believed 'that it will [the draft originally said 'doth'] breed a boldness in the new knights to crave support to maintain this degree'.[101]

Of course, the earl of Desmond's erratic behaviour, his substantial indebtedness as well as his obvious status as 'the sick man of Munster' had led the captains to mentally rehearse his demise and the opportunities that might result from it. We have already noted Stanley's request in 1583 that his hold over Castlemaine might be consolidated, with the aim of making it 'a town of English'.[102] Even as early as October 1579, Stanley, flushed with glory after being dubbed a knight in the field, had intimated to Walsingham 'that the queen's majesty may rather gain by the wars of Munster than lose any part of her charges'.[103] Significantly, on the same

---

crown in Munster. For an excellent account of the fate of St Leger's colonising ambitions and his abortive attempts to secure the presidency of Munster during the second Desmond rebellion see David Edwards, 'St Leger, Sir Warham (1525? –1597)', *Oxford Dictionary of National Biography* (Oxford, 2004).

[100] Ciaran Brady has noted the effort that Sir Henry Sidney went to in both his dispatches from Ireland and his petitionary 'memoir of service' to present a country as populated with named potentates with whom the crown could do business with, Brady (2002), pp. 1–37.
[101] Walsingham to Waterhouse, 8 November 1579, SP63/70/10.
[102] Stanley to Walsingham, 2 March 1583, SP63/100/1; Stanley to Burghley, 25 December 1583, SP63/106/33.
[103] Stanley to Walsingham, 12 October 1579, SP63/69/53.

day, Malby wrote a letter remarking that the earl was so beyond remedy that 'there is no good part in him to make a good subject of. He is so far in as, if her majesty will take advantage of his doing, his forfeited living will countervail her highness's charges'. It is easy to imagine Stanley and Malby battle-sore and elated around a fire in Adare parcelling out the earldom between themselves and their cronies. Things did not work out that way, however. The idea that 'the lands of the traitors will be made bear [the queen's] charges wherein may be planted better subjects' was certainly pursued, but neither Malby, Pelham nor Stanley benefited.[104] The subsequent attainders by act of parliament in 1585–6 came to bear heaviest on the English-Irish community with only thirty-eight of the 136 attainted individuals being of Gaelic-Irish lineage.

EDUCATIVE VIOLENCE AND EXPEDIENCY

A further argument advanced for devastating violence throughout Elizabeth's reign was its utility as both an example and an aide-memoire, not for those suffering the punishment but for those who witnessed its execution. Gilbert's use of decapitated heads ostensibly had this aim, although it savoured more of violation and mockery of the defeated enemy. He himself cited Diogenes' refusal to be concerned about the fate of his own corpse as evidence that the dead would not care about his exemplary use of their heads. Montaigne, in his essay 'On cruelty' – and indeed 'cruelty' was the very word Malby used to describe his own severity – similarly argued for the public mutilation of corpses in the cause of exemplary justice as preferential to the practice of public torturing of offenders to death. Compassion demanded that death should be sudden, the demands of good government demanded that people should be cowed by the spectacle of mortified human carrion.[105] In any case,

---

[104] The sentence quotes from a letter from Sir Henry Wallop to Walsingham, January 1580, SP63/71/1. A petition by Jacques Wingfield and members of his family for lands in the plantation did not succeed see 'Petition of Jacques Wingfield', 24 May 1586, SP63/124/40. Some captains became minor undertakers like George Thornton, who received 1,500 acres. One captain that did particularly well was Sir George Bourchier, an old hand in the province who received 12,880 acres. Captain Francis Barkley came somewhere in between with 7,000 acres. See 'The proceedings of the undertakers in Munster' 29 October 1589, SP63/147/51i. See MacCarthy-Morrogh (1986), pp. 54–5.

[105] Gilbert's reference to Diogenes' lack of concern about the fate of his corpse is taken from *The apophthegmes of Erasmus, translated into English by Nicolas Udall* (London, 1542) sig. 154 r. Udall's translation was republished in 1564. See also Montaigne, *The complete essays*, ed. M. A. Screech (London, 1991), p. 472.

Gaelic Ireland had long employed mutilation of hostages as a means of gaining a political edge over opponents, hence Shane O'Neill's threat in 1564 to 'strike off Con O'Donnell's son's leg' unless a fortification held by O'Donnell confederates was ceded to him, Rory Óg O'More's severing of Henry Harrington's fingers when he kidnapped the captain in 1577 and the dismembering of John Grace and Redmond Dillon by malcontents in Connacht in 1589.[106] In 1581 Colonel Gilbert's half-brother Walter Ralegh wrote to Walsingham from Cork asking that Gilbert's return to Munster might be 'rightly looked into' because he had 'never heard nor read of any man more feared then he is among the Irish nation'.[107] Malby after harrying the *mac an iarlas* in 1586 was pleased to tell Walsingham that 'the earl's sons are brought to cry *peccavi*' and that 'how contrary it is to common opinion to rule this nation by courtesy'.[108] However, more often than not, the exemplary aspect of violence had a short-term aim based primarily on practical economic and strategic concerns. Just as Gilbert's brutality had guaranteed the speedy surrender of outstanding rebels, Malby's ruthlessness while besieging Shane MacHubert sparked a similar wave of capitulation among the MacWilliam Burkes. In this context, repudiation of discretionary mercy was justified by the savings made for the crown and the concomitant limitations the effect of the actions placed on insurgency and suffering in terms of both duration and area. The utility of killing surrendered defenders who often outnumbered the besieging force needs no explanation, but contemporaries recognised that Grey de Wilton's controversial actions at Dún an Óir had been carried out with a broader exemplary intent. Perhaps the most revealing reading of the rationale behind Grey's actions was enunciated by George Bohuy, an English agent in the Low Countries, to William Herle, Burghley's creature, in April 1581, when he lamented that 'Ireland still remaineth in her old state, the rebellions nothing diminished, nor the rebels terrified by the slaughter of the Spanish and Italians at the fort.' The futility of it all led Bohuy to continue: '[the rebellions in Ireland, in spite of Dún an Óir, had] increased so that some begin to be of opinion that a peace by pardoning them will be better than so unprofitable a war.'[109]

---

[106] For Shane's threat see Wrothe to Leicester, 23 July 1564, SP63/11/35. For the killing of Grace and Dillon and the subsequent discovery of their hands see Theobald Dillon to Bingham, 23 October 1589, SP63/147/23.
[107] See E. Edwards, *Life of Ralegh*, 2 vols. (London, 1868), Vol. II, p. 12.
[108] Malby to Walsingham, 7 and 17 March 1577, SP63/57/33, 40.
[109] Bohuy to Herle, 25 April 1581, BL MS Cotton Galba C VII fol. 127r–128v.

The limits of rhetoric 239

Throughout Europe, contemporary guidebooks to military strategy and policy increasingly set the parameters of conduct in the field in terms of securing military advantage rather than proper and honourable behaviour. The English translation of General de Bellay's *Instructions for the warres* published in 1589 set its third book over to show by 'what means a lieutenant general may bring his wars to an end in short time', where de Bellay dealt approvingly with the use of 'force mingled with fraud' to take a town under siege.[110] Similarly, Richard Robinson in 1576 cited Cyrus's military advice that 'he that would win & have the upper hand and victory, must entrap and take his enemies by all manner of policy whatsoever, either by secret ambushes, or deceit and fraud, yea by rapine, theft, and pilfery they must be spoiled, robbed & impoverished.'[111] Yet, in the context of military strategy in Ireland, 'force mingled with fraud' did not have to be employed solely with an eye to economy and short-term advantage. As was often the case on such occasions, the strands of chivalric and monarchical concerns as well of those of *raison d'état* were so tightly woven together that it was often difficult to tease out where one ended and the other began. Monarchical sanction could be solicited for breaches of promise. M. E. James has shown that the legitimation of the duke of Norfolk's breach of promise on the king's behalf during the Pilgrimage of Grace was a sign of how political demands underpinned by monarchical authority could transcend chivalric ethics.[112] Consequently, the idea was current that a 'dishonourable' settlement or agreement made by a monarch was not binding should more propitious circumstances afford themselves.

For example, Sir Warham St Leger counselled Elizabeth in 1583 that a tactical truce with the Munster rebels might prove useful by pointing to the example of Henry VIII and the Kildare rebellion of 1535. Henry VIII, St Leger stated, saw that the rebellion 'could not be suppressed without great effusion of blood and consummation of a marvellous mass of treasure [and so] concluded a peace, although somewhat dishonourable, whereby in time he paid them home for their undutiful behaviour and thereby quieted the English Pale for many years'.[113] These sentiments must have been common at the time because Sir Henry Wallop also remarked that 'if Elizabeth had thoroughly punished these traitors and conspiracies as her father did that of Thomas Fitzgarret, it would have

---

[110] De Bellay, W., *Instructions for the warres* trans. P. Ive (London, 1589), pp. 212, 223.
[111] Robinson, R., *A moral methode of civil Pollicie* (London, 1576), p. 79.
[112] James (1978), pp. 22–32.
[113] St Leger to Elizabeth, 8 May 1583, SP63/102/16.

kept them in fear to offend in many years after as that example hath done', adding that 'for from his attainder and his partners there was never rebellion nor conspiracy in the Pale until within this two or three years'.[114] Sir Thomas Fitzgerald had surrendered to Lord Deputy Leonard Grey on promise of a royal pardon but was subsequently executed at Tyburn along with his five uncles for high treason.[115]

It is important to stress that neither a vulgarly conceived 'Machiavellian moment' nor a crisis in humanism were required to facilitate morally ambiguous action in Ireland.

THE BUSINESS OF COMMISSIONS

The political calculation involved in proceeding with 'force mingled with fraud' as a discrete strategy can be presented as more sophisticated than that employed in the cases of actions done under the auspices of commissions of martial law, but the use of such powers often entailed a good deal of cunning. It would be inaccurate to associate the execution of martial law solely with indiscriminate violence at the hands of English military men aimed merely at killing and dividing the spoils. Perusal of the commissions of martial law issued throughout Elizabeth's reign in Ireland shows that a large proportion of them were granted to local English-Irish potentates such as the earl of Kildare and Roland Eustace, Viscount Baltinglass or to sheriffs who were natives of the Pale.[116] Occasionally, they were issued to Gaelic-Irish figures such as Barnaby Fitzpatrick, baron of Upper Ossory, Sir Dermot mac Teig, captain of Muskerry in Cork and Owen MacHugh O'Dempsey.[117] Of course, in an Ireland riddled with 'night stealths', cattle raids, murders and freelance distraint of goods intended to force arbitration, it is unsurprising that the terms under which the commissions were issued emphasised martial law as a means of social control. Gentlemen or freeholders who possessed 40s per annum's worth of land or £10 worth of goods acquired without fraud were generally exempted. In terms of procedure, theoretically a

---

[114] Wallop to Walsingham, 6 March 1583, SP63/100/5.
[115] McCorristine, L., *The Revolt of Silken Thomas* (Dublin, 1987), pp. 121–31.
[116] *Fiants*, Vol. II, 953, 1196.
[117] *Fiants*, Vol. II, commissions in 1567 were issued to Sir Donogh MacCarthy Reagh of Carbery (1010) and Sir Dermot MacTeig, captain of Muskerry (1019) 1196. In 1571 Owen Mac Hugh O'Dempsey (1782) Ross MacGoughegan, sheriff of Westmeath (1833) and Donell Omaghery O'Ferrall, sheriff of Longford were in receipt of commissions.

proclamation of martial law would be 'published' on a parish church stating that after a set number of days any idle person or 'vagabond' found in the area specified in the commission was to be imprisoned, unless he or she was accompanied by 'some honest man of English apparel'. If there were deemed to be a 'reasonable or just cause' why those apprehended should be put to death, the commissioner had the power to carry out the execution after examining the suspect before the 'next gentleman of worship' or the head officer of the next town. Once 'sufficient matter of death' was found, it was up to the commissioner whether to carry out the execution. Any person caught aiding or abetting an 'outlaw', 'open thief', 'murderer' or 'rebel' could have his or her goods seized, and once the charge were proved, those goods would be divided up, with two-thirds going to the crown and one-third going to the commissioner. Any suspect found at night without 'an honest man' in tow might be 'used at the discretion of the commissioner' and, if they were caught in the act of any 'stealth, robbery or murder', could lawfully be hanged.

A potentially remunerative aspect of the commission was the allowance it made for the commissioner, when about the business of punishing malefactors, to take meat or drink for his horses and men. However, the terms of the commission usually placed a limit on this licence specifying that the commissioner could use the allowance for the space of only one or two nights in each barony or place 'so as not to be oppressive'.[118] Typically, however, the commissioners were also given power to treat with rebels and enemies, to grant safe conducts to facilitate those negotiations and 'to conclude good orders with them under the instructions of the Lord Deputy'. On occasions, the usual limitations on the commissioners' actions were waived: Captain William Collier, for instance, at the end of November 1574, received such a commission to use within the Pale over the following two months, presumably to deal with Gaelic-Irish incursions emanating from the revolt of Rory Óg O'More in Laois. Each executor of martial law, given the discretionary nature of the powers that went with the commission and the high level of emphasis that the commission placed on his discernment, was bound to bring his personal beliefs on law, order and authority, his familiarity with and agenda for local politics, his partiality for certain people and his dislike of others as well as his own psychological inclinations to bear on his use of the powers.

[118] *Fiants*, Vol. II, 1196.

And, of course, the emphasis placed on the commissioners' discretion became the most lucrative aspects of these commissions, whether they permitted the execution of martial law, assizes according to oyer and terminer and gaol delivery, the enforcement of purveyance (cess) or the commutation of Gaelic-Irish exactions into cash or payments in kind. Most commissioners' indecisiveness could probably be allayed by bribery and tractability. Consequently, it was bad business practice to devastate the country, because causing undue havoc and annoyance was tantamount to killing the goose that lays the golden egg. For instance, the vignette we have of the conduct of Harpoole and his confederates around Forth O'Nolan, Rathvilly and the manor of Clonmore in 1570 is instructive. Many of those who lived there, mostly Gaelic-Irish freeholders, husband-men and kern, were particularly annoyed because, even though they had paid extortionate fines in cash and kind to receive pardons, they had never received them. The procedural ambiguity that resulted enabled Harpoole and his lackeys to come around repeatedly, 'with great force' demanding more fines because, in the absence of the promised pardons, the insecurity of the inhabitants was at a premium. Some, such as Joan Mac Murrough, a widow of Killenbride, were forced to pay fines (in her case of 13s 4d) for pardons, 'which [they] never sought'. Others were indicted spuriously for felonies, convicted by packed juries under the Harpoole cosh and forced to pay fines for further pardons. The process thereby was kept in permanent momentum. Forth O'Nolan was subjected to the distraint of thirty kine and sixty sheep for Harpoole and thirty-nine kine and forty-eight sheep for the lord deputy (out of which he allegedly took nine kine and nine sheep for himself), and the area was infested by 'strange kern' for whom he levied a cess so severe that many inhabitants could no longer afford to pay their rent. Even the poorest of cottiers had to hand over a hen each.[119] Whatever about the rapacity of Harpoole's operation, the fact that complaints about it managed to make their way into state papers is significant. If informal exactions interfered with subjects' capacity to pay rent, they certainly did not serve the highest good.

And, indeed, when the winding down of the seneschal system was mooted in Fitzwilliam's instructions of October 1592, the abuse of commissions of martial law came in for particular official censure. Although complaints against the extortions of seneschals, constables and captains had been lodged and officially investigated, as was the case with Harpoole,

---

[119] 'The book against Robert Harpoole' SP63/33/39.

English perpetrators of martial-law abuses were as least as likely as the most well-connected Irishman to receive an official pardon wiping away their indiscretions. The hardening of metropolitan attitudes towards the seneschals and similar officers stemmed less from the stated desire to normalise the shiring process in Ireland (where that sort of normalisation often amounted to an abstraction) than the crown's growing desire to secure forfeited lands, goods and chattels, which, it feared, had been squirreled away by opportunistic captains. In 1592, the use of martial law by officers where common law might do the trick was officially deemed 'dishonourable' to the crown. Even the captains' commissions of oyer and terminer were deemed to pose an occasion for scandal; only arbitration by mutual consent of two parties would be permitted. Letters were to be sent to the seneschals revoking their commissions. It was envisaged that the lord deputy and council should thereafter determine whether the authority to execute martial law should be ceded to one officer or another. But for all this, Whitehall's concern about the 'oppression of the people' centred on the 'discharge of prisoners under arrest' not their massacre, as well as the implications of the general pardons that sheriffs were wont to give out to their idle henchmen following their term of office. Scrutiny centred on clemency secured through bribery and the collusive brigandage that resulted, rather than violent brutality – the business of manufacturing both the threat and the protection from it. The financial tyranny and misappropriation that resulted from these commissions was the problem, not any unyielding severity against those who could be 'proven' to be rebels. The old loopholes remained. It was reaffirmed as a matter of course that the suppression of rebellion, the retention of any of her majesty's castles or the 'forcible withstanding of the queen's majesty's authority' occasioned the use of martial law. *Plus ça change.*[120] Whatever about the sincerity of these instructions, their impact (especially in the recently shired counties of Connacht) was minimal.

---

[120] Cambridge University Library (ULC), MSS Kk, fols. 44v–45r. 'Elizabeth R, articles containing sundry things to be considered of by the LD and council in Ireland to be answered to her majesty. Anno 1592 (October)'. On the problem of the sheriff's idle henchmen see article 6: 'no pardons hereafter [should] be granted as hath been in former times to any without respect to the quality of their persons and crimes, which liberty to the contrary hath been a direct cause of increase of offenders, and hath boldened the sheriffs and others to commit great disorders and injuries in the time of their offices. And therefore no pardons to be granted but in open council, with subscription of the councillors names according to former custom. And it would be also be provided that the sheriffs do not ride with great numbers of idlemen under colour of exhibiting their offices, oppressing thereby the people not only by eating upon them (in taking horse meat and man meat) but also by taking bribes and fines for composition with the offenders'.

PERSONAL GRUDGES AND VENGEANCE

Naturally, martial law and the judicial system had both been used to lethal effect when political structures had broken down, most notably during the second Desmond rebellion, a time of total war. After his revocation in 1583, Grey de Wilton sent an *apologia* for his viceroyalty to Elizabeth. He was particularly resentful that the 'plumes' he earned in prosecuting the rebels now 'garnish[ed]' the earl of Ormond. As had been the case in the northern rebellion of 1569, diligence in her majesty's service was being measured by a headcount. It was this context that led him to make his infamous statement: 'the number of slain in this service of note comes to 1485 not accounting those of meaner sort, neither executions by law, nor killing of churls, the account of which is besides number.' In totting up the numbers, he produced a list of actions by the captains of Ireland not as passive governors but as fully mobilised and ruthless soldiers. This included Captain Humphrey Mackworth's despatching of forty-four of the O'Mores; William Russell's and Thomas Masterson's slaughter of eighty of the Kavanaghs; and his own pursuit of David Barry, which resulted in the death of 120 rebels.[121] But yet, despite that sterling service, Elizabeth preferred to proceed more cautiously by promulgating a general pardon and appointing the earl of Ormond as lord general of Munster, who, in turn, offered lavish protections to the earl of Desmond's desperate followers. This proved a remarkably successful policy that ended the war but disgusted Lord Grey.[122] Munster suffered dreadful privation and famine because of the conflict over those years. Captain Edward Stanley reported to Ormond in April 1583 that in

---

[121] Grey to Elizabeth, 1583, SP63/102/62. However, in May 1582, Grey had had to defend Captains Cosby (Francis's son) and Humphrey Mackworth from 'some dislike' that Elizabeth held against them for 'treasonable parts . . . against the Irish in entrapping and betraying them', Grey de Wilton to Walsingham, 7 May 1582, SP63/92/10. Grey's defence of young Cosby against charges of using entrapment stressed the captain's poverty: 'As for the other, Cosby, I mean of my credit Sir, since my coming neither directly nor otherwise hath he ever hurt man, and besides so poor, as hardly bread he is able to put into his own mouth and families so far from ableness to entrap any other by banqueting'. Mackworth defended his killing of the O'Mores at a parley by alleging that one of them ran at him with a knife, Mackworth to Walsingham, 7 May 1583, SP63/92/14.

[122] See Grey de Wilton to Elizabeth, 1583, SP63/106/62 where he points out that Ormond's policy was effective merely because Grey's severity in killing the tillers of the soil and scorching the earth had so reduced the rebels that the reasons why they were flocking to take up the lord general's protections was no 'Sphinx's riddle'. See Edwards (2003), p. 233 for reference to Ormond's rival estimate that far from being lenient he had killed 5,650 rebels. For the text of the general pardon (excluding the earl of Desmond) issued on 19 April 1581, see SP63/82/42.

Dingle 'the poorest sort hath been driven to eat the dead men's bodies which were cast away in the shipwreck'.[123]

Accounts of the actions at Smerwick, Rathlin Island and elsewhere have already shown us that the desire to wreak revenge for fatalities inflicted on crown forces could be invoked as just cause for reprisals. Such hunger for vengeance could obliterate whatever inclination towards clemency might have been found among the captains, and focused retributive actions carried out using martial law often had as much to do with a desire for personal satisfaction along the lines of the *lex talionis* as concern for good government. For example, Churchyard tells us that following the killing of Thomas Smith Jr 'by the revolting of certain Irishmen of his own household, to whom he overmuch trusted' both Nicholas and John Malby were intent on exacting revenge on his assassin Neil Mac Brien Artho (Mac Brian Fertagh).[124] The brothers asked the earl of Essex for leave to enter Lecale. Essex, 'not knowing their minds' (an indication of official disapproval for personal vendetta), allowed John to go there with sixty-four horsemen. Consequently, John killed thirty-five of Neil's 'best men'. This retribution, Churchyard indicated, was given divine approval when one of the casualties Con MacMaloeg (perhaps Con MacNeill Óg) 'who before caused master Smith to be eaten up with dogs after he had been boiled' was himself left as carrion among wolves for a week and subsequently while, being keened by friends, 'by mischance' caught fire

[and] the dogs in the town, smelling this dead body ran in and took it out of the house, and so tore it to pieces ... which [we are assured] was a thing to be much marvelled at, and thought to be sent from God as a terror to all tyrants.[125]

In essence, the vengeance of the captains was more likely to be personal rather than general, its concern being less the preservation of law and order in the polity and more the infliction of visible pain and suffering on particular individuals. In 1578, for example, Sir William Drury as lord president of Munster cursorily related that he had executed approximately eighty people by both 'justice and martial law' but was particularly proud of killing 'one so dear to James Fitzmaurice, as when he heard of his death he wept'. Similarly, the earl of Essex, in a letter to Walsingham, took

---

[123] Captain Edward Stanley to Ormond, 28 April 1583, SP63/102/49i.
[124] Essex to the privy council, 20 October 1574, SP63/42/55, where Essex notes that Thomas Smith's death gave the Irish great cause to rejoice.
[125] Churchyard [1579] sigs. Fiii, r.–Fiii, v.

explicit pleasure in having inflicted grief on Sorley Boy MacDonnell through Norris's and Drake's foray onto Rathlin Island, noting with glee that the distressed chieftain had impotently witnessed the slaying of his clan's women and children from the mainland.[126] Malby's unrestrained satisfaction at the killing off of Shane Reagh Burke's sons in 1581 ('that lineage is clean extinct, which were as evil disposed persons as ever lived') speaks for itself.[127] The intimate nature of politics and violence in Ireland meant that personal vendetta, and the language that went with it, could easily result. Sir Edmund Butler, when out in rebellion in August 1569, wrote to the earl of Ormond about a pyrrhic assault by his gallowglasses on Sir Peter Carew, remarking that if he, himself, had been at their head 'I doubt not, but Peter might have lost his better eye'.[128] A certain amount of this vengefulness on the part of English soldiers can probably be put down to fear among the rank and file of the dangers that Irish service posed to those who felt exposed both on the field and in the garrison. As we have seen, following the massacres at Rathlin and Smerwick, both Essex and Grey alleged that pressure for severity came from the troops themselves, incensed because they had sustained casualties. Death from natural plagues, like the flux, was endemic, but death in action was far from unknown. For instance, twenty English soldiers were killed by Leinster insurgents in 1581 after they had ('by their own folly', according to Wallop) left the castle of Clohamon to take a prey. Nicholas Malby's soldiers, as we have seen, were killed in time of truce in March 1577 by John Burke, and, similarly, four years beforehand, Captain William Collier's band wandering without food in Thomond suffered fatalities when they were ambushed.[129]

---

[126] Drury to the privy council, 24 March 1578, SP63/60/25; Essex to Walsingham, July 1575, SP63/52/79, Essex noted that a spy told him that 'Sorley put most of his plate, most of his children, and the children of the most part of his gentlemen, with their wives, into the Rathlin with all his pledges, which be all taken and executed . . . to the number of 600'. Significantly, Essex, in his letter to Elizabeth, written on the same day, omitted all reference to Sorley's grief and stressed the enterprise's accordance with the law of war.
[127] Malby to Walsingham, 11 April 1581, SP63/82/24.
[128] Sir Edmund Butler to Ormond, 24 August 1569, SP63/29/47i.
[129] See Wallop to Walsingham, 13 May 1581, SP63/83/13 on the ambush at Clohamon; Fitton's articles against the earl of Clanricard, 8 May 1573, SP63/40/37i; see also Malby to Walsingham, 10 September 1579 SP63/69/17 on the killing of Captain Richard Price by the troop of kern he was leading into battle. See also the letter from Recorder Thomas Arthur and Alderman Stephen Whit of Youghal to Malby in late 1579, SP63/70/32ii for reference to the killing of twelve of Captain Apsley's men in Limerick. Of course, crown casualties were merely a fraction of deaths in Elizabethan Ireland.

Yet, the distinction between primal vengeance and justice was well known even if the actual actions undertaken in the name of each, and their result, could be the same, i.e. the extra-judicial killing of her majesty's subjects, hence the restraint that can be found in many soldiers' accounts of their actions. The contemporary account of the virtues commonly held vengeance to be an irreducibly bad thing. This was especially the case in a more civil society. In Wales, for instance, the earl of Pembroke deemed his own forbearance in refusing to intrigue against his social inferior Sir John Perrot as a particularly virtuous achievement, remarking that 'desire of revenge is a sign of a mean, weak and an abject mind; for that none do rejoice in revenge more than women.' He added further that 'we see many times that forgetting and forgiving of injuries *especially when there is power to revenge* doth gain more good will, than the giving of great rewards' (my italics).[130] Whereas vengeance demanded crude obliteration of the offender merely as a blood price, violent actions in the name of justice contained an inherent statement of faith in the polity. Bradshaw's acute scrutiny of the idea of justice in Edmund Spenser's *Faerie queene* underlines this. In Book V, Canto 9, when Duessa, who represents Licence, is put on trial by Mercilla, the goddess of Mercy, the counsels of the allegorical attorneys Pity, Regard for Duessa's womanhood and Nobility of birth, as well as Grief are dismissed, but the vengeful prosecution of Zeal for the full retributive exaction of justice against the defendant is also discounted. Mercilla disregards any acknowledgement of Duessa's status as an individual and condemns her to death, not with rancorous intent but in accordance with the dispassionate demands of justice and mercy. The Aristotelian mean between vengeful justice and pity is thus conceived of as a mercy that prioritises the claims of right order and reformation of the polity.[131] But, whereas some cast this type of reasoning as the result of 'rhetorical ploys' and 'fine distinctions' used by an almost 'scholastic' Spenser to pervert the idea of mercy in defiance of humanistic norms, it appears that, prior to the 'gentle poet's' flourishing, such ideas about the clinical claims of severe justice were common in the writings of military captains. Offenders against the state's (and crown's) honour and security, as we have seen,

---

[130] Rawlinson (1728), p. 43. Perrot showed no such aristocratic restraint, not even in his dealings with crown officers. See Alban Stepneth's disapproving account of Perrot threatening the constables of Haskard in Wales with martial law in 'Alban Stepneth's allegations' SP63/42/41.

[131] See Bradshaw (1987), pp. 80–3. Also see Pelham and the Irish council to the privy council, 26 November and 13 December, 1579 *Walsingham letter book*, pp. 243 and 248, for the case of Captain Hollingworth, accused of seeking revenge without commission.

were deemed to be beyond the claims of pity, a conclusion that could be garnered from a myriad of sources such as the laws of war, political thinking in relation to the privileges of monarchy within the polity or constitution and republican views on the correct relationship between the individual and the *res publica*.

Yet, even when detailing those abstractions that justified violent action, we should not discount the capacity for violence to be motivated by an unalloyed appetite for destruction.[132] Montaigne must have been thinking of soldiers he himself commanded when he wrote of his horror at those 'who would commit murder for the sheer fun of it . . . for the one sole purpose of enjoying the pleasant spectacle of the pitiful gestures and twitchings of a man dying in agony'.[133] The besetting vice of mankind has always been less the urge to kill than the desire to have another's life in its hands. Yet, among the state papers for 1572 (although assigned by their recent editor to a date in the 1580s), a letter exists that describes martial law used casually as a means of entertainment. It details forays punctuated by arson and looting of livestock in south Wicklow and north Wexford by Leinster garrisons whose penetration into the mountainous fastnesses was facilitated by the help of Irish guides. In this case, a guide offers the company of soldiers 500 head of cattle, or entry into a glen 'to have some killing', which, we are told, 'Captain Hungerford and Lieutenant Parker rather chose'. The narrator relates that 'at the break of the day they entered in and had the killing of divers, what they were I know not . . . they slew many churls, women and children.'[134] Despite the recent dating of this letter to the 1580s, similar occurrences, as we have seen, were current in 1572. In that year, a distressed Lord Deputy Fitzwilliam wrote to Burghley indicating that the garrison had got out of his control. Significantly, the viceroy, eschewing praise for severe practice, was more concerned about the fate of his immortal soul before God than for those subjects slain during his viceroyalty:

I will pass over usual matters as burning, killing and spoiling wherewith I am troubled and even in conscience pinched almost every hour of the day for God I fear me will demand at my hands the shameful effusion of innocent blood

---

[132] Humphrey Gilbert, for instance, was undoubtedly a dangerous and sociopathic character, who encouraged the same qualities in his soldiers. See the letter of Sir Owen O'Sullivan to Leicester, 25 October 1579, SP63/69/72 where O'Sullivan complains of Gilbert's conduct at his house on his brief return to Munster in 1579. 'After his going away', O'Sullivan noted 'some of his men did kill a proper merchant man out of Cork who was fishing in this harbour (Bearhaven)'. See also Rory Rapple, 'Gilbert, Sir Humphrey (1537–1583)', *Oxford Dictionary of National Biography* (Oxford, 2004).
[133] Montaigne (1991), p. 484. [134] Account of foray in Leinster, SP63/36/31.

whereat I may shake the scabbard with the sign of a sword but have not the sword to draw indeed and whereon when I look beside or wink and with a wounded soul pass over horrible injuries or give such remedies that as good never a whit as never the better.[135]

It is in considering the conscience of a lord deputy that the necessity for strategies of justification becomes personally understandable.

---

[135] Fitzwilliam to Burghley, 21 October 1572, SP63/38/20.

CHAPTER 7

Unlimited indemnity: delegates versus viceroys

> As your honour knoweth: where a practice is joined with an authority how available the same may be to compass what is expected.
> Sir Richard Bingham to Walsingham, 4 September 1589

In 1594, Oxford's university press produced Richard Beacon's *Solon his Follie*. Beacon's work, a dialogue between Pisistratus and Epimenides on the topic of reforming corrupt commonwealths, was a thinly disguised treatment of the problems of Elizabethan Ireland. With its university imprint, *Solon* stands as the academic high water mark of Irish studies in the late sixteenth century. The polemic has recently attracted the interest of intellectual historians because Beacon, an English planter in Munster, stands as the clearest example we have of a full reception of Machiavelli in Elizabethan England. Markku Peltonen, in particular, has outlined the extent of Machiavelli's influence on Beacon. Not only were many of the examples Beacon employed to illustrate his arguments culled wholesale from the *Discorsi*, much of his analysis of the political problem that Ireland posed for the crown followed exactly the same internal logic as Machiavelli's meditations on Livy.[1] In terms of the developing situation in Ireland, the year of publication is particularly suggestive: in 1594, Ireland was already on the verge of tumbling into that stop-start conflict, later called the Nine Year's War. Of course, Beacon could not predict the enfolding events that triggered this cataclysm nor its main result, the

---

[1] Peltonen (1995), pp. 75–102. The pioneering reassessment of Beacon was Brendan Bradshaw's 'Robe and sword in the conquest of Ireland' in Cross et al. (1988), pp. 139–68; see also Vincent Carey, 'The Irish face of Machiavelli: Richard Beacon's *Solon his Follie* and republican ideology in the conquest of Ireland' in Morgan (ed.) (1999) and Clare Carroll's analysis of Beacon's text, sources and the traditions he drew on in the introduction to Carroll's and Carey's edition of *Solon* (Binghamton, NY, 1996). For the importance of Beacon's work in the development of reason of state theory in England and the influence Machiavelli exerted over him see G. Baldwin, 'The self and the state, 1580–1651', unpublished Ph.D. thesis (Cambridge University, 1998), pp. 40–4.

breaking of the native veto over crown policy, but he was nonetheless sure that Ireland was an entirely corrupt commonwealth; the institution of new laws alone would not suffice to reform it; indeed, if any good were to come out of the country it would have to stem from root and branch re-formation of the kingdom as a mixed polity. Once the kingdom emerged pristine, conditioned by a new constitution, he suggested, the defeated population would ever after seek peace. Yet, it would not be a cakewalk. Beacon conceded that devastating extra-legal action by crown officers would be needed along the way to sustain the process; reason of state demanded this. When Beacon argued for this contingency, he summoned up the actions of a particular officer as exemplary: those of Sir Richard Bingham.[2]

Among all the Elizabethan captains, Richard Bingham, president of Connacht from 1584 to 1596, has had a particularly black reputation in Irish nationalist historiography, serving almost as an identikit for the 'typical' rapacious, bloodthirsty dog of war. During the nineteenth century, the dim view taken by Irish nationalists and English liberals of Sir Richard's descendants, most notably Field Marshal George Charles Bingham, the third earl of Lucan, coloured historiographical views. George Charles was an extreme instance of the abuses associated with late-ascendancy landlordism in Ireland. Like his predecessor, he had courted controversy. He was notorious throughout the world at large for ordering the charge of the Light Brigade, while in Ireland his attempt to preserve his own livelihood in Mayo during the Famine by forcing the clearance of tenants, irrespective of their age or health, stuck in the public mind.[3] Broad public acquaintance with the name of Richard Bingham had also arisen because of the rather unearned prominence in nationalist historiography of the 'pirate queen' Gráinne O'Malley. The story of O'Malley's famed personal submission and petitioning of Elizabeth I during June 1593 in defiance of Sir Richard's harassment, proved a useful parable for non-separatist Irish nationalism as it seemed to endorse the virtues of loyalty to the monarch and faith in the will of the metropolis to see fair play done to Ireland despite the slanders of servitors on the ground. The imaginative possibilities posed by the spectacle of an Irish 'queen', a personification of the nation, coming face to face

---

[2] Beacon, R., *Solon his follie* (Oxford, 1594), p. 8, 17, 91. Beacon depicts Bingham as a figure shrewdly willing to 'put [traitors and rebels] to death without lawful indictment' rather than 'damage the commonweal', concluding that 'so as in this action and in all other parts of his government, he hath showed himself to be the person, which Archilocus describeth in these his verses: *He is both champion stout of Mars his warlike band / And of the Muses eke, the arts doth understand.*'
[3] Woodham Smith, C., *The reason why* (New York, 1953), pp. 114–29 and I. Hamrock's *The famine in Mayo: a portrait from contemporary sources 1845–50* (Castlebar, 2004), pp. 35, 132–5.

with an English queen – Elizabeth's clemency being a gesture of sisterly solidarity – seemed particularly suggestive. Separatists such as Patrick Pearse, while discarding the Elizabethan context, retained the emblematic 'Gráinne', and along with her they implicitly retained the emblematic English brute: Bingham. The fascination with the 'pirate queen' has not abated; continued interest arises from her anomalous position as a female leader in a man's world.[4]

Wonted historiographical and political polarities, of course, resulted in a markedly different view of Bingham by historians of a more Unionist bent. For instance, Hubert Thomas Knox ('formerly of the Madras Civil Service') produced the two most exhaustive treatments of Bingham's career: 'Sir Richard Bingham's Government of Connaught' in the *Journal of the Galway archaeological and historical society* and his *The history of the County of Mayo to the close of the sixteenth century* (1908). Knox was the first historian to address in such detail the, often bewildering, sequence of events that made up Bingham's career; his chronological rigour was matched only by his unshakeable conviction that Sir Richard was fundamentally humane and just: 'not only was he upright in his own dealings, but he kept his subordinates strictly within their duties.' In this assessment, Knox was following Richard Bagwell's tendency in *Ireland under the Tudors* to take the president's accounts of his own actions at face value, expressing consistent sympathy for his beleaguered status. The stance is plausible. Even Hiram Morgan, certainly no Unionist, has recently characterised Bingham's career as 'firm but fair'.[5]

However, despite this, Bingham has retained his emblematic status. For example, Brendan Bradshaw asserted en passant in his article 'Sword, word and strategy in the reformation of Ireland' that Bingham stood as a 'representative' garrison hardliner, and this assertion has been taken as read by other historians, notably Mitchell Leimon and Bernadette Cunningham.[6]

---

[4] Patrick Pearse famously referred to O'Malley in his poem 'Óró sé do bheatha 'bhaile' where he imagined the mythical Gráinne routing the foreigners. See more recently Anne Chambers's biography *Granuaile: the life of times of Grace O'Malley, c. 1530–1603* (Dublin, 1981) which has been in print continuously since 1981. Strangely enough Bingham has featured in two musical by-products of public interest in O'Malley, first the composer Shaun Davey's 'Granuaile' suite, and second *The Pirate Queen* composed by Alain Boublil and Claude-Michel Schönberg, the creators of *Les Misérables*, which ran for just over two months on Broadway. As a result, Sir Richard Bingham must be the only Elizabethan captain in Ireland with two show tunes devoted to him.

[5] Knox, H. T. *The history of the county of Mayo to the close of the sixteenth century* (Dublin, 1908), p. 262; Morgan, H., *Tyrone's rebellion* (London, 1993), p. 189.

[6] Bradshaw, B., 'Sword, word and strategy in the reformation of Ireland', *HJ* 21 (1978), p. 480. Both Mitchell Leimon and Bernadette Cunningham treat Bradshaw's categorisation of Bingham and other soldiers as 'garrison hardliners' as sufficient explanation for their actions and views.

But can Bingham's opinions and modus operandi really stand metonymically for the opinions and modus operandi of the 'garrison milieu' in Elizabethan Ireland as a whole? Certainly, his career and his correspondence contained patterns of thought that chime with the experiences and methods of other captains; however, the tone of Bingham's letters, and, ultimately, his attitude to his own actions were distinct. Even his contemporaries regarded him as something quite exceptional. No amount of categorisation can avoid the fact that throughout his career as governor of Connacht, Bingham attracted an unprecedented amount of controversy, exciting both passionate loyalty and intense hatred as well as provoking tremendous fear. Longevity ensured that Bingham's career in the late 1580s and early 1590s survived both the scrapping of much of Sir Henry Sidney's vision and the passing of Walsingham's pre-eminence over Irish patronage.

Considering the energy with which Bingham served as president in Connacht, it is surprising to note that he was fifty-seven when he took it up, older indeed than his predecessor Sir Nicholas Malby who had died in office at the relatively youthful age of fifty-five.[7] Bingham and Malby shared some other similarities. Malby, as we have seen, could point to an impressive military career on the Continent, which took in fighting at St Quentin, Newhaven and the siege of Malta. Bingham began to follow a martial career around the age of twenty in the duke of Somerset's campaigns in Scotland; subsequently, according to Thomas Churchyard, he also fought at the battle of St Quentin against the French in 1557 in a band led by the notorious Thomas Stukeley, and, thereafter, like many English captains (Malby included), he continued to fight on the Continent, serving with the Venetians at Lepanto and then in Hungary in the early 1570s.[8] By the late 1570s, again according to Churchyard, he was lieutenant under Colonel Candish of a regiment of 1,200 Englishmen fighting in the employ of the states general, and had a fearsome reputation as a harsh disciplinarian.[9]

See M. M. Leimon, 'Sir Francis Walsingham and the Anjou marriage plan, 1574–1581', unpublished Ph.D. thesis (Cambridge University, 1989), p. 93; Bernadette Cunningham, 'The composition of Connacht' in *IHS* (1984) Vol. 24, p. 8. My criticism of Bradshaw's statement about Bingham, which is an aside, in no way affects my regard for his argument as a whole.

[7] Bingham was seven years younger than Burghley, four years older than Walsingham, five years older than his queen; many of the most influential figures in Irish government were also approximately the same age, for example Sir Henry Sidney, Sir John Perrot, and Sir William Fitzwilliam.

[8] According to his epitaph in Westminster Abbey Bingham fought at Lepanto with the Venetians. See Knox, *JGAS* Vol. V, I, (1907–8), p. 27.

[9] See Thomas Churchyard's *Churchyard's Choise* (1579), sig. Hi, r, for reference to Bingham's service at Newhaven in 1563; see Ai, v for reference to Bingham's part with the Imperial army in the Siege of Heading, and Civ, r for his service at St Quentin in Sir Thomas Stukeley's troop. See sigs. Si,

The similarities continue. Both Malby and Bingham had been judicially condemned to death: Malby for coining in 1562, while Bingham had been condemned for treason by a jury in Surrey in February 1563 for his part in the conspiracy centred around Arthur Pole, the Cardinal's nephew which had aimed at smuggling Pole into Flanders in order to proclaim him duke of Clarence; the plot had also sought to depose Elizabeth and raise up Mary Stuart with the collusion of the duke of Guise and the papacy. Bingham was arrested with his accomplices in a tavern beside St Olaf's in Southwark close to London Bridge in October 1562. Whereas Pole perished in the Tower in 1570, Bingham received a pardon, perhaps the fruit of willingness to inform on his colleagues or an indication of a Janus-like role in the conspiracy from the start. Commanded to appear before Sir Nicholas Bacon, keeper of the great seal every Michaelmas until 1571, Bingham was under some pressure to keep his promise to 'behave faithfully towards the crown'.[10]

Significantly, both Malby and Bingham had a devoted patron in Sir Francis Walsingham. As Mitchell Leimon has shown, Walsingham's initial contacts with Malby had been through Edward Waterhouse, the long-serving Irish administrator, in 1574, when both Waterhouse and Malby were associated with the first earl of Essex's 'Enterprise of Ulster'. Later in the 1570s, Walsingham entrusted Malby with the administration of his ever-widening clientele in Ireland.[11] It is more difficult to determine when Walsingham came into contact with Bingham. Richard's return to England in 1573 after campaigning abroad was heralded by Ralph Lane, who wrote the covering note to a letter that Bingham had written to Burghley (which is now missing) demanding a crown pension. Lane, who had been instructed to forward the letter to both the earls of Warwick and Leicester, apologised to the lord treasurer that 'the poor man was iron-bellied at the writing of it' and asked him to 'bear with his errors and accept his dutiful meaning'. Lane suggested that 'some £30 a year pension out of her majesty's coffers' would see the returning warrior 'preserved for the service of her majesty'.[12] As we have seen, by the following year, Bingham was tantalising Guerau de Spes, the Spanish ambassador, with an offer to seize Rotterdam (William of Orange's headquarters at the

---

r–Ti, r for an account of Bingham's service as lieutenant general of Candish's regiment, especially his lack of trust in the abilities of his soldiers and his problems enforcing his authority on the troops.
[10] For the details of Bingham's condemnation see his pardon in *CPR Eliz.*, 1566–7, pp. 63–4. Malby's condemnation on 6 August 1562 is referred to in Henry Machyn's diary, see *The diary of Henry Machyn, citizen and merchant-taylor of London*, ed. J. G. Nichols, (London, 1848), p. 290.
[11] Leimon (1989), pp. 83–5. [12] Lane to Burghley, 27 October 1573, SP12/92/42.

time) for Philip II. Spes suitably charmed, told Philip that Bingham, disaffected with the Dutch, was a Catholic surrounded by Catholic officers. It is most probable that it was around this time that Bingham came to know Walsingham, who had recently been appointed principal secretary alongside Sir Thomas Smith.[13] Whatever about their first contact, Walsingham was loyal to the 'iron-bellied' man of Dorset ever after, and it was their relationship, more than anything else, that enabled Bingham to assert himself so stridently: Walsingham's devotion to him proved exceptional. In the first instance, it was Walsingham who ensured that Bingham, then 'a miserable suitor' in England, was appointed governor of Connacht after Sir Nicholas Malby's demise.[14]

But there were also marked differences between Malby and Bingham. Malby, as we have established, was an old hand in Ireland, having served in and around Kilkenny during Mary's reign and subsequently in Carrickfergus, a posting that required constant contact with neighbouring Gaelic-Irish clans, notably the O'Neills of Clandeboy.[15] Bingham had never served in the sister kingdom before, apart from a short period as a naval officer off the coast of Kerry during the second Desmond rebellion. This lack of Irish experience prior to 1580 marked Bingham off from the Irish military establishment dominated by men of approximately the same generation cohort: Nicholas Bagenal, Thomas Masterson, Robert Harpoole and Warham St Leger, each of whom had secured a post in Ireland as viceregal clients or had secured promotion within the Irish garrison.[16] Previously, some newcomers had met with a welcoming reception, for example Sir William Drury, the renowned governor of Berwick, who on his arrival as president of Munster in the mid-1570s had already been assured of fellowship because Sir Francis Walsingham had enjoined his clientele in Ireland (at that period very neatly organised) to cooperate with him; on the other hand, figures such as Sir Edward Fitton and, to some extent, Sir William Pelham had not been so fortunate and had

---

[13] Lane to Burghley, 27 October 1573, SP12/92/42.
[14] Bingham to Lady Walsingham, 14 June 1585, SP63/114/27, where he describes his life in England prior to appointment as governor of Connacht in those terms.
[15] *Churchyard's Choise*, sig. Dii, v, for Malby's service in Kilkenny, and sigs. Eii, r–Eiv, r for some details of his service in east Ulster in the 1570s.
[16] All these figures are named as part of the garrison at 31 March 1586. See 'Book of the garrisons', SP63/123/21. Bagenal is first mentioned in Irish state correspondence in 1542, see lord deputy to the king, SP60/10/86; Masterson, Harpoole and Malby are mentioned in the 'consignation of Leix' of 1556, SP62/1/21, Warham St Leger arrived in the mid-1560s, being mentioned in a memo of Cecil's SP63/14/10.

suffered as a result.[17] Fitton's manifest failure as the first president of Connacht had resulted from a combination of the native population's boycott of crown government and lukewarm support from Dublin. A decade later, Pelham's vulnerability during his brief term as lord justice led to him being disgraced by the queen, jostled by a by times friendly but often predatory Nicholas Malby and shunned by the earl of Ormond.[18] In short, Ireland was a daunting prospect for a new crown officer. Most of those already serving there had their own modus vivendi, which they guarded jealously. Without a combination of both some metropolitan and grass-roots support, it was easy to be destroyed. In such an environment, Bingham was bound to find establishing himself in Connacht an uphill climb.

There were, in truth, many 'Connachts' during the Elizabethan period. The province could be defined in a diversity of ways in line with a number of organising principles: region, dynasty, administrative designation and orientation towards power brokers within and without the province proper. The difficulty of abstracting one of these analytical strands from the others is considerable; in the 1580s, the political process in Connacht involved a renewed attempt to plait them all together. In the mid-1570s, Sidney had aimed to comprehend the area within an anglicised administrative framework, hence the splitting of the province into counties, Mayo, Galway, Sligo, Leitrim, Roscommon and Thomond. In 1577, Nicholas Malby, the president of Connacht, began collecting composition and, despite the subversion of Sidney's best-laid plans to institute the tax in the country as a whole, he continued (loudly) to adhere to the idea of a self-financing provincial administration after his own very personal fashion up to his death in 1584.[19]

Each county had its own long-established grandees, wonted holders of power both within and beyond the wonted sphere of influence of their kin group or sept. These figures, throughout the 1570s and 1580s, realised that relations with the crown were reaching that psychological stage where one took risks in 'negotiation' with an eye to receiving not only interim advantage but also a larger portion of the cake when all would be settled: a violent manifestation of controlled intensity in good time might ensure

---

[17] Leimon (1989), pp. 84–9. On the tension between Malby and Drury on matters to do with territory, see Whyte to Malby, 1577, SP63/59/70.
[18] For a succinct treatment of Fitton's presidency see Brady (1994), pp. 137–9, 182–6. The discord between Malby and Pelham can be picked up in Malby to Walsingham, 29 February 1580, SP63/71/64. Pelham's woes are lamented in Fenton to Walsingham, 3 January 1580, SP63/71/2.
[19] For a treatment of Sidney's composition strategy and its ramifications see Brady (1994), pp. 140–58.

that the general settlement would reflect permanently in favour of your dynasty, or perhaps more importantly, your hereditary line within that dynasty. Since the 1570s, most of the grandees of Connacht had claimed loyalty to crown government, the optimistic flavour of Sir Henry Sidney's policy of political construction during that period had been marked by the number of knighthoods he bestowed on prominent gentlemen throughout the province. For instance, in Iar-Chonnacht, the extreme west of the province, Sir Murrough Ne Doe O'Flaherty had been assisted to leadership of his dynasty by the crown, sundering his opponents within the lordship. In Sligo, Sir Donal O'Conor had managed to assert his autonomy and secure his landed interest in spite of the O'Donnells' wonted interest in northern Connacht. Sir Brian O'Rourke's relationship with the crown was notoriously temperamental: on the one hand, he submitted to Sidney in 1576, was knighted by him in 1579 and agreed to pay rent on his lands to the crown, but, on the other hand, he grew ever more restive in the early 1580s when his brother-in-law the earl of Desmond was forced into rebellion against the crown; furthermore, his lordship was heavily militarised. Under Malby's regime, the Clanricard Burkes of Galway and the O'Briens of Thomond had upped the ante. The subsequent bloody prosecution of them, as we have seen, resulted in Ulick Burke (one of the fractious brothers that made up the duo known as the *mac an iarlas*) and Donnchadh O'Brien, both poachers turned gamekeepers, succeeding to the respective earldoms, settling them under the crown in something approaching a mutually beneficial manner.

Of all the large political units, the 'lower' MacWilliam Burke lordship of Mayo was most vulnerable to manipulation not only by its neighbours but also by the crown. Unlike the earls of Desmond and the 'upper' MacWilliam Burkes of Clanricard, the MacWilliams of Mayo, induced to submit to Henry VIII in the 1530s, had not received an 'English' title, a circumstance that left the dynasty exposed: the unilateral suppression of the indigenous title by the crown would deal a fatal blow to the honour of the sept. Furthermore, the MacWilliam Burkes were politically fragmented; although the title of 'MacWilliam' remained in existence, in reality the dynasty boasted a number of prominent 'gentlemen' among whom power was often evenly balanced, none of whom was able to exert true hegemony over the lordship. Malby's attempts in 1580 to secure an agreement on the leadership of the dynasty between the brother of the previous 'MacWilliam' Risteard MacOliverius and the *tánaiste* Risteard an Iarainn resulted in a settlement that lasted for only two years before the lordship dissolved into strife. More than any other major Connacht dynasty, the lower MacWilliam Burkes cultivated links with Scottish mercenaries and long-established gallowglass clans, such as the Clandonnells. Otherwise, the relations of the smaller lordships, such as the O'Maddens, O'Kellys and MacDermotts of Roscommon, or the Joyces and Clangibbons of north Connemara with the crown consisted of submitting to diplomacy, although they participated in armed demonstrations alongside stronger neighbouring dynasties.

Bingham took up the governorship of Connacht at a momentous time: the pacification of south Connacht and Clare, established by his predecessor, was being secured, under the overall aegis of Sir John Perrot, with the institution of the 1585 composition of Connacht, a replacement for that of 1577.[20] This was to be a meticulous survey, eventually to encompass all Connacht lordships, which determined the amount of revenue to be paid to the crown by each tenured inhabitant of the province by way of a tax on land. As before, the wealth collected was designed to finance the maintenance of a crown administration and garrison in the province, thereby eliminating the need for crown officers to coerce the inhabitants into purveyance arrangements to supply the forces – that is, to cess them. The financial spring-cleaning the composition provided was supposed to be accompanied by the suppression of honorific Irish titles, deemed an obstacle to the rationalisation of government in Connacht. However, as Bernadette Cunningham has pointed out, the composition of 1585 – certainly in Clanricard and Thomond where it achieved its greatest success – tended to fix rank-ordering in the province by allowing the larger grandees to hold substantial demesne lands, known as 'freedoms', exempt from composition rent, as well as a guaranteed revenue levied from the landholders of the province.

The aim was to secure similar deals with each and every lord in Connacht. Although Bingham was nominally the chief commissioner of the composition, it was the English-Irish commissioners Sir Nicholas White and Thomas Dillon, both favourites of Perrot (appointed in 1584) who had put the greatest effort into the initiative: the deal they secured in Clanricard and Thomond was savagely criticised by Sir Richard once he felt secure enough to raise his voice, because he alleged that it exempted too much land from the tax, and he desired leave to alter the terms of the agreement.[21]

---

[20] Cunningham, B., 'The composition of Connaught in the lordships of Clanrickard and Thomond, 1577–1641', *Irish Historical Studies* 24 (1984), pp. 1–14.
[21] Bingham to Walsingham, 5 February 1586, SP63/122/64, where Bingham asks for licence to go through the composition books again and draw the arrangement 'to more certainty'.

It is certain that in 1585 Bingham felt quite powerless to influence the survey and institution of the tax; he had only recently arrived in Connacht, after all. Although he never got the opportunity to recast the arrangement, he would subsequently, in a marked volte-face, flaunt the composition and its fruits as evidence of his superiority in the practice of Irish government.[22]

From his first arrival, Bingham paraded an awareness of the misery of the 'poor' in Connacht. By adopting this attitude, he was placing himself in the tradition of English concern for the Irish commons that stretched from at least the early Henrician period down to Sir William Gerrard. This registered with horror the abject poverty of the common order and churls of Ireland and placed the blame for their misery at the door of the indigenous aristocracy and their 'Irish exactions'.[23] In a letter to Lady Walsingham ('familiar' correspondence with her was an infallible indication of favour with the principal secretary), he wrote of 'the poverty which so continually follows me, crying for justice', adding 'scarcely they will give me leave to eat any meat.' But alongside these humanitarian noises was Bingham's desire for more financial support; the ebbing economic tide in Connacht had caused all boats to drop: in short, the poverty of the common orders and the rapacity of the magnates were placing limits on his financial horizons, which meant, of course, that he needed more money.[24] The province's wealth, it seemed, had already been parcelled out in seigneurial grants to Irish magnates, including those from outside the province. The earl of Ormond's claim on prise wines in Galway city, for instance, threatened to eat up any revenue generated by Connacht's only urban centre of real consequence. By early 1585, Bingham's views on the Irish aristocracy had become calcified:

I will say these great men and great authorities (other than in the prince only) [are] the chiefest thing that we that be her Majesty's ministers here and in general all the people – save a very few – do pluck at and seek to pull down by all good means possible.[25]

Later, Bingham would joke at his subversive reputation, but there was more than a trace of ironic and vengeful satisfaction in his tone when he

---

[22] Bingham to Burghley, 6 March 1592, SP63/163/51, where Bingham compares Lord Deputy Fitzwilliam's settlement of Monaghan unfavourably with the Composition of Connacht. In *Solon his Follie* Beacon lauded the stabilising nature of the Composition, see Beacon (1594), p. 87.
[23] For the longevity of this concern, see Cusack to the privy council, 1541, *SP Hen VIII*, Vol. III, p. 327.
[24] Bingham to Lady Walsingham, 14 January 1585, SP63/114/27.
[25] Bingham to Walsingham, 8 February 1585, SP63/114/72.

remarked on the grandees' disdain for those sweepings of Gaelicised society with which he consorted: 'for the regard I had to better the state of the meaner tenants and common people the principal gentlemen termed me Captain of the churls.'[26]

Although Bingham could indulge in inverted snobbery when he was in correspondence with Whitehall, day by day he had to deal with a number of established interest groups. First, as already rehearsed, there were the native dynasties, English-Irish and Gaelic-Irish, and their collaterals. The earls of Clanricard and Thomond were secure in their loyalty, which even withstood the strains caused by severe assizes held at Galway in 1586, but Bingham looked askance at the others, on one hand noting their *froideur* towards the English and, on the other, resenting the pressure Lord Deputy Perrot placed on him to pursue a policy larded with 'fair words and sweet promises'.[27] Second, Connacht contained a sizeable group of those of English birth: military captains, office-holders who had served under Fitton or Malby, as well as many of Malby's own tenants on his Roscommon lands, people who knew the intricacies of governing Connacht and had lived there under Sir Nicholas's stewardship – figures such as Nicholas Mordaunt, Thomas Woodhouse and Malby's brother-in-law George Castell. Last, there were an array of English-Irish office-holders and opportunists from the Pale who had 'returned' to the lost province of the medieval colony: for example, Robert Dillon, former constable of Loughrea; Theobald Dillon, collector of the composition rent, who established himself among the MacCostello dynasty as a type of protector stressing 'common' English-Irish roots between himself and the long Gaelicised clan; not to mention Thomas Dillon and Sir Nicholas White, whose concern to secure the composition was indicative of another aspect of this traditional English-Irish *Drang nach Westen*. Similarly, in 1584, John Browne of Kilpatrick received a patent (along with an Englishman Robert Fowle) to renovate Athenry town, but Walsingham appended a postscript indicating his hope that the petitioners would broaden their horizons and that their 'scope [might be] enlarged over all the province, namely to choose their seat where they may find it, so it be no hindrance to her majesty, nor offence, nor wrong, to any private person'.[28] The

---

[26] Bingham to Burghley, 12 December 1586, SP63/127/26.
[27] Bingham to Walsingham, 7 August 1584, SP63/111/53; See also Bingham to Burghley, 7 March 1585, SP63/115/18, for Bingham's indication of willingness to use 'the mild and gentle form of government'.
[28] 'Petition of Robert Fowle and John Browne', *CPRI*, Vol. II, pp. 74–6. Other examples of internal migration include William Bowen and Christopher Garvey, nephew of the bishop of Kilmore.

attitude of the more seasoned English-Irish inhabitants of Connacht towards these Palesmen on the make is well summed up by the Galway chieftain Tibbot MacAug's mockery of the English-Irish captain of horse Thomas Dalton: 'it seemed he had neither land nor living in his own country seeing he came to serve in Connacht.'[29] The erstwhile Lord Deputy Sir Henry Sidney had found it easy to praise all three groups promiscuously because of their collective indispensability to his programme to summon up a sophisticated political society.[30] He had envisaged a situation where the magnates threatened by the crown garrison would resort to the legal options offered by the English-Irish administrators and thereby forsake their arbitrary exactions and unruly private armies. Without a commanding figure to enforce this coherent vision, each group lived with each other in a somewhat ad-hoc manner.

First, Bingham had to deal with the legacy of his predecessor. Bingham inherited a difficult financial situation, which, he soon realised, it was not in his interest to play down in public. Malby's 'good and serviceable estate' had been maintained because he had been on the take, spending all the money garnered from the composition on his housekeeping and, despite receiving pay from the exchequer for his footmen and horsemen, forcing the country to support the army themselves. According to Bingham, Malby's accounts dealing with the composition money and rents due to the Queen had neither 'a beginning, middle or ... ending'.[31] To give him the same money as his predecessor and expect him to be able to do his job, he claimed, was preposterous. Furthermore, he had not been given the command of all the bands of footmen and horsemen in the province, a good proportion of horsemen having been bestowed instead on Francis Barkley, the provost marshal.

The new boss had little respect for the old arrangements. The supposed disparity between Malby's landed wealth as governor and his own lot became an obsession for Bingham. From the start, he entered into a dispute with Malby's widow Tamsin and son-in-law Anthony Brabazon over the leasehold to Roscommon Castle which brought with it administration of Sir Nicholas's cherished estate, where Bingham was on his arrival renting 'office space' from the Malbys in an arrangement which

---

[29] Whyte to Malby, 1577, SP63/59/70. For more about Tibbot MacAug, a 'gentleman' given a commission by Malby, see Malby's answer to Edward Whyte, April 1582, SP63/91/58.
[30] See Brady (2002), pp. 87–91 for Sidney's praise of the amenability of the Gaelic-Irish of Connacht and the capability of the military captains there, and pp. 67–8, 76 and 96 for the high regard in which he held the Dillon family as a whole.
[31] Bingham to Walsingham, 7 August 1584, SP63/111/54.

he claimed, with maintenance and trimmings thrown in, cost him £300 per annum. Furthermore, Bingham told Walsingham he needed the £60 per annum the estate generated to finance his administration and continued his persistent agitation, casting the possession of Roscommon as his right. The Malby family, although in disarray (the widow Malby had hastily found a new beau and her son Henry ran away from school in Oxford) managed to garner strong support within the Irish administration: Archbishop Loftus of Dublin and Edward Waterhouse each took the part of Brabazon against Bingham.[32] Even Walsingham sought reconciliation between Bingham and the Brabazon interest.[33] Perrot also took the part of the Malbys, granting himself the wardship of Henry Malby, a wardship that Bingham had gone to 'vicious' lengths to discover. Bingham portrayed this action as just another aspect of the viceroy's general unwillingness to cede him the full extent of military and financial entitlements owed him in Connacht. The relationship between lord deputy and provincial governor slid slowly but inexorably into acrimony. Officers had hated viceroys before, but the sheer concerted and consistent bitterness with which Bingham approached his dealings with Perrot was phenomenal.

Wilful, paranoid and charmless, Sir John Perrot in some ways resembled Bingham. One thing in particular made him more odious to his colleagues on the Irish council: he had vision. A keynote of his approach to government was his association with the cadre of Palesmen, many of them former intimates of Sir Henry Sidney, who manned the legal offices of the State; Lucas Dillon, chief baron of the exchequer; Robert Dillon, second justice in Connacht and Nicholas White, master of the rolls – men who wanted to anglicise Ireland after their own image and interest, in many ways a reworking of Sir Henry Sidney's programme of government for Ireland in the late 1570s. Perrot's capacity for making unfashionable allies was complemented by his gift for making sworn enemies. His plans to turn St Patrick's Cathedral and its revenues into a university excited the horror of Archbishop Loftus of Dublin; his relations with the vice-treasurer Sir Henry Wallop (a long-time client of Walsingham) soured when he publicly belittled Wallop's part in the survey of escheated lands in Munster following the Desmond rebellion; and his high-handed

---

[32] Perrot to Walsingham, 2 April 1585, SP63/116/4, where the viceroy reports that 'such that wished [Lady Tamsin Malby] well here do greatly mislike with her that she has bestowed herself upon one of her men'.

[33] See Wallop to Walsingham, 7 March 1586, SP63/123/9.

manner and moodiness quickly eliminated whatever neutrals remained.[34] As far as relations between the viceroy and his governor in Connacht were concerned, Bingham persisted in referring sympathetically to Perrot in his letters to Burghley until January 1586, whereas he had been scornful about him in communications to Walsingham from the very start.[35] Yet, given the fractious relationship Bingham had with partisans of the previous provincial administration in Connacht as well as the unenthusiastic attitude of the Dublin administration towards his attempts at self-aggrandisement, the demonisation of Sir John Perrot and the organisation of a campaign among crown officers to oust and destroy him provided an excellent opportunity for him to come in from the margins and develop real bonds with influential colleagues.

Coincidentally, the MacWilliam lordship of Mayo was showing signs of unrest. These were a by-product first of an internal succession dispute following the death of the 'MacWilliam' Risteard MacOliverius, and second of the desire to assert the value of the various ancestral customs and titles of the lordship likely to be dismantled by the inevitable composition arrangement, as well as an apparently shrewd desire to wring the maximum number of pardons for members of the lordship as a remedy against the ravages of sessions run under English law.[36] Unfortunately for the MacWilliams, their hopes for a spectacular demonstration of power coincided with Richard Bingham's desire to prove himself. Bingham later maintained that the conflict began when gentlemen and freeholders of Mayo refused to attend judicial sessions which had been convened for the 'perfection' of the composition of Mayo in Donamona, near Roscommon Castle in September 1585.[37] One of those who stayed away, Thomas Roe Burke, subsequently died in disputed circumstances. According to Bingham, when a sub-sheriff had attempted to take him in as a pledge for good behaviour, he had resisted arrest and had been killed. Both Francis Barkley, Connacht's provost marshal, and Theobald Dillon, the receiver of composition rents, stated that Bingham's account of this killing was a

---

[34] Wallop to Burghley, 26 April 1586, SP63/123/52, where Wallop lists his charges against Perrot who 'most desireth to deal in all things absolutely'; see also Wallop to Walsingham, 26 and 31 May 1586, compounded in SP63/124/53.

[35] See Perrot's endorsement of Bingham's judgement and methods in Perrot to Walsingham, 19 January 1586, SP63/122/32, and Bingham's high praise for Perrot's unpopular Ulster policy, Bingham to Burghley, 7 March 1585, SP63/115/18.

[36] See both Bingham to Burghley, 6 October 1586, SP63/126/53–53i and 'A true discourse of the causes of the late rebellion of the Burkes', 16 November, SP63/126/83.

[37] Bingham to Burghley, 6 October 1586, SP63/126/53–53i.

blatant lie and that the governor had actually provoked the crisis in Mayo through extra-legal harassment.[38]

Accordingly, in early spring 1586, Barkley and Dillon charged Bingham with malpractice before the Irish council. Perrot upheld their allegations and demanded that they be investigated. Bingham countered by accusing Barkley and Dillon, 'men English and Englished' of encouraging defiance among the MacWilliam Burkes by promising them viceregal pardons which would be given out once Bingham had been thoroughly undermined (he sullenly wrote) 'for that the Lord Deputy loved not [Bingham], but would do anything to cross and disgrace [him]'.[39] In short, Perrot was pursuing a vendetta against him.

The longest continuous account of Bingham's conduct in this period is his own deftly composed *apologia*, penned in September 1586, which, understandably, presents him as both severe and restrained: a model adherent of due process.[40] Opposition to Perrot within the Irish council ensured that Bingham's every action was readily supported by Wallop, not only in letters to their shared patron Walsingham but also to Burghley; Loftus, previously at daggers drawn with Wallop, also came to support him, and Bingham, an adept self-publicist, kept a constant volume of letters from various supporters flowing to Whitehall. Theobald Dillon's attempted retaliation on this score (Barkley quickly withdrew his allegations) was to pose as a valued client of the principal secretary on the basis of a brief introduction to Walsingham sometime in 1582 while Nicholas Malby was at court.[41]

Whatever about the genesis of the rebellion, the situation worsened in the summer of 1586 as the sons of Mayo grandees continued to defy Bingham. In retaliation, he killed a number of prominent figures using both civil and martial law, most notably Edmund Burke of Castlebar, the

---

[38] Relations between Bingham and Dillon did not have to be this bad. According to Walsingham's notes of letters received in 1585, SP63/115/8i, the principal secretary was requested by Sir Richard to write a letter of thanks to Theobald Dillon for his 'courtesy'.

[39] Bingham did not tire from sending his account of his actions against the MacWilliams and the Scots to all and sundry: to Wallop (SP63/126/57, 18 October 1586) to Perrot (SP63/126/34ii, 30 September 1586) and, crucially, to Burghley (SP63/126/53i, 6 October 1586). Burghley also received copies from Lord Chancellor Archbishop Loftus (SP63/126/34, 30 September 1586) and Geoffrey Fenton (SP63/126/31, 29 September 1586). See also *Cal. Car. MSS, 1575–1588*, 'A letter from a gentleman to his friend, of certain services done by Sir Richard Bingham', pp. 429–34, which is a paraphrase of Bingham's letter.

[40] Bingham to Burghley, 6 October 1586, SP63/126/53–53i.

[41] Theobald Dillon to Walsingham, 27 January 1583, SP63/99/37; Malby to Walsingham, 4 May 1583, SP63/111/4, where Malby commends Dillon; Theobald Dillon to Walsingham, 4 May 1583, SP63/111/5. Barkley would survive to denounce Bingham again.

aged *tánaiste*. He continued to pursue his opponents, using troops given him by the earl of Clanricard and a small number of English footsoldiers. According to Bingham, Perrot attempted to contain the insurrection by telling him to give protections to all the rebels, a command which Bingham openly interpreted as a typically shameful one – less disgraceful in relation to himself than to the honour of the crown. These protections – Perrot's doing – allowed the malcontents to increase their strength, while standing aloof from the institutions of crown government.[42] Perrot, no doubt mindful of the cold reaction his 1585 expedition against the Scots in Ulster, deemed by many a waste of resources, had earned from Whitehall and Dublin, claimed that his concern to bring hostilities to a halt in Mayo came from the desire to achieve the composition arrangement planned without disruption, thereby placing crown government there on a firmer political and financial footing. Despite reports that the strengthened rebels (comprising 800 troops) were attempting to bring in Scottish troops to assist them – even promising the Scots lands in Mayo as payment – Bingham, in an ostentatious show of obedience to the viceroy, continued to abide by the letter of his order and refused to take any action without an *explicit* command to do so. The country was under threat of Scottish invasion and, according to Bingham, was being ransacked by men who openly invoked the Spanish king as their sovereign, yet he did nothing.

When Perrot and the council eventually gave him permission to act, Bingham harried both south Mayo and Connemara, and then executed the pledges of the Lower MacWilliam Burkes. In a crucial 'propaganda coup', Bingham's severity in Connacht was accompanied by ostentatious thrift: he used booty spoiled from the countryside to pay his companies and kern, rustling 5,000 head of cattle while campaigning. In the face of such an onslaught, various members of the MacWilliam Burkes and their dependants came to Bingham to submit and give fresh pledges for good behaviour. The governor used his advantageous position to secure worthwhile hostages, eldest sons where possible, handed over with understandable reluctance.

The subsequent invasion of the Scots under the leadership of Donal Gorm MacDonnell and Alastair MacDonnell, lured by the MacWilliams' promise of lands, allowed Bingham to play to his strengths in the most

---

[42] It is very noticeable that throughout his discourse of service Bingham repeats individual allegations against Perrot with great frequency in a way that might make the reader believe that each repetition is in fact a new allegation. It seems certain that this rhetorical device is deliberate, see Bingham's discourse SP63/126/53i *passim*.

unambiguous manner. Bingham crushed them at the battle of Ardnaree on 22 September, leading a force of 500 foot and ninety horse (mostly 'entertained soldiers', as Bingham had sent away Irish troops supplied by the earl of Clanricard and the local risings out, deeming them a liability rather than a help) against close to 2,000 Scots, a victory so complete that Captain Thomas Woodhouse, a former intimate of Malby's, wrote: 'I was never since I was a man of war, so weary with the killing of men, for I protest to God, as fast as I could I did but hough them and paunch them.' At least 1,400 Scots were killed that day, according to Bingham, besides horse-boys, 'women, churls, and children'.[43] Ironically, this victory brought an even pettier dimension to the enmity between president and viceroy. It was alleged that Perrot, who had defeated the Scots in Antrim in March 1586, had grown jealous, even in anticipation, of Bingham's attempt to secure martial glory against the same foe and consequently insisted on dealing with the threat in Connacht personally. He led an army from Dublin for the purpose. The majority of the Irish council, by now weary of their fractious and unbiddable lord deputy compounding their criticisms of this initiative with their objections to the profligacy of his earlier tour against the Scots of Antrim, but Perrot, eager to embarrass Bingham, persisted. By the time the lord deputy had reached Mullingar, word came of the victory at Ardnaree. Further assistance would be superfluous.[44] Rather than return to Dublin with his tail between his legs, Perrot pressed on into Galway, searching for evidence of improprieties and complaints against the president.[45] Unsurprisingly, this provoked hysterical outrage from Bingham.

Bingham short-circuited these manoeuvres by getting his sundered opponents to write attesting to his innocence. The 'true discourse of the causes of the late rebellion of the Burkes' is a remarkable document signed (or, to be more accurate, marked) by eighteen notables from the MacWilliam lordship. In it, the MacWilliam Burkes cleared Bingham of

---

[43] Even the account of the Four Masters points to the magnitude of Bingham's achievement at Ardnaree. *ARÉ*, (Dublin, 1990), Vol. V, 1849–1855. See Bingham's own account written around 6 October 1586, SP63/126/53i.

[44] Bingham interpreted Perrot's subsequent despatch of soldiers to court who had served in Sorley Boy MacDonnell in Ulster in March 1585 as a malicious slight against his own service against the Scots at Ardnaree. Bingham told Burghley: 'It is well known that Sorley Boy and his son were but followers of James MacDonnell's sons' adding disingenuously 'I write not about this to your honour . . . as having an intent to blazon the service . . . I did it of purpose to let your Lordship understand the truth, that I may not be disgraced by mine enemies', Bingham to Burghley, 12 December 1586, SP63/127/26.

[45] Bingham to Wallop, 18 October 1586, SP63/128/57.

all charges. Thomas Roe's death, they claimed, far from being provoking, 'was no part of our quarrel', which had as its 'only ground and principal beginning' 'the taking away of the said MacWilliamship and the division of the lands and inheritance'. They accused Francis Barkley and Theobald Dillon of working against Bingham, commanding the Burkes to be 'upon our keeping and not to come to any officer'. Furthermore, they alleged that Barkley, having whipped up a sense of desperation among them, attempted to capitalise on it by pressuring them into joining him on a military expedition to Flanders, 'which [they alleged] seemed so strange unto us that we knew not in the world what to do, but did choose rather to go forward in our folly and die in our native country'. They even denied that Bingham's cold-blooded execution of pledges might have intensified the rebellion: 'we never grounded any part of our quarrel in revenge of the same, for that we knew it ought to be so.' In short, the president's government, they admitted, while severe, was fair. He did not billet his troops upon the county, and all his preys and booties were 'lawfully taken'.[46]

Bingham's victory at Ardnaree seems to have brought the New English and the military captains to a new understanding with their president, and the unremitting severity he displayed on that day might have been thought a helpful adjunct to the metropolitan strategy of placing continued pressure on James VI after the ousting of the earl of Arran in July in the lead up to Mary Stuart's trial for plotting Elizabeth's assassination in October. With such devastation being visited on Scots – even in Ireland – it was clear that the young king of Scotland had little room for manoeuvre; he certainly could not seriously intervene on behalf of his beleaguered mother even as she faced death. Bingham now began to feel confident enough to surround himself with his own creatures, rather than relying on the officers he inherited from Malby. His own inner circle became settled: figures such as Thomas Woodhouse; Francis Dalton; John Birt; Edmund MacCostello; George Goodman; the new attorney of Connacht Gerald Comerford, a one-armed lawyer from Kilkenny who had had '[sundry parts of his body] most cruelly mangled maimed and wounded' during the Desmond rebellion; Captain Greene O'Molloy, whose impromptu exactions and billeting in County Mayo under Nicholas Malby had been subject to enquiry; not to mention three more captains, Richard Mappowder (probably a neighbour of Bingham's from

---

[46] 'A true discourse of the causes of the late rebellion of the Burkes', 16 November 1586, SP63/126/83.

Dorset), Daniel Daly and Henry Eyland.[47] Eyland's controversial conduct as sheriff of Roscommon gave Bingham another opportunity to display his independence and influence.[48] In autumn 1586, Eyland was accused of 'hanging and ransoming many of her majesty's subjects contrary to law', of 'extortious taking of their goods and chattels'. His roll of excess, which included the hanging of William MacPiers MacCostello probably a protégé of Theobald Dillon, became the subject of charges before the court of castle chamber in Dublin.[49] Sir Nicholas White, reflecting on Eyland's spree, remarked that he was the sort of crown officer 'that make her majesty's laws hateful to her people and have been too long borne withal'.[50] But Eyland, rather than turning up at court as the *subpoena* commanded, absconded to England. Bingham took Eyland's part in defiance of Ireland's prerogative court.

While the Eyland controversy threatened to stink up the air, Bingham took full advantage of the prevailing wind of success since Ardnaree. He even took the opportunity to advance his own interest in spite of the greater designs of his supposed political allies and advocates. *Non sufficit orbis*, the world is not enough, may have been the slogan of Philip II, but *non sufficit Ballymote* was Bingham's. At Bingham's first taking up of office, Perrot had given him leases of the castles of Ballymote and Boyle

---

[47] Woodhouse's band had been discharged and sent to Flanders with a different captain. He looked to Bingham to secure his overdue wages, see Woodhouse to Fenton, 23 September 1586, SP63/126/31iv. Comerford had been ambushed while attempting to secure defections from the earl of Desmond's confederates to the earl of Ormond's crown-sponsored forces; the wounds had been inflicted by men who had served under Sir John of Desmond: Comerford's petitions, 31 December 1583, SP63/105/39–40. For the Comerfords see D. Edwards *The Ormond Lordship in Co. Kilkenny, 1515–1642* (Dublin, 2003), pp. 40–1, 247. Goodman, an Englishman who had settled in Loughrea, was a commissioner in the composition alongside Theobald Dillon, see *Fiants*, Vol. II, 4732; For Greene O'Molloy's penurious presence in Mayo under Malby see SP63/72/45, 62; for the enquiry into Malby's payment of Greene and other 'bands of Scots, English and Irish' and evidence of a falling out between O'Molloy and the then president over pay see the copy of the enclosures concerning the enquiry into Malby's manner of payment, SP63/116/5, 2 April 1585. O'Molloy played a central role in putting together the Crown force that fought at Ardnaree, 'A discourse of the services done by Sir Richard Byngham in the county of Mayo', SP63/126/53i. Mappowder is the name of a triangular parish of 1,900 acres adjoining Melcombe Horsey the parish in which Bingham's Melcombe, the homestead of the Bingham family, was located. It is reasonable to think that Richard Mappowder hailed from this parish although parish registers dating from 1654 onwards name no one in the parish bearing that name, see www.dorset-opc.com/index.htm. For a description of the manor house of Bingham's Melcombe as well as its location see the Royal Commission on Historical Monuments (England), *An inventory of historical monuments in the county of Dorset*, III, Central Dorset, 2, (1970), pp. 163–7.

[48] Eyland succeeded Robert Nugent as sheriff of Roscommon. Nugent's shrievalty is referred to in his pardon of 21 March 1586 in *Fiants*, Vol. II, 4835.

[49] Knox, H. T., *A history of the county of Mayo to the close of the sixteenth century* (Dublin, 1908), p. 318.

[50] White to Burghley, 29 November 1586, SP63/226/90.

in Connacht because he was chief commissioner of the composition. By 1586, he had made clear his dissatisfaction with these leaseholds, and (Henry Malby's wardship having eluded him) he consequently agitated for a grant of the castle of Athlone as his right, remarking that it had belonged to Fitton and Malby before him. He disparaged the estates he had: '[Ballymote] may be a house for the chief officer to rest in for a month . . . when he shall have occasion to repair thither to the frontiers of the province, yet all the world knoweth it is no place to keep house in continually.' Boyle, on the other hand, had 'no house, stick, nor stone standing . . . and the land is all waste.'[51] The arrangements concerning the leasehold of Athlone were complex and contentious and proved to be not merely a cause of tension between Bingham and Perrot, but a cause of disagreement within the Walsingham affinity in Ireland. The lease of Athlone was held by Sir Henry Wallop. Bingham had stopped agitating for it while Wallop was hectoring Barkley, Dillon and Perrot on his behalf to Whitehall, but the more comfortable Sir Richard of early 1587 returned to the question petitioning Burghley as well as Walsingham for Athlone.

The subsequent wrangling took on a characteristically petty tone. When Wallop suggested that Bingham could govern the province from Galway in the same way as his Munster counterpart Sir John Norris did from Cork, he retorted that the affluent Wallop might as well be content with merely *some* of his Irish estates. The perennial comparison with Malby's former status was made, as if a moral imperative could be inferred from it.[52] Wallop gave up the fight in April 1587, his ostentatious thanks to Burghley for his 'mild and favourable' attitude towards his continued stake in Athlone 'though all reason, law and conscience do concur, and fortify your lordship's opinion in that behalf' amounted to a meek, but clear protest against his abandonment in this matter by Walsingham. As recompense for his unilateral magnanimity, Wallop asked for the fee-farm of the house and land of Enniscorthy and other boons. Bingham, once again, had got what he wanted.[53]

---

[51] Bingham to Walsingham, 5 February 1586, SP63/122/64i.
[52] 'The answer of Sir Richard Bingham to Mr Treasurer Wallop's letter touching the house of Athlone', 15 February 1587, SP63/128/43.
[53] The queen's patent dated 3 December 1587 directing that Bingham be granted the use of Athlone determined that 'at the time of the departure of the lord deputy from England, it was by his instruction ordered that Athlone House should be kept in his own hands, and that he should reside there as one of the aptest places for his abode, for the government of the whole realm; but that since his entrance into the government of Ireland, he had not disposed himself to reside there, but appointed a vice-constable to look to the ward'. See *CPRI*, II (Dublin, 1862), p. 153.

Theobald Dillon's official humiliation must have been particularly sweet for the provincial president. Bingham was acquitted of all charges by the Irish council in February 1587. Dillon's accusations were deemed 'malicious', caused by his 'vexation and dislike' for Bingham's government, while Bingham, in the words of the council's verdict, had 'his credit and authority in government and charge no whit abated, but rather increased'.[54] In time, Dillon would beg Walsingham to intercede for him with Bingham, 'whereof I never intended or attempted [anything] towards him notwithstanding the jealousy of his conceit over credulous to the calumniations of such as maligned me and abused him.'[55]

Lord Deputy Perrot, aware that he was trapped in a web of hostility and scorn, stood on his personal honour in a last, rather desperate, attempt to daunt the provincial president. On the evening of Sunday, 19 February 1587, Bingham was interrupted – the day before his acquittal – while at dinner with Chief Justice Gardener by the constable of Dublin Castle Stephen Seagrave who was brandishing a white truncheon. The constable brought a message that Perrot was now 'ready for the combat'. Bingham later claimed to have been confused by this challenge although Seagrave's 'giving of the lie' stated that Sir Richard had been heard to say openly that he would have killed Perrot except for the fact that he was viceroy.[56] The 'combat' never took place, but the challenge allowed Bingham to be unbuttoned in his condemnation of the lord deputy, especially in correspondence with Burghley, denouncing him as a friend of the 'tyrannical great ones' stating that the viceroy's revocation would do more good for crown government in Ireland than the immediate despatch of 1,000 fresh well-trained recruits.[57]

Perrot, incandescent with rage, grew ever more erratic over the following months, and – crucially – metropolitan attitudes towards him became more and more contemptuous.[58] By contrast, Bingham, by agreeing to

---

[54] Acquittal of Sir Richard Bingham, 20 February 1587, SP63/128/50. Wallop concurred with the rest of the counsellors 'for as many articles as I was the hearing of'. See Theobald Dillon to Walsingham, 15 July 1588, SP63/135/86, where Dillon tells how Bingham on his return to Ireland from the Low Countries 'promised for your sake to esteem and use me well, in hope whereof I live the better contented having hitherto no cause to distrust the same'.

[55] Theobald Dillon to Walsingham, 15 July 1588, SP63/135/86.

[56] Bingham to Burghley, 26 February 1587, SP63/128/60. In 1590 Lord Deputy Fitzwilliam refused to reappoint Seagrave constable of Dublin Castle because of an alleged offence he committed against Silvester Cowley, a one-armed man, in order to secure the job, 17 May 1590, SP63/152/32.

[57] Bingham to Burghley, 26 February 1587, SP63/128/60.

[58] For Perrot's physical assault on the aged knight marshal Sir Nicholas Bagenal during council business see 'Speeches passed between the Rt Hon lord deputy and Sir Nicholas Bagenal' 15 May 1587, SP63/129/84 and Sir Nicholas White's account of the same, SP63/129/93i.

serve under the earl of Leicester in the Netherlands, ensured that his stock with the great and the good had never been higher. But before he left Ireland, he tried to secure his interests in Connacht from whatever depredations Perrot might inflict upon them in his absence, and he was single-minded and shameless about achieving this. Two months after his departure from Connacht, the privy council wrote to Perrot with horrible condescension demanding indemnity of Bingham's intimates from 'hard measure ... delivered to them by you'; men who were 'in no small fear, some of them dreading to lose their office, some others fearing that severe punishment shall be laid on their bodies, and some that their livings and goods shall be seized on, by virtue of judgement and orders passed against them rigorously'.[59] Bingham was to be immune from all actions against him, especially those taken on Theobald Dillon's behalf. Perhaps the most notable evidence of the strength of Bingham's sway over Connacht was a letter of George Castell's, the formerly staunch Malby partisan, to Burghley in which he not only repined at Bingham's absence but railed against the president's brief replacement by Sir Thomas Lestrange in an ethnocentric rant, indicative of the growth of a belligerent New English presence in Connacht:

> To us poor Englishmen that would live in the country [his absence] shall be a great plague and (without God be merciful unto us) our utter undoing ... We could hardly get justice, though Sir Richard stood to us, and now we look for none at all, for our justice is an Irishman, all the officers Irish, Sir Thomas Strange, now in Sir Richard's place, married to an Irish woman the justice wife's mother; so that what the one sayeth the other will affirm, so that we stand in great fear that we shall be forced to leave the country. This is not my voice alone ... but almost every man, especially the poor, and your Honour knoweth: *vox populi vox Dei est.*[60]

Castell's enthusiasm (which, whether sincere or not, did not last) may have stemmed from the need to endear himself to Bingham, the new leaseholder of the castle of Athlone, where he served as constable.[61]

---

[59] Privy Council to Perrot, July, SP63/130/57.
[60] Castell to Burghley, 30 June 1587, SP63/130/26. See *Fiants*, Vol. II, 5021, 'Commission for martial affairs in Connacht' 14 July 1587, where Lestrange is designated to be general of the forces of Connacht in the field.
[61] Castell to (Burghley?), 1589, SP63/148/52. Where he alleged that Bingham, after apprehending five survivors of the Armada in Connacht – four Spaniards and one Italian – kept the Italian, 'Hippolyta', as a protected guest, allowing him 'liberty to ride around the country at his pleasure' and paying his expenses. Hippolyta had supposedly even kept a private library in Athlone, and was, no doubt, an irritating presence for Castell, constable of the castle.

By this stage, however, Bingham had proven that he could effectively protect those who served him, thereby making membership of his clientele a coveted quantity in Connacht. For instance, Henry Eyland benefited remarkably from Bingham's charmed political connections.[62] Bingham alleged that everything about the original verdict against him was suspect. The court had met out of term, had passed its judgement despite the fact that Lord Chancellor Loftus, Chief Justice Gardener, Vice Treasurer Wallop and the lord bishop of Meath Thomas Jones had objected, and the writ was not *ad respondendum;* that is, it had not required Eyland's immediate arrest and transportation to Dublin. Eyland, 'a man of the best religion', had fled only when he heard that all he owned was to be given in prey to 'his mortal enemy' Theobald Dillon, Bingham's constant scapegoat. Every other matter in the case was mopped up by Bingham on the one hand taking responsibility for delegating these tasks to his sheriff – 'if any punishment is to be afflicted upon any it is upon myself and not upon Eyland: for he did them by a provincial order from me and the rest of Her Majesty's Commissioners' – and on the other absolving Eyland from responsibility for what his underlings did, 'haply his ministers under him at the time . . . have offended the law in the execution of their charges' – a remarkable fragmentation of the chain of command. The privy council, having already determined that Eyland could enjoy total indemnity until Bingham returned, demanded a retrial before the castle chamber – one that could really only go one way.[63] Bingham's audacity reached its zenith when he defended himself from charges that his soldiers were spoiling Connacht in his absence by implausibly alleging that Perrot had deliberately sent in 'loose and idle men . . . terming themselves my soldiers' in the hope of giving the president's government a bad name.[64]

During this period, another of Bingham's obsessions came to light. Having devastated those office-holders who refused to bow to him in everything and also having – apparently – entirely cowed the MacWilliam Burkes through the activities of his brother George, he turned his attention north-eastwards to Connacht's border with Ulster with a view to placing the area under his control by means of a network of garrisons

---

[62] Sir Nicholas White to Burghley, 29 November 1586, SP63/126/90.
[63] Bingham met the fugitive Eyland at Chester in March 1588, and sent him as a bearer to court with his special appeal on his behalf, see Bingham to Burghley, 13 March 1588, SP63/134/14. For the privy council's demand of indemnity for all of Bingham's intimates see privy council to Perrot, July 1587, SP63/130/57.
[64] Bingham to Burghley, 24 February 1588, SP63/133/79.

commanded by family members and associates. The death of Sir Donal O'Conor Sligo, a long-standing friend of crown government in Connacht, was seized upon as a particularly good opportunity to advance his own interests under the appearances of advancing the strategic interests of the crown.[65] George, lately appointed sheriff of Sligo by his brother, forcibly occupied the castle and town of Sligo, inciting protest from the dead chieftain's nephew, Donough O'Conor, the aspiring heir.[66] George's actions seemed particularly scandalous, it appeared that he was pursuing his own aims with a total disregard for a native subject's tried and tested reputation as a loyalist.

Few Gaelic-Irish magnates had proved quite as amenable to English government as Sir Donal. In 1567 during the high spring of Sir Henry Sidney's first viceroyalty he had personally submitted to Elizabeth at Hampton Court surrendering all his lands, receiving them again by letters patent.[67] By proving his explicit loyalty to the crown, he had managed to mitigate the harshness of a long-standing arrangement paying 'yoke and services' to his northern neighbours the O'Donnells: an understanding had been ratified as recently as 1539.[68] Despite this, both Sir Richard and George Bingham blocked Donough's claim to his uncle's title. They alleged that both Sir Donal and Donough were illegitimate and therefore unable to inherit, despite the fact that Malby had always assumed that all lands would proceed after Sir Donal's death to 'the heirs male of the body of his father'.[69] Mindful of the assurances given during Sir Henry Sidney's viceroyalty, O'Conor Sligo appealed to the earl of Leicester in February 1588 to complain that George Bingham had 'no less desire to the profits of my living, than delight in the pleasure of my houses [and aims] to undo me and overthrow my state'.[70] The Binghams stressed the

---

[65] For Sidney's good disposition towards Sir Donal see his 1583 memoir, Brady (2002), pp. 57, 88.
[66] In 1580, O'Conor Sligo's property included the barony of Carbery, including the castle and manor of Sligo with royalties as well as profit of leet and court baron, the barony of Tireragh, the barony of Maghereleyny, the half barony of Cowlovynn, as well as lands called Sliocht Moriertagh, Sliocht Briain, Sliocht Tirrelagh O'Conor, and Cowrine Moygenny. O'Conor Sligo also held the baronies of Tireriel and Corren of the manor of Ballymote. See 'Lands belonging to Sir Donnell for term of his life and after to the heirs male of the body of his father', 4 January 1580, SP63/71/6.
[67] For details of O'Conor Sligo's submission see *CPRI*, Vol. I, pp. 495, 509.
[68] For the 1539 arrangement with O'Donnell which stipulated that O'Conor Sligo should give military service, should submit to O'Donnell's counsel in all things, should hand over control of Sligo castle and town with its customs and burgages and should actively assist O'Donnell's officers in levying tribute, see Simms (1987), p. 113.
[69] See 'Lands belonging to Sir Donnell for term of his life and after to the heirs male of the body of his father', 4 January 1580, SP63/71/6.
[70] Donough O'Conor to Leicester, 17 February 1588, SP63/133/64. Perrot to Walsingham, 18 March 1588, SP63/134/29, Perrot described Donal as 'appertain[ing] to the Earl of Leicester'.

strategic importance of Sligo as 'the door and key' between Connacht and Ulster, 'the only straight and mouth through which the Scots ordinarily accustom to annoy the province', presented both as a complement to Sir John Perrot's attempted partition of Tír Conaill and an undermining of his conciliatory attitude to O'Conor Sligo.[71] The president counselled that the crown not only had a right but a duty to take possession of them. Bingham even made so bold to suggest that, even if Donough could be found to be legitimate, that he might be prevailed upon to swap Sligo for Ballymote, which had been gutted by a troop of kern in early October 1588.[72]

Perrot, prior to his departure, had appointed a commission to inquire into the tenure of the lands after Sir Donal's death. It was made up of trusted lieutenants, Sir Robert Dillon, Sir Lucas Dillon and the bishop of Meath Thomas Jones with a local jury. It found in favour of Donough's legitimacy and his right to hold the lands, after which the inquisition was returned to the chancery and Perrot awarded livery of the premises to Donough.[73] Bingham denounced the commission as partial; it had been formed, he alleged, solely to arrive at the conclusion it did: why else had he himself, the crown's chancellor in Connacht, been excluded from its membership, or, for that matter, Chief Justice Robert Gardener and Connacht's justiciar Nicholas Walsh?

Bingham pursued his own counter-manoeuvres. First, on his return to England after campaigning in the Low Countries, he managed to get Elizabeth to give an oral assurance that she believed that George Bingham should not hand over Sligo Castle to Donal. Despite this, Perrot claimed that any delay in handing over Sligo amounted to contempt of *his* authority as viceroy. Second, a crown escheator was procured, who worked ex officio at Bingham's behest. Unsurprisingly, he declared that all the lands should go to the queen. Bingham suggested to Burghley that a concession should be made: all lands should be given to Donough, but Sligo town and castle should be kept for the queen. After Perrot's departure, Bingham secured a second commission *a melioris inquirandi* from the new viceroy, Sir William Fitzwilliam, which found that Donough was a bastard.[74] A host

---

[71] See Bingham to Burghley, 24 February 1588, SP63/133/79, sent from Chester; Bingham to Burghley, 15 May 1588 SP63/135/26. Morgan (1993), p. 53.
[72] Bingham to Burghley, 6 March, 1588, SP63/134/3, sent from Chester; Bingham to Fitzwilliam, 14 October 1588, abstracted at SP63/137/10 xiii. Donal O'Conor Sligo had deftly combined his loyalty to the crown with his obligations to Calvagh O'Donnell by joining the confederation against Shane O'Neill.
[73] Perrot to Walsingham, 18 March 1588, SP63/134/29.
[74] Instructions to Sir William Fitzwilliam, 8 March 1588, SP63/134/11.

of allegations suggested that the second commission was more partisan than the first, that Bingham had seized a dissenting member of the second commission's jury by the beard and threatened him with a traitor's death unless he ceased his opposition; Bingham's supporters countered that if the juror in question was treated in such a manner it was only because he deserved it; this was the sort of transparently flawed and overbearing argument that Bingham had grown accustomed to prevailing with in the past. The eleven others who were empanelled for the second commission, according to Bingham's detractors, were a mixum-gatherum 'of the adverse part ... notorious murderers, most of no residence in the country, the rest of no freehold'.[75] Worse still, the second commission's business was transacted clandestinely, under cover of being a session for gaol delivery. Despite this, Bingham airily asserted that the first commission *must* have been crooked if both the escheator and a second jury had found against it, and this ruling prevailed.[76] But even Bingham acknowledged that the 'taking of this from Donough O'Conor may breed a suspicion in the Irishry that we seek all from them and so not only make them unwilling to surrender any lands to her majesty, but also incite them to stirs and disquietness' but nevertheless assured Burghley that 'the people of this province are so dejected and made subject to the sword as there is no doubt or fear to be conceived of one or the other'.[77]

In the midst of this procedural chicanery, the dregs of the 1588 Spanish Armada skirted the coasts of Connacht. Bingham's role in extirpating the sodden Spaniards on the beaches and rocks within his territory was impressive and no doubt influenced Fitzwilliam's indulgence of his sleight of hand concerning Sligo. Initially, many crown officials feared that the influx of Spanish mariners would result in an emboldening of disaffected elements among the Irish and a rash of alliances between the refugees and Irish septs. Geoffrey Fenton remarked that the kern who burned Ballymote had declared that they did so for Philip of Spain; Bingham made

[75] The case of Donough O'Conor Sligo, 1589, SP63/136/53.
[76] Donough would petition regularly for restitution of Sligo, but without success, for example his letter to the privy council of October 1590, SP63/155/23. Ultimately, O'Conor Sligo threw in his lot with O'Donnell in 1599, as the four masters later attested, see *ARÉ* (1599) Vol. VI, p. 2141, 'O'Conor Sligo (Donough mac Cathail) continued in friendship and amity with O'Donnell from the time that the governor was slain to the end of this year. It was a change for the better and a shelter for him, to come over to this friendship from the cold, slow and unprofitable promises made him [by the English] from year to year.' 'Ua Concobair Sligeach Donnchadh Mac Cathail Óg do bheith i muintearas agus i gcaradh Uí Domhnaill ón aimsir anseo marbhadh ar gobernóir go dtí na seo. Ba haithrisadh ar glan, agus ba coim ria cioth dósomh tocht isin caradh sin ó na fuairthingealltoibh imri ettarchacha no geallta dó ó bhlian go bliain go sin.'
[77] Bingham to Burghley, 15 May 1588, SP63/135/26.

much play of the danger that might have issued if O'Conor Sligo had been in a position to hand Sligo over to the Spanish – an entirely hypothetical scenario, of course.[78] But Bingham's preferred prophylactic against any major alliance between armed elements of Connacht society and the Spaniards was the mass recruitment and use of indigenous troops while investigating the extent of the incursion. His successes therein further bolstered his reputation, but, despite his hitherto charmed existence, Bingham now had to deal with a new viceroy.

The reasons for Fitzwilliam's return to Ireland as lord deputy in July 1588 can be understood, perhaps, in the context of the changing political climate that followed the execution of Mary Stuart in early 1588, especially among the Protestant party at court. The Catholic reversionary interest had lost its dynastic focus, which had profound political ramifications both at the centre and the peripheries. In the short term, some of the brittle indulgence found between notables of the Protestant party at court on matters of patronage now became less pressing. Walsingham's precarious health, especially from late 1588 onwards, led Burghley to look again at the sister kingdom, and the principal secretary's clients there, in a less collegiate spirit than hitherto; his appreciation of the opportunities that Ireland offered for personal patronage and wealth had been pricked by his experiences with the Munster plantation. Leicester's death in early September 1588 also made a major difference to metropolitan power and influence in Irish matters: all parts of the late Sir Henry Sidney's network of contacts woven together in the late 1560s and mid-1570s were now atomised, and, with Leicester's demise, figures such as O'Conor Sligo and O'Farrell lost their final guarantor at court. Prior to Mary Stuart's death, the appointment of Perrot as viceroy had seemed appropriate: a man committed to a consistent agenda for the reform of Irish government who looked and acted like Sidney. The contrast with William Fitzwilliam's laissez-faire approach, inflected with ingrown deviousness could hardly be greater. As Burghley's client, Fitzwilliam was well supported at court.[79]

By the time Sir William Fitzwilliam had been sworn in, Bingham seemed confident that the pattern of personal dominion he had established in northern Connacht was secure, and, despite the change at the top, he assumed that Fitzwilliam would be forced to tolerate him; indeed, the way the new deputy had indulged and facilitated the violation of common-law norms in Sligo indicated that Bingham would be given

[78] Fenton and George Bingham to Richard Bingham, 6 October 1588, SP63/137/15.
[79] MacCarthy-Morrogh (1986), pp. 38–9.

carte blanche. Early in 1589, crown government's first concern was the rumours that Sir William Stanley, who had lately handed Deventer over to the Spanish, would be steering a course to the south-east of Ireland with his Irish troops. This fear was particularly intense because of the defector's first-hand knowledge of the kingdom's vulnerabilities.[80] But for all this, Fitzwilliam retained a studied laziness and haughtiness. In 1589, it looked as if Bingham could not be easily daunted. There was no need for him to attempt to trespass on Fitzwilliam: he was supreme in Connacht, and Walsingham's indulgence meant that his influence had to be heeded. But neither Fitzwilliam nor Burghley were content to let that be.

In March, the MacWilliam Burkes were out in arms again. Caught between the hostility of the earl of Clanricard, Bingham and Roger O'Flaherty from Iar-Chonnacht, they demonstrated their repudiation of the developing state of affairs by killing both John Browne of the Neale, County Mayo and Daniel Daly, both of whom were recognised as some of the president's closest, and consequently most hated, subordinates.[81] The Burkes made it clear that their actions were first and foremost a protest against Bingham's arbitrary abuses: their lands were being seized 'without order of law'; the president's sheriffs' and sub-sheriffs' massively bloated retinues constantly demanded to be supported; bailiffs and kerns in the crown's service were spoiling the country; worst of all, Bingham had totally disregarded the protections he had given them. They had copies of his commissions issued to Browne and Daly, each of whom had proved indecently hasty in executing pledges to prove this last point. This disregard had been exemplified by the execution, under martial law, in 1588 of Euston MacDonnell, a gallowglass who had complained of the 'oppression of [Bingham's] soldiers'. They also demanded that the crown recognise the existence of a unitary chieftainship – a MacWilliamship – the only hope they had of preserving the integrity of the sept and its territory against the constant depredations of Bingham and the other members of his extended family, who were increasingly infiltrating themselves into shrievalties and crown fortifications in northern Connacht. In the face of this defiance, Bingham and the attorney of Connacht, Gerald Comerford, justified their subsequent harsh actions by alleging that the rebels were

---

[80] Fitzwilliam and council to the privy council, 30 January 1589, SP63/140/51.
[81] For the course of the rebellion, see Thomas Nolan to Bingham, 19 March 1589, SP63/143/12ii; Comerford to Fitzwilliam, 29 March 1589, SP63/143/12vi. For the value of the young earl of Clanricard to the crown in Connacht, see the letter by Nicholas Mordaunt to Fitzwilliam, 21 May 1589, SP63/144/50i which tells of Clanricard's charge on O'Rourke's men 'the bullets flying about his ears'.

sustained in their insurgency by the casuistry of a Spanish priest and some Spaniards who had evaded arrest in 1588.[82]

Significantly, in April 1589, Fitzwilliam and Bingham managed to ignore their budding differences to pursue a shared aim of discommoding O'Rourke, the most troublesome remnant of the political settlement that Sidney had forged in Connacht.[83] Bingham had long wanted him gone. Fitzwilliam, who, at the same time, was pursuing a diffuse set of aims in Ulster, granted the president a commission to attack O'Rourke and the MacWilliam Burkes. The earl of Clanricard, his hold on his territory strengthened by the composition, was impeccably loyal to the president and proved perennially willing to devote his martial resources to Bingham's designs. In a bid to justify the action, both Bingham and Fitzwilliam told Burghley the notorious story of O'Rourke's alleged desecration of an 'image of a tall woman' bearing the slogan 'QUEEN ELIZABETH', which was hacked by gallowglasses' axes, dragged behind a horse with a halter around its neck, in parody of the procedure used against traitors, and defecated upon.

Fitzwilliam and Bingham's cooperation in spreading calumny signalled an attempted détente between president and viceroy which, given northern Connacht's susceptibility to Scottish influence, may have had something to do with the crown's concern to act in parallel with James VI's moves against prominent Catholics, especially the earl of Huntly. Whereas military action against the O'Rourkes, forcing the rebarbative Sir Brian out of his lordship, may have suited Fitzwilliam's purposes in Ulster, the escalation of conflict in Mayo among the MacWilliam Burkes did not. The scale of disturbances in spring 1589 prompted Fitzwilliam to assert himself by reopening investigations into Bingham's misdemeanours in Connacht, seeking a negotiated settlement rather than a return to the president's normal bludgeoning practices. The reasons he gave were pragmatic: unless he dealt with the question of Bingham in Connacht, no peace was possible. A commission to examine the evidence against Sir

---

[82] Jones to Burghley, 13 May 1589, SP63/144/30; Report of commissioners into Connacht, 14 May 1589, SP63/144/34i. For a copy of Bingham's explanation for the execution of Euston MacDonnell, see 10 April 1589, SP63/143/17; Bingham to Fitzwilliam, 24 March 1589, SP63/143/12iii. Comerford to Bingham, 15 March 1589, SP63/143/12iv; Comerford to Fitzwilliam, 29 March 1589, SP63/143/12vi.

[83] For the embattled nature of Sidney's legacy in Connacht see the letter of endorsement that Sir Henry Harrington (Sidney's nephew) wrote for Fergus O'Farrell, whose attempt to become the leading figure in his sept 'according to the composition made in the time of Sir Henry Sidney's government' was being frustrated by allegations that he was an ally of O'Rourke's, Harrington to Walsingham, 13 February 1589, SP63/141/23; Loftus and Irish councillors to the privy council, 17 December 1589, SP63/149/41.

Richard and to pacify the province was appointed, manned by Thomas Jones, the bishop of Meath; John Garvey, the bishop of Kilmore; Sir Nicholas White, master of the rolls; Sir Robert Dillon, chief justice and Sir Thomas Lestrange: a line-up that was not only very similar to that of the initial commission that had found in favour of Donough O'Conor Sligo in 1587 but amounted to a roll-call of Bingham's opponents in the Dublin administration.[84] Fitzwilliam, himself, visited the province but disassociated himself from Sir Richard by indicating that he did not want him to publicly attend on him there – an indelible sign of official disapproval designed to undermine the viability of Bingham's continuance in office. Fitzwilliam also ordered that Bingham was to desist from using martial law until he returned to finish his viceregal circuit through Connacht.

Bingham – true to form – got Walsingham to stand for him, hence the letter which Fitzwilliam received from Whitehall which not only derided official deference to the complaints of the MacWilliam Burkes but warned the Deputy, as if he needed reminding, that the president of Connacht was 'not so weakly friended' as he might think.[85] Bishop Jones received a similar note from the principal secretary warning him: 'if you had been so wise either in divinity or policy as you would be taken to be, you might easily have considered that such loose persons as they are that broke out in Connacht could and should in no better sort be repressed than by the sword.' Walsingham added that Bingham would 'stand upright there, in spite of all your malice', finishing indignantly, 'I am sorry that a man of your profession should under the colour of justice carry yourself so maliciously'. Fitzwilliam, frustrated by Bingham's strongarm tactics, mendacity and obstructionism, denounced him to Burghley in the strongest terms imaginable: 'I fear if there be an *atheist* upon earth, [Bingham] is one, for he careth not what he doeth, nor to say anything (how untrue soever) so it may serve his turn' (my emphasis).[86]

The MacWilliam Burkes had long hoped that Fitzwilliam's accession to the lord deputyship, and the tensions that were emerging, might enable them to gain some advantage against Bingham and, as a result, *retracted* their previous signed endorsement of the president's account of the events

---

[84] Sir N. White to Burghley, 7 April 1589, SP63/143/7. For Bingham's complaints about the same see Bingham to Walsingham, 6 April 1589, SP63/143/6.

[85] Walsingham to Fitzwilliam, 8 July 1589, SP63/145/55.

[86] Fitzwilliam to Burghley, 17 December 1589, SP63/149/43. See also Fitzwilliam's commentary of October 20, 1589, SP63/147/29 *viz.*, 'this man is shameless' on Bingham's letter to Burghley of 5 October 1589, SP63/147/9 during the official investigation into Bingham's government of Connacht and his subordinates that year. Walsingham to Jones, 24 June 1589, SP63/145/21; Bingham to Walsingham, 24 June 1589, SP63/145/22.

of 1585–7, choosing to back-date their grievances to the time of his arrival in the province. Realising that they had to be as devious as their president, they made sure that their book of complaints was read into the council book on 8 November 1589, despite the strong support given to Bingham by the earl of Clanricard and most of the notables of County Galway.[87] But now the MacWilliams's long-rehearsed accusations about the execution of Thomas Roe Burke, Richard Óg Burke, Moyler and Tibbot Burke and Edmund Burke in 1586 were compounded by the inclusion of material concerning the homicidal treatment of pledges in that year, most of whom, they said, were 'infants, the eldest of them being but of the age of 14 years' who most 'devilish and Turkishly' executed while Bingham, the Bishop of Kilmore and the earl of Clanricard were at supper. Added to this were many tales about Bingham's cronies, John Browne, John Merbury and Daniel Daly, and the depredations they had exacted in contravention of the agreed composition in north Connacht. In support of their argument, the MacWilliam Burkes showed the investigators a commission composed by Bingham and despatched without the necessary countersignatures to John Browne, telling him that the 'protected' MacWilliam Burkes had broken their protections and thereby mandating him to 'levy soldiers ... prosecute ... prey, burn and spoil'.[88] The Mayo Burkes hoped that this instance of shoddy procedure which not only facilitated death and rapine but also frustrated the smooth functioning of the composition, would prove to be the undoing of the president. Yet, the Burkes' distrust for even the commissioners' *bona fides* was so great (or so they claimed) that they refused to hand this evidence over to them saying that they preferred to carry or send it directly to the queen. A copy was taken.

All in all, the Burkes argued that their insurgency was motivated by despair. No pardon or protection they could procure at whatever expense seemed to suffice in Bingham's eyes: 'The governor sought their destruction *for their goods and not their reformation*' (my italics). They could only become more amenable if Bingham was removed '[for] they thought Sir Richard a devil and all that followed him to be devils that sought to deceive Her Majesty and her people'. They were happy to work with and 'yield their obedience' to anyone other than him and his cronies.[89] In

---

[87] 'Attestation by Ulick Burke, earl of Clanricard etc', 20 October 1589, SP63/147/27.
[88] The Burkes' book of complaints, 20 November 1589, SP63/148/15; Book of matters presented by juries versus Bingham, 24 November 1589, SP63/148/20.
[89] Report of commissioners into Connacht, 14 May 1589, SP63/144/34i.

essence, they alleged, Bingham was using martial law in a slapdash way to facilitate cattle-rustling on an industrial scale throughout County Mayo. Larceny was the aim, death and destruction the inevitable by-products. The officers who assisted the president in this were either his relatives, his allies – such as the earl of Clanricard – or opportunistic captains, of both English and Gaelic-Irish extraction. Bingham, replying to allegations about his creatures, asserted that very few of the sheriffs of Connacht had received their offices through him, having been appointed by Perrot; however, all this bluster could not hide the fact that in northern Connacht members of the Bingham family featured disproportionately on the crown's pay-roll.[90]

Not that Sir Richard cared. While the commissioners tried to compile evidence for their enquiry, Bingham was spectacularly uncooperative. On their arrival in Connacht, he refused to get out of bed to see them. More significantly, wherever the commissioners were collecting material and might have needed the protection of crown troops, they found that Bingham had assigned them elsewhere. When Robert Dillon entreated Bingham's cooperation, Sir Richard tersely replied, 'I will make stay until we see what good you can do', and departed. His absolute contempt for Fitzwilliam's commission was demonstrated in Newcastle Abbey outside Galway city where the commissioners had agreed to meet the Burkes. While they were waiting, three associates of the Binghams entered the abbey, 'apparelled in women's mantles and caps, and the third in a black gown . . . challenging to themselves the names of her majesty's commissioners, one said: "I am the bishop of Meath"; another said "I am the bishop of Kilmore"; and another said, "I am Sir Robert Dillon" . . . the three . . . actors then in that disguised sort went through the streets of Galway, saying thus, "room for the queen's commissioners" . . . "reverence for the queen's commissioners".'[91] Crown government was mocking itself. Despite the commissioners' efforts and the enormity of the allegations against the president, the main dispute that arose from the enquiry centred on a matter of procedure, the question of where Bingham could receive a fair trial: Galway, Dublin or Westminster.

The lord deputy took a personal interest in the commission's attempts to shoehorn Bingham out of Connacht. He involved himself in the

---

[90] Bingham to Walsingham, 4 September 1589, SP63/146/31. See SP63/146/35ii, a roll of sheriffs and subsheriffs of Connacht divided into Perrot appointees (by far the majority), Fitzwilliam appointees and Bingham appointees.
[91] Report of commissioners into Connacht, 14 May 1589, SP63/144/34i.

investigations about Bingham's subordinates' conduct of their campaign against the Joyces and Clangibbons in Connemara, two septs that had made a show of rebellion in concert with the MacWilliam Burkes. His interrogation of Captain William Mostyn in the summer of 1589 is telling, as Mostyn was obviously so discomfited that he cobbled together a disjointed story full of elisions and omissions. According to Mostyn, Sir Richard had proclaimed both septs to be traitors and had then appointed his own brother John as 'general of the field'. What followed was the wholesale spoliation of the area by an army of 200 kern and Gaelic-Irish lightfootmen led by Mostyn, Nicholas Mordaunt, Ambrose O'Madden and that old stalwart Grene O'Molloy.

Four years later, complaints about this campaign would form a central part of Gráinne O'Malley's dossier of grievances against Bingham, because her eldest son Owen MacDonnell O'Flaherty had been a casualty. According to Mostyn's 1589 account, Owen MacDonnell O'Flaherty had been arrested for trying to entrap crown forces; he had invited them to cess themselves on his followers, who were taking refuge on a fortified island, with the aim of cutting their throats. O'Malley would later allege that Sir Richard Bingham had personally counselled Owen, a man noted for his loyalty to the crown, to retire with his followers and all their goods and chattels to that fortified island in order to avoid the fury of John Bingham's campaign. Later, in a show of typical perfidy, Owen and eighteen of his chief followers had been arrested while revelling with crown troops, invited merely to enjoy his hospitality. Grene O'Molloy had then kept Owen bound fast in a cabin, inflicting twelve deadly wounds on him. Four years earlier, Mostyn, somehow aware that things had not quite been done by the book, had accepted that the killing of civilians on the island had been unfortunate, but, he alleged, Owen's ulterior motive had necessitated stern action. Mostyn, displaying both ignorance and distaste, tried to mitigate the supposed enormities. He stated:

upon my first coming into the island I saw four or five dead bodies killed by some of the soldiers and as I heard there was a woman who swimmed to recover a boat and was strucken with a staff or a stone and so drowned by some of the soldiers. I was angry at it; but it was said, they used some resistance and were entering into boats to take [to] the sea.[92]

---

[92] 'Examination of Captain William Mostyn', SP63/145/46; 'Answer of Grace O'Malley to the articles of interrogatory', July 1593, SP63/170/63.

He claimed not to know precisely how Owen was killed; it had happened in a mêlée that broke out at night after the alarm was raised. Similarly, the death of Theobald O'Toole, a ninety-year-old, although distasteful was excusable: he had been hanged swiftly during the initial defensive action on the island, so swiftly that John Bingham's explicit command that 'the old man' be spared had come too late. Either way, the amount of wealth taken was substantial: 4,000 cows, 500 stud mares and horses and 1,000 sheep according to O'Malley. Here Mostyn's and O'Malley's accounts were in total agreement. Tellingly, the spoils were taken to Sir Richard, still ensconced just outside Galway city. He, and he alone, had the job of dividing the spoils.

The success or failure of attempts to restrain Bingham relied more on developments in Whitehall than elsewhere. One of the strangest fruits of the hostility that had built up between Fitzwilliam and the president was a brief and tremendously opportunistic reconciliation, facilitated by Walsingham, between Bingham and Perrot.[93] As Hiram Morgan has pointed out, Perrot, although back in London, at this stage had become an important influence on Irish affairs. Walsingham was consulting with him secretly and with old allies in Dublin, such as Sir Nicholas White, who were intent on using every means available to make Fitzwilliam squirm.[94] Fitzwilliam, a past master at disparagement, had already complained of how despatches from Connacht were full of 'every vain and trifling rumour ... without regard either of truth or probability', inveighing against correspondents who were 'countenanced and cherished' for no other reason than their capacity to write biased reports.[95] But Fitzwilliam's denunciation of his critics, aimed in part at Bingham's habit of running to Walsingham with advantageous gossip, innuendo and allegations, was alluding to a type of politics that had quickly become a pattern.

---

[93] For disputes about where Bingham's case could be held, see Fitzwilliam to the privy council, 2 September 1589, SP63/146/28; about the difficulties of getting people to testify against Bingham in Dublin, an evident sign of distrust for the crown, Fox to Walsingham, 24 October 1589, SP63/147/36; Merbury to Burghley, 27 September 1589, SP63/146/56, where the suggestion is made that Bingham could only find justice at a tribunal held in England; Fitzwilliam to Burghley, 24 October 1589, SP63/147/35; Statement about bias of Fitzwilliam and Irish Council against Bingham, November 1589, SP63/148/37.

[94] Waterhouse to Walsingham, 30 August 1589, SP63/146/18; Bingham to Perrot, 25 August 1589, SP63/146/14. See Fitzwilliam's outrage at Perrot's interference in Irish affairs, Fitzwilliam to Burghley, 24 October 1589, SP63/147/35. Castell to (Burghley?), 1589, SP/148/52. For the continuing feud between Castell and Bingham see the note at SP63/148/53 and Castell to Burghley, 8 July 1592, SP63/166/5.

[95] Fitzwilliam to Burghley, 29 April 1589, SP63/143/45.

Henceforth, the stories would increase in their grotesqueness. Indeed, as Morgan has shown, the political climate of the time was one where opportunism, allegation and counter-allegation, used to the greatest effect by Burghley, Fitzwilliam and Hatton, reigned supreme. Burghley, more than anyone else, set the tone. By the summer of 1589, he could not abide any favourable reports about Perrot. Fitzwilliam's predecessor was a marked man, and Bingham's hand in his attempted rehabilitation had been horribly miscalculated.[96]

Throughout all these intrigues, the situation in Mayo remained intractable. Fitzwilliam, himself facing pointed queries from Whitehall about the arbitrariness of his conduct in Monaghan, continued his persecution of Bingham and his government, although it fast became clear that his campaign against the president appeared increasingly odd to Elizabeth given that the MacWilliam Burkes appeared to be committed to rebellion.[97] Fitzwilliam had hoped that his personal presence in Connacht would inspire the disaffected to testify in bulk against their president; however, the internal political dynamic of the sept of the MacWilliam Burkes, their desire to capitalise on Bingham's apparent disgrace by gaining recognition of the integrity of their clan grouping and many of its old forms, meant that the viceroy became increasingly frustrated. They had re-established the Gaelic-Irish Brehon law jurisdiction throughout Mayo, were ostentatiously displaying their Catholic allegiances and were reinstating their chieftainship. Their stated distrust of crown government, especially their reluctance to travel to Dublin to testify against Sir Richard, effectively scotched Fitzwilliam's attempts to drive Bingham out of office. Because no witnesses appeared to uphold the material in the Commissioners' report or Burkes' book of complaints, Bingham was acquitted and his innocence publicly proclaimed. When, in January 1590, prominent figures among the MacWilliam Burkes – Edmund Burke of Cong and Marcus MacDonnell, Walter Kytagh Burke and the Blind Abbot William Burke – refused to heed a proclamation to submit to the viceroy on the twelfth of the month demanding to receive a safe-conduct which would cover not only their journey to the deputy but their departure from his presence as well, Fitzwilliam and the Irish council lost all patience with the situation and resignedly handed over charge of an offensive to

---

[96] Morgan, H., 'Extradition and treason trial of a Gaelic lord: the case of Brian O'Rourke', *The Irish Jurist*, 22 (1987), pp. 285–301.
[97] Privy Council to Fitzwilliam, 19 November 1589, SP63/148/14.

Bingham as the queen had only recently suggested.[98] Reinforcements were assigned to him in early February after which augmented crown troops in Connacht numbered over 800 foot and 300 kern. But, despite these resources being placed at Bingham's disposal, relations between the president and viceroy were not harmonious: throughout the first month of the 1590 campaign, Bingham refused to communicate with Fitzwilliam, and, indeed, the lord deputy complained to Burghley that any news available from Bingham's campaign usually reached the streets of Dublin ten days before he got any word from the president.[99] By late March, the MacWilliam Burkes and Clandonnells had submitted to Bingham, allowing him to turn his attention to young Brian O'Rourke, who was keeping up the fight in Roscommon, after his father, in a fit of false optimism, had fled in the hope of gaining sanctuary at the court of James VI of Scotland.[100]

Because of all this campaigning and the onset of a bad dose of the flux, it was as late as 6 April before Bingham got a chance to write to Walsingham at length about the campaign and his own tribulations.[101] He attempted to entertain the secretary with tales from the conflict; the impressive amounts of cattle seized, the amount of corn burned and, especially, the near-comic circumstances in which the Blind Abbot William Burke had lost his leg and died. Bingham, however, did not know that he was writing this letter to a dead man. Walsingham had died on that very day. Without knowing the futility of his actions, he sent a more detailed recapitulation of the campaign to the secretary on 21 April. Word of Walsingham's death finally reached Ireland later that week.[102]

Walsingham's death, hardly unanticipated, was a remarkable disruption to Bingham's sense of security. Over the next year, it emerged that certain of Bingham's strategic manoeuvres, especially his reconciliation

---

[98] Edward Whyte to Nicholas White, 20 October 1589, SP63/147/28; Fowle to Fitzwilliam, 4 January 1590, SP63/150/23iii.
[99] Fitzwilliam to Burghley, 28 February 1590, SP63/150/78; Note of the forces appointed for Sir Richard Bingham, SP63/150/87; 1 February, SP63/151/4.
[100] Bingham to Walsingham, 6 April 1590, SP63/151/57.
[101] For the seriousness of the 'flux' and its effect on the crown garrison in Ireland see Barnaby Googe to Cecil, 11 March 1583, SP63/100/14: 'For my own part I can very well away with the discommodity of the country saving only the deadly flux [it] being the daily extinction of our countrymen; neither spareth she any whit her own inhabitants, albeit I have heard it reported to your lordships by some of great countenance that it is only an accident to camps whych is untrue being so extreme as no physick here will help it. *I was never more afraid of my schoolmaster than I am of it* and yet I trust in God to stay it' (my italics).
[102] Fitzwilliam to the privy council, 29 April 1590, SP63/151/90.

with Perrot, had been terribly ill conceived, leaving him politically exposed.[103] Indeed, it is indicative of how Bingham was left to hang in anticipation that it was May 1591 before he could write to Burghley telling him of his relief at receiving a message which stated icily that even though 'Bingham [had] lost a friend [in Walsingham], yet should he ever find an honourable friend in him [Burghley].'[104] After Walsingham's death, Connacht's president would never regain the indemnity he had become accustomed to. In truth, Walsingham's demise had a much broader impact on metropolitan attitudes to Irish policy. Correspondence from this period, especially Burghley's, shows an increased willingness to indict the regimes imposed by martial officers throughout the country. Of course, Bingham, who had long been accused of rendering northern Connacht ungovernable, was one obvious candidate for constraint under a new, supposedly more clement, orthodoxy. This proposed scaling-back of martial rule in Ireland held a number of attractions for Fitzwilliam: first, it allowed him to roll back a layer of unwieldy personnel that he had inherited, many of whom did not warm to him or his parsimonious ways; second, the policy went hand in hand with a desire to economise by cutting garrison numbers in Ireland; third, it allowed him to ape Perrot's high-mindedness somewhat; the ever-more-common positing of a scandalous contradiction between the character of the captains' local administration and the hoped-for spirit of common-law jurisdiction in state correspondence seemed in line with his predecessor's concerns to assuage Irish-born loyalists by emphasising due process, a just composition to support an accountable garrison and on increased engagement with Gaelic-Ireland (especially Ulster) to both pacify and anglicise the kingdom. All this proved a convenient cloak for self-aggrandisement within the administration by both the viceroy and other figures, especially the council's secretary, Geoffrey Fenton. Furthermore, these concerns allowed Fitzwilliam to throw his weight around a bit more amongst his subordinates. As early as July 1589, Bingham had been privately warned by the viceroy to put aside his abuse of martial law and prioritise the use of the common-law apparatus in Connacht. Yet, for all Fitzwilliam's hatred of the crown's man in Connacht, it could not be denied that Bingham's regime was cheap. An assessment of military expenditure in Ireland made in January 1590 showed that Bingham's bruising tactics combined with the composition had brought the province to a state of self-sufficiency,

[103] Bingham to Burghley, 2 November 1591, SP63/161/5.
[104] Bingham to Burghley, 27 May, SP63/158/23.

although the fear that Bingham's conduct would spark a cataclysmic and expensive situation remained. Furthermore, Bingham's long-standing disregard of the collegiate theory that had originally animated the idea of provincial presidencies opened up opportunities for real savings. Indeed, it was mooted that the allowance made from the exchequer for the diet of the provincial president and his council could easily be abated because 'there [was] seldom any assembly of council [in Connacht], neither is there any necessity to have any other councillors than the chief justice and the attorney who [already] have large fees from her Majesty.'[105]

In what may have been a pointed gesture against Bingham's abuses in October 1591, Elizabeth, operating, more likely than not, at Burghley's prompting, deplored the predatory use of martial law by military officers, exhorting her administration in Ireland to embrace the usual civil means of local administration.[106] The president's lack of concern about the distrust for crown government in Ireland generating among Gaelic and Gaelicised lords further afield was utterly typical, but it worried the lord deputy. Bingham would return to hammer the MacWilliam Burkes once again in 1592 following their further ham-fisted attempts to garner help from Scots: at that time, a more disparaging tone was apparent in Bingham's descriptions of his prevaricating opponents. They were 'a handful of beggarly and cowardly wretches', whose desperation had led them to act less as men than 'beasts, heartless and much ashamed'. He had mortally injured the MacWilliam Burkes and devastated whatever chances they had had of achieving any worthwhile agreement with the crown from a position of local strength, creating a power vacuum that he obviously hoped would be entirely plugged by himself, his brothers and their intimates.[107]

Fitzwilliam's eye was fixed on developments in Ulster where he was attempting to harness what remained of Perrot's initiatives for the Gaelic-Irish lordships to his own purpose. Perrot had put great effort into upgrading the crown's relations with the lords of Ulster, renewing surrender and regrant arrangements with O'Reilly, Magennis and O'Donnell, forming new ones with Maguire and MacMahon. In a bid to ensure that the lords in Ulster would cease to employ Scottish mercenaries, a full-blown system of composition, modelled on Connacht's, had been

---

[105] 'Matters for good service in Ireland', January 1590, ULC Kk, 20r.
[106] ULC Kk, sig. 44v–45r.
[107] Bingham and the council of Connacht to Fitzwilliam, 2 July 1592, SP63/166/4ii. Note also Bingham's incredulity at the undue importance he believed Fitzwilliam ascribed to the MacWilliam Burkes in summer 1589, Bingham to Walsingham, 22 June 1589.

inaugurated: Ulster was shired; the office of sheriff was instituted in each lordship/county; the administration of the O'Neill lordship was divided between Turlough Luineach and Hugh, Baron of Dungannon (subsequently to be elevated to the title of earl of Tyrone); and the command of over 1,000 crown soldiers was handed over to the lords of Ulster to take up the military role previously fulfilled by Scots. However, after Perrot's revocation, the framework of government within the shires had increasingly come under strain. Under Fitzwilliam, the captains, his own appointments, often serving as sheriffs, were used to manipulate politics within the traditional lordships to disastrous effect. By early 1589, Hugh MacMahon had utterly rejected Captain Humphrey Willis's presence in his lordship, driving him and his soldiers to seek refuge in Monaghan Abbey. This repudiation of the sheriff was but a prelude to Fitzwilliam's invasion of Monaghan and forced partition of the MacMahon lordship. In Strabane, Captain Merriman, serving under Turlough Luineach, became a key opponent of the earl of Tyrone, not only facilitating the return to Ulster of Shane O'Neill's son Hugh Gavelagh but also constantly insinuating that Tyrone was intriguing with Spain. Turlough Luineach had also employed Captain Bowen obnoxiously to gain sway among the O'Donnells.[108] Two others, Hugh Mostyn and Henry Bagenal of Newry also assisted Hugh Gavelagh in his subversive campaign within the O'Neill lordship. The earl of Tyrone's summary hanging of Hugh Gavelagh by martial law, although it undercut the MacShanes's attempts to discommode him provided yet another plank on which to oppose the use of martial law *tout court* throughout the country.

Despite Bingham's apparently more intimate engagement with crown administration at the highest level, serving as a commissioner examining the case against Sir Robert Dillon, Perrot's old ally, accused of provoking O'Rourke into rebellion, he still had to field allegations about his manner of governing Connacht. Particularly problematic were the facts of his black reputation and the continued consolidation of Castlebar and Sligo as fiefdoms of his brother George, especially given the developing political situation in Tír Chonaill and Fermanagh.[109] Although Sir Hugh O'Donnell had long had a cordial enough relationship with the crown, since the late 1580s his wife Fionnuala (Iníon Dubh) had increasingly taken a pre-eminent role in the lordship, acting as a proxy for her son Red Hugh, imprisoned in Dublin, destroying possible opponents to his claim

---
[108] Morgan (1993), p. 122.
[109] 'Demands to be moved for the Queen', 20 November 1592, SP63/167/22xxi.

to the chieftainship. Once Red Hugh escaped from Dublin Castle in 1592 (through the connivance of Fitzwilliam and Tyrone), Tír Chonaill became a magnet for papal bishops. A confessionalised Catholic ideology was flourishing in north Connacht and south Donegal, and the adherents of this new alliance viewed Bingham with particular repulsion. In O'Donnell's territory, Nial O'Boyle, bishop of Raphoe, would be joined in 1592 by Edmund Magauran, archbishop of Armagh spirited into the O'Donnell lordship by Hugh Maguire; the Church in Connacht was represented by the exiled archbishop of Tuam, James O'Hely.

Donegal had long attracted disaffected refugees from Bingham's Connacht, such as Brian Óg O'Rourke; Bingham's conduct as president of Connacht had facilitated their radicalisation. His actions and those of his family, not to mention his constant insistence on unequivocal victory coupled with a reputation for brutality, had created the circumstances in which a critical mass of radicalised Gaelic and Gaelicised Irish potentates – deprived of whatever benefits they had formerly accrued from the pursuit of 'surrender and regrant' arrangements with the crown – acquired a radicalised Catholic ideology seeking to create a confederacy allied to the Spanish war effort. The experience of dealing with Bingham had, indubitably, coloured the chieftains' attitude to the presence of English-born sheriffs in Ulster, notably Captain Willis, whom Fitzwilliam unsuccessfully attempted to impose as sheriff of Donegal and who in spring 1593 was appointed sheriff of Fermanagh where he attempted to discommode Hugh Maguire in every way possible. When the garrison's presence in Ulster was augmented by Henry Bagenal's enhanced presence in post-partition Monaghan, the presence of crown troops seemed an ever more pressing threat. Tyrone found himself increasingly hemmed in by a chain of garrisons – Carrickfergus, Blackwater, Newry, Monaghan – which were not under his command. Ballymote, at that time one of George Bingham's boltholes, was, once again, burned to the ground by Brian Óg O'Rourke and Maguire's son. Maguire complained to Fitzwilliam that ever since his accession to the chieftainship of Fermanagh the Binghams had harried his country – cruel harassment on one flank which was now complemented by Henry Bagenal's trespasses on the other. Maguire initially sought and received Tyrone's protection, submitting through him to the viceroy, and asked the earl to secure from Fitzwilliam a guarantee of Bingham's future 'good demeanour' towards him, but by September he appeared to break ranks with his sponsor and raided Monaghan, thereby incurring heavy retaliation. By the end of 1593, crown forces were campaigning against Maguire and subsequently seized his Enniskillen stronghold. Over time, the extent to which the lord of Fermanagh was acting as a proxy of the earl of Tyrone increasingly changed from being a matter of speculation and rumour to one of certitude.

The story of the outbreak of war, first in Ulster and then throughout Ireland, as Morgan states, 'is one of the most complex and baffling episodes in Irish history', involving layer upon layer of machination and bluff which, thankfully, has been recounted elsewhere.[110] What is germane here is the degree to which Bingham had helped bring it all about, especially by virtue of his role in creating a situation where two predatory 'organisations' existed in the north-west, the radicalised O'Donnell lordship and the Bingham interest, which circled around each other, vying for control over the demoralised septs of north Connacht. The tension was in no way helped by the remarkable quid pro quo Bingham had secured for his final betrayal of Perrot, the benefits of which he hoped to bring to bear on the border between Connacht and Ulster. The sustained campaign of denunciation against Perrot, in which Bingham had been a belated participant, had also taken down the former viceroy's cousin, Sir Thomas Williams, the clerk of the check and muster-master and the man chosen to be his replacement proved to be a very old friend of Bingham's, indeed the ally who had first mooted him as a client to Burghley in 1573: Sir Ralph Lane.[111] Now, twenty years later, they both promoted a scheme whereby Lane, with his influence on military expenditure, would fortify and take charge of the strategic lands in the pivotal triangle of Beleek, Ballyshannon and Bundoran, which lay between Loch Erne and the west coast: in one fell swoop, menacing Maguire's territory, cutting off O'Donnell's access into northern Connacht and giving the Binghams breathing space to consolidate their control over their interests.[112] This initiative, which would have been contentious at the best of times, could only be explosive in 1593. The apparent endgame hitherto in evidence in Connacht, allowing Clanricard and Thomond safely graze while taking a predatory view of those lordships where political development was either inchoate or subject to internal dispute, seemed to be being reproduced in Ulster. Tyrone could stand as a Clanricard or Thomond, one powerful enough, one whose sept had done a deal with the crown sufficiently far enough back that he was bound to be a linchpin. After all, the crown had

---

[110] Morgan (1999), p. 139.
[111] Bingham to Burghley, 16 December 1590, SP63/156/10; Bingham to Burghley, 23 March 1590, SP63/157/49.
[112] Bingham to Burghley, 17 April 1593, SP63/169/16.

gone to such lengths over decades to ensure Hugh's succession to the earldom. Septs such as the O'Donnells, Maguires and MacMahons could look at the treatment meted out by Bingham and his sheriffs to the MacWilliams and O'Conor Sligo and form their own conclusions as to whether the pattern would be replicated in their own province, even down to the detail of being hounded by subalterns from within Gaelic society.

But if elements both in Gaelic Ulster and within the administration were already estranged from Fitzwilliam, his relations with captains already established in Ireland were also horribly strained. In 1590, a band of seventy-seven foot soldiers who had marched from Limerick to protest at the arrears on their pay had attempted to impede the viceroy's passage out of Dublin Castle.[113] On that occasion, there had been concern that the sword of state might be snatched from the hands of its ceremonial bearer, but the mutineers, their confidence undermined by Fitzwilliam's *hauteur*, submitted meekly.[114] The notorious captain Thomas Lee, a strong, if opportunistic, voice of opposition to Fitzwilliam's government outlined in his *A brief declaration of the government of Ireland* how Fitzwilliam had venally tampered with the garrison's entitlements, spurning the 'great offers of ... well known and experienced servitors ... [such as Bingham, Sir Henry Duke and Lee himself] to make choice of such base men as Conell, Fuller, and Willis, whose behaviour ... being such as a well advised captain of that kingdom would not admit into any office in his company'. As far as Lee was concerned, Willis was emblematic of all that was wrong with Fitzwilliam's ruinous engagement in Ulster politics, having

with him three hundred of the very rascals and scum of that kingdom, which did rob and spoil that people, ravish their wives and daughters, and made havoc of all; which bred such a discontentment as that the whole country was up in arms against them, so as if the earl of Tyrone had not rescued and delivered him and them out of the country, they had been all put to the sword.[115]

The irony of championing Bingham as exemplary while fastidiously denouncing the depredations of Willis and other captains might have

---

[113] Relation by George Carew, 28 May 1590, *Cal. Car MSS, 1589–1600*, p. 32.

[114] Carew later wrote to Sir Walter Ralegh that the mutiny arose from 'the unequal manner of paying the garrison, for the new companies are paid weekly to the uttermost farthing, and the old bands seldom imprested ... the late companies ... being for the most part their boys [are] better paid than themselves', Sir George Carew to Ralegh, 31 May 1590, *Cal Car MSS, 1589–1600*, p. 37. The matter of pay, specifically his refusal to bestow sterling pay, on the troops had generated particular problems.

[115] Lee, T., 'A brief declaration of the government of Ireland' in *Desiderata Curiosa Hibernica* (1772) Vol. I, p. 106.

caused others to falter, but not Lee. Fitzwilliam's ruinous appointments, he alleged, ultimately derived from his cupidity, his 'greedy desire . . . [which] made him careless of . . . those good servitors who would freely offer themselves'. Fitzwilliam was to blame for every ill to be found in Ireland, and all his opponents, Lee suggested, were, to a man, exemplary figures, no matter how strange they were as bedfellows – he praised both Tyrone and Bingham for instance. Under Fitzwilliam, the characteristic wail went up from the captains: 'What encouragement . . . can a man have to offer himself in the wars of that country, who shall neither get honour, reward, nor payment for his labour?'[116]

Of course, the kernel of Lee's plan was his offer to use his connections with O'Donnell, Maguire, O'Rourke and MacMahon to secure renewed consent for the placing of crown troops in Ulster, replacing Fitzwilliam's pets – 'men of no worth' – with disaffected captains such as William and Henry Warren, Anthony Brabazon, Nathanial Smith, Dudley Loftus, George Bourchier and Henry Duke.[117] All in all, he alleged, Fitzwilliam showed himself to be studied in his negligence, shameless in his self-aggrandisement and penny-pinching in his administration, adulterating the martial character of the garrison in Ireland by appointing 'base commanders over [troops] that deserved not the pay of one of the soldiers', 'cowardly captains . . . to bring . . . in cows to convert into angels', all at a time when resoluteness in military matters was required. For Lee, in 1594, and, as we have already seen, for Richard Beacon, Sir Richard Bingham could be readily seized upon as a supposed exemplar of all the qualities lacking in crown government in the face of the increasing mobilisation of Gaelic Ulster for conflict. Elizabeth, more and more receptive to criticism of Fitzwilliam, informed the Irish council in March 1594 that 'in case of the Deputy's sickness continuing or his death', Chief Justice Robert Gardener and Sir Richard Bingham were to be appointed as Lords Justice', which appeared to be a strategic victory for the ailing viceroy's opponents, ready to retrospectively scrutinise the conduct of Fitzwilliam's conflict should he be revoked or become indisposed.[118] There seemed to be the chance that the slide towards a full-scale war would serve Bingham's ambitions; an increasingly militarised situation required an enhanced role for a martial man, after all, but by 1595 – over a decade after hostilities

---

[116] Lee (1772), pp. 124, 136–7.
[117] Morgan, H., 'Tom Lee: posing peacemaker' in *Representing Ireland: literature and the origins of conflict, 1534–1660*, eds. B. Bradshaw, A. Hadfield, W. Maley (Cambridge, 1993), pp. 132–65.
[118] Elizabeth to Fitzwilliam and the Irish council, 14 March, 1594, SP63/173/85.

with Spain had begun – there were a number of English military commanders recently blooded on the Continent at the crown's disposal. The appointment of the forty-two-year-old Sir William Russell, formerly Leicester's lieutenant general of horse and governor of Flushing, as lord deputy, in May 1594, seemed to be a declaration of intent. Although a man with some experience of service in Ireland, Russell's viceroyalty was an indubitable disaster. Just prior to his swearing in in August, Maguire, with the assistance of Cormac MacBaron O'Neill, Tyrone' brother, won a devastating victory over George Bingham at the Ford of the Biscuits, and his quick acceptance of Tyrone's cursory submission in Dublin indicated that in spite of his martial reputation, Russell was not the finest strategic mind. The reverse was also indicative of the increasing challenge that the O'Donnells and their confederates were bringing to bear on the Binghams' hold over northern Connacht.

The startling nature of the Gaelic insurgency underlined the necessity of taking a strong military approach to the crisis. A new commander of the army was required. Sir Henry Wallop and Sir Robert Gardener suggested their old ally Bingham, but the president of Connacht, who had been so exotic and experienced in 1585, a decade later looked provincial and entrenched. He was sixty-seven. Burghley and Robert Cecil wanted their client Sir John Norris, the president of Munster, to take up the post. By this stage, Norris had quite simply become the foremost English soldier in the continuing war against Spain. Having emerged from Leicester's Low Countries expedition with his prowess vindicated, he had led the crown's attempted 1589 attack on Lisbon and, since 1593, had served as lord general of the English forces in Brittany. Archbishop Loftus, another of Bingham's supporters, objected to Norris's appointment on the basis that his undoubted 'valour and wisdom' did not quite measure up to the suitability of Bingham's muck-stained credentials. Although Norris was suitable to be used in a war against a 'mighty prince', Bingham was the 'fitter man' for 'this broken and running service': he had had experience holding the line in northern Connacht against Ulstermen and his entourage, was more plebeian than the 'many gallant gentlemen [that] usually do accompany Sir John' and would be cheaper to support. Most importantly, Loftus argued, Norris might not be as easily handled or directed as Bingham, which may be 'a great hindrance to the service'.[119] But by this stage, Norris's veteran troops were arriving in Waterford from Brittany, and Norris's appointment was a fait accompli. The fact that by

[119] Loftus to Robert Cecil, 19 March 1595, SP63/178/97.

June the confederates had not only taken Enniskillen but had also seized Sligo Castle and were overrunning Mayo and Roscommon made Sir Richard's reputation appear at a discount.

The descent of O'Donnell on Sligo in June 1595 heralded the return of fugitives to each of the lordships, ready to repay old scores. With Bingham's grip loosened, Theobald MacWalter Kittagh, a MacWilliam amenable to O'Donnell's designs, was inaugurated in Mayo in December, and loyalty to the crown within the province of Connacht was effectively confined to the territories of the earls of Clanricard and Thomond.[120] Bingham's supposed achievements were swept away, and his resulting vulnerability prompted the wonted pattern of allegations against his government to ratchet up again; on this occasion, it was Bingham's earliest opponents in Connacht, the English of Roscommon, Theobald Dillon, Anthony Brabazon and young Malby who all procured witnesses to testify against him in front of the Lord Deputy Russell in Galway during the winter of 1595. Bingham's attempts to gain leverage by appealing to both Burghley and Robert Cecil proved of limited success, and investigations into the conduct of his government were handed over to Sir John Norris and Sir Geoffrey Fenton. Norris, despite his martial profile, had been sent to Ireland to conciliate. He had good reason to think that placating the Irish was a viable strategy; he aimed not only to separate Tyrone from O'Donnell and his confederates but also to re-establish Connacht as a loyal province.

In order to achieve the latter result, he determined, with the connivance of Sir Geoffrey Fenton and the approval of his metropolitan patrons, to sacrifice Bingham: this was perhaps the only means of allowing the province to retain a sense of itself autonomous of O'Donnell's claims. Sir Richard's isolation became even more apparent in the run-up to O'Donnell's submission to the crown on 18 October 1595. In correspondence with Burghley in late September, Fenton explicitly began measuring Bingham for his winding sheet, hoping 'to stay the rage of Connacht' by allowing the 'wavering' population there another opportunity to have their grievances redressed. Bingham's hard measure, he argued, had only served to swell the numbers of the Ulster confederates' forces with well-informed guides and spies. Fenton proposed that he should initially be removed from the presidency, under colour of his relocation to service in France, the Low Countries or at sea, and a full investigation could subsequently be held into his government, an investigation

---

[120] Brabazon to Russell, 29 December 1595, SP63/186/12ii.

that would exclude Henry Wallop and Robert Gardener from its make-up because of their partiality. While Fenton scantily disguised each figure in the letter with a moniker, the names he used spoke volumes for his opinions: while he gave Norris the name 'Scipio', and Russell 'Menelaus', he called Bingham 'Improvido'. The president of Connacht was not deemed to be the intelligent or formidable opponent as he had seemed to be years before during Perrot's viceroyalty but was merely a stupid and improvident irritation to be got rid of.[121]

The charges that had been levelled before Russell and Fenton in Galway in November 1595 about Bingham's government came from a narrow group of deponents but were familiar in their import: Bingham had allegedly allowed subordinates such as John Bingley and William Fildew generous leeway in imposing themselves and their bands upon the country; his sheriffs were low-born illiterates; and he was accused of selling clemency to those willing to pay. Even Ulick Burke, brother of the earl of Clanricard, whose assassination of Captain George Bingham in Sligo Castle had caused the gaping breach in Connacht's defence against the Ulster confederates, had, allegedly, been able to purchase his enlargement. Again, the composition of the commission doing the investigating and the question of where its deliberations would take place were all important. In May, Bingham was summoned to Dublin so that his opponents in the province could come forward and testify against him. But events had got out of hand, and the rebels, setting the agenda themselves, seemed to be relatively unconcerned with this wrangling within the administration.[122] By early July, when Sir Richard was summoned by the new lord deputy William Burgh to answer complaints against his administration, it was clear that both Norris and Fenton were set on his removal. Norris, already president of Munster, had explicitly lined his own brother Henry up for Sir Richard's job, a strategy that Bingham, no stranger to nepotism, could recognise but one that seemed politically significant as it gave the Norrises control of two of Ireland's four provinces.[123] In August, the queen ordered that Bingham be tried before a commission in Athlone but mitigated the unanimous hostility of its make-up by insisting that Robert Gardener be

---

[121] Fenton to Burghley, 21 September 1595, SP63/183/44. Fenton called Wallop 'Rigido' and Gardiner 'Amoroso'.
[122] Lord deputy and council to the privy council, 16 July 1596, SP63/191/25; 'Note of divers things wherewith Sir Richard Bingham is charged', SP63/191/25i.
[123] Norris to Robert Cecil, 27 November 1595, SP63/183/89. By this time Sir John, general of the crown army, had already received authority over all military appointments, a privilege which was normally a viceregal prerogative.

appointed. On 23 August, faced with a set of conditions surrounding the trial dictated to him by Fenton, Bingham, without seeking permission, absconded to England. The initial ignominy surrounding his arrival there, his committal to the Fleet pending investigation, seems to have been a calculated risk. It is difficult to disagree with Hubert Knox's assessment that the condition Norris put down that during the trial Bingham should not reside in Athlone Castle but somewhere 5 or 6 miles outside the town was a fig leaf that barely obscured his hope, maybe even his plan, that some rebel or old enemy might pay off an old score and rid Irish government of this meddlesome captain for once and for all. Bingham, probably inured to such tricks opted for temporary disgrace in England rather than fatal exposure in the Connacht countryside.[124] Besides, the steady rise of the young earl of Essex since 1593 had restored a counterweight to the *regnum Cecilianum* at Whitehall, a development particularly apparent in matters of martial patronage. This polarisation of politics proffered opportunities to disaffected figures, increasing their chances of finding a patron willing to champion their causes. Where Essex had previously been content to allow Burghley to control Irish matters, by the second half of the 1590s, his overwhelming desire to not only be the pre-eminent patron of the military but also to prove himself the consummate politician forced him to engage ever more actively in Irish matters.

Bingham, once he was enlarged from the Fleet, entered into the factionalised environment that appertained at court and took up the role that Irish servitors had filled in the past, that of sagacious adviser. Bingham's experience provided particularly useful leverage against the Dublin administration to those who wished to use it. And the earl of Essex, who had assiduously attempted since his admission to the privy council in February 1593 to annex all aspects of military patronage to himself, found in Bingham's disgrace an instance that could serve as a powerful symbol of all that had gone wrong with Burghley's Irish policy since the appointment of Sir William Fitzwilliam. Despite his own fraught relations with the queen at the time, Essex and his creatures promoted Bingham, who increasingly stood as an emblem of martial stolidity against the flaccidity and capitulation of crown government in Ireland. This seemed never more relevant than in late August 1598 following the nadir in the crown fortunes in Ireland occasioned by Sir Henry Bagenal's defeat and death at the battle of the Yellow Ford. This unprecedented military humiliation at the hands of the Irish led to the loss of up to 2,000 crown troops, but

---

[124] 'Reasons why Richard Bingham went to England', 30 September 1596, SP63/193/51.

Bagenal's death opened up the position of marshal of the Irish army. Bingham's seamless appointment to the post by the privy council on 28 August 1598 – the day before Burghley's funeral – seemed significant.

Now seventy and in ill-health, Bingham served Essex's purposes – as he had Beacon's four years earlier – as the model of ruthless severity in the service of the crown, yet this view, particularly affecting in the earl's world of chivalric dash, hardly chimed with Bingham's career, which, although marked with examples of great cruelty, had been seen by many contemporaries as marked by indifferent service and much selfishness. His appointment as marshal, just five months before his death, was a glorious end to a long career and was portrayed as such on the cenotaph commemorating him in Westminster Abbey, erected by his servant, the reviled John Bingley. Unsurprisingly, the small square slab in the south wall of south aisle did not mention any of the official suspicion and disapproval that had consistently attached itself to him but painted a picture that corresponded with a worthy chivalric *cursus honorem:* after fighting in the Mediterranean, in France and the Netherlands, he became the governor of a province, Connacht,

where he overthrew the Irish Scots, expelled the traitor O'Rourke, suppressed diverse rebellions and that with small charges to her majesty, maintaining that province in flourishing good estate by the space of thirteen years finally, for his good service was made marshal of Ireland and general of Leinster where at Dublin, in an assured faith in Christ he ended this transitory life.[125]

The truth was, however, that Bingham had served the crown as a licensed grotesque. This was not only true administratively, but physically: Nicholas Lestrange noted that Bingham was of 'very small stature' and had occasionally been called 'dandy prat' to his chagrin.[126] And, while he probably served as the physical inspiration for Spenser's creation of Talus, the man of iron, Artegall's enforcer of justice, in Book V of the *Faerie Queene*, in truth his base cunning meant that all such attempts to idealise him, whether by Beacon, Walsingham, Essex or the 'gentle poet' strain credulity. If Spenser's Talus had resembled Bingham more, he, perhaps, would have reduced the Amazons to submission, appointed his brother as

---

[125] See Knox, *JGAS*, Vol. V, I, (1907–8), p. 27.
[126] Bingham's portrait in the National Portrait Gallery confirms L'Estrange's anecdote. Tallness was, of course, deemed a boon for military service and, of course, the adjective 'tall' was frequently used as a moral descriptor to mean the same as 'upright'. Bingham, himself, praised a Mr Prise for being 'serviceable and tall' in a letter to Walsingham. Bingham to Walsingham, 14 January 1590, SP63/150/8.

their superintendent, set up a brothel and continued piecemeal exactions at will.

Fitzwilliam pointedly called Bingham an 'atheist', a man of no conscience. That Bingham was an inveterate liar even by the mendacious standards of Anglo-Irish state correspondence in this period is beyond doubt.[127] It is impossible to know precisely when Bingham lied, but his capacity to manufacture coherent and unambiguous justifications for his appeals and arguments was consistent. The patterns established in Bingham's early career in Connacht were enduring. An unusual figure, he entered his office with little Irish experience or status (he had only recently been knighted) at a time when the province was firmly in the hands of a cartel of interests, made up at the centre of English-Irish and English and at the peripheries of aspiring Gaelic-Irish which had been establishing itself there for almost a decade; furthermore, this cartel of interests had been formed, endorsed and supported by the lord deputy and his kitchen cabinet. He did not have the same military resources as his predecessor, nor the same landed resources, nor did the crown officers already established there initially show much enthusiasm for his presence; indeed, the opposite was the case: the Malbys and their closest intimates never fully reconciled themselves to Bingham, although the English presence in Roscommon inaugurated by his predecessors remained coherent and strong and as late as 1596 tried to do for him. Despite all these handicaps, Bingham devastated opponents with impunity, including the very viceroy who had appointed him. Usually, he chose his opponents wisely. Repeated attempts to dislodge him, undertaken by the MacWilliam Burkes among others, tacitly encouraged by many prominent elements in the Dublin administration were unsuccessful – six substantial dossiers of grievances were lodged against him in 1589 alone, and repeated commissions manned by unsympathetic officials failed to manage his demise until Norris and Fenton arrived with the unalloyed intention of destroying him, even by assassination. The keystone of Bingham's initial success had been the unassailable height of Walsingham's regard for him. His military prowess not only brought him victory at Ardnaree – an invasion by foreigners after all – but ensured that he was cherished by a principal secretary whose mind was on the role that England would play in the fight for reformed religion in Europe. Ultimately, it was a reputation for Continental warfare that got him there, but it took a man with a more immediately arresting reputation – Sir John Norris – to

---

[127] Fitzwilliam to Burghley, 17 December 1589, SP63/149/43.

undermine him. Bingham's prompt response to the Spaniards who were shipwrecked on the west coast after the Armada showed that he was valuable, but, perhaps, also signalled the fixed nature of his presence there. Under Fitzwilliam's dispensation, Bingham's low cunning did not leave him, but it remained untrammelled by any grand design, other than his own advancement in northern Connacht, the assertion of his insatiable appetite for pre-eminence and the establishment of an affinity made up of family members and a collection of English, English-Irish and Gaelic-Irish swordsmen.

Many people were casualties of the rise of Sir Richard Bingham, but the damage he wreaked on the tottering legal constitution of the kingdom of Ireland was more harmful still. This is not to say that Bingham had ideological intent when he pursued the shaming of due process and the rendering ridiculous of the privileges of her majesty's subjects in Ireland. These were merely by-products of his cupidity for honour and pre-eminent power. Chinks in the Irish polity were levered open one by one by Bingham in his successive bids to gain footholds to facilitate his ascent. The commissions set up to investigate Bingham all failed to make a cast-iron case against him because of a lack of witnesses. This could be interpreted two ways: first (and most obvious), Bingham and his associates were probably past masters at intimidation, and, second, many figures in Elizabethan Connacht might have preferred to live in a venal and corrupt polity that allowed them to purchase license at will to do pretty much anything rather than suffer the rigours of a less biddable, rigid common-law based system.

Of course, preferment in Ireland was ultimately arbitrated in Whitehall, rather than from Dublin – the lack of a viceregal court allowed Walsingham to rally, in the teeth of Perrot's and Fitzwilliam's opposition, to Bingham's call but also ensured that once Walsingham died Bingham could never reclaim his wonted indemnity. He had supporters within the Dublin administration as well, and his bequest of his 'ambling grey mare' to Robert Gardener and his pistol to Henry Wallop smacks more of the allocation of keepsakes than the bestowal of serious assets.[128]

Ultimately, it did not matter what end justified the means; Bingham's conduct and wonted impunity meant that the office of lord deputy and the idea of a self-contained policy agenda for Ireland were once more objects of scorn. It is significant that the story of Bingham's rise to true possession of his office can be told without much reference to the policies

---

[128] Bingham's will, PCC PROB/11/94.

which Perrot hoped to establish through his parliament of 1585–6. Similarly, although Sir Richard had the use of the composition revenues of Clanricard and Thomond, he was not in accord with, nor had much interest in, the vision of those foremost in instituting it, those doyens of the English-Irish administrative class, White and Dillon. Indigenous loyalty was pocketed without gratitude. The 'truth' suffered as well. Whereas Nicholas Malby had been mendacious in a bid to stave off metropolitan intervention in his field of operations, Bingham, during the heyday of his dependence on Walsingham, lied to facilitate such intervention, to fabricate myths of coherence that could justify it. Malby was happy to have his lies forgotten; Bingham wanted his lies underwritten. Every court in Ireland, every tested servant of the crown, every grandee looking for encouragement to engage with crown administration, indeed the very crown administration itself, could not be confident of prevailing against Bingham, whose conscience – in so far as he had any – was merely the lawyer to his will and whose powerful protector had been for so long willing to enforce that will.

Conclusion

In so many ways, Elizabeth's constables, seneschals and presidents seemed merely to aspire after the pattern of life which had been enjoyed by fifteenth- and sixteenth-century landed gentry back home in England. In short, they sought to be lords of land and men, to attain the standing and dignity that so many of them had not been able to achieve in England because of the untimely death of their parents, the sequence in which they had been born or some other misfortune. Despite David Trim's argument that the martial officers of Elizabethan England prioritised the 'fighting [of] Jacob's wars' (the smiting of the enemies of reformed religion) above all else, each of these men were never more like Jacob than when struggling against the legacy of their own Esaus – their older brother entitled to everything – carving out their own patrimony by fair means or foul.[1] Like their exemplars in Kent, Lincolnshire and Somerset, these men on their arrival in Ireland not only acquired manors but sought through the use of ad-hoc commissions to implement law and order through judicial procedure in the monarch's name. Resembling the gentry of the 1450s *Boke of Noblesse*, Ireland's English-born seneschals, constables and provincial presidents each took pride in being 'a captain or a ruler at a session or a shire day'.[2] According to their own stated credo, their presence prevented the country, already riven by forcible entry and theft from degenerating further into faction and crime. But for all this, their presence in Ireland, initially envisaged as but a component of the English-Irish dream for a resuscitation of the medieval English colony throughout the country, developed its own momentum, mode of procedure and ideology. To call them 'practitioners of Tudor policy' in Ireland and thereby the agents of 'strategies of brutal repression' is to posit too much

---

[1] Trim (2002), p. 36.
[2] Harriss (2005), p. 168. See *The Boke of Noblesse*, ed. J. G. Nichols, Roxburghe Club (London, 1860), p. 168.

political coherence in the garrison. They could be brutal but when it came to policy, no matter what they purported to be doing, they suited themselves.[3]

At the lowest level of political interaction, these captains must have appeared to many of the Irish as but one authority among a panoply of others; the others, generally of indigenous provenance, invoked ancestral right, factional alliance or the need to promote the might and ambition of disaffected and charismatic individuals such as Shane O'Neill or Rory O'More. But, despite the claims that these other authorities could attempt to make upon the political allegiance of Irishmen and Irishwomen, they could never, in the eyes of the office-holding captains, claim parity with the authority that they themselves invoked: their actions, both venal and proper, were carried out behind the bulwark of the assertion that they were delegates of the sole imperial authority in the land, the royal *imperium*, against which there was no right to resist. This, they believed, at once raised them above the hurly-burly of Irish politics and gave them the mandate to suborn their local rivals, annex their strength and secure a monopoly on the execution of law and order that corresponded with the proper monopoly on force and arbitration that the crown was entitled to. Thus, English officers set themselves up as arbiters of local issues and disputes in Irish society competing with indigenous authorities, and sometimes other English officers. Often a group of these competitors would organise themselves as a cartel, thereby bringing a personally profitable type of stability to a region that facilitated the 'equitable' division of rents, resources and revenues amongst themselves, as well as providing recognisable channels through which the queen's subjects could petition for possible redress if they felt unduly harassed and exploited, but this was hardly the queen's law as the English-Irish lawyers of the Pale would have had it.

Rather than operate under the hegemony of English law and trial by jury, local politics, while hosting the classical English legal forms, was in reality dominated by arrangements such as that which Harpoole enjoyed with Davells. Not only did the two constables pool their military resources, they also affected to respect the property rights of each other's dependants. For instance, after Gillpatrick Mac Sheera of Bishopscourt near Kells had his garran horses stolen in September 1574, he got his brother, a tenant of Davells, to request his landlord to ask Harpoole to return them.[4]

---

[3] Edwards, D., 'Ideology and experience: Spenser's *View* and martial law in Ireland' in *Political ideology in Ireland, 1541–1641* ed. H. Morgan.
[4] 'The examination of Donnel O'Magher . . . taken the 16th of November 1574' Bodl. Carte MSS, 56/532. *Fiants* III, 6706.

Bingham's government in Connacht displayed the same self-serving devotion to venality carried out under the banner of effective crown government. Even the supposed official downgrading of martial law in the early 1590s seems to have had little impact on Bingham's local methods. As late as June 1596, it was alleged that he had given authority to each of his sheriffs to grant bail for any felony to anyone, without any requirement to bring them before a legal officer. The hazy distinction between bribes and on-the-spot fines was the order of the day. Those who could pay were pardoned. In truth, it was clemency, expensive clemency, rather than severity that was the main problem of martial-law jurisdiction as far as the crown and 'right-thinking' subjects were concerned, if such a category really existed in Elizabethan Ireland. The captains' jurisdiction had become a racket overarching a nest of local rackets, siphoning funds off their proceedings. Occasionally, political necessity demanded that the collusive doors of clemency be closed, but the fetishisation of crown authority by these déclassé Englishmen led effortlessly to the commodification of that authority and, by extension, to the constant temptation to a type of simony: the sale of the sacrament of the monarch's forgiveness to those with the deepest pockets. So, commissions equalled power, and, in Ireland, power equalled wealth. And many of these captains, especially provincial presidents, trusted in their own competence to bestow highly charged commissions, such as those of martial law, upon subordinates.[5] Their vocal identification with the monarch's honour and their solicitousness in relation to it, glorying in its glory, hurting at the slurs visited on it, became their alibi against allegations of tyranny, arbitrariness and fraudulent conduct.

As has been demonstrated, the extent of the captains' vanity about their own political importance as expressed in state correspondence was second to none. But, of course, the degree to which one can trust the paper trail they left behind them is open to question. A wide range of, by now largely inscrutable, motivations lay behind these communications. Either they used their accounts of their efforts (both violent and peaceful) as a cover for systematic venality, or, indeed, they actually did the severe, not to mention the clement, things they said they did in the spirit they said they did them, advancing the civil benefits of crown rule and government. Was their braggadocio about the severity of their government really

---

[5] For instance it was alleged that Malby had granted authority 'by his own warrant' to execute martial law to subordinates including Nicholas Mordaunt, Grene O'Molloy and Edward Mostyn, see Edward Whyte to the privy council, 12 April 1582, SP63/91/24.

sincere or was this effusiveness by times employed as a distraction to cover a pattern of lucrative clemency? It depended on each captains' different motives and aims at a particular moment in time, but mercy certainly paid. What mattered above all, even more than wealth, was the question of where delegated *imperium* and personal honour intersected. Meinecke's truism that 'Man takes a wholehearted pleasure in power itself and, through it, in himself and his heightened personality' has a particular relevance when applied to the rule of English martial men in Ireland.[6] These governors entrusted with the task of securing the well-being of the state using power, were meant, of course, to moderate their exercise of authority with the commitment to ethics and justice expected of a Christian governor. In Ireland, however, ethics and justice were at a discount from long before the advent of the captains, and, in the starker dispensation that appertained, one where systematic restraints were under-developed, power was exercised in such a way that it was impossible to know precisely how and where utilitarian and idealistic motives meshed and dovetailed or to discern where zeal for the prince's prerogative in Ireland ended and wholesale avarice began. At the end of the day, the captains' loyalty was primarily to themselves and the monarch from whom they got their power and then, and only then, to Ireland as a functioning *res publica*.

Despite this, the seneschals, constables and captains were adept at stitching themselves into the fraying tapestry of local Irish politics, but this did not mean that they in any way abandoned their reflexive belief in the cultural superiority of England and English ways and the cultural inferiority of Irish customs and the Irish. Although the instability of Irish politics provided opportunities, the way in which factionalism and theft stalked the land was obviously retrograde, a throwback to an English *status quo ante*, the horrors of the Wars of the Roses. In common with the majority of their European contemporaries, the English officers held that social systems were formative, that in a conflict of different social systems, the superior system would prevail, and that, in an Irish context, English institutions were normative.[7] But no matter how much the seneschals, constables and presidents may have abstractly disdained Gaelic-Irish customs and societal norms, most of them exhibited broad tolerance of

---

[6] Meinecke, F., *Machiavellism: the doctrine of raison d'état and its place in modern history*, trans D. Scott (New Haven, Conn., 1957), p. 4.
[7] A paraphrase of the candid description of early modern English attitudes to Irish society offered by Aidan Clarke and R. Dudley Edwards in 'Pacification, plantation, and the catholic question, 1603–23' in *NHI*, Vol. III, p. 187.

the Gaelic-Irish themselves, especially those who were not commanding traditional positions of power: that is to say, they consorted widely with déclassé, disaffected and vulnerable elements of Gaelic-Irish society. Ironically, this habit of fraternising with the Gaelic-Irish was often facilitated by the captains' easy disparagement of that culture and the formative effect it had on Irishmen and Irishwomen.[8] The impulse behind most of these alliances was generic and was a result of commonly received patterns of thought among the chivalry of Europe.

The broad cultural context in which these alliances make most sense was best enunciated by George Pettie, the author/translator of *The civill conversation of M. Stephano Guazzo* (1581). Pettie declared it to be a commonplace that 'every one will look for as much pre-eminence every way', adding that the best way a man could ensure this pre-eminence was by 'consorting with his inferiors [so that] he shall be the chief man amongst them and rule the company as he list, neither shall [he] be forced to say or do anything contrary to his mind, which liberty is seldom allowed him being amongst his equal'. 'I do with my inferior what I list and dispose with him at my pleasure, so that I find the company of my equals to be, as it were, servitude, and of my inferiors liberty.' This is what Harpoole, William Piers, Nicholas Malby and Richard Bingham, 'the captain of the churls', professed. Service as a seneschal, constable or president around the country tallied with Pettie's statement that

for the most part a gentleman maketh his abode in a village or manor whereof he is lord where he seemeth to be a king for that he is there obeyed and nothing done contrary to his pleasure. Which he shall not have in a city, where he is much less respected.

The impulses of Englishmen of gentle birth or men aspiring to the manners of those of gentle birth propelled the captains, once they had acquired their manors, usually dissolved monasteries or concealed crown lands, to gather a motley court of Art Duffs, William Begs and Shane Oges around them wherever they were stationed.[9] An elusive feeling of pre-eminence was easier to secure that way.

Curbs, however, frustrated their notions and their ambitions. Constables, seneschals and sheriffs had to accept with resignation that Elizabeth's

---

[8] Malby was alleged to have fostered his child among the Irish. See Edward Whyte to the privy council, 12 April 1582, SP63/91/24. Harpoole, as we have seen, married into the Byrne sept.
[9] Pettie, G., *The civill conversation of Mr Stephano Guazzo* (London, 1581), Vol. II, pp. 44–5. See also James (1978), pp. 2–12. It should not be assumed that these Gaelic-Irish figures felt that they were inferior to the captains.

respectful attitude towards her Irish aristocracy – the constituency most profoundly challenged by the crown officers' conceit – limited their powers of discretion and freedom of action. The annoyance that this provoked provided the context for some of the captains' shrillest outbursts in correspondence. The queen's personal interventions in Irish politics, although few, and her expressions about her preferences for her other kingdom, of course, naturally trumped their abstracted exercise of crown authority and jurisdiction. Their hostility to the native elite, especially the earl of Ormond, was, of course, inflected by anxiety about their authority and standing in society. The presence of native potentates around them, especially English-Irish and Gaelic-Irish figures with English titles, constantly frustrated the captains' attempts to secure pre-eminence in local politics. Who was Francis Cosby or, indeed, (Sir) Nicholas Malby when compared with a peer such as Ormond or, indeed, any other peer – Thomond, Clanricard, Clancar or Tyrone? For all the captains' sniping at seigneurial interests, including the, now illegal, exactions that Irish potentates had employed for centuries, the social distinction between the peerage and themselves remained. An illustration of this came in 1591. Arnold Cosby, son of Francis Cosby, was tried before Lord Justice Fleetwood and subsequently executed for stabbing and killing Baron John Burke of Castleconnell – hardly a significant figure – outside Wandsworth, inflicting twenty-five wounds in the process. In a near-contemporary account of the trial, Cosby was described as one 'Irish born' who had given 'unto the said Lord Burke sundry very base terms and unseemly words [...] as no noble gentleman would have put up at the hands of so mean a man as Arnold Cosby'.[10] Elizabeth's consistent disparagement of the practice of dubbing men in the field in Ireland shows how paltry Irish service was deemed to be.

Ireland certainly did not prove to be a centre for a Protestantised 'new' chivalry which sought to reconcile honour, wisdom and religion. By contrast, wonted lip-service to the drabbest commonplaces of Europe's traditional martial virtue and practice was the norm. Sifting through the work of Philip Sidney or Edmund Spenser for the key to the captains' attitude will always prove to be unsatisfactory. This is not to suggest that it was impossible to follow the chivalric virtues in Ireland, to display prowess as Bingham did at Ardnary, to distribute largesse as Harpoole did to Art Beg, to be frank as Fitton was to Fitzwilliam in the matter of the pardon for Thomas Roden's murderer, to be courteous as captains were

[10] *The arraignment, examination, confession and judgement of Arnold Cosby* (London, 1591).

any time they enquired after the health of Lady Walsingham, above all to be loyal to the monarch, the fount from which they got their power. Spenser's austere ideological fervour was alien to them. Similarly the highbrow enthusiasms of Philip Sidney will offer us no clear window into the minds of these men. If we seek to find a figure whose charisma seemed to find expression in the ethos of the English captains one would be forced to admit that there was something peculiarly Henrician about their touchiness and their swagger, their imperial pretensions and their wrath when they felt their righteous authority was trespassed upon.[11]

The peculiarities of Ireland facilitated this cupidity towards power. These men sorted through the studied ambiguities and ill-defined paradoxes of English political and constitutional thinking and came to adopt a view of their own delegated authority that eschewed any thing that countenanced the splitting of sovereignty or *imperium*. *Imperium*, to their mind, was discreet and autonomous, like Bodinian sovereignty, and, when delegated, it became the most precious thing of all: the guarantee of pre-eminence. This question of the seizure of delegated *imperium* and the problems surrounding it were not confined to Ireland. Francis Drake's opportunistic and arbitrary execution of Thomas Doughty, formerly his 'equal companion', during the circumnavigation of 1578 – an action accompanied by the vaunting of a supposed commission from Elizabeth giving him supreme authority over the fleet – bears the familiar signs of the personal appropriation of *imperium*. When facing down Doughty's friends who questioned his authority to take such actions before the sentence was passed, Drake cried, 'I have not [. . .] to do with you crafty lawyers, neither care I for the law, but I know what I will do.' Some accounts of Drake's action suggested that he, himself, wielded the axe that beheaded Doughty and cast the head away with a yell of 'Long live the queen of England' or 'Lo, there is an end to traitors.' His own account of the action complained that the dead man had been implicated in the 'taking away of my good name', an action which he asserted was tantamount to mutiny. Typically, the line between personal honour and crown honour was blurred.[12]

---

[11] See T. F. Mayer 'On the road to 1534: the occupation of Tournai and Henry VIII's theory of sovereignty' in Hoak (1995), p. 18–19 for a meditation on the shift between feudal and imperial ideas of sovereignty and their implications for crown officers early in Henry VIII's reign.

[12] Kelsey, H., *Sir Francis Drake: the queen's pirate* (New Haven, Conn., 1998), pp. 106–9 and Pedro de los Rios's 1580 account of the testimony of Nuño da Silva in *New light on Drake* (London, 1914), pp. 378–9. Famously Drake claimed on the day of Doughty's execution that he had left his royal commission behind him in his cabin. Kelsey plausibly assumes that no such commission

Men such as Drake, Bingham and Malby may not have been professional sophists or sophisticates – ink rarely stained their fingers and then only when they wrote their self-serving dispatches to Whitehall – but there was a coherent political vocabulary and tradition within their intellectual range. This vocabulary and tradition, which eschewed models of a mixed constitution that sought to carve *imperium* up, served them well by allowing them to place themselves above or 'aside from' that law. It allowed them to reconcile their actions with their idea of themselves in much the same way as the civic republicanism of Cecil and his circle served their own selfless and selfish ends. From 1558 to 1603, England was kingless. We know that for those mid-Tudor survivors that dominated the privy council well into the 1580s this state of affairs proved to have its advantages, offering them the opportunity 'to contemplate the world and its affairs with some independent detachment, by means of [their] own collective wisdom and with the Queen absent'.[13] Coincidentally, the government of the kingdom of Ireland, negligently ruled by the same 'absentee', was also dominated by English mid-Tudor survivors, but they were of a different stamp. They were, if anything, in a more radical state of 'independent detachment' than the office-holders in Whitehall. Although the 'absence' of the monarch in Ireland was a product of unavoidable geographical constraints, rather than gender, the result was less 'headless conciliar government' than many-headed monarchical government.

---

existed. The jury Drake convened did not find Doughty guilty of treason, but, despite this, after canvassing his crew, Drake had him executed.

[13] Collinson (1997), pp. 118–19.

Bibliography

PRIMARY SOURCES

MANUSCRIPT MATERIAL

The Public Record Office, London

SP10: State papers, Domestic, Edward VI.
SP11: State papers, Domestic, Philip and Mary.
SP12: State papers, Domestic, Elizabeth I.
SP61: State papers, Ireland, Edward VI.
SP62: State papers, Ireland, Philip and Mary.
SP63: State papers, Ireland, Elizabeth I.
Prerogative Courts of Canterbury, wills.

The British Library, London

Cotton MSS: Titus B. X, B. XI, B. XII, B. XIII.
Egerton MSS: 2642.
Lansdowne MSS, 11, 12, 25, 98.
Additional MSS, 4160, 4786, 15891, 32379, 48015, 37536.

Bodleian Library, Oxford

Carte MSS, 55, 56, 57, 58.
Perrot MSS.

Northampton Record Office

Fitzwilliam (Milton) C 92.
Fitzwilliam (Milton) I 67.

PRINTED WORKS

Printed sources, annals, contemporary or near contemporary writings

A brefe declaration of certein principall articles of religion set out by order and auc-thoritie as well of the right honorable Sir Henry Sidney knyght (Dublin, 1566).

Bibliography

A golden mirrour, conteining certain pithy and figurative visions (London, 1589).
Allen, W., *A copie of a letter (written by) W. Allen concerning the yeelding of Daventrie* (Antwerp, 1587).
Annála Rioghachta Éireann, Annals of the kingdom of Ireland by the four masters ed. J. O'Donovan, 7 vols. (Dublin, 1856).
Annals of Loch Cé, 2 vols., ed. W. Hennessy (London, 1871).
Ariosto, Ludovico, *Orlando Furioso*, 2 vols. (Milan, 1974).
Ascham, R., *English works of Roger Ascham: Toxophilus, report of the affaires and state of Germany, and The scholemaster*, ed. W. A. Wright (Cambridge, 1904).
Aubrey, J., *Aubrey's Brief Lives*, ed. O. Lawson-Dick (London, 1949).
Barston, J., *Safegarde of societie* (London, 1576).
Beacon, R., *Solon his Follie* (Oxford, 1594).
  Solon his Follie., ed. V. Carey and C. Carroll (Binghamton, NY, 1996).
Becon, T., *A new pollicy of warre* (London, 1542).
Bellay, W. de, *Instructions for the warres*, trans. P. Ive (London, 1589).
Blandie, W., *The castle or picture of pollicy* (London, 1581).
The boke of St Albans (1486) (facsimile edition, London, 1881).
Bonet, H., *The tree of battles*, ed. G. Coopland (Liverpool, 1949).
Boswell, J., *Boswell's life of Johnson*, 6 vols. (Oxford, 1934).
A brefe declaration of certein principall articles of religion set out by order and aucthoritie as well of the right honorable Sir Henry Sidney knyght (Dublin, 1566).
A briefe discoverie of Doctor Allen's seditious drifts (London, 1588).
Calendar of Border Papers, 1560–94 (Edinburgh, 1894).
Calendar of the Carew Manuscripts preserved at Lambeth, 1515–1624, 6 vols. (London, 1867–73).
Calendar of Patent Rolls, Elizabeth I to 1575, 6 vols. (London, 1939–73).
Calendar of State Papers Domestic, 1547–1603, 8 vols. (London, 1856–72).
Calendar of State Papers Foreign 1547–1603, 25 vols. (London, 1863–1956).
Calendar of Scottish State Papers
Calendar of State Papers, Ireland, 1509–1592, 4 vols. (London, 1860–85).
Calendar of State Papers, Ireland, 1571–75, ed. M. O'Dowd (London, 2000).
Calendar of State Papers: Rome, 1558–71 (London, 1916).
Calendar of State Papers: Spanish, 1485–1603, 7 vols. (London, 1862–1954).
Calendar of State Papers: Scotland, 1547–1603, 13 vols. (London, 1898–1952).
Calendar of State Papers: Venetian 1555–56 (London, 1877).
Calendar of Patent Rolls Henry VIII, Edward VI, Mary and Elizabeth, Ireland ed. J. Morrin, 2 vols. (London, 1861–2).
Camden, W., *The history of the most renowned and victorious Princess Elizabeth*, ed. W. MacCaffrey (Chicago, Ill., 1970).
Castiglione, B., *The courtyer of Count Baldessar*, trans. T. Hoby (London, 1561).
Cervantes, M. de., *Don Quijote* (New York, 1999).
Caxton, W., *The boke of the ordre of chyvalry or knyghthode* (1484) (facsimile edition, Amsterdam, 1976).
Churchyard, T., *Churchyard's chippes* (London, 1575).
  A lamentable and pitiful description of the wofull warres in Flanders (London, 1578).

Bibliography

A generall rehearsall of warres called Churchyardes choise (London, 1579).
A pleasaunte laborinth called Churchyardes chance (London, 1580).
A scourge for rebels (London, 1584).
Churchyardes Challenge (London, 1593).
A wished reformacion of wicked rebellion (London, 1598).
Cicero, *De officiis* (Cambridge, Mass., 1997).
Cicero, M. T., *Letters to Atticus*, 4 vols. (Cambridge, Mass., 1999).
Collins, A., *Letters and memorials of state – from the De Lisle and Dudley papers*, 2 vols. (London, 1746).
A complete collection of state trials, ed. T. B. Howell (London, 1816).
Correspondence of Robert Dudley, earl of Leycester during his government of the Low Countries in the years 1585 and 1586, ed. J. Bruce (London, 1844).
Correspondentie van Robert Dudley, graaf van Leycester 1585–7, ed. H. Brugmans, 3 vols. (Utrecht, 1931).
Cox, R., *Hibernia anglicana* (London, 1689).
Croft, J., 'The autobiography of Sir James Croft', ed. R. Ham, *Bulletin of the Institute of Historical Research*, vol. L, no. 121, pp. 48–57.
Cyvile and uncyvile life (London, 1579).
De l'Isle and Dudley Papers, vol. II, Historical Manuscript Commission (London, 1934).
Desiderata Curiosa Hibernica ed. J. Lodge, 2 vols. (Dublin, 1772).
Digges, L. and Digges, T., *An arithmeticall warlike treatise named Stratiotocos compendiously teaching the science of numbers as well in fractions as integers* (London, 1590).
The Digest of Justinian ed. T. Mommsen, P. Kruegar, trans. A. Watson (Pennsylvania, Pa., 1985).
Elyot, T., *The boke named the Gouvernour* (London, 1992).
Erasmus, D., 'Querela pacis' trans. B. Radice in A. H. T. Levi (ed.), *Collected works of Erasmus*, vol. 27. (Toronto, 1986).
Apophthegmes, that is to saie, prompte, quicke and sentencious saiynges [. . .] translated into Englyshe by Nicolas Udall (London, 1542).
Ferne, J., *The blazon of gentrie* (London, 1586).
Fenton, G., *A forme of Christian pollicie* (London, 1574).
Froude, J. A., *The history of England from the fall of Wolsey to the defeat of the Spanish Armada*, 12 vols. (London, 1870).
English seamen in the sixteenth century (London, 1907).
Short studies on great subjects (Oxford, 1924).
Foxe, J., *Acts and Monuments of John Foxe*, ed. J. Pratt, 7 vols. (London, 1855).
Fulbecke, W., *The parallele of conference of the civil law, the canon law and the common law of this realm of England* (London, 1601).
Gates, G., *The defence of militarie profession* (London, 1579).
'Gerrard papers: Sir William Gerrard's notes of his report on Ireland, 1577–8', ed. C. McNeill, *Analecta Hibernica*, II (Dublin, 1931).
The government of Ireland under Sir John Perrot (London, 1626).

Greville, F., *The Prose Works of Fulke Greville, Lord Brooke*, ed. J. Gouys (Oxford, 1986).
Grey de Wilton, A., *A commentary of the services and charges of Lord Grey of Wilton by his son Arthur Grey of Wilton*, ed. Grey Egerton de Malpas (-London, 1847).
Hakluyt, R., *The principall navigations, voiages and discoveries of the English nation*, 3 vols. (London, 1600).
Hall, A., *A letter sent by F.A. touching the proceedings in a private quarrel and unkindness* (London, 1576).
Hartley, T., *Proceedings in the parliaments of Elizabeth I, 1558–1581* (Leicester, 1981).
Harvey, G., *Marginalia*, ed. G. Moore-Smith (Stratford, 1913).
Works, 3 vols. (London, 1884).
Gabrielis Harveii Gratulationum Valdinensium libri quatuor Ad illustriss. Augustissimamque principem Elizabetam (London, 1578).
Haynes, S. (ed.), *A collection of state papers*, 2 vols. (London, 1740).
Herbert, W., *Croftus sive de Hibernia liber*, ed. A. Keaveney and J. Madden (Dublin, 1922).
Hooker, J., 'Life of Sir Peter Carew' in *Calendar of Carew MSS preserved at Lambeth* (London, 1867).
Parliament in Elizabethan England: John Hooker's 'Order and Usage' ed. V. Snow (New Haven, Conn., 1977).
Irish Fiants of the Tudor Sovereigns during the reigns of Henry VIII, Edward VI, Philip & Mary, and Elizabeth I., 3 vols. (Dublin, 1994).
Johnson, S., *Samuel Johnson: the major works*, ed. D. Greene (Oxford, 1984).
Lambarde, W., *Eirenarcha or the office of the justice of the peace [. . .]* (London, 1582).
William Lambarde and local government, ed. C. Read (Ithaca, NY, 1962).
Legh, G., *The accedens of armory* (London, 1568).
Letters and Papers, foreign and domestic, Henry VIII, 21 vols. and addenda (London, 1862–1932).
Liber Munerum Publicorum Hiberniae ed. Rowley Lascelles, 2 vols. (London, 1852).
Lost Lives, eds. D. McKitterick, Seamus Kelters, Brian Feeney and Chris Thornton (Edinburgh, 1999).
Luther, M., 'Whether soldiers too can be saved', in *Luther's Works*, ed. R. Schultz, vol. 46 (Philadelphia, Pa., 1967).
Machiavelli, N., *The Discourse of Livy*, trans. J. and P. Bondanella (Oxford, 1997).
L'Arte della guerra (Rome, 2001).
Machyn, H., *The diary of Henry Machyn*, ed. J. Gough Nichols (London, 1848).
Maurice, J., *Le Blason des armoiries de tout les chevaliers de l'ordre de la Toison d'Or* (La Haye, 1665).
Montaigne, M. de, *The complete essays*, ed. M. A. Screech (London, 1991).
Montluc, B. de, *The commentaries of Messire Blaise de Montluc, mareschal of France* (London, 1624).
More, T., *Utopia*, ed. E. Surtz and J. Hexter (New Haven, Conn., 1965), pp.
Moryson, R., *An exhortation to styrre all Englyshe men to the defence of theyr countreyes* (London, 1539).

New light on Drake: a collection of documents relating to his voyages of circumnavigation, 1577–1580 trans. and ed. Zelia Nuttall (Hakluyt Society, 2nd ser., 34) (London, 1914).
Newbolt, H., *Admirals all* (London, 1897).
Nicolas, N., *The memoirs of Sir Christopher Hatton* (London, 1846).
O'Sullivan Beare, P., *Historiae Catholicae Iberniae compendium* (Lisbon, 1621).
Ó hUiginn, T., *The bardic poems of Tadhg Dall Ó hUiginn*, ed. E. Knott, 2 vols. (London, 1922).
Patterson, W. B., *King James VI and I and the reunion of Christendom* (Cambridge, 1997).
Peck, F. (ed.), *Desiderata Curiosa or a collection of divers scarce and curious pieces*, 2 vols. (London, 1732–5).
Peckham, G., *A true reporte, of the late discoueries, and possession, taken in the right of the Crowne of Englande, of the new-found landes: by that valiaunt and worthye gentleman, Sir Humfrey Gilbert Knight* (London, 1583).
Pisan, Christine de, *The book of the fayttes of armes and of Chyvalrie*, trans. W. Caxton, ed. A. Byles (London, 1932).
Plutarch, *The lives of the noble Grecians and Romanes compared*, trans. T. North (London, 1579).
Polemon, J., *All the famous battels that have been fought in our age throughout the world* (London, 1579).
Proctor, J., *The historie of Wyatt's rebellion* (London, 1554).
Queen Elizabeth and her times, ed. T. Wright, 2 vols. (London, 1838).
Ralegh, W., *A report of the truth of the fight about the Iles of Acores, this last sommer betwixt the Revenge, one of her Maiesties shippes, and an Armada of the King of Spaine* (London, 1591).
Rawlinson, R., *The history of that most eminent statesman, Sir John Perrot* (London, 1728).
Relations politiques des Pays-Bas et de l'Angleterre ed. Kervyn de Lettenhove, 11 vols. (Brussels, 1882–1900).
Rich, B., *A right exelent and pleasant dialogue, betwene Mercury and an English soldier: containing his supplication to Mars* (London, 1574).
Allarme to England, foreshadowing what perils are procured where the people live without regard of Martial Law (London, 1578).
Riche his farewell to the military profession (London, 1581).
Robinson, R., *A moral methode of civile policie* (London, 1576).
A learned and true assertion of the original life, acts and death of the most valiant and renowned Prince Arthur, king of great Brittaine (London, 1582).
St German, C., 'St German's doctor and student', ed. T. Plucknett and J. Barton, *Selden society* 91 (London, 1974).
Sallust, trans. J. C. Rolfe (Cambridge, Mass. 1931).
Sidney, H., 'Memoir' in *Ulster Journal of Archaeology*, first series, 11 (1855), pp. 33–52, 85–109, 336–57; 5 (1857), pp. 299–322; 8 (1866), pp. 179–95.
A viceroy's vindication: Sir Henry Sidney's memoir of service in Ireland, 1556–78, ed. C. Brady (Cork, 2002).

Sidney, P., *Miscellaneous prose of Sir Philip Sidney*, ed. K. Duncan-Jones and J. Van Dorsten (Oxford, 1973).
Smith, T., *De republica anglorum*, ed. M. Dewar (Cambridge, 1982).
The statutes at large passed in the parliaments held in Ireland, 13 vols. (Dublin, 1786).
State papers: King Henry VIII, vol. II (London, 1834).
Staunford, W., *An exposition of the king's prerogative collected out of the great abridgement of Justice Fitzherbert* (London, 1567).
Stubbs, J., *John Stubbs' gaping gulf*, ed. L. Berry (Charlottesville, Va., 1968).
Stowe, J., *A summarie of Englyshe Chronicles* (London, 1565).
Tudor Economic Documents eds. R. H. Tawney and E. Power (London, 1935).
Ussher, J., *The whole works of most reverend James Ussher*, 17 vols. (Dublin, 1848).
The vocacyon of Johan Bale (New York, 1990).
The voyages and colonising enterprises of Sir Humphrey Gilbert, ed. D. B. Quinn, 2 vols. (London, 1940).
Wadsworth, J., *The English Spanish pilgrime* (London, 1630).
Walshe, E., *The ordre and duety of fyghting for our countrey* (London, 1545).
The Walsingham letter book or register of Ireland 1578, eds. J. Hogan and N. McNeill O'Farrell (Dublin, 1959).
The whole volume of statutes at large which at anie time heretofore have beene extant in print... (London, 1587).
William of Ockham, *Dialogus inter militem et clericum*, ed. A. Jenkins Perry (London, 1825).
Whetstone, G., *The rock of regard* (London, 1576).
  The honorable reputation of a souldier (London, 1585).
  A mirror of treue honour (London, 1585).
  The censure of a loyall subject (London, 1587).
Whitehorne, P., *The arte of warre* (London, 1560).
  Certain ways for the orderyng of souldiers in battleray (London, 1560).
  Of the Generall Captaine and of his Office (London, 1563).

SECONDARY SOURCES, BOOKS AND ARTICLES

Adams, S., 'The Dudley Clientele and the House of Commons, 1559–86' in *Parliamentary History*, vol. 8, pt 2 (1989), pp. 216–39.
  'The Dudley Clientele, 1553–1563' in G. Bernard (ed.), *The Tudor Nobility* (Manchester, 1992), pp. 241–65.
  Leicester and the court (Manchester, 2002).
  'Stanley, York and Elizabeth's Catholics', *History Today*, 37:7 (1987), pp. 45–50.
Adnitt, H., 'Thomas Churchyard' in *Transactions of the Shropshire Archaeological Society*, vol. III (1880), pp. 1–68.
Alford, S., 'Reassessing William Cecil in the 1560s' in J. Guy (ed.), *The Tudor Monarchy* (London, 1997), pp. 223–53.
  The early Elizabethan polity: William Cecil and the British succession crisis, 1558–1569 (Cambridge, 1998).

Alsop, J. D., 'Towerson, Gabriel (*bap.* 1576, *d.* 1623)', in *Oxford Dictionary of National Biography* (Oxford, 2004).
Andrews, K. R., N. Canny and P. Hair (eds.) *The westward enterprise: English activities in Ireland, the Atlantic and America* (Liverpool, 1978).
Appleby, John C., 'Towerson, William (*d.* 1584) *Oxford Dictionary of National biography* (Oxford, 2004).
Archer, I., *The pursuit of stability: social relations in Elizabethan London* (Cambridge, 1991).
Ayton, A., 'English Armies in the fourteenth century' in Anne Curry and Michael Hughes (eds.), *Arms, armies and fortifications in the Hundred Years' War* (Woodenbridge, 1999), pp. 21–33.
Bagwell, R., *Ireland under the Tudors*, 3 vols. (Dublin, 1890).
Baker, J. H., 'Bendlowes, William (1516–1584)', *Oxford Dictionary of National Biography* (Oxford, 2004).
Baldwin, R. C. D., 'Aldersey, Thomas (1521/2–1598)', *Oxford Dictionary of National Biography* (Oxford, 2004).
Barnard, T., *Cromwellian Ireland: English government and reform in Ireland 1649–1660* (Oxford, 2000).
Bayley, C. C., *War and society in Renaissance Florence: the 'De Militia' of Leonardo Bruni* (Toronto, 1961).
Beier, A., *Masterless men* (London, 1985).
'Biographical memoir: James Croft' in *The retrospective review*, vol. 15 (1827), pp. 469–98.
Bellamy, J., *The Tudor law of treason* (London, 1979).
The end of bastard feudalism (London, 1989).
Bottigheimer, K., 'The failure of the reformation in Ireland: une question bien posée', *Journal of Ecclesiastical History*, 36 (1985), pp. 196–207.
Boulton, G., *The knights of the crown* (London, 1987).
Boynton, L., *The Elizabethan militia* (London, 1967).
Braddick, M., *State formation in early modern England c. 1500–1700* (Cambridge, 2000).
Bradshaw, B., 'The opposition to the ecclesiastical legislation in the Irish reformation parliament', *Irish Historical Studies* 16 (1969), pp. 285–303.
The dissolution of the religious orders in Ireland under Henry VIII (Cambridge, 1974).
'Cromwellian reform and the origins of the Kildare rebellion', *Transactions of the Royal Historical Society*, vol. 5, no. 27 (1977): 69–93
The Irish constitutional revolution of the sixteenth century (Cambridge, 1979).
'Sword, word and strategy in the reformation of Ireland', *Historical Journal*, vol. 21 (1978), pp. 475–502.
'Edmund Spenser on justice and mercy', in Tom Dunne (ed.) *The writer as witness: Historical Studies XVI* (Cork, 1987), pp. 76–89.
'Robe and sword in the conquest of Ireland', in C. Cross, D. Loades and J. Scarisbrick (eds.), *Law and government in Tudor England* (Cambridge, 1988), pp. 139–62.

'Nationalism and historical scholarship in modern Ireland', *Irish Historical Studies*, vol. 26: 104 (1988–9), pp. 329–51. Bradshaw, B., 'Transalpine Humanism', in J. H. Burns and M. Goldie (eds.), *The Cambridge history of political thought, 1450–1700* (Cambridge, 1991), pp. 95–131.

'The English reformation and identity formation in Ireland and Wales', in B. Bradshaw and P. Roberts (eds.) *British consciousness and identity: the making of Britain 1533–1707* (Cambridge, 1998), pp. 43–111.

Bradshaw, B., and J. Morrill (eds.) *The British problem: 1534–1707* (London, 1996).

Brady, C., 'Faction and the origins of the Desmond rebellion of 1579', *Irish Historical Studies*, vol. 22: 88 (1981), pp. 289–312.

'Spenser's Irish crisis: humanism and experience in the 1590s', *Past & Present*, vol. III (1986), pp. 17–49.

'Conservative subversives: the community of the Pale and the Dublin administration, 1556–86' in P. J. Corish (ed.), *Radicals, rebels and establishments* (Belfast, 1986), pp. 11–32.

The chief governors: the rise and fall of reform government in Tudor Ireland, 1536–88 (Cambridge, 1994).

'Constructive and instrumental: the dilemma of Ireland's first new historians', in C. Brady (ed.), *Interpreting Irish history: the debate on historical revisionism* (Dublin, 1994), pp. 3–31.

Shane O'Neill (Dundalk, 1996).

'The captains' games', in T. Bartlett and K. Jeffery (eds.), *A military history of Ireland* (Cambridge, 1996), pp. 136–59.

Brigden, S., *New worlds, lost worlds: the rule of the Tudors, 1485–1603* (London, 2000).

Brooks, R., *Cassell's battlefields of Britain and Ireland* (London, 2005).

Burke, P., *The fortunes of the courtier* (Cambridge, 1995).

Bush, M., *The government policy of Protector Somerset* (London, 1975).

Caball, M., 'Faith, culture and sovereignty: Irish nationality and its development, 1558–1625', in B. Bradshaw and P. Roberts (eds.) *British consciousness and identity* (Cambridge, 1998), pp. 112–39.

Canning, J. P., 'Introduction: politics, institutions and ideas' and 'Law, sovereignty and corporation theory' in J. H. Burns *The Cambridge history of medieval political thought* (Cambridge, 1988), pp. 341–65, 454–76.

Canny, N., *The Elizabethan conquest of Ireland: a pattern established* (Hassocks, 1976).

'Why the reformation failed in Ireland: une question mal posée', *Journal of Ecclesiastical History*, vol. 30 (1979), pp. 423–49.

'Edmund Spenser and the development of Anglo-Irish identity', *The yearbook of English Studies* 13 (1983), pp. 1–19.

Kingdom and colony: Ireland in the Atlantic world (Baltimore, Md., 1988).

Making Ireland British: 1580–1641 (Oxford, 2001).

Carey, V., 'John Derricke's *Image of Irelande*, Sir Henry Sidney and the massacre of Mullaghmast, 1578', *Irish Historical Studies*, vol. 31, no. 123 (1999), pp. 305–27.

'The Irish face of Machiavelli: Richard Beacon's *Solon his Follie* and republican ideology in the conquest of Ireland', in H. Morgan (ed.), *Political ideology in Ireland, 1541–1641* (Dublin, 1999), pp. 83–109.
Chambers, A., *Granuaile: the life of times of Grace O'Malley, c. 1530–1603* (Dublin, 1981).
Cobb, R., *Police and the people: French popular protest, 1789–1820* (Oxford, 1970).
Collinson, P., *Archbishop Grindal, 1519–1583: the struggle for a reformed church* (London, 1979).
 'The monarchical republic of Queen Elizabeth I', in J. Guy (ed.), *The Tudor monarchy* (London, 1997), pp. 110–35.
 '*De republica anglorum*': *or history with the politics put back* (Cambridge, 1990).
Colvin, H. M., 'Castles and government in Tudor England', *EHR*, vol. 327 (1968) pp. 224–34.
Cooper, J. P., *Land, men and beliefs: studies in early modern history* (London, 1983).
Coss, P., *The knight in medieval England, 1000–1400* (Gloucester, 1993).
Coward, B., 'The Stanleys, Lords Stanley and earls of Derby', *Chetham Society* (1983).
Cruickshank, C., *Elizabeth's army* (Oxford, 1966).
 Henry VIII and the invasion of France (London, 1990).
Cunningham, B., 'The composition of Connaught in the lordships of Clanrickard and Thomond, 1577–1641', *Irish Historical Studies*, vol. 24:93 (1984), pp. 1–14.
Curtis, E., *A history of Ireland* (London, 1960).
Davies, C., 'England and the French War, 1557–9', in Jennifer Loach and Robert Tittler (eds), *The mid-Tudor polity 1540–1560* (London, 1980), pp. 159–85.
Day, J. F. R., 'Death be very proud: Sidney, subversion, and Elizabethan heraldic funerals', in Dale Hoak (ed.), *Tudor political culture* (Cambridge, 1995), pp. 179–203.
Duffy, E., *The voices of Morebath: reformation and rebellion in an English village* (New Haven, Conn., 2001).
Edwards, D., 'The Butler revolt of 1569', *Irish Historical Studies*, vol. 28: 111 (1992–3), pp. 228–55.
 'Beyond reform: martial law and the Tudor reconquest of Ireland', *History Ireland*, vol. 5, no. 2 (1997), pp. 16–21.
 'Ideology and experience: Spenser's *View* and martial law in Ireland', in H. Morgan (ed.), *Political ideology in Ireland, 1541–1641* (Dublin, 1999), pp. 127–57.
 'St Leger, Sir Warham (1525?–1597)', *Oxford Dictionary of National Biography* (Oxford, 2004).
Edwards, E., *Life of Ralegh*, 2 vols. (London, 1868).
Edwards, R. D., *Church and state in Tudor Ireland* (Dublin, 1934).
Ellis, S., *Reform and revival* (London, 1986).
 Tudor frontiers and noble power: the making of the British state (Oxford, 1995).
Elton, G., *The Tudor revolution in government* (Cambridge, 1953).

Reform and renewal (Cambridge, 1973).
Reform and reformation: England 1509–58 (London, 1977).
The Tudor constitution (Cambridge, 1982).
'Arthur Hall, Lord Burghley and the antiquity of Parliament', in *Studies in Tudor and Stuart politics and government*, vol. III (Cambridge, 1983), pp. 254–73.
Esler, A., *The aspiring mind of the Elizabethan younger generation* (Durham, NC, 1966).
Falls, C., *Elizabeth's Irish wars* (London, 1950).
Fissel, M. C., *English warfare, 1511–1642* (London, 2001).
Fletcher, A., 'Honour and officeholding in Elizabethan and Stuart England', in A. Fletcher and J. Stevenson (eds.), *Order and disorder in early modern England* (Cambridge, 1985), pp. 92–116.
Ford, G. A., *The Protestant reformation in Ireland, 1590–1641* (Frankfurt, 1985).
Fox, A., and J. Guy, *Reassessing the Henrician age: humanism, politics and reform* (Oxford, 1986).
Garrett, C., *The Marian exiles* (Cambridge, 1938).
Garrisson, J., *A history of sixteenth-century France, 1483–1598*, trans. R. Rex (London, 1995).
Gilmore, M., *Argument in Roman law in political thought, 1200–1600* (Cambridge, Mass. 1941).
Grafton, A., and Jardine, L., 'Studied for action: How Gabriel Harvey read his Livy', *Past & Present*, vol. 129 (1990), pp. 30–78.
Greenblatt, S., 'To fashion a gentleman: Spenser and the destruction of the Bower of Bliss', in *Renaissance Self-Fashioning: from More to Shakespeare* (Chicago, Ill., 1980), pp. 157–92.
Guy, J., *Tudor England* (Oxford, 1990).
(ed.) *The Tudor Monarchy* (London, 1997).
'The 1590s: the second reign of Elizabeth I?', in J. Guy (ed.), *The reign of Elizabeth I: court, culture and the last decade* (Cambridge, 1995), pp. 1–19.
Habakkuk, H. J., 'The market for monastic property, 1539–61' *Economic History Review*, second series, vol. 10, no. 3 (1958), pp. 362–80.
Hadfield, A., *Spenser's Irish experience: wild fruit and savage soil* (Oxford, 1997).
Hammer, P., *The polarisation of Elizabethan politics: the political career of Robert Devereux, 2nd earl of Essex, 1585–1597* (Cambridge, 1999).
Elizabeth's wars: war, government and society in Tudor England, 1544–1604 (London, 2003).
Hammerstein, H., 'The continental education of Irish students in the reign of Queen Elizabeth I', in T. D. Williams (ed.), *Historical Studies VIII* (Dublin, 1971), pp. 137–53.
Hamrock, I., *The famine in Mayo: a portrait from contemporary sources 1845–50* (Castlebar, 2004).
Harriss, G., *Shaping the nation: England, 1360–1461* (Oxford, 2005).
Hayes-McCoy, G., *Scots mercenary forces in Ireland, 1565–1603* (Dublin, 1937).
Irish battles (London, 1969).

Helgerson, R., *Forms of nationhood: the Elizabethan writing of England* (Chicago, Ill., 1992).
Hoak D. (ed.), *Tudor political culture* (Cambridge, 1995).
Hogan, J., 'Shane O'Neill comes to the court of Elizabeth I', in Séamus Pender (ed.), *Féilscribhínn Torna* (Cork, 1947), pp. 154–70.
Hudson, W. S., *The Cambridge connection and the Elizabethan settlement of 1559* (Durham, NC, 1980).
Hutton, R., *The rise and fall of merry England* (Oxford, 1994).
James, M. E., 'English politics and the concept of honour, 1485–1642', *Past & Present supplement 3* (1978).
Johnston, D., 'Richard and the submissions of Gaelic Ireland', 22:85, *Irish Historical Studies* (1980), pp. 1–20.
Kamen, H., *Philip of Spain* (New Haven, Conn., 1997).
Kaeuper, R., *Chivalry and violence in medieval Europe* (Oxford, 1999).
Keen, M., *Chivalry* (New Haven, Conn., 1984).
England in the later Middle Ages (Oxford, 1997).
Kelley, D. E., 'Elizabethan political thought', in J. G. A. Pocock (ed.), *The varieties of British political thought, 1500–1800* (Cambridge, 1993), pp. 47–79.
Kempshall, G., *The common good in late medieval political thought* (Oxford, 1999).
Kingdon, R., 'Calvinism and resistance theory, 1550–1580', in J. Burns and M. Goldie (eds.), *The Cambridge history of political thought, 1450–1700* (Cambridge, 1994), pp. 193–246.
Knafla, L. A., 'Common law and custom in Tudor England: or, "the best state of a commonwealth"', *Law, Literature and the settlement of Regimes, Proceedings of the Folger Institute Center for the History of British Political Thought*, vol. II (Washington DC, 1990), pp. 171–86.
Knecht, R. J., 'Francis I, *Defender of the Faith*', in E. W. Ives, R. J. Knecht and J. J. Scarisbrick (eds), *Wealth and power in Tudor England* (London, 1978), pp. 106–27.
Knox, H. T., *A history of the county of Mayo to the close of the sixteenth century* (Dublin, 1908).
'Sir Richard Bingham's government of Connaught', *Journal of the Galway Archaeological Society*, vol. iv (1905–76) parts 3–4, pp. 161–76, 181–97, and vol. v (1907–8) part 1, pp. 1–27
Kraye, J., 'Moral philosophy', in C. Schmitt (ed.), *The Cambridge history of Renaissance philosophy* (Cambridge, 1988), pp. 303–86.
Lander, J., *Crown and nobility, 1450–1509* (London, 1976).
Lennon, C., *The lords of Dublin in the age of Reformation* (Dublin, 1989).
Sixteenth-century Ireland: the incomplete conquest (Dublin, 1994).
Lloyd, H. A., *The Rouen Campaign, 1590–2: politics, warfare and the early modern state* (Oxford, 1973).
Loades, D., *Two Tudor conspiracies* (Cambridge, 1965).
John Dudley, duke of Northumberland (Oxford, 1996).
Loeber, R., *The geography and practice of English colonisation in Ireland from 1534 to 1609* (Athlone, 1991).

'An architectural history of Gaelic castles and settlements, 1370–1600', in P. Duffy, D. Edwards and E. Fitzpatrick (eds.), *Gaelic Ireland* (Dublin, 2001), pp. 271–314.

Luscombe, D. E. and G. R. Evans, 'The twelfth century renaissance', in J. H. Burns (ed.), *The Cambridge History of Medieval Political Thought* (Cambridge, 1988), pp. 306–38.

Lydon, J., *The making of Ireland: from ancient times to the present* (London, 1998).

MacCaffrey, W., 'The Crown and the new aristocracy', *Past and Present*, vol. 30 (1965), pp. 52–64.

The shaping of the Elizabethan regime (Princeton, NJ, 1968).

'The Newhaven Expedition', *The Historical Journal*, vol. 40, no. 1 (1997), pp. 1–21.

McCall, H. B., 'The rising in the north: a new light upon one aspect of it', *The Yorkshire Archaeological Journal*, vol. 18, pp. 74–87.

MacCarthy-Morrogh, M., *The Munster Plantation* (Oxford, 1986).

MacCormack, A., *The earldom of Desmond 1463–1583: the decline and crisis of a feudal lordship* (Dublin, 2005).

McCorristine, L., *The revolt of Silken Thomas* (Dublin, 1987).

MacCulloch, D., 'Bondsmen in Tudor England' in C. Cross, D. Loades, J. J. Scarisbrick (eds.), *Law and government under the Tudors: essays presented to Sir Geoffrey Elton on his retirement* (Cambridge, 1988), pp. 91–109.

Tudor church militant (London, 1999).

McFarlane, K. B., *The nobility of later medieval England*, ed. J. P. Cooper and J. Campbell (Oxford, 1973).

'The Wars of the Roses', in K. B. McFarlane, ed. *England in the fifteenth century* (London, 1981), pp. 231–61.

McGlynn, M., *The royal prerogative and the learning of the inns of court* (Cambridge, 2003).

McLaren, A. N., *Political culture in the reign of Elizabeth: Queen and commonwealth, 1558–85* (Cambridge, 1999).

Maley, W., 'Dialogue-wise: some notes on the Irish context of Spenser's View', *Connotations*, 6, 1 (1996): 67–77.

Mallett, M., *Mercenaries and their masters: warfare in Renaissance Italy* (London, 1974).

Mayer, T., *Thomas Starkey and the commonweal* (Cambridge, 1989).

'On the road to 1534: the occupation of Tournai and Henry VIII's theory of sovereignty', in D. Hoak (ed.), *Tudor political culture* (Cambridge, 1995), pp. 11–30.

Mercer, 'Fane, Sir Thomas (*d*. 1589)', *Oxford Dictionary of National Biography* (Oxford, 2004).

Moody, T. W., F. X. Martin and F. J. Byrne (eds.), *A new history of Ireland*, vol. III: *Early modern Ireland 1534–1691* (Oxford, 1976).

Morgan, H., 'The colonial venture of Sir Thomas Smith in Ulster, 1571–75', *Historical Journal*, vol. 28: 2 (1985), pp. 261–78.

'Extradition and treason trial of a Gaelic lord: the case of Brian O'Rourke', *The Irish Jurist*, vol. 22: 2 (1987).

Bibliography

    Tyrone's rebellion: the outbreak of the Nine Years War in Tudor Ireland (Woodbridge, 1993).
    'Tom Lee: posing peacemaker', in B. Bradshaw, A. Hadfield and W. Maley (eds.), *Representing Ireland: literature and the origins of conflict, 1534–1660* (Cambridge, 1993), pp. 132–65.
    'The fall of Sir John Perrot', in J. Guy (ed.), *The reign of Elizabeth I: court and culture in the last decade* (Cambridge, 1995), pp. 109–25.
    (ed.) *Political ideology in Ireland, 1541–1641* (Dublin, 1999).
Motley, J., *The rise of the Dutch Republic*, 3 vols. (London, 1896).
Muldrew, C., *The economy of obligation* (London, 1998).
Nolan, J., *Sir John Norreys and the Elizabethan military world* (Exeter, 1999).
O'Brien, C. (ed.), 'Feagh McHugh O'Byrne: the Wicklow Firebrand', *Journal of the Rathdrum Historical Society*, vol. I (1998).
Ó hEithir, B., *The begrudger's guide to Irish politics* (Dublin, 1986).
O'Rahilly, A., 'The massacre at Smerwick (1580)', *Cork University: Historical and Archaeological papers*, 1 (Cork, 1938).
Osborn, W., *Young Philip Sidney: 1572–77* (New Haven, Conn., 1972).
Pallares-Burke, M. L. G., *The new history: confessions and conversations* (Cambridge, 2002).
Palliser, D. M., *The age of Elizabeth: England under the late Tudors, 1547–1603* (London, 1992).
Parker, G., *The Dutch Revolt* (London, 1990).
    The grand strategy of Philip II (New Haven, Conn., 1998).
Patterson, W. B., *King James VI and I and the reunion of Christendom* (Cambridge, 1997).
Peltonen, M., *Classical humanism and republicanism in English political thought 1570–1640* (Cambridge, 1995).
Quinn, D., *Ralegh and the British empire* (London, 1947).
    The Elizabethans and the Irish (Ithaca, NY, 1966).
    England and the discovery of America, 1481–1620 (New York, 1974).
Rapple, R., 'Gilbert, Sir Humphrey (1537–1583)', *Oxford Dictionary of National Biography* (Oxford, 2004).
Read, C., *Mr Secretary Cecil and Queen Elizabeth* (London, 1965).
    Lord Burghley and Queen Elizabeth (London, 1965).
Roberts, P., 'Elizabethan players and minstrels and the legislation of 1572 against retainers and vagabonds', in A. Fletcher and P. Roberts (eds.), *Religion, culture and society in early modern Britain* (Cambridge, 1994), pp. 29–5.
Rodger, N. A. M., 'Queen Elizabeth and the myth of sea-power in English history', *Transactions of the Royal Historical Society*, sixth series, XIV, pp. 153–74.
Ronan, M. V., *The reformation in Ireland under Elizabeth* (Dublin, 1930).
Rosenberg, E., *Leicester, patron of letters* (New York, 1955).
Rowse, A. L., *The expansion of England* (London, 1955).
Royal Commission on Historical Monuments (England), *An inventory of historical monuments in the county of Dorset*, vol. III, Central Dorset, Part 2 (1970).
Russell, F. H., *The just war in the middle ages* (Cambridge, 1975).

Ryan, L. V., *Roger Ascham* (Stanford, Calif., 1963).
Said, E., *Representations of the intellectual* (London, 1994).
Salmon, J., 'Catholic resistance theory', in J. Burns and M. Goldie (eds.), *The Cambridge history of political thought, 1450–1700* (Cambridge, 1994), pp. 219–53.
Scott, J., *England's troubles: seventeenth-century English political instability in European context* (Cambridge, 2000).
Shagan, E., 'Protector Somerset and the 1549 rebellions: new sources and new perspectives', *English Historical Review*, vol. 114 (1999), pp. 34–63.
  ' "Popularity" and the 1549 rebellions revisited', *English Historical Review*, vol. 115 (2000), pp. 121–33.
Sharpe, K., and P. Lake, *Culture and politics in early Stuart England* (London, 1994).
Shaw, W., *The knights of England*, 2 vols. (London, 1906).
Simon, J., *Education in Tudor England* (Cambridge, 1966).
Simpson, R., 'Biography of Sir Thomas Stucley', in *The school of Shakespere* (London, 1878), pp. 1–139. Skinner, Q., *Foundations of modern political thought*, 2 vols. (Cambridge, 1978).
Skinner, Q., 'Political philosophy', in C. Schmitt (ed.), *The Cambridge history of Renaissance philosophy* (Cambridge, 1988), pp. 389–452.
  Reason and rhetoric in the philosophy of Hobbes (Cambridge, 1996).
Slack, P., *From reformation to improvement: public welfare in early modern England* (Oxford, 1999).
Starkey, D., *The reign of Henry VIII: personalities and politics* (London, 1985).
  'Representation through intimacy: a study in the symbolism of monarchy and court office in early-modern England', in J. Guy (ed.), *The Tudor monarchy* (London, 1997), pp. 42–77.
Strong, R., 'Queen Elizabeth and the order of the garter', in *The Tudor and Stuart Monarchy: Pageantry, painting and iconography*, 3 vols. (Woodbridge, 1995), vol. II, pp. 55–87.
Stone, L., *The crisis of the aristocracy* (Oxford, 1965).
  Family and fortune: studies in aristocratic finance in the sixteenth and seventeenth centuries (Oxford, 1973).
Thirsk, J., *The rural economy of England* (London, 1984).
Thorp, M., 'Religion and the Wyatt rebellion of 1554', *Church History*, vol. 47, no. 4 (1978), pp. 363–80.
Thomas, D., 'Leases in reversion on the crown's lands, 1558–1603', *Economical Historical Review*, vol. 30, no. 1 (1977), pp. 67–72.
Thompson, G., *Lords lieutenant in the sixteenth century* (London, 1923).
Treadwell, V., 'The Irish parliament of 1569–71', *Proceedings of the Royal Irish Academy*, 65 sect. C (1966), pp. 55–89.
  'Sir John Perrot and the Irish parliament of 1585–6', *Proceedings of the Royal Irish Academy* 85 sect. C (1985), pp. 259–308.
Trim, D., 'Gates, Geoffrey (*fl.* 1566–1580)', in *Oxford Dictionary of National Biography* (Oxford, 2004).

'Seeking a Protestant alliance and liberty of conscience on the Continent, 1558–85', in Susan Doran and Glenn Richardson (eds.), *Tudor England and its neighbours* (London, 2005), pp. 139–77.
Ullmann, W., *A history of political thought: the Middle Ages* (London 1970).
Wagner, J. A., *The Devon gentleman: the life of Sir Peter Carew* (Hull, 1998).
Ward, B. M., *The seventeenth earl of Oxford 1550–1604* (London, 1928).
Wark, K., 'Elizabethan recusancy in Cheshire', *Chetham Society* (1971).
Waugh, E., *The sword of honour trilogy* (London, 1994).
Webb, H. J., *Elizabethan military science: the books and the practice* (Madison, Wisc., 1965).
Wendel, F., *Calvin: the origins and development of his religious thought* (London, 1969).
Wood, J., *The king's army: warfare, soldiers and society during the wars of religion in France, 1562–76* (Cambridge, 1996).
Woodham Smith, C., *The reason why* (New York, 1953).
Wooding, L., *Rethinking Catholicism in Reformation England* (Oxford, 2000).
Worden, B., *The sound of virtue: Philip Sidney's* Arcadia *and Elizabethan politics* (New Haven, Conn., 1996).
Williams, P., *The council in the marches of Wales* (Cardiff, 1958).
The Tudor Regime (Oxford, 1981).
Wright, L., *Advice to a son: precepts of Lord Burghley, Sir Walter Raleigh and Francis Osborne* (Ithaca, NY, 1962).
Wyndham, K. S. H., 'Crown land and royal patronage in mid-sixteenth century England', *Journal of British Studies*, vol. 19, no. 2 (1980), pp. 18–34.

UNPUBLISHED THESES

Baldwin, G., 'The self and the state, 1580–1651' (Cambridge University, Ph.D. thesis, 1998).
Doran, S., 'The political career of Thomas Radcliffe, 3rd earl of Sussex, 1526?–1583' (University of London, Ph.D. thesis, 1975).
Leimon, M., 'Sir Francis Walsingham and the Anjou marriage plans, 1574–1581' (Cambridge University, Ph.D. thesis, 1989).
Murray, J., 'The Tudor diocese of Dublin: episcopal government, ecclesiastical politics and the enforcement of the reformation, c. 1534–1590' (University of Dublin, Ph.D. thesis, 1997).
Trim, D., 'Fighting "Jacob's warres": the employment of English and Welsh mercenaries in the European wars of religion: France and the Netherlands, 1562–1610' (University of London, Ph.D. thesis, 2002).

Index

act for the kingly title, the (33 Hen VIII, c. 1), 140–1
Affane, battle of, 212
Agard, Francis, 151, 171
Agrippa, Henry Cornelius, 68
Aguirre, Juan de, 102
Alcazar, battle of, 118
Alciatus, Andreas, 191
Aldersey, Thomas, 63
Alford, Stephen, 8
Anjou match, 89, 91, 104, 152, 153, 205
appetitive living,
   condemnation of by 'commonwealth' men, 43
   condemnation of by Erasmian humanism, 29–30
   condemnation of in Stoic moral philosophy, 27
Arnold, Nicholas, lord justice of Ireland, 108, 148, 156
Ascham, Roger, 33, 43, 46, 47–8, 53, 58
Audeley, captain, 65
Augustine, 21

Babington, Antony, 120
Bagenal, Henry, 288, 289, 296
Bagenal, Nicholas, 58, 115, 145, 156, 164, 165, 171, 255
Baker, J. H., 9
Barkley, Francis, 261
baronial rebellion,
   taming of, 31
Becon, Thomas, 38–40
Bell, Robert, 196
Bellingham, Edward, lord deputy of Ireland, 141
Bendlowes, William, 63
Bernard of Clairvaux, 21
Berwick, 49, 55, 59, 70, 71, 99, 110, 123, 149, 176
Bingham, George, 272, 288
Bingham, George, 'a cousin', 295

Bingham, John, 282
Bingham, Richard, 5, 16, 58, 106, 119, 214, 217, 250–300, 305
   an 'atheist', 298
   as 'captain of the churls', 260
Bingley, John, 295, 297
Birt, John, 267
Bodin, Jean, 198
Bohuy, George, 238
Bonet, Honoré, 21
Boulogne, 36, 46, 64, 113
Bourchier, George, 146, 292
Bowen, Captain, 288
Bowes, George, 206
Brabazon, Anthony, 292, 294
Bradshaw, Brendan, 247
Brady, Ciaran, 143, 147, 149
Braham, Humfrey, 46
   his treatment of gentility, 44
Brandon, Charles, first duke of Suffolk, 35, 36, 113
Browne, John, 260
Burchet, Peter, 206
Burgh, William, lord deputy of Ireland, 295
Burke, Edmund, 264
Burke, John (Castleconnell), 306
Burke, Richard, second earl of Clanricard, 106
Burke, Risteard an Iarainn, 214
Burke, Risteard MacOliverius, 263
Burke, Shane McHubert, 214
Burke, Thomas Roe, 263
Burke, Ulick, third earl of Clanricard, 106, 159, 192, 212, 218, 219, 228, 257
Burke, William, 178, 285
Butler, Edmund, 188, 220, 246
Butler, Thomas, tenth earl of Ormond, 101, 116, 120, 150, 172, 209, 220, 244, 256
Byrne, Edmund, 87

Calais, 48
Camden, William, 206

324

Index

Canny, Nicholas, 143
Carew, Peter, 58, 83, 164, 174, 220, 246
  as informer, 108
  his biography, 55
Carey, Henry, first Baron Hunsdon, 90, 109
Carey, John, 123
Castagna, Giambattista, future pope Urban VII, 117
Castell, George, 260, 271
Castiglione, Baldissare, 30
Caxton, William, 23–4
Cecil, Robert, 293, 294
Cecil, William, first Baron Burghley, 33, 40, 43, 46, 49, 53, 54, 55, 61, 62, 65, 99, 100, 116, 142, 152, 163, 208, 230, 248, 254, 269, 275, 293, 294
  as political actor and thinker, 6–9
  friendship with Roger Ascham, 47–8
  his antipathy to martial men, 19–20
  his importance setting the tone of Elizabeth's reign, 46–7
Cervantes, Miguel de, 95
Charles V, 35, 86, 88, 96, 113
Chatterton, Thomas, 233
Cheevers, Christopher, 186–7
Cheke, John, 33, 43, 46, 83, 108
Chester, Edward, 103
Chichester, John, 108
chivalric orders,
  Calatrava, 94, 117
  Garter, 92
  Golden Fleece, 93
  Holy Spirit, 94
  Santiago, 94
  St Michael, 93
  use of, in diplomacy, 93
'Chivalric policy', 81
chivalric virtues, 22–3
  courtoisie,
    Castiglione's treatment of, 30
  franchise, 23, 54
  largesse, 23, 34, 99
  loyauté, 87
  prouesse, 23, 34, 66, 77, 95
Chivalry,
  breach of word for advantage, 239–40
  description of, 24
  effects of fourteenth century military tactics on, 25
Christine de Pisan, 21
Church of Ireland,
  high commission and court of faculties of (1577),
  membership, 156

Churchyard, Thomas, 20, 47, 55, 86, 99, 200, 245
  justifies his martial themes, 74
  lack of confessionalisation in his works, 91–2
  on the opposition of the pen to the sword, 76
  praises caste system, 76
  praises Philip II for his *largesse*, 97
Cicero, 26, 29, 78
civic republicanism,
  education in civic virtues, 26–7
  emphasis on citizenship and *negotium*, 26
  endorsement of the idea of a civic militia,
  its expression in an English context, 37–8, 39
  Whetstone attempts compromise with traditional martial values, 78
  increasing use of vocabulary of, in Henrician England, 37–40
  intolerance of professional men at arms, 28–9
  place of martial endeavour in, 27–9
  revival of, 25–8
Clinton, Edward, eighth Baron Clinton and Saye, 49
coign and livery, 131, 134–5
Colet, John, 33, 83
Colley, Henry, 171, 235
Collier, William, 150, 241, 246
Collinson, Patrick, 6, 8
Comerford, George, 267
Comerford, Gerald, 277
Commines, Philippe de, 197–9
'commonwealth' thinking, 42–3
  disapproves of vagrancy, 43
composition, 141, 145, 167, 203, 258
Conell, captain, 291
confessionalisation, 91
Cosby, Arnold, 306
Cosby, Francis, 58, 61, 145, 171, 220, 222, 235, 306
Coss, Peter, 24
court politics, 30
Cranmer, Thomas, 37, 38
Croft, James, lord deputy of Ireland, 109–11
Cromwell, captain, 65
crown forces in Ireland,
  distribution of soldiers, 148
crown fortifications in Ireland,
  Athlone, 141, 143, 148, 269, 296
  Ballinasloe, 143
  Ballymote, 268, 289
  Blackwater, 147, 289
  Boyle, 268

crown fortifications in Ireland (*cont.*)
  Carlow, 115, 142, 145
  Carrickfergus, 100, 143, 146, 222, 224, 289
  Castlemaine, 119
  Coleraine, 147
  Derry, 87, 112, 149
  Dungarvan, 151
  Ferns, 116, 142, 151
  Fort Governor, 141
  Fort Protector, 141
  Galbally, 143
  Leighlin, 54, 115, 142
  Lismore, 119, 143
  Loughrea, 143
  Monaghan, 289
  Monasterevin, 145
  Newry, 115, 289
  Roscommon, 143, 263
  Wexford, 115
Cusack, Thomas, 115
Cyrus, 239

Dalton, Francis, 267
Daly, Daniel, 267
Daniel, John, 108
Darcy, Thomas, 40
Davells, Henry, 151, 221, 302
Toledo, Fernando Álvarez de, duke of Alva, 73
Denny, Edward, 61, 180
Deventer, 121
Devereux Walter, first earl of Essex, 103
Devereux, Robert, second earl of Essex, 296
Devereux, Walter, first earl of Essex, 143, 210, 215, 216–17, 224, 229–33, 245
Digges, Thomas, 81, 122
Dillon, Lucas, 262, 274
Dillon, Redmond, 238
Dillon, Robert, 186, 192, 260, 262, 274, 279, 281, 288
Dillon, Theobald, 260, 263, 264, 267, 269, 270, 271, 272, 294
Dillon, Thomas, 258, 260
Don John of Austria, 73, 96
Drake, Francis, 216, 307
Drury, William, lord justice of Ireland, 49, 58, 60, 70, 148, 151, 152, 163, 176, 177, 184, 194, 207, 245, 255
Dudley, Ambrose, earl of Warwick, 49, 64, 68, 101, 152, 205, 254
Dudley, John, duke of Northumberland, 36
Dudley, Robert, earl of Leicester, 62, 103, 114, 152, 153, 165, 188, 225, 254, 271
Duke, Henry, 291
Dumoulin, Charles, 191

Edinburgh, siege of, 60
Education,
  for citizenship, 27
  Gilbert's 'chivalric' curriculum, 81
  reception of humanist *cursus* in England, 32–4
Edward III, 25, 92
Edward VI, 37, 40, 60, 73
Egerton, Charles, 146
Elizabeth I, 88, 204, 215
  her dislike for the dubbing of knights in the field, 236
  her dislike of Henry Sidney, 188–9
  her views on severity, 205–7
  lack of munificence to martial men, 50, 59, 70–1, 98, 108, 235, 237
  rumour of her lack of interest in plantation, 230
  status as unmarried woman limits familiarity with martial men, 55, 125–6
Elizabethan martial men,
  ambiguous attitude to clemency, 224–9
  and lands in Ireland, 235–7
  and vengeance, 245–8
  as writers,
    stress their lack of eloquence, 64, 76
  at a discount, 105
  casualties of primogeniture, 55–7
  Cecil's patronage of, 153
  clash with Elizabeth I over use of force, 204–8
  confessionalisation of, and Ireland, 153–62
  detachment on religious matters, 84–5
  financial difficulties of, 60–4
  fraternisation with the Gaelic-Irish, 219–24
  in Ireland,
    leases and landholding, 147
  international connections of, 95–126
  Leicester's patronage of, 152
  Protestant zeal and motivation attributed to in historiography, 15–17
  trends in the historical treatment of, 10–17
  Walsingham's patronage of, 151–2, 254
Ellis, Steven, 131
Eltoftes, Edmund, 164
Elton, Geoffrey, 6
Elyot, Thomas, 30–3
England,
  unpreparedness for war, 71
English-Ireland, 128–32
  English-Irish intervention in Connacht, 261
  Palesmen,
    reform literature, 135–8
    their fetishisation of due process, 167–9
  the Pale, 130–2
enterprise of Ulster, 101, 181, 229–33, 254

Index

Erasmian humanism,
  rise of, 29–31
Erasmus, Desiderius, 29
errantry, 27, 94–5
Eustace, James, third viscount Baltinglass, 118
Eustace, Roland, second Viscount Baltinglass, 168, 240
Eyland, Henry, 268, 272

Faction in Ireland,
  mirroring English politics, 188
Fane, Francis, first earl of Westmoreland, 56
Fane, Thomas, 56
Farnese, Alexander, duke of Parma, 111
Fawkes, Guy, 124
Fenton, Edward, 205
Fenton, Geoffrey, 275, 286, 294, 295, 296, 298
Ferrault, Jean, 191
Field of Cloth of Gold, 34
Fildew, William, 295
Fitton, Edward, 153, 156, 164, 166, 172, 173, 183, 214, 229, 255
Fitzalan, William, eighteenth earl of Arundel, 49
Fitzgerald, Gerald, eleventh earl of Kildare, 115
Fitzgerald, Gerald, fourteenth earl of Desmond, 163, 175, 204, 207, 226
Fitzgerald, James Fitzmaurice, 175, 211, 212
Fitzgerald, John, 204
Fitzgerald, Thomas, tenth earl of Kildare, 240
Fitzpatrick, Barnaby, 220, 240
Fitzwilliam, William, lord deputy of Ireland, 56, 87, 99, 101, 152, 153, 157, 165, 166, 170, 174, 193, 203, 208, 209, 214, 215, 225, 232, 242, 248, 274, 275, 276, 277, 278, 291, 296
Fletcher, Anthony, 164
Flodden, battle of, 36, 39
Flower, William, 86
'flux,' the,
fortifications,
  early modern views on, 213
Fowle, Robert, 260
Foxe, John, 158
Francis I, 34, 35, 191
Frobisher, Martin, 83, 119
Fuller, Captain, 291

Gaelic Ireland, 132–5, 169–71
  freeholders within, 144
  Gaelic Irish,
    political strategy of, in relation to the crown, 229
  Gaelic Irish, submit to crown by proxy, 227
  'tanistry', 134
Gamme, Robert, 59

Gardener, Robert, 270, 272, 274, 292, 293, 295, 299
Gardiner, Stephen, 37, 56, 157
Gargrave, Thomas, 206
Garvey, John, 279
Gascoigne, George, 82
Gates, Geoffrey, 76–8
Geneva Bible, 72
Gentillet, Innocent, 197–9
Gerrard, Thomas, 119
Gerrard, William, 151, 193, 259
Gifford, Gilbert, 120
Gilbert, Humphrey, 58, 79–84, 119, 150, 180, 185, 194, 220, 238, 240
  constitutional dispute with Thomas Smith, 196–9
  finances of, 62–3
  his appropriation of the absolute prerogative, 195, 212
  his conduct as colonel in Munster, 201
  his contribution to the 1571 parliament, 195–6
  his patent as colonel in Munster, 210–11
Giles of Rome, 27
Goodman, George, 267
Googe, Barnaby, 185
Grace, John, 238
Grace, Shane, 149
Gregory XIII, pope, 117, 118
Greville, Fulke, 213
Grey, Arthur, fourteenth Baron Grey de Wilton, lord deputy of Ireland, 152, 154–5, 165, 194, 209, 212, 224, 227, 239, 244
Grey, Leonard, lord deputy of Ireland, 115, 139, 240
Grey, William, thirteenth Baron Grey de Wilton, 40, 49
Grindal, Edmund, 46
Guaras, Antonio de, 91, 102
Guerau de Spes, 101, 102, 106, 107
Guise, 88–9
Guy, John, 6

Haddon, Walter, 33, 82, 240
Hales, John, 41
Hall, Arthur, 207
Hammer, Paul, 14, 49
Harpoole, Robert, 145, 221, 222, 242, 255, 302, 305
Harrington, Henry, 146, 166, 223, 226, 238
Harriss, Gerald, 25
Harvey, Gabriel, 73, 82, 83, 240
Hatton, Christopher, 90, 99, 206, 284
  interest in martial matters, 69
Hawkins, John, 206

Hawkwood, John, 28
Hayes, Edward, 83
Henrician era,
  a golden age for English chivalry, 20, 34–7
Henry II, 87, 93, 95, 96, 98, 113
Henry III, 104
Henry VIII, 53, 88, 239
  appropriation of heraldic jurisdiction, 35
  champion of both chivalric ethos and
    Christian humanist ethos, 55, 84
Herbert, William, first earl of Pembroke,
    49, 114
Herle, William, 102, 105, 106, 238
Hill, Christopher, 12
Hoak, Dale, 6
Holinshed, Raphael, 81
Honour,
  impact of personal disgrace, 3–5, 54
  local reputation boosted by martial
    service, 66
  monarchical/state honour,
    clemency a threat to, 224–9
    development of in Henrician era, 35–6
    identification of captains in Ireland with,
      208–12
  individual defence of by way of duel, 87–8
  siege warfare and, 212–17
  the Irish context, 210
Hooker, John, 52, 54, 81, 83, 186
Howard, Charles, second baron Howard of
  Effingham, 90
Howard, Henry, 68, 91
Howard, Henry, earl of Surrey, 37
Howard, Thomas, fourth duke of Norfolk, 102,
  110, 188
Howard, Thomas, third duke of Norfolk, 35, 36,
  49, 138, 239
Hungerford, captain, 248

illegitimacy, 57
Imperium, 85
  absolutist tendencies of the Tudor
    monarchy, 190
  appropriation of, 195
  delegation of, 163–4, 189
  Henry VIII maximises the scope of his, 34–5
  merum imperium,
    as the power of the sword, 175, 182
    delegation of, 191–3
  proposal to cede it to the Irish peerage, 181
  royal prerogative,
    extent of, 196–9
  royal prerogative,
    absolute and ordinary, 195, 197
  viceroy of Ireland as *pro-rex*, 189, 192

Ireland,
  crown policy in, 203–4
  crown policy in,
    lukewarm view of plantation, 234
    reservations about martial law, 240–3
    fear that crown might lose, 209
Isidore of Seville, 21

James VI, 123
James, M. E., 20, 239
John of Salisbury, 21
Jones, Thomas, 272, 274, 279

Kavanaghs, 116, 119, 128, 141, 142, 187, 244
Keatings, 222
Keen, Maurice, 24
Kelley, Donald, 9
Kinsale, battle of, 212
Knighthood,
  idea that knights should be governors, 23
  its changing status in English society, 24–5
  source of social stability, 24
  theories about its provenance, 20–4
Knollys, Francis, 46
Knox, H. T., 252, 296

Lane, Ralph, 254, 290
Latimer, Hugh, 33
Laudabiliter, 127
leases in reversion, gifts of, 59
Lee, Thomas, 291, 292
Leimon, Mitchell, 151, 152, 252, 254
Leith, siege of, 49, 110
Lestrange, Nicholas, 297
Lestrange, Thomas, 271, 279
lex digna, 197, 199
Lincolnshire rebellion, 36
Livy, Titus, 28, 199
Loftus, Adam, 119, 151, 262, 272, 293
Loftus, Dudley, 292
Louis XI, 197
Lull, Raymond, 22, 76

mac an iarlas, 106, 159–60, 179, 192, 212, 218,
  227, 228, 238, 257
Mac Murrough, Joan, 242
MacCarthy, Donal, first earl of Clancar, 176,
  211, 235
MacCostello, Edmund, 267
MacCostello, William MacPiers, 268
MacDonnell, Alastair, 265
MacDonnell, Donal Gorm, 265
MacDonnell, Euston, 277
MacDonnell, Sorley Boy, 216, 231, 245
McFarlane, K. B., 37

Index

Machiavelli, Niccolò, 38, 76, 83, 85, 180, 213, 240, 250
   his belief that England was organised militarily along republican lines, 37
   reception of idea of *virtù* in England, 84
Mackworth, Humphrey, 244
MacMahon, Hugh, 288
MacVicar, Donal, 149
MacWilliam Burkes, 137, 160, 214, 217, 238, 257, 264, 265, 272, 277, 278, 279, 282, 284, 287, 298
Magauran, Edmund, 289
Magna Carta, 187
Maguire, Hugh, 289
Malby, Henry, 262
Malby, John, 86, 94, 95, 245
Malby, Nicholas, 5, 86, 94, 119, 144, 147, 148, 158–61, 163, 165, 171, 178–9, 183, 185, 204, 207, 212, 214, 215, 218–19, 223, 227, 237, 245, 246, 255, 305
   Gaelic Irish assessment of, 96
   his wife Tamsin, 105, 261
   international career and its implications, 100–6
Malory, Melchisidech, 207
Malory, Thomas, 23
Malta, siege of, 96
Mappowder, Richard, 267
Marlowe, Christopher, 84
martial career,
   benefits of, 58
martial law, 146, 169, 171, 178, 182, 184, 185, 186, 195, 202, 206, 210, 215, 221, 231, 240, 241, 242, 244, 245, 247, 248, 264, 277, 279, 281, 286, 287, 288, 302, 303, 317
   captains erect protection rackets using, 240–3
   commissions of, 142
   plea to its jurisdiction, 186–7
martial men,
   and plain speech, 64, 76
   courtiers mimic, 73
   disparagement of by Henrician and Edwardian reform party, 40
   incompatibility with commonwealth, 28, 45–6
   instruments of God's judgement, 65
   pursuits in peacetime, 81
   skills required to be a good officer, 67
   their vices, 28, 65, 77, 78
martial profession,
   biblical endorsement of, 72
   opportunities for upward mobility, at the French court, 52, 58
   pre-eminence of, 70, 76, 77
   unchristian nature of, 29
Mary I, 43, 48, 86, 215
Mary, queen of Scots, 40, 102, 176, 276
Masterson, Thomas, 116, 145, 244, 255
Medley, William, 62
Melanchthon, Philip, 33
mentalities, 2, 18
Merriman, Nicholas, 288
Michiel, Giovanni, 108
Mildmay, William, 103
military expenditure,
   Elizabeth I's 1558–63, 50
mobilisation of troops,
   occasion for financial oppression by princes, 65, 197
mobilisation of troops in England,
   corruption in practice, 67
   development of, 38
   preserves social conservatism, 66
monarchical republic, 6, 8, 10
Montaigne, Michel de, 215, 237, 248
Montmorency, Philip de, count of Horne, 90
Moore, Edward, 146, 222
Mordaunt, Nicholas, 161, 260, 282
More, Thomas, 29
Morgan, Hiram, 99, 284, 290
Morison, Richard, 38–40, 46
Mostyn, William, 282
Mostyn, Hugh, 288

Newhaven, 49, 64, 96, 101, 152
Nicholls, Kenneth, 133
Nobility,
   difference between Aristotelian and Ciceronian definitions of, 26, 31
Norris, John, 120, 148, 152, 216, 269, 293, 294, 295, 298
Northern Rebellion of 1569, 50, 161
Nugent, William, 155, 160

O'Boyle, Nial, 289
O'Brien, Conor, third earl of Thomond, 173
O'Brien, Donnchadh, fourth earl of Thomond, 257
O'Brien, Turlough, 178
O'Byrne, Fiach MacHugh, 119, 223
O'Byrne, Hugh MacShane, 225
O'Byrne, Owen Dowlagh, 221
O'Carroll, William, 177, 220
O'Conor Sligo, Donal, 273
O'Conor Sligo, Donough, 274, 279
O'Conor, Brian, 233
O'Conor, Rory, 141

O'Dempsey, Owen MacHugh, 220, 240
O'Donnell, 'Red' Hugh, 17, 289
O'Flaherty, Murrough Ne Doe, 257
O'Hanlon's country, 233
O'Hely, James, 289
O'Madden, Ambrose, 282
O'Malley, Gráinne, 282
O'Meagher, Donal, 222
O'Molloy, Greene, 267, 282
O'More, Giollaphadraig, 141, 233
O'More, Lysagh MacKedagh, 149
O'More, Rory, 223, 238, 241
O'Neill, Brian MacPhelim, 224, 229–33
O'Neill, Cormac MacBaron, 293
O'Neill, Hugh Gavelagh, 288
O'Neill, Hugh, second earl of Tyrone, 17, 288, 290, 291, 293, 294, 306
O'Neill, Shane, 112, 115, 151, 157, 208, 212, 238, 288
O'Neill, Turlough Luineach, 150, 209, 213, 224, 231, 288
O'Rourke, Brian, 160, 173, 257, 278
O'Rourke, Brian Óg, 289
O'Toole, Phelim, 227
O'Toole, Theobald, 283

Panderus, 136–8
pardons,
    as used in Ireland, 218–19
    benefit of clergy in Ireland, 217
    Irish exploit them to gain political advantage, 229
    lucrative use of by captains, 240–3
    Malby's use of, 228
    theory of, 217–18
Parker, lieutenant, 248
Parker, Matthew, 153
Paul IV, pope, 107
Pavia, battle of, 53
Peckham, Henry, 108
Pelham, William, lord justice of Ireland, 3–5, 49, 58, 61, 62, 118, 148, 152, 159, 164, 165, 193, 194, 204, 207, 208, 209, 255
Peltonen, Markku, 8, 250
Perrot, John, lord deputy of Ireland, 58, 99, 107, 108, 147, 150, 157, 164, 174, 175, 181, 192, 212, 213, 216, 247, 258, 262, 263, 264, 265, 266, 268, 270, 271, 274, 276, 281, 286, 287, 290, 295, 300
    attempted reconciliation with Bingham, 283
    unpopularity of, 262
Peryam, William, 186
Petrarch, Francesco, 28
Pettie, George, 305

Philip II, 43, 48, 87, 96, 99, 106, 118, 122
Piers, William, 100, 146, 150, 171, 224, 305
Pilgrimage of Grace, 35
Pinkie Cleugh, battle of, 40, 88, 142
Plunkett, James, 186
Plutarch, 27, 83
Pollard, John, 108
postglossators, 21, 26
pre-eminence, 22, 25, 27, 29, 32, 47, 84, 164–7, 187, 202
    accommodation with bid for civic glory, 78
    assertion of, celebrated by Elizabethan martial men, 79–84
    English martial men vie for, 48
    importance of *imperium* in bids for, 85
    innate urge to assert, 75
    privy council, 9, 31, 33, 36, 54, 60, 102, 110, 111, 122, 146, 148, 156, 159, 161, 163, 166, 176, 196, 208, 209, 210, 214, 224, 228, 234, 236, 245, 246, 259, 271, 272, 275, 277, 278, 283, 284, 285, 295, 296, 303, 305, 308
provincial presidencies, 143, 173, 174, 187, 287
    and extension of English law, 172–9
    presidents and pre-eminence, 305
    presidents as delegates, 171, 191
    presidents' commissions, 169, 180
    presidents described as 'monarchs', 181
Pypho, Robert, 146

Quinn, D. B., 12
Quintilian, 26, 84

Radcliffe, Henry, 146
Radcliffe, Thomas, third earl of Sussex and lord lieutenant of Ireland, 50, 91, 141, 152, 184, 205, 234
Radcliffe, Thomas, third earl of Sussex and lord lieutenant of Ireland, 49
Ralegh, Walter, 83, 238
Randolph, Edward, 16, 49, 56, 58, 62, 65, 110, 111–12
Randolph, Thomas, 56, 99
Rathlin island,
    massacre on, 216–17, 246
Read, Conyers, 7
reduction of Leinster, 141
Rich, Barnaby, 51–2, 55
    works complaining about plight of martial men, 63–73
Ridley, Nicholas, 33
Ridolfi, Robert, 102
Robinson, Richard, 239
Rokeby, Ralph, 172

Index 331

Rowse, A. L., 13
Russell, Francis, second earl of Bedford, 49
Russell, William, lord deputy of Ireland, 78, 244, 293, 294, 295

St John's College, Cambridge, 46
St Leger, Anthony, lord deputy of Ireland, 139
St Leger, Warham, 146, 164, 235, 239, 255
St Quentin, battle of, 48, 88, 110
Sallust, 45, 64
Scotland, 36
Scots in Ulster, 209, 212, 216–17
Seagrave, Stephen, 270
Sebastian, king of Portugal, 118
seneschals, 171, 225
  and pre-eminence, 305
  as delegates, 188, 193
  desire to phase out, 242
  profile in local politics, 301
  their commissions, 142, 169, 180
Seymour, Edward, duke of Somerset, 36, 37, 213
  his policies, 40–1
Seyssels, Claude de, 191
Sforza, Francesco, 28
Shakespeare, William, 17
shiring, 256
Shute, John, 49
Sidney, Henry, lord deputy of Ireland, 100, 101, 105, 144, 149, 150, 165, 167, 172, 193, 203, 208, 218, 261, 262
  alleged Spanish intrigue, 104
  Caesarean posturing of, 189
  disapproval of plantations, 234
  religious policy of, 153
Sidney, Philip, 2–3, 61, 122, 180, 188, 213
Simms, Katharine, 132
Skeffington, William, lord deputy of Ireland, 138
Skinner, Quentin, 9
Slack, Paul, 41
Smerwick, 154, 155, 245
Smith Jr, Thomas, 82, 143, 240, 245
Smith, Nathanial, 292
Smith, Thomas, 7, 9, 31, 33, 41, 48, 53, 82, 143, 180, 181, 196, 240
Spenser, Edmund, 247, 297
Stafford, Thomas, 215
Stanley, Edward, 244
Stanley, Edward, third earl of Derby, 118
Stanley, Ferdinando, fifth earl of Derby, 125
Stanley, Rowland, 122
Stanley, William, 99, 118–25, 236, 237, 277
Star Chamber, 31
Starkey, Thomas, 32
Strelley, Philip, 59

Strongbow and first English invaders of Ireland, 127
Stukeley, Thomas, 61, 75, 84, 113–18
surrender and regrant, 141

Talbot, George, fourth earl of Shrewsbury, 35
'tanistry', 144
Taxis, Juan Baptista de, 122
Thirsk, Joan, 55
Throckmorton, Nicholas, 46
Tournai, 35, 39, 64
tower houses, 212–14
Towerson, William, 63
Tremayne, Edmund, 54, 174
tripartite social stratification, 22, 75
  Erasmian humanism's opposition to, 30
Tudor political thinking,
  historiography of, 5–10

Vaughan, Cuthbert, 49, 65
Vere, Edward de, seventeenth earl of Oxford, 73, 76
violence,
  ambivalent views of in history writing, 13–14
  as used by captains in Ireland, 201–49
  difficulties writing historically about, 201–3
  exemplary violence, 239
  indispensable for maintenance of social stability, 24, 32, 76
  revenge as motive, 245–8

Wadsworth, James, 124
Wallop, Henry, 119, 152, 166, 205, 223, 226–7, 262, 269, 272, 293, 295
Walsh, Nicholas, 274
Walsingham, Francis, 3, 83, 100, 103, 111, 117, 151, 153, 164, 177, 205, 208, 218, 236, 238, 253, 262, 263, 264, 269, 276, 300
  his death, 285
  his loyalty to Bingham, 255, 277, 279
Walsingham, Ursula, 259
Warren, Henry, 292
Wars of the Roses, 31
Waterhouse, Edward, 151, 180, 193, 205, 225, 236, 262
Wentworth, Peter, 196
Weston, Robert, lord justice of Ireland, 171
Whetstone, Geoffrey, 78–9, 87
White, Nicholas, 61, 101, 116, 145, 153, 175, 222, 262, 268, 283
Whyte, Edward, 192, 234
William, prince of Orange, 93, 105, 188
Williams, Philip, 99
Williams, Thomas, 290

Willis, Humphrey, 288, 289, 291
Wilson, Thomas, 103
Wingfield, Jacques, 56, 157–8, 186
Wolsey, Thomas, 33
Woodhouse, Thomas, 260, 266, 267
Worden, Blair, 91

Yaxley, Robert, 59
Yellow Ford, battle of, 212
York, Rowland, 121, 122
younger sons, 53, 57, 58
   Gilbert's educational proposal and, 81
   plight of in Tudor England, 55–7

CAMBRIDGE STUDIES IN EARLY MODERN
BRITISH HISTORY

Title in series

The Common Peace: Participation and the Criminal Law in Seventeenth-Century England*
CYNTHIA B. HERRUP

Politics, Society and Civil War in Warwickshire, 1620–1660*
ANN HUGHES

London Crowds in the Reign of Charles II: Propaganda and Politics from the Restoration to the Exclusion Crisis*
TIM HARRIS

Criticism and Compliment: The Politics of Literature in the England of Charles I*
KEVIN SHARPE

Central Government and the Localities: Hampshire, 1649–1689*
ANDREW COLEBY

John Skelton and the Politics of the 1520s*
GREG WALKER

Algernon Sidney and the English Republic, 1623–1677*
JONATHAN SCOTT

Thomas Starkey and the Commonweal: Humanist Politics and Religion in the Reign of Henry VIII*
THOMAS F. MAYER

The Blind Devotion of the People: Popular Religion and the English Reformation*
ROBERT WHITING

The Cavalier Parliament and the Reconstruction of the Old Regime, 1661–1667*
PAUL SEAWARD

The Blessed Revolution: English Politics and the Coming of War, 1621–1624
THOMAS COGSWELL

Charles I and the Road to Personal Rule*
L. J. REEVE

George Lawson's 'Politica' and the English Revolution*
CONAL CONDREN

Puritans and Roundheads: The Harleys of Brampton Bryan and the Outbreak of the Civil War
JACQUELINE EALES

An Uncounselled King: Charles I am the Scotish Troubles, 1637–1641*
PETER DONALD

The Early Elizabethan Polity: William Cecil and the British Succession Crisis, 1558–1569*
STEPHEN ALFORD

The Polarisation of Elizabethan Politics: The Political Career of Robert Devereux, and Earl of Essex*
PAUL J. HAMMER

The Politics of Social Conflict: The Peak Country, 1520–1770*
ANDY WOOD

Crime and Mentalities in Early Modern England*
MALCOLM GASKILL

The Church in an Age of Danger: Parsons and Parishioners, 1660–1740
DONALD A. SPAETH

Reading History in Early Modern England
D. R. WOOLF

The Politics of Court Scandal in Early Modern England: News Culture and the Overbury Affair, 1603–1660*
ALASTAIR BELLANY

The Politics of Religion in the Age of Mary, Queen of Scots: The Earl of Argyll and the Struggle for Britain and Ireland*
JANE E. A. DAWSON

Treason and the State: Law, Politics and Ideology in the English Civil War*
D. ALAN ORR

Pamphlets and Pamphleteering in Early Modern Britain
JOAD RAYMOND

Preaching during the English Reformation
SUSAN WABUDA

Patterns of Piety: Women, Gender and Religion in Late Medieval and Reformation England
CHRISTINE PETERS

Popular Politics and the English Reformation*
ETHAN H. SHAGAN

Mercy and Authority in the Tudor State*
K. J. KESSELRING

Unquiet Lives: Marriage and Marriage Breakdown in England, 1660–1800
JOANNE BAILEY

Images and Cultures of Law in Early Modern England: Justice and Political Power, 1558–1660[*]
PAUL RAFELD

The Gospel and Henry VIII: Evangelicals in the Early English Reformation[*]
ALEC RYRIE

Sir Matthew Hale, 1609–1676: Law, Religion and Natural Philosophy
ALAN CROMARTIE

Crime, Gender and Social Order in Early Modern England
GARTHINE WALKER

Print Culture and the Early Quakers
KATE PETERS

Ireland and the English Reformation: State reform and Clerical Resistance in the Diocese of Dublin, 1534–1590
JAMES MURRAY

London and the Restoration, 1659–1683
GARY S. DE KREY

Defining the Jacobean Church: The Politics of Religious Controversy, 1603–1625
CHARLES W. A. PRIOR

Queenship and Political Discourse in the Elizabethan Realms
NATALIE MEARS

John Locke, Toleration and Early Enlightenment Culture
JOHN MARSHALL

The Devil in Early Modern England
NATHAN JOHNSTONE

Georgian Monarchy: Politics and Culture, 1714–1760
HANNAH SMITH

Catholicism and Community in Early Modern England: Politics, Aristocratic patronage and Religion, 1550–1640
MICHAEL C. QUESTIER

The Reconstruction of the Church of Ireland: Bishop Bramhall and the Laudian Reforms, 1633–1641
JOHN MCCAFFERTY

The 1549 Rebellions and the Making of Early Modern England
ANDY WOOD

Parliaments and Politics During the Cromwellian Protectorate
PATRICK LITTLE AND, DAVID L. SMITH

Hobbes, Bramhall and the Politics of Liberty and Necessity
NICHOLAS D. JACKSON

Europe and the Making of England, 1660-1760[*]
TONY CLAYDON

Hunning and the Politics of Violence before the English Civil War
DANIEL C. BEAVER

[*]Also published as a paperback